ANTI-CORRUPTION IN A DISCORDANT WORLD

As the United Nations Convention against Corruption celebrates 20 years, there could be a sense that anti-corruption discourses, policies, and practices are settling into a stable, consensus-driven phase. This edited volume argues they are not.

Bringing together perspectives from around the world, this book captures the turbulent contemporary practice of anti-corruption. It shows it to be an arena in which domestic and transnational politics play out, shaping outcomes in often unpredictable ways. The purpose and means of this policy field are disputed and reinterpreted. Populist and illiberal leaders hijack anti-corruption to target opponents, restrict media and civil society, or even legitimise authoritarian rule. However, new forms of collective action and technology are emerging to forge novel paths forward.

Through various chapters, ranging from Russia to Brazil and Sri Lanka to the United Kingdom, the book shines a light on the contestation and abuse of contemporary anti-corruption, as well as on the innovation emerging to tackle one of the world's most pressing problems. The book looks to the future to consider the anti-corruption we need to meet the challenges of a discordant world.

This book will be an essential read for students, researchers, professionals, and activists interested in how anti-corruption practice unfolds in a volatile age.

David Jackson is Principal Advisor at the U4 Anti-Corruption Resource Centre at the Chr. Michelsen Institute (CMI), Norway. He has published works in peer-reviewed academic journals, such as *Development Studies*, *Public Integrity*, and *Southeastern and Black Sea Studies*, and contributed chapters on future research agendas, social norms, and corruption in the Middle East to several edited volumes.

Inge Amundsen is Senior Researcher Emeritus at the Chr. Michelsen Institute (CMI), Norway. He was Director of the U4 Anti-Corruption Resource Centre from 2002 to 2006, and he has edited a book on the topic of political corruption in Africa.

David Aled Williams is Principal Advisor at the U4 Anti-Corruption Resource Centre and Senior Researcher at the Chr. Michelsen Institute, Norway. He coordinates U4's thematic work on Corruption and Anti-Corruption Efforts in Natural Resources and Energy Sectors. He is author of *The Politics of Deforestation and REDD+ in Indonesia: Global Climate Change Mitigation*, published by Routledge (2023).

"*Anti-Corruption in a Discordant World* offers a realist's perspective on global corruption, arguing against 'toolkits' and quick-fix reforms by showing that progress against corruption will entail prolonged contestation, clear understanding of how power is abused, and reform innovations rather than revisiting 'best practices' that may not be appropriate everywhere. The book arrives at the right time: if the US is stepping back from the fight against global corruption, these voices from many parts of the world deserve our close attention."

Michael Johnston, *Emeritus Charles A. Dana Professor of Political Science, Colgate University, USA*

"This timely and incisive volume unpacks the messy realities of anti-corruption, posing urgent questions about who benefits from anti-corruption efforts and how new ideas emerge in adverse conditions. Essential reading for scholars and development professionals alike."

Fahmida Khatun, *Executive Director at Centre for Policy Dialogue, Bangladesh*

"For the world to be a better place, the fight against corruption is a fight that must be sustained and won. *Anti-Corruption in a Discordant World* presents lucid and scholarly interrogations of the many faces of corruption and shows how to combat it."

Emmanuel Oladipo Ojo, *Associate Professor at Ekiti State University, Nigeria*

"*Anti-Corruption in a Discordant World* is a timely volume moving away from prescriptive accounts of what anti-corruption is in an ideal world by looking at it as it is in a complex and messy world. This allows the readers to reflect on real-life problems through an illuminating conceptual frame. This book will surely contribute to better anti-corruption policies in their diverse contexts."

Mihály Fazekas, *Professor at Department of Public Policy at Central European University, Austria*

Routledge Corruption and Anti-Corruption Studies

The series features innovative and original research on the subject of corruption from scholars around the world. As well as documenting and analysing corruption, the series aims to discuss anti-corruption initiatives and endeavours, in an attempt to demonstrate ways forward for countries and institutions where the problem is widespread. The series particularly promotes comparative and interdisciplinary research targeted at a global readership.

In terms of theory and method, rather than basing itself on any one orthodoxy, the series draws broadly on the tool kit of the social sciences in general, emphasizing comparison, the analysis of the structure and processes, and the application of qualitative and quantitative methods.

Corruption and Development in Nigeria
Edited by Ọláyínká Àkànle and David O. Nkpe

Corruption Proofing in Africa
A Systems Thinking Approach
Edited by Dan Kuwali

Corruption, Ethics, and Governance in South Africa
Issues, Cases, and Interventions
Edited by Modimowabarwa Kanyane

Deconstructing Corruption in Africa
Edited by Ina Kubbe, Emmanuel Saffa Abbdulai, and Michael Johnston

The Digitalisation of Anti-Corruption in Brazil
Scandals, Reforms, and Innovation
Fernanda Odilla

Judicial Anti-Corruption Campaigns
Prosecutions in Italy, Brazil, and Romania
Nedim Hogic

Anti-Corruption in a Discordant World
Contestation, Abuse, and Innovation
Edited by David Jackson, Inge Amundsen, and David Aled Williams

For more information about this series, please visit: www.routledge.com/Routledge-Corruption-and-Anti-Corruption-Studies/book-series/RCACS

ANTI-CORRUPTION IN A DISCORDANT WORLD

Contestation, Abuse, and Innovation

Edited by David Jackson, Inge Amundsen, and David Aled Williams

Routledge
Taylor & Francis Group
LONDON AND NEW YORK

Designed cover image: Silvia Jackson

First published 2026
by Routledge
4 Park Square, Milton Park, Abingdon, Oxon OX14 4RN

and by Routledge
605 Third Avenue, New York, NY 10158

Routledge is an imprint of the Taylor & Francis Group, an informa business

British Library Cataloguing-in-Publication Data
A catalogue record for this book is available from the British Library

ISBN: 978-1-032-87299-5 (hbk)
ISBN: 978-1-032-87298-8 (pbk)
ISBN: 978-1-003-53192-0 (ebk)

DOI: 10.4324/9781003531920

Typeset in Galliard
by Deanta Global Publishing Services, Chennai, India

CONTENTS

FIGURES

TABLES

CONTRIBUTORS

Sahabuddin Ahmed is a lecturer in the Department of Political Science, Dhaka International University, Bangladesh. His primary research interests are in urban governance, corruption, political economy, and democracy.

Hasan Muhammad Baniamin is an assistant professor at the South Asian Institute of Policy and Governance (SIPG) and at the Department of Political Science and Sociology, North South University, Bangladesh. He obtained a PhD from the University of Bergen, Norway, and has published articles in journals such as *Public Administration*, *Public Organisation Review*, *International Political Science Review*, and *International Journal of Public Administration*.

Daniela Cepeda Cuadrado is a senior anti-corruption adviser at the U4 Anti-Corruption Resource Centre. She is a public policy professional with extensive experience in the areas of anti-corruption, human rights, health, and sustainable development. She has worked with several organisations, including the UN system, multilateral and bilateral agencies, academia, think tanks, and civil society.

Bayar Dashpurev is a doctoral student at the Max Planck Institute for Social Anthropology, Germeny, where he is involved in the project 'Environmental Rights in Cultural Context'. He was a lecturer in law, teaching environmental law, mining law, and public administrative law at the School of Law, the National University of Mongolia, and the German-Mongolian Institute for Resources and Technology. His research primarily focuses on the socio-legal aspects of environmental protection and resource extraction through an interdisciplinary lens, combining legal and anthropological approaches.

Rebecca Dobson Phillips is an assistant professor in Politics at the Centre for the Study of Corruption based at the University of Sussex, UK. Her research focuses on corruption, integrity, and public standards, with an emphasis on relationships of power, to explore the foundations of effective, legitimate, and just forms of governance.

Cheri-Leigh Erasmus is a co-CEO of Accountability Lab, a global translocal network. She currently co-chairs the Steering Committee of the Transparency, Accountability and Participation (TAP) Network, and has written frequently about good governance and equity in the development sector.

Guilherme France is a PhD candidate in Political Science at the Institute for Social and Political Studies at the Rio de Janeiro State University, Brazil. He holds a Master's in International Law from the Rio de Janeiro State University and a Master's in History, Politics, and Cultural Assets from the Getulio Vargas Foundation.

Carolina Gerli is a PhD candidate in Political and Social Sciences at the University of Bologna, Italy. Her research explores AI in anti-corruption, particularly public sector applications across the EU. She has an academic background in public management and professional experience in government digital transformation.

Blair Glencorse is a co-CEO of Accountability Lab, a global translocal network which he founded in 2012. He is also a former co-Chair of the Open Government Partnership and a member of the World Economic Forum's Global Future Council on Governance.

Alexey Konov is a director of the Anti-Corruption Center at the HSE University (Moscow, Russia) and editor-in-chief of the Anti-Corruption Portal. For over 20 years, he has been involved in developing, promoting, and monitoring the implementation of anti-corruption legislation in Russia as well as regularly participating in international anti-corruption forums, including UNCAC CoSP and G20 ACWG.

Fernanda Odilla is an assistant professor at the Department of Political and Social Sciences at the University of Bologna, Italy. She holds a PhD in Public Policy and Social Sciences and an MA in Criminology from King's College London. Her research interests include the use of digital technologies to promote integrity and curb corruption.

Ramesh Ramasamy is a senior lecturer in Political Science at the University of Peradeniya, Sri Lanka. He obtained his PhD under the NORHED project on

Governance and Policy Studies in South Asia. His research interests are mainly in the quality of government, corruption, institutional trust, public service delivery, and citizenship rights.

Gabriel Rojas-Salazar is an associate professor in the Public Administration Department at the Center for Research and Teaching in Economics (CIDE) and a researcher in the Transparency, anti-corruption and digitalization initiative of the Monterrey Institute of Technology and Higher Education (ITESM) in Mexico.

Nurul Huda Sakib is serving as a professor at the Department of Government and Politics, Jahangirnagar University, Bangladesh. Dr Sakib received his PhD from the Department of Government and International Relations, The University of Sydney, Australia, in 2018. His current research interests are corruption, anti-corruption, political communication, democracy, and elections in South Asia.

Jean Scrimgeour is a co-CEO of Accountability Lab. She joined the Lab in 2017. Before joining the Lab, she worked as a public affairs and democratic governance specialist in the United States, the United Kingdom, and Southern Africa and has written widely on peacebuilding, good governance, and non-profit management.

Thomas Shipley is a research fellow at the Centre for the Study of Corruption in the United Kingdom. His research interests include questions concerning the role of international financial and development institutions in supporting and evaluating anti-corruption reforms.

Guilherme Siqueira is a PhD candidate in Business Ethics and Legal Studies at the Wharton School of the University of Pennsylvania, USA. He holds Bachelor's and Master's degrees in law from the University of São Paulo, Brazil.

Luis Roberto Vargas-Pineda is a PhD student at the University of Nevada, Las Vegas, USA. Roberto Vargas has worked in Mexico's Federal Supreme Audit and the Secretariat of Finance and Public Credit as a specialist in Performance Auditing, Performance Evaluation, Open Data, and Fiscal Transparency.

ACKNOWLEDGEMENTS

This book is a collective endeavour, and there are many individuals at several institutions whom we would like to thank for enabling this project to come to fruition. Our sincere thanks go to the Routledge editorial board for appreciating the potential of our idea for this volume, to the editor at Routledge, to those who peer reviewed our initial proposal and the individual chapters. This book would not have been possible without support from our home institution, the Chr. Michelsen Institute (CMI), and its U4 Anti-Corruption Resource Centre, and our thanks go to all our colleagues who have given us the space and support to pursue this project at the institute. We are particularly thankful to Guillaume Nicaise for enabling us to present our emerging work at CMI's Corruption Research Group. We are profoundly grateful to all chapter authors for their engagement with our vision for this volume, their interpretations and re-interpretations of our ideas, and for their comments and contributions not just on other chapters but on our introduction too. Beyond our home institution and chapter contributors, we are also grateful for good conversations with colleagues within the broader anti-corruption research and practice communities on new frontiers, methods, and questions of evidence and theory. Lastly, but by no stretch least, we warmly thank our respective families who provided nourishment and encouragement for the long-haul work that producing such a book entails.

PART I

Introduction

1

ANTI-CORRUPTION IN A DISCORDANT WORLD

Contestation, Abuse, and Innovation

David Jackson, David Aled Williams, and Inge Amundsen

Introduction

Corruption is recognised as harming democracy, economic growth, and social cohesion. Thus, *anti-corruption* has become one of the most important public policy agendas of contemporary politics, and the move from problem acknowledgement to the institutionalisation of responses has been relatively swift. Most states around the world now have national anti-corruption strategies that aid and abet a growing plethora of international agreements – only eight UN member states have not yet signed the *United Nations Convention against Corruption* (UNCAC). International dialogue has advanced into joint action, including in the recovery and returning of stolen assets. Minimising corruption is part of the *Sustainable Development Goals* (SDGs), and anti-corruption is supported by a transnational community of practitioners – some say industry – that shapes, articulates, and helps put into effect an ever-evolving range of measures.

The focus of this book is not corruption in itself, but anti-corruption. Societal responses to corruption and its harms have become far more diverse and sophisticated. Digital technologies have reimagined administrative procedures; practical instruments have become highly specialised – such as for procurement and contracting – and formerly isolated anti-corruption activities have become integrated into sector strategies. This ongoing development takes place as the anti-corruption community pays more attention to non-technical aspects, such as social norms, gender, the role of indigenous communities, and the environment, as well as transnational links and connections.

Corruption was once a taboo topic, now a global agenda to tackle corruption has emerged with seemingly unchallenged linearity. Indeed, as UNCAC

DOI: 10.4324/9781003531920-2

celebrates 20 years, there could be a sense that anti-corruption discourses, policies, and practices are settling into a stable, consensus-driven phase. This edited volume argues that they are not.

With discordance more pronounced in international and domestic politics, the way anti-corruption plays out in practice is also getting more unpredictable and varied. International anti-corruption regulations may have 'confusing and alienating' impacts when applied across diverse contexts (Feikema 2024). Increasingly sophisticated and diverse forms of collective organisation against corruption are recast as 'foreign agents' or part of 'western plots' by illiberal leaders (Arriola, Rakner, and Van de Walle 2023). The wisdom of technical solutions is contested by some observers doubting whether these are possible before economic growth (Khan 2005; Khan, Andreoni, and Roy 2019). Western tax money which has sustained the agenda is confounded by leading banks, consultants and PR firms, even NGO initiatives, helping corrupt leaders launder reputations and money (Van Vuuren et al. 2018). While the achievement of better anti-corruption outcomes is possible in some settings, in others anti-corruption efforts are used to bolster corrupt leaders by 'frying small fish', or, through an emphasis on 'terrorist financing' or 'tax evasion', into tools that restrict space for media and civil society (Amundsen 2019; Amundsen and Jackson 2021).

From a European perspective, turbulence in global politics may have escalated since the beginning of 2025; but for others around the world, political uncertainties have been routine and unremarkable. This book's starting point is that anti-corruption in the modern era has always been confronted by discordance – but now the trend is broadening and deepening. The book aims to gather empirical evidence on the many paths anti-corruption has been taking in a discordant world. It aims to provide the reverse image of anti-corruption: rather than ponder how anti-corruption should be adapted to context, we want to show *how context has been distorting, deforming, and enriching anti-corruption*.

A more self-reflective approach that emphasises realism over solutionism and linear projections of progress has been argued for several years. Critics have, for example, called out the 'narrow, outdated and incomplete' narratives that frame an understanding of the means and ends of anti-corruption (Johnston and Fritzen 2021: 150). At the heart of this is a call for a better understanding of how anti-corruption hits the ground. Analysis shows how an agenda with increasingly sophisticated guidance abstracted from multiple real-world contexts has been implemented in ways that overlay rather than engage with the realities of context, resulting in unfeasible agendas with voided thinking about how change can happen in a particular location (Grindle 2017; Jackson 2020; Mungiu-Pippidi 2023; Khan et al. 2019).

Critical voices have pointed out the contradictions of a policy field urgently promoted by mostly Western powers, who often articulate lofty precepts such as 'zero-tolerance' but have in some instances been more selective, even complicit, when anti-corruption threatens national corporate interests, political allies, and access to natural resources (Van Vuuren et al. 2018; Brown and Cloke 2004). Others have identified the inconsistencies of practice whereby activities, strategies, and campaigns targeting corruption are rooted in the discourse of social justice and democratic transformation but are unable or unwilling to challenge unjust systems of power (Johnston and Fritzen 2021; Rothstein 2021).

There is certainly a practical need to think about the kind of anti-corruption we need in an increasingly discordant world. The more that anti-corruption has been embraced as a global agenda, supported by a growing wave of reform packages, research, international agreements, conferences, and specialised institutions and NGOs, the more doubts have been raised over the efficacy of the approaches taken (Johnston and Fritzen 2021; Mungiu-Pippidi 2023).

Progress and regress happen at the same time. Understanding why and in what ways this occurs in anti-corruption is the aim of the book. In a discordant world, three conceptual lenses are used in this book to understand anti-corruption *as it is* rather than *how it is supposed to be*:

- *Contestation* aims to understand both the positive and negative diversity, dissent, and evolution of anti-corruption practices, challenging the idea of a self-evident consensus and of a static, 'one route' of anti-corruption.
- *Abuse* aims to show how anti-corruption is wrapped up in systems of power, and how anti-corruption can be weaponised in power struggles and become integrated into other forms of power abuse – for protecting a regime and for attacking its opponents.
- *Innovation* aims to demonstrate how locally grounded and context-specific initiatives can respond to contestation and abuse, showing a way forward in adverse settings, beyond the standard approaches.

This introductory chapter first explains in what ways the world is more discordant, before outlining how the book defines corruption and anti-corruption. The remainder of the chapter goes into more detail about how we operationalise the concepts of contestation, abuse, and innovation.

Why This Matters: Anti-Corruption in a Discordant World

Is the world more discordant (i.e., unstable, unpredictable, disagreeing) now than at any other time since the end of the Cold War? If so, what does this have to do with anti-corruption and in what ways?

The relatively stable period since the 1990s, characterised by an international neoliberal order underpinned by American hegemony, has arguably come to an end (Mearsheimer 2019; Economist 2024). Perspectives differ on whether the world is still largely unipolar, firmly multipolar, or verging on anarchy in international affairs (Lehti and Pennanen 2020). Yet we can discern at least six major recent dimensions of discordance. These are: (i) de-democratisation and entrenchment of autocratic rule; (ii) the manipulation of information across borders; (iii) an increase in worldwide deaths from armed conflicts and related population displacements; (iv) disillusionment with conventional politics in liberal democracies; (v) the triple climate, biodiversity, and pollution crisis leading to displacements, extreme weather events and socio-environmental conflicts; and, not least, (vi) rising voices that the current international order is ill-equipped to deal with these challenges and must be reshaped. Let us briefly look at each of these six dimensions in turn.

As of 2023, the share of the world's population living in autocracies had increased to 71 per cent, up from 50 per cent in 2003. In 2023, the number of countries autocratising was 36, with only 18 countries democratising (V-Dem 2024: 7; Our World in Data 2024a). Putin's Russia is the most prominent recent example of autocratisation, with Pierre Hassner noting in 2008 that it 'has gone from a mixture of oligarchy, democracy, and anarchy, to a regime of autocracy with some fascist features' (Hassner 2008: 5). Indonesia's *reformasi* era of democratic reforms is widely considered to have given way to a period of de-democratisation (Croissant and Haynes 2021); Hungary, Turkey, El Salvador, and Tunisia are cited examples of countries to have recently taken an autocratic turn, along with the nine Sub-Saharan African countries that experienced state coups since 2020 (Levitsky and Way 2025; Chin 2021).

Second, states and non-state actors are again (like in the Cold War) exporting *disinformation* and manipulating public discourse, notably using social media, but also other direct means, to push 'fake news' or sabotage society. Schiffrin (2017) argues that the initial enthusiasm for social media and the positive role it appeared to play in the Arab Spring protests has given way to the realisation that it also offers autocrats a means of widely communicating 'big lies'. Examples include Russian interference in the UK's 2016 referendum on leaving the European Union (Brexit), in the 2016 presidential elections in the United States, and in the more recent elections in Georgia and Moldova (McGaughey 2018; Mueller 2019; Orenstein 2024).

Third, in addition to continued threats from both domestic and foreign terrorism, various forms of *armed conflict* around the world have increased over the past decade. From around 2010, there have been several years in which total deaths in armed conflicts exceeded 100,000, with 2022 seeing nearly 237,000 such deaths worldwide (Our World in Data 2024b). While many of these conflicts remain internal to states, they also include situations in which major powers support opposing sides in intrastate conflicts (Davies et al. 2023). This rise in conflict may be both a cause and consequence of a more discordant world.

Fourth, we have recently observed increased *disillusionment* with conventional politics in older liberal democracies. The reasons for this 'crisis of liberal democracy' are many and complex, but Kutlay and Öniş (2023) suggest it is partly explained by rising competition between different regime types under global capitalism. Notably, Russia and China are moving in the direction of state-led capitalism (Kutlay and Öniş 2023), and this model has motivated the rise of authoritarian populism in the European periphery (e.g., Hungary, Turkey) and other parts of the world (e.g., Indonesia, Venezuela, and several Sahel countries). Populism has also made headway in Western liberal democracies, associated with increased polarisation, violence, and authoritarianism. The most prominent example so far in the west is the rise as US president of Donald Trump and the attack on the US Capitol in 2021, widely viewed as an example of insurrection or domestic terrorism (Trautman 2021). The UK, too, saw its first cases of political assassination after a quarter of a century gap (i.e., members of parliament Jo Cox in 2016 and Sir David Amess in 2021), while democratic institutions in Germany are contending with the re-emergence of ethno-nationalist populism, with the far-right party **A***lternative für Deutschland* (AfD) ruled in 2024 by a court as suspected of extremism.

Fifth, the world now also faces a triple crisis from *climate change, biodiversity loss, and pollution*, as well as connected public health challenges (Scheffran 2025). These changes are, in turn, having major impacts on human health, farming systems, and on the very stability of societies. The direct impacts of this triple crisis are not equally distributed around the world, but they have indirectly caused significant hardship and loss of life, as well as social conflicts.

Sixth, and as if to make matters worse, there is a realisation that the *current international order is ill-equipped* to deal with the above challenges. Scholars who posit that the world has already passed into multipolarity with the strategic competition between China and the US, note, for example, that order across the world is in big trouble. Mearsheimer (2019) notes this is partly because the hegemon at the heart of any international liberal order must itself be a liberal democracy, which was and will be in some doubt in Trump's America. These strains affect not only Western and non-Western relations, but relations within the west and among its allies too. Although remnants of the post-World War II multilateral architecture, such as NATO and the UN system still exist, their relevance for solving multiple simultaneous global crises is being questioned and weakened.

While put together, these six factors make a compelling case for increased post-Cold War discord and disorder on a global scale, although people and countries experiencing better times and prospects today (for example, because of decolonisation and/or peace) may disagree that life now is more discordant or disorderly. Also, international cooperation and collaboration across very different regime types still occur.

However, if the world is more discordant today in some ways, and not in others, what does this have to do with anti-corruption, the focus of this book? Superficially, international cooperation cedes way to competition, the rules-based international system is denounced, challenged, and undermined, and the rise of discord in the form of increased authoritarianism and conflict makes corruption itself much more challenging to address. This endangers the international cooperation necessary to address corruption, and it makes anti-corruption weaponised in international competition and in the political terminology of de-democratising regimes and autocracies. Our argument is that in this more discordant world, the common assumptions as to how different societies pursue anti-corruption must be fundamentally revisited.

The dominant underpinning of anti-corruption supported by Western governments, embedded in multilateral organisations, aid agencies, and NGOs, has been to make other states more like liberal democracies, or at least to make trading with them more predictable and rules-based. Western-backed technical reforms and funding programmes targeting foreign countries have typically aimed at improving laws, policies, and institutions along Western notions of 'good governance' and 'free trade'. Though there has been a recent 'realist' turn in anti-corruption policy and practice towards working more politically to achieve results, this turn has coincided with significantly reduced space for pursuing democratic or political anti-corruption goals in many non-Western countries.

At the same time, interest in pursuing anti-corruption goals has not diminished, and preventing or reducing corruption is an aim in a large variety of countries and societies around the world. This leads us to ask whether we sufficiently understand the varied realities of anti-corruption as it is nowadays pursued around the world, and how anti-corruption is being abused to pursue other goals, such as protecting regimes and silencing its critics and political opponents. And, if some anti-corruption practice enables the abuse of power, rather than holding it to account, what new kinds of anti-corruption could meet the challenges of this more discordant world?

What Kind of Problem Is Corruption?

We view corruption, at its core, as a problem of social order. While conventional normative social theory posits that people not only follow the rules of their societies but make them a part of themselves and the way they live, the strategic interactionist turn in social theory argues that people everywhere sometimes fail to follow rules and can instead use them for their own interests (Edgerton 2022). While rules regulate conflicts between societal and personal interests, deviations occur, and these are at the heart of definitions of corruption (Rose-Ackerman 1978; Buchan and Hill 2014).

Popular corruption definitions, such as those promulgated by Transparency International and the World Bank, for instance, highlight deviations between the public good and private gain. The World Bank defines corruption as the 'abuse of public office for private gain' while Transparency International (TI) views corruption as 'the abuse of entrusted power for private gain'. Nye (1967), too, suggests that corruption is 'behaviour which deviates from the formal duties of a public role because of private-regarding (personal, close family, private clique) pecuniary or status gains'.

However, as pointed out in more recent debates on the character of social order, all societies allow for exceptions to rules and these exceptions, in themselves, also constitute social rules i.e., rules about exceptions to rules (Edgerton 2022). Thus, if corruption involves failing to follow rules in the interests of society, it can also mean rule-following in the interests of a societal sub-set, such as a family dynasty, a dictatorship, or a group of cronies. This is recognised by Robbins (2000) in his understanding of corruption based on a study of India's forest sector, in which he identifies corruption as 'a system of normalised rules, transformed from legal authority, patterned around existing inequalities, and cemented through cooperation and trust'. The canny ability of corruption to solve certain problems facing societal sub-groups has, indeed, been viewed as integral to its longevity and resilience as a strategy for social interaction (Marquette and Pfeiffer 2015).

Yet even if corruption helps maintain social cohesion or creates wealth for some people under certain circumstances (e.g., by maintaining economic predictability under a ruling elite), we argue, along with others (such as Persson et al. 2019), that it serves to undermine the achievement of broader societal interests in the long run. For instance, while different studies find that corruption can be associated both with increases (Rabnawaz 2015) and reductions (Wong 2023) in income inequality (in the latter case by growing opportunities in the informal economy), it is also associated with lower spending on health and education (Ananta et al. 2023). In other words, corruption radically undermines efforts to create a just and caring social or public order that prioritises individual human security and well-being. It also plays a significant role in destroying the foundations of the liberal rules-based international order.

How Do We Define Anti-Corruption?

A main argument of this book is that, if corruption is a problem of social order, the kinds of social order we pursue condition the kinds of *anti-corruption* we get. For instance, an autocrat pursuing an authoritarian order with no political competition is likely to employ a form of anti-corruption that is selective and disciplines lower cadres and/or eliminates opponents. This, however, offers no prospect of this form of anti-corruption limiting dictatorial rule, no matter how corrupt it is. Likewise, democrats seeking a liberal political and social order with a high degree of protection for individual rights are likely to employ forms of anti-corruption consistent with this goal.

Considering this, we do not define *anti-corruption* with reference to a prescribed set of activities, institutions, laws, or policies, but rather view it as a process involving a spectrum of means, ends and actors. Anti-corruption describes an unending process by which different actors ostensibly work through various means to minimise the negative impacts of corruption in society, politics, and the economy, but *whose real motivations and ultimate outcomes remain to be empirically tested.*

These means may include both direct and indirect anti-corruption interventions or practices, such as the creation of an anti-corruption body, improving the state's fiscal discipline, or digitalising public services. They may be motivated by a genuine desire to achieve integrity outcomes, or they may arise from less praiseworthy goals, such as tackling a political opponent regardless of actual evidence of wrongdoing.

If anti-corruption refers to anything that ostensibly minimises corruption's impacts on society, politics, and the economy, directly or indirectly, in all regime types, this implies anti-corruption can also uphold social orders many readers would undoubtedly find unjust. This is precisely why we argue in this book for a deeper empirical engagement with the practice of anti-corruption around the world today, via the concepts of contestation, abuse, and innovation.

Three Conceptual Lenses

Just as we observe deep divisions in how corruption is understood, we observe contestation in how anti-corruption is understood and expressed in different contexts. We see contestation in what the goals of anti-corruption really are, and consequently in how and by whom anti-corruption should be pursued. We also observe the abuse of anti-corruption, since strategies pursued under the banner of anti-corruption can involve significant harm to individuals, groups, or societal values. We can, however, also observe innovation in anti-corruption. That is: efforts to map effective pathways to prevent, disrupt, or minimise corruption even in hostile settings.

These facets of anti-corruption play out simultaneously and interact. Contestation can be the prelude to abuse: anti-corruption can be reframed and co-opted into the logics of power abuse and become politicised, for instance when traditional anti-corruption measures are framed as being part of 'foreign agents' influence or covert political plots. Contestation can also be a prelude to innovation, when the official anti-corruption discourse is delegitimised, and dissent opens space for alternative understandings and solutions.

Abuse and weaponisation of anti-corruption can trigger the search for innovative and strategic responses.

This book is organised into three sections that reflect these heuristics. This book's eleven chapters all empirically engage with the concepts of contestation, abuse, and innovation in anti-corruption. Addressing a range of thematic and geographic contexts, they each explore how these concepts manifest themselves, pointing to new kinds of anti-corruption needed to meet the challenges of this discordant world. They collectively raise both new concerns and new pathways for anti-corruption, which, in the book's conclusion, we attempt to summarise, adding our own reflections on anti-corruption in this more discordant world.

Contestation

Anti-corruption is not a set of prescriptions, but a policy arena wrapped up in systems of power, of personal and group-interests, of bargaining, and of matters of social justice and basic social values. It is therefore subject to contestation; a concept whose operationalisation depends largely on discipline (Dunn 2008; Wiener 2017).

Contestation is the first lens by which we examine anti-corruption's evolution, one that helps to see beyond the projection of consensus. We use contestation in neutral terms as referring to the act of challenging, disputing, or opposing a particular idea, norm, authority, or practice.

According to some authors, the global, normative understanding of anti-corruption has developed via consensus and close collaboration between technical experts, civil society and diplomats (Joutsen and Graycar 2012). The norms expressed by UNCAC, overall, have not been met with much categorical opposition, despite these norms adhering to a liberal political agenda, an agenda which in other policy fields, such as human rights, has elsewhere been criticised for its neo-colonialism and hypocrisy (Rothstein 2021). However, while this normative vision of good governance rests on consensus, the reality of practice is that we see much more diversity and division than is often captured.

As a starting point, we hypothesise that contestation manifests itself in the application of standards and concepts, in discourses around justifications and in disputes around who are the corrupt and who are the victims, as well as around priorities and solutions. National governments and powerholders, activists and citizens, academics, private firms, interest groups as well as multilateral organisations are all part of this contestation.

Contestation can be highly localised, for example about how states domestically enact global normative agendas, and the kind of local norms and discourses brought up by domestic actors that distort its implementation. Lesch's study of the German parliament's protracted incorporation of UNCAC into

German law exemplifies how debates brought up 'normative questions about the role of German MPs as "public officials" and the very meaning of a legal concept of political corruption' (Lesch 2021: 614).

Academic and policy arguments feed into re-interpretation. There are contestations over appropriate subjects of reform and much disagreement over who is more corrupt, such as whether corruption is a corporate problem or a national governance issue. There are contestations over conceptual metrics, with, for instance some countries resisting the Corruption Perceptions Index because it fuels stereotypical perceptions (Gutterman and Lohaus 2018; Baumann 2020), and there are contestations over the normative fit and the extent to which standardised forms of anti-corruption can match local contexts (Funaki and Glencorse 2014; Heilman and Ndumbaro 2002).

Anti-corruption is also coloured by political ideology, triggering more far-reaching re-interpretations. Populist politicians, for example, have reshaped the basic rationale of anti-corruption, framing it as a necessary crusade against alleged corrupt elites and bureaucracies exploiting the common man and woman. Populist anti-corruption is presented as anti-establishment politics. Mendilow and Phélippeau suggest that populist leaders can even get away with some corruption, if this is done in the interests of the people against 'the malign deep state actors' (Mendilow and Phélippeau 2021).

National and nationalist ideology also matters. China, for example, interprets anti-corruption mostly as maintaining political purity, obedience, and discipline (Lang 2019). Autocrats have contested anti-corruption as a plot against national values. A noteworthy instance of a direct kind of contestation is the way Vladimir Putin, in the run-up to the full-scale invasion of Ukraine, claimed that Ukraine's internationally supported Ukraine's National Anti-Corruption Bureau (NABU) was part of an anti-Russian drive in Ukraine (Mungiu-Pippidi 2023).

Four chapters in this book examine how contestation is playing out in a discordant world. Rojas-Salazar and Vargas-Pineda describe in their chapter on populism and anti-corruption policies in Mexico how the former populist regime redefined corruption as a 'moral perversion' deeply embedded in the state apparatus, and how the populist leader presented himself as the only saviour and moral keeper, in contrast to the corrupted elite. In her chapter focused on post-Brexit Britain, Dobson Phillips argues that significant contestation threatened to undermine the integrity of long-established anti-corruption norms and also provoked a deeper reflection on the character and prevalence of corruption in British society. In their chapter on the 'Operation Car Wash' in Brazil, France and Siqueira show how a huge corruption investigation became contested and was turned into criticism of the key case investigators and prosecutors. This contestation arose from a diverse set of challenges to anti-corruption policies and practices, which deserve a detailed analysis, not only because of its impacts in the Brazilian context, but also due to its potential connections to wider contestation efforts worldwide. Finally, Shipley in his chapter on Monitoring, Evaluation, and Learning (MEL) systems within aid organisations disputes the idea that this is a policy field that is progressing via self-reflection. Drawing on original evidence, Shipley demonstrates how a lack of internal reflections risks reinforcing approaches to anti-corruption programming which may be harmful.

Abuse

Whereas we know – through the vast and ever-increasing literature on corruption – what *corruption* is, what its drivers and consequences are, there is far less research on how *anti-corruption* has been twisted and thwarted, used and abused, for political purposes. Some research is done on the politisation of anti-corruption in specific countries (see for instance Carothers 2022; Engler 2020; Pavlova 2020; Zhu and Zhang 2017; Sberna and Vannucci 2013), and there is a large body of anecdotal evidence, but we need to analyse the abuse of anti-corruption more systematically.

Anti-corruption in the form of prosecution of individuals and firms – according to the law – is not the concern here, nor is bureaucratic mismanagement or allegations of corruption directed against political rivals and opponents when part of an open debate. This can be considered as 'normal' political procedure – or what we describe as the contestation of anti-corruption.

Abuse of anti-corruption is about misdirection: it is when different actors apply the rhetoric of anti-corruption – and apply the measures usually understood as anti-corruption – for *other* purposes than to minimise the impact of corruption in society, politics, and the economy. These other purposes are narrow group-interests or self-interest: when anti-corruption is politically instrumentalised to serve the power, status, and wealth ambitions of certain politicians and power holders, and not the common good. Abuse implies an egregious misuse of anti-corruption measures. One example is when anti-corruption laws are implemented with political bias, to target corrupt rivals and opponents of the regime at the same time as corrupt regime insiders and supporters are not.

In addition, abuse of anti-corruption has the side-effect of making corruption more likely to occur in the future. This is because the abuse of anti-corruption involves severe consequences for the body politic. Abuse is often a part of, or leads to, democratic backsliding as it inconsistently applies the rule of law and therefore damages it, undermines the credibility and autonomy of enforcement agencies and the government institutions of oversight and control, and it undermines checks and balances. Abuse is when anti-corruption is weaponised to de-legitimise and stifle the opposition, to dismantle the institutional systems of checks and balances, and to change the rules of the game to lock in powerholders' advantages. It is also abuse when it is distorted to reduce transparency and to serve as a smokescreen to distract attention from more pressing policy issues, the real corruption problems, and the most corrupt actors. The abuse of anti-corruption spreads disinformation in the public realm.

It is important to note that the abuse of anti-corruption is usually *but one element in a broader set of power abuse*, which typically includes repressive legislation, the politicisation of the judiciary and the state bureaucracy, media restrictions, manipulation of elections, disinformation, intimidation, threats, and (ultimately) violence. Two books with telling titles illustrate this point well: *How Democracies Die* (Levitsky and Ziblatt 2018) and *How to Rig an Election* (Cheeseman and Klaas 2019).

The incentives for abusing anti-corruption – power, status, and wealth – can usually be inferred from the outcome: boosted power positions, entrenched power structures, reduced space for public participation and influence in politics, and economic privileges for the few – the regime insiders and their cronies and supporters. The problem with abuse of anti-corruption is that it increases political and economic disparities.

Anti-corruption can be abused to benefit the powerholders in many ways. A common and well-known method is the politisation and weaponisation of anti-corruption, by reframing, redefining, and retargeting anti-corruption so that it does *not* address the corrupt practices of the powerholders and their supporters, cronies, and private companies and pecuniary interests, but delegitimises and targets their rivals and competitors. Anti-corruption institutions, laws, and regulations can be weaponised and used to smear, expel from office, and silence political rivals and the opposition, civil servants, civil society, and the media. The anti-corruption agenda can also be topped up with allegations of 'terrorist financing', 'tax evasion', 'capital flight', and other incorrect justifications (distorting the facts, smear campaigns, fake news).

This method can have the desired side-effect of boosting the legitimacy of powerholders, by claiming that 'everybody else' or selected groups and individuals are corrupt, and by showing that they are 'serious' in fighting corruption. Even the targeting of non-political entities (i.e., by 'frying the small fish', like the lower bureaucracy and certain socio-cultural groups) can launder the reputation and strengthen the power of powerholders.

A biased implementation of anti-corruption can also include exceptions (leniency, 'pardon') of various sorts for individual members of the ruling elite and its core constituents. Allegations of corruption can be used to entice opposition leaders and rivals to change sides, when 'pardon' is granted for doing so. A biased implementation can also make corrupt practices like gift-giving, vote buying and 'handouts', special remuneration and advancement for loyal bureaucrats, capital flight, secret contracting, etc., tolerated and exempt from normal anti-corruption procedures – when serving the interests of the power holders.

Another method is to nominate political loyalists to head the government's anti-corruption institutions, and/or to create new anti-corruption institutions controlled by the powerholders (Amundsen 2019: 16, 17). Yet another is to delegitimise anti-corruption measures altogether when it hurts the interests and supporters of the powerholders. This can, for instance be done by claiming that it is biased, unconstitutional, unproportional, etc. Thus, when politically opportune, anti-corruption can be rolled back selectively or completely, for instance by destroying the effectiveness of checks and balances, altering the legislation, and by politicising or dismantling the institutions of oversight and control (Amundsen 2019: 17). By this, impunity is secured for the powerholders and their core supporters and cronies.

The abuse of anti-corruption can also open new business opportunities for the powerholders and their core supporters, cronies, and businesses. When the anti-corruption agenda is hijacked to target selected or competing firms, this opens for take-overs and for preferences for the companies owned by the powerholders and their business partners (Amundsen 2019: 17). Pecuniary interests can be the ultimate rationale for holding power, and the goal of abusing anti-corruption.

This outline of the many forms of abusing anti-corruption is not an exhaustive list, and not necessarily in order of severity. Three chapters in this book will examine how abuses unfold with reference to specific contexts.

As argued by Ramasamy and Baniamin, Sri Lanka's 'Executive Presidential System' was another source of abuse of anti-corruption by a semi-authoritarian regime that became a kleptocracy by using, among other abuses, anti-corruption rhetoric prior to elections and the nomination of loyalists to positions in the anti-corruption commissions. Dashpurev, in his chapter on Mongolia's coal theft case, argues that the state's strategic absence from managing the resource-rich South Gobi region should be viewed as a case of anti-corruption abuse because of selective enforcement. Konov in his chapter 'All the Kings Men' shows how anti-corruption efforts in Russia had selective enforcement built into the mechanics of the system, highlighting how the reforms reflected the intricate political economy of Russia's ruling system.

Innovation

Although innovation has been understood and defined differently throughout history (Taylor 2017), we start by loosely defining innovation in the context of anti-corruption as a creative process that brings about new forms of anti-corruption practice, whether that be novel collaborations, discourses, analytical tools, or strategic action. In this book, we will look at how innovative anti-corruption can take place in specific contexts of contestation and abuse, when the conventional anti-corruption measures are met with resistance, ridicule, de-legitimisation, manipulation, hijacking, and weaponising.

Rather than innovation as aligning with de-contextualised 'best practice', the book aims to explore innovation as a response to when traditional approaches to anti-corruption have shown few successes, are no longer serving their purposes, or are backfiring. The assumption being that innovation is needed to make anti-corruption work in hostile or passive environments.

We pay attention to innovative anti-corruption that can be built on a mix of foundations. Above all, innovation is locally driven. It grows up as an answer to location-specific forms of power abuse and inaction (the local political economy factors and incentive structures). Innovation therefore keys into opportunities presented by time and space in specific contexts. Taking advantage when windows of opportunity occur (historical factors and watershed events) can be a source of innovation. USAID, for instance, argued in its Dekleptification Guide that moving rapidly and aggressively in historic windows of opportunity is necessary to fight kleptocrats and can make reforms harder to reverse (USAID 2022). Localised innovation tends to anticipate challenges, seeking early forms of prevention. In contexts of de-democratisation, this can mean identifying and acting against anti-democratic politicians and their strategies before they manage to wing-clip institutional checks and balances and stifle the opposition, civil society, and media, and manipulate elections (Amundsen and Jackson 2021).

Innovation grows from new forms of collaboration: actors finding new partnerships and drawing mutual inspiration. The 'usual suspects' involved in anti-corruption work, i.e., the international and national NGOs, civil society organisations, professional associations, anti-corruption commissions, and citizens can probably maximise the impact and raise the pressure for change by adding new actors in collective action.

Sometimes, 'strange bedfellows' can be central and surprising allies. We have, for instance seen how the Nigeria Police Force (NPF) – an institution infamous for being outright corrupt – has partnered with Nigeria's anti-corruption commission (the Economic and Financial Crimes Commission, EFCC) in its efforts to curb police corruption (PSC 2008: 1). Transnational networks can help local NGOs use legislation and policy to pressurise corrupt leaders. This was the conclusion of a research article from 2014 that analysed Transparency International as a transnational NGO back in 2014 (Gutterman 2014). That international organisations might help in-country reformers at critical junctures in time has also been argued by Guerzovich et al. (2020).

Innovation in anti-corruption may draw on new technologies which can be used to analyse the corruption problem and to disclose corrupt practices. Artificial Intelligence (AI) can potentially uncover hidden and corrupt relationships, do real-time analyses of transactions, and can be used for more precise risk-scoring and prediction models (Jaiyeola 2023). Big data can be analysed to identify patterns in everything from tax evasion to social networks and can be extended into new areas and be implemented in new strategies and by a wider set of users. Investigative journalists have, for instance used big data analytics on the Pandora Papers to uncover some of the biggest corruption scandals. Crowdsourcing platforms can be deployed for collecting information (Jaiyeola 2023). Blockchain is still regarded as a platform for illicit trade, money laundering, tax evasion, and corruption, as individuals do not have to disclose their identity when participating in a transaction and the transactions are made very quickly. However, some observers also see its potential for anti-corruption (Muci 2023; Kaplan 2021).

Alternative analytical perspectives can also help generate new forms of practice. Novel language can cast light on the consequences of corruption and possibilities of change in energising and inspiring ways. Bringing in perspectives from diverse traditions, such as human rights or gender, can fashion more powerful forms of argument and action. Novel heuristics enlighten how corruption can be structured and therefore how it should be addressed.

Four chapters in this book show these elements are put into practice. Sakib, Ahmed, and Amundsen in 'Civil Society in an adverse environment' retrace how Transparency International Bangladesh innovated through new forms of interacting in the public space and with government. Cepeda Cuadrado in 'Anticorruption with a Human Rights Lens' shows how in Latin American countries that innovation emerged through new forms of collaboration between human rights and anti-corruption agendas that responded to various opportunities to act. Erasmus, Glencorse and Scrimgeour in their chapter on 'Translocalism' show how translocalism can help refine how collective action in anti-corruption is structured, making an argument for how collective action can become more resilient in a discordant world. Exploring the potential for artificial intelligence to lead to anti-corruption innovations, Gerli and Odilla describe the various production processes by which these tools emerge.

References

Amundsen, Inge (2019): Extractive and power-preserving political corruption. In: Amundsen, I. (ed.): *Political Corruption in Africa*. Cheltenham: Edward Elgar Publishing Ltd.

Amundsen, Inge and David Jackson (2021): *Rethinking Anti-Corruption in De-Democratising Regimes*. Bergen: Chr. Michelsen Institute (U4 Issue 2021:5). (www.cmi.no/publications/7743-rethinking-anti-corruption-in-de-democratising-regimes).

Ananta, P., M. E. B. M. Kamal and N. Mohamed (2023): *Public Spending, Corruption, and Human Development: Empirical Evidence in Middle-Income Countries*. European Proceedings of Social and Behavioural Sciences. Conference paper, November 2023. (https://doi.org/10.15405/epsbs.2023.11.48).

Arriola, Leonardo R., Lise Rakner and Nicolas Van de Walle, eds. (2023): *Democratic Backsliding in Africa? Autocratization, Resilience, and Contention*. Oxford: Oxford University Press.

Baumann, H. (2020): The corruption perception index and the political economy of governing at a distance. *International Relations*, 31(1), 504–523 (https://doi.org/10.1177/0047117819897312).

Brown, E. and J. Cloke (2004): Neoliberal reform, governance and corruption in the south: assessing the international anti-corruption crusade. *Antipode*, 36(2), pp.272-294.

Buchan, B. and L. Hill (2014): *An intellectual history of political corruption*. London: Palgrave Macmillan.

Buchan, B. and L. Hill (2014): *An intellectual history of political corruption*. Springer.

Carothers, Christopher (2022): Taking authoritarian anti-corruption reform seriously. *Perspectives on Politics,* 20(1), 69–85.

Cheeseman, N. and B. Klaas (2019): *How to Rig an Election*. Croydon: Yale University Press.

Chin, J. J. (2021): Coups d'Etat in the COVID-19 era. *Brown Journal of World Affairs*, 28, 161.

Croissant, A. and J. Haynes (2021): Democratic regression in Asia: Introduction. *Democratization*, 28(1), 1–21. (https://doi.org/10.1080/13510347.2020.1851203).

Davies, S., T. Pettersson and M. Öberg (2023): Organized violence 1989–2022, and the return of conflict between states. *Journal of Peace Research*, 60(4), 691–708.

Dunn, Kevin C. (2008): Never mind the bollocks: The punk rock politics of global communication. *Review of International Studies,* 34(S1), 193–210.

Economist (2023): 2024 will be a stressful year for those who care about liberal democracy. *The Economist*. November 13th.

Edgerton, R. B. (2022): *Rules, Exceptions, and Social Order*. Berkeley and Los Angles: University of California Press.

Engler, Sarah (2020): "Fighting corruption" or "fighting the corrupt elite"? Politicizing corruption within and beyond the populist divide. *Democratization*, 27(4), 643–661.

Feikema, Liesbeth (Elisabeth Titia) (2024): Anti-corruption law as a fiction: The illusion of serving morality by controlling it through rules and regulations with an international reach. *Global Perspectives*, 5(1), 115472.

Funaki, Y. and B. Glencorse (2014): Anti-corruption or accountability? International efforts in post-conflict Liberia. *Third World Quarterly*, 35(5), 836–854. (https://doi.org/10.1080/01436597.2014.921433).

Grindle, M.S. (2017): Politics and policy implementation in the Third World.

Guerzovich, Florencia, María Soledad Gattoni and Dave Algoso (2020): *Seeing New Opportunities: How Global Actors can Better Support Anticorruption Reformers*. Open Society Foundations, report, November 2020.

Gutterman, Ellen (2014): The legitimacy of transnational NGOs: Lessons from the experience of Transparency International in Germany and France. *Review of International Studies*, 40(2), 391–418.

Gutterman, E. ānd M. Lohaus (2018): What is the "anti-corruption" norm in global politics? In Kubbe, I., Engelbert, A. (eds): *Corruption and Norms* (pp. 241–268). Springer International Publishing. (https://doi.org/10.1007/978-3-319-66254-1_12).

Hassner, Pierre (2008): Russia's transition to autocracy. *Journal of Democracy*, 19(2), 5–15. (https://www.journalofdemocracy.org/articles/russias-transition-to-autocracy/).
Heilman, B. and L. Ndumbaro (2002): Corruption, politics and societal values in Tanzania: An evaluation of the Mkapa administration's anti corruption efforts. *African Journal of Political Science*, 7(1). (https://doi.org/10.4314/ajps.v7i1.27322).
Jackson, D. (2020): *How change happens in anti-corruption. A map of policy perspectives.* Bergen: U4 Anti-Corruption Resource Centre, Chr. Michelsen Institute (U4 Issue 2020:14).
Jaiyeola, Alhaji Razak (2023): *Deploying Emerging Technology to Fight Corruption.* International Federation of Accountants (IFAC) Content Series, 13 January 2023. (www.ifac.org/knowledge-gateway/building-trust-ethics/discussion/deploying-emerging-technology-fight-corruption).
Johnston, Michael and Scott Fritzen (2021): *The Conundrum of Corruption. Reform for Social Justice.* Oxon: Routledge.
Joutsen, Matti and Adam Graycar (2012): When experts and diplomats agree: Negotiating peer review of the UN convention against corruption. *Global Governance: A Review of Multilateralism and International Organizations*, 18(4), 425–439.
Kaplan, Mehmet (2021): Cryptocurrency and corruption: Auditing with blockchain. In: Aksoy, T., Hacioglu, U. (eds): *Auditing Ecosystem and Strategic Accounting in the Digital Era.* Cham: Springer Verlag.
Khan, Mushtaq, Antonio Andreoni and Pallavi Roy (2019): *Anti-Corruption in Adverse Contexts: Strategies for Improving Implementation.* Working Paper. SOAS.
Khan, Mushtaq H. (2005): Markets, states and democracy: Patron–client networks and the case for democracy in developing countries. *Democratization*, 12(5), 704–724.
Kutlay, M. and Z. Öniş (2023): Liberal democracy on the edge? Anxieties in a shifting global (dis)order. *Alternatives*, 48(1), 20–37. (https://doi.org/10.1177/03043754221096511).
Lang, B. (2019): *China and Global Integrity-Building: Challenges and Prospects for Engagement.* U4 Issue.
Lehti, M. and H. R. Pennanen (2020): Beyond liberal empire and peace: Declining hegemony of the West? In: Lehti, M., Pennanen, H. R., Jouhki, J. (eds): *Contestations of Liberal Order.* Cham: Palgrave Macmillan. (https://doi.org/10.1007/978-3-030-22059-4_2).
Lesch, M. (2021). Multiplicity, hybridity and normativity: Disputes about the UN convention against corruption in Germany. *International Relations*, 35(4), 613–633. (https://doi.org/10.1177/0047117820965662).
Levitsky, S. and D. Ziblatt (2018): *How Democracies Die.* New York: Penguin Books.
Levitsky, S. and L. A. Way (2025): The path to American Authoritarianism: What comes after the democratic breakdown? *Foreign Affairs*, 36.
Marquette, H. and C. Pfeiffer (2015): *Corruption and Collective Action,* Developmental Leadership Program and U4. Available at: https://www.u4.no/publications/corruption-and-collective-action.
McGaughey, E. (2018): Could brexit be void? *King's Law Journal*, 29(3), 331–343.
Mearsheimer, J. J. (2019): Bound to fail: The rise and fall of the liberal international order. *International Security*, 43(4), 7–50.

Mendilow, J. and É. Phélippeau (2021): *Populism and Corruption: The Other Side of the Coin.* Cheltenham and Northhampton (MA): Edward Elgar Publishing.
Muci, Frank (2023): *Can Blockchains Reduce Corruption?* A NYE Special (commentary), 31 December 2023. (https://frankmuci.substack.com/p/can-blockchains-reduce-corruption).
Mueller, R. S. (2019): *Complete Report on the Investigation Into Russian Interference in the 2016 Presidential Election.* U.S. Department of Justice, Washington, D.C. March 2019.
Mungiu-Pippidi, A. (2023): *Rethinking Corruption.* Cheltenham: Edward Elgar Publishing.
Nye, J. S. (1967): Corruption and political development: A cost-benefit analysis. *The American Political Science Review*, 61(2), 417–427.
Orenstein, M. (2024): *Russia's Hybrid Warfare: Disinformation and Interference in Moldova.* FPRI: Foreign Policy Research Institute. United States of America.
Our World in Data (2024a): *People Living in Democracies and Autocracies, World.* Political regimes are based on the classification by Lührmann et al. (2018) and the estimates by V-Dem's experts (People living in democracies and autocracies, World (ourworldindata.org)).
Our World in Data (2024b): *Deaths in Armed Conflicts, World.* Conflict Data Explorer – Our World in Data.
Pavlova, E. (2020): *Corrupt governance: Self-defeating anti-corruption rhetoric and initiatives in Russia.* New Perspectives, 28(2), pp.205-222.
Persson, A., B. Rothstein and J. Teorell (2019): Getting the basic nature of systemic corruption right: A reply to Marquette and Peiffer. *Governance*, 32(4), 799–810.
PSC (2008): *Combating Corruption in the Nigeria Police.* A Presentation. Independent Corrupt Practices & Other Related Offences Commission, August 2008.
Rabnawaz, A. (2015): Corruption, inequality and economic growth. *Developing Country Studies*, 5(15), 106–111.
Robbins, P. (2000): The rotten institution: Corruption in natural resource management. *Political Geography*, 19(4), 423–443.
Rose-Ackerman, Susan (1978): *Corruption: A Study in Political Economy.* Cambridge/MA: Academic Press.
Rothstein, B. (2021): *Controlling corruption: The social contract approach.* Oxford University Press.
Sberna, Salvatore and Alberto Vannucci (2013): "It's the politics, stupid!". The politicization of anti-corruption in Italy. *Crime Law Soc Change*, 60, 565–593. (https://doi.org/10.1007/s10611-013-9480-8).
Scheffran, J. (2025). Planetary boundaries, polycrisis and politics in the anthropocene: Climate pathways, tipping cascades and transition to sustainable peace in integrative geography. In *Towards Rethinking Politics, Policy and Polity in the Anthropocene: Multidisciplinary Perspectives* (pp. 339–444). Cham: Springer Nature Switzerland.
Schiffrin, A. (2017). Disinformation and democracy: The internet transformed protest but did not improve democracy. *Journal of International Affairs*, 71(1), 117–126. (https://www.jstor.org/stable/26494367).
Taylor, S. P. (2017): What is innovation? A study of the definitions, academic models and applicability of innovation to an example of social housing in England. *Open Journal of Social Sciences*, 5, 128–146. (https://doi.org/10.4236/jss.2017.511010).

Trautman, L. J. (2021): Democracy at risk: Domestic terrorism and attack on the US capital. *Seattle University Law Review*, 45, 1153.
USAID (2022): *Dekleptification Guide. Seizing Windows of Opportunity to Dismantle Kleptocracy.* Prepared by a USAID task team. Washington DC, September 2022. (www.usaid.gov/document/usaid-dekleptification-guide).
V-Dem (2024): *Democracy Report 2024. Democracy Winning and Losing at the Ballot.* By Nord, Marina, Martin Lundstedt, David Altman, Fabio Angiolillo, Cecilia Borella, Tiago Fernandes, Lisa Gastaldi, Ana Good God, Natalia Natsika, and Staffan I. Lindberg. University of Gothenburg: V-Dem Institute. March 2024.
Van Vuuren, Hennie, Michael Marchant, Anine Kriegler and Murray Hunter (2018): *Apartheid Guns and Money: A Tale of Profit.* London: C Hurst & Company.
Wiener, Antje(2017):A theory of contestation—A concise summary of its argument and concepts. *P*
olity, 49(1), 109–125.
Wong, M. Y. (2023): Economic development, corruption, and income inequality: The role of the informal sector. *Politics*, 45(2). (https://doi.org/10.1177/02633957221148951).
Zhu, Jiangnan and Dong Zhang (2017): Weapons of the powerful: Authoritarian elite competition and politicized anticorruption in China. *Comparative Political Studies*, 50(9), 1186–1220. (https://doi.org/10.1177/0010414016672234).

PART II

Contestation

2

POPULISM, DISCOURSE, AND CHANGE

Anti-Corruption Policies in Mexico

Gabriel Rojas-Salazar and Luis Roberto Vargas-Pineda

Rhetoric and Ideological Battles

In his inauguration speech, Andrés Manuel López Obrador (AMLO), President of Mexico 2018–2024, declared that during his mandate, "a peaceful and orderly transformation will be carried out, but at the same time deep and radical, because corruption and impunity that prevent the rebirth of Mexico will be ended" (2018). His intention to position corruption as a central and urgent problem was evident. This discourse would mark his entire administration; however, there are questions about what his real interests were, how they materialized, and how AMLO has used his discourse to push an agenda of reforms highly supported by a large sector of the citizenry but with a minimal impact to reduce corruption as shown by the data from the National Institute of Statistics, Geography and Information (INEGI) (2021; 2023) and in the 2024 Corruption Perception Index (Transparency International 2025). This discourse aimed at questioning and defaming opponents based on the construction of a narrative where the opposition was pointed out as guilty of the problem is not exclusively from populist politicians but certainly is exacerbated in populist regimes.

This chapter acknowledges that corruption is a complex and evolving phenomenon shaped by social and political discourses. These discourses, endorsed by political actors, not only influence public policy but also impact the public's perception of corruption. How corruption is defined and addressed affects anti-corruption policies, which are inherently political. In democracies, different actors with conflicting perspectives shape anti-corruption policies, while in populist regimes, the dynamics can be quite different. Populist leaders may challenge the policy process by promoting mechanisms based more on

DOI: 10.4324/9781003531920-4

political aspects instead of technical ones and by promoting direct democratic processes such as referendums or voting to legitimize these policies (Collin 2019; Mohrenberg et al. 2021; Zaslove et al. 2021).

The anti-corruption discourse benefits a populist regime that can be instrumentalized to gain power and criticize political opponents. Furthermore, as Mudde (2004) and Mudde and Kaltwasser (2017) argues, due to the ideological ambiguity of populist movements, the policy definitions and alternatives might be similar to the ones proposed by their political opponents, but the chance to point to these contradictions is silenced down in comparison to non-populist regimes. However, since the discursive strength of populism is strong, these proposals can be entirely accepted; thus, policy proposals that were previously unacceptable are approved and defended, although in this process, based mainly on discourse, little is studied on policy outcomes (Pritchett 2023).

This chapter examines how AMLO's government has used anti-corruption rhetoric in broader ideological battles, particularly criticizing neoliberalism. By framing corruption as a result of neoliberal policies, the administration often targets political opponents based on moralistic approaches. This blurring of lines between corrupt actors and opposition groups bolsters the government's moral authority while undermining institutions designed to combat corruption, such as the National Anti-Corruption System (NAS) or the National Institute for Transparency, Access to Information and Protection of Personal Data (INAI). This chapter also explores how AMLO has shifted the discourse on corruption, making previously unacceptable policy changes seem legitimate using the *Overton Window*, a model that describes how ideas are shaped and evolve through time, going in cycles; thus, the Window shows how ideas that seem politically unacceptable in one moment, later could be accepted and have a high level of legitimacy.

It is relevant to mention that the Overton window seems absent from academic literature on corruption and anti-corruption policies. However, this does not imply that this model cannot be utilized to analyze how public opinion, political elites, policymakers, and activists framed and understood these phenomena. On the contrary, literature provides stories about changes in the perception of corruption, suggesting shifts in the Overton window.

The chapter is divided into five sections. In the first section, we outline how populism reconfigures what is public and how the populist discourse can define corruption and identify and design alternatives for its solution. This section also explains this chapter's relationship with this book's framework.

The second section explains the *Overton Window* as a valuable model for tracing discursive changes over time. This model shows how ideas that may be unacceptable become accepted and legitimate over time. We argue that this method can show the paradoxes and ambiguities in the political changes that populist movements promote.

The third section examines the changes in discussions about anti-corruption policies and strategies in Mexico from 2015 to the presidential elections in June 2024. This timeframe is selected because it starts with establishing the NAS, a system that resulted from a broad discussion following an anti-corruption scandal. It also covers the administration of AMLO, which represents a shift in institutions based on populist reasoning. We will analyze speeches at conferences, official documents, and news articles demonstrating the key trends and beliefs of the most influential political figures during this period.

In the fourth section, we present the discourses and how they have changed, showing that AMLO's proposals used to be considered unacceptable, even by his party. At the same time, they now enjoy legitimacy and broad support from the political actors in power. In that sense, the Overton Window illustrates how discursive changes occurred, especially in contexts of high political ambiguity, such as populist governments.

The chapter closes with some brief reflections on the anti-corruption discourse and its marked changes in the context of populist governments. Hence, this chapter provides a clear idea of how populist regimes can utilize anti-corruption discourses to impose their views, values, and ideology but without engaging in anti-corruption policies that deal with corruption and how populist regimes can benefit from corrupt systems and practices to gain and preserve power (Mendilow 2021).

Corruption in the Context of Populist Regimes

Corruption as a public problem is socially constructed, so its definition and conceptualization vary depending on a specific zeitgeist's social and political factors. For AMLO's government, corruption is entangled with neoliberalism; the perspective defends the Mexican people who were betrayed by the technocratic elites, who overturned the scale of values and the political and economic system. Thus, neoliberalism is a flagrant enemy along with the members of these elites, which include opposition politicians, prominent businessmen, academics who question the government's actions, activists, and members of civil society. To illustrate this point, speeches and official documents are collected. In SFP communiqué 042 (2019b), it is stated that state austerity "gathers the best of our country's history and moves away from the application of neoliberal austerity that affects social rights". In another SFP communiqué (2019c) – the 116th – , it is expressed that "[t]he worst inheritance of neoliberalism is corruption". Finally, in the Second Government Report, AMLO commented that "conservatives are angry because there is no more corruption and they lost privileges" (Presidencia de la Republica 2024).

For that reason, the link between populism and corruption is especially relevant. Populist leaders, by appealing directly to "the people", often present themselves as authentic representatives of the interests of the discontented masses, confronting political elites who, according to them, are inherently corrupt (Jancsics 2024). In this sense, the populist discourse seeks to discredit the traditional political class, using corruption as a rhetorical weapon to polarize society (Busby et al. 2018; Cheeseman and Peiffer 2024; Kubbe and Loli 2020). However, this strategy can lead to the erosion of democratic control mechanisms and a centralization of power, where the leader and his close circle become unaccountable and with absolute impunity. Thus, the populist narrative reduces the effectiveness of institutional checks and balances and alters how anti-corruption policies are conceived, shifting them towards more moralistic and less institutionalized approaches (Dussauge-Laguna 2022), as the way to end corruption depends on individual morals, as AMLO defended in his speech.

"Populist platforms" adopt different policies to reduce the power of the elites, while in reality, those policies benefit the same elites, even ending in altering equilibria, exacerbating inequality or unfairness (Mendilow 2021; Müller 2019). How do populist actors achieve this? Mendilow (2021) argues that they manipulated widespread resentment, helping them to win office, and then they masked corrupt acts perpetrated by themselves and their collaborators. A similar idea is proposed by Arellano-Gault and Rojas-Salazar (2021) when they explain the concept of the original contradiction in anti-corruption policy in contexts under systemic corruption, which consists of how the actors with more power are the ones that are in charge of implementing, developing, and sustaining the anti-corruption reforms. Yet, they are the ones that benefit the most from the corrupt system. Hence, they are unlikely to promote effective anti-corruption reforms, as this would contest their status quo (Morris 2022).

The relationship between populism and corruption is intensified when populist governments redefine anti-corruption policies from a "direct democracy" perspective. Instead of strengthening traditional oversight mechanisms, such as professional audits or collaboration with external actors, populism presents corruption as a "moral perversion" that can be corrected through a movement that fosters the national identity, highlighting values such as honesty or loyalty (Cheeseman and Peiffer 2024; Engler 2020). This simplistic narrative may generate widespread support in the short term but often weakens democratic institutionality in the long term, as well as technical efforts to reduce corruption while instrumentalizing it for their own ends, such as the appropriation of public goods and the abuse of power for their benefit. By concentrating power on the leader and delegitimizing institutions and opponents, populist governments create an environment where accountability is minimal, which can exacerbate the corruption problems they initially set out to combat (Arellano-Gault and Rojas-Salazar 2021; Bauer et al. 2021; Dussauge-Laguna 2022).

Additionally, they can promote practices such as patrimonialism, patronage, and the spoils system that reinforce the political logic of representativeness at the expense of institutionalization and robustness of career civil services (Arellano-Gault 2021; Bauer and Becker 2020; Peters and Pierre 2020; Dussauge-Laguna 2022). In this regard, Kossow (2019) argues that populist leaders use anti-corruption discourse to divert attention and justify their actions, usually oriented to hiring people who are part of their movement, as they will be loyal and supportive of the populist leader.

Populism is ideologically contradictory and ductile (Meny and Surel 2002; Stanley 2008). In that sense, there are diverse populist movements and expressions. Bauer and Becker (2020), Bauer et al. (2021), Bauer (2023), Dussauge-Laguna (2022), and Moynihan (2022) illustrate how populism contributes to the dismantling of the administrative apparatus, similar to the process of emptying the state, which arose from the privatization of the public apparatus based on political ideas, such as reducing the state since it is part of the elites, a technical one based on "efficiency" and cost opportunity. Populist leaders might consider the institutional settings redundant and expensive, and finally, a symbolic one, in which populist leaders might want to put forth a portrayal in which they are going to solve the problems; they have the best solutions without the help of incompetent bureaucrats (Kossow 2019).

Regarding political discussions, populism is a narrative strategy that uses communication tactics to gain the support of a vulnerable, underrepresented group of voters (Groza and Groza 2017: 149). These tactics are employed by a charismatic leader who encourages the public to participate in collective action in political parties or "movement parties". This is achieved by using emotional storytelling that promises to provide direct representation (Retamozo 2014).

Populist leaders also use the concept of "the people" to justify illegal policies, pursue political polarization, and demonize the opposition (Dussauge-Laguna 2022: 780). Their discourse thrives in the tensions between populist rhetoric and political pluralism, where any opposition is quickly identified as a rival deprived of any legitimacy; furthermore, the moralization of political conflicts presents "elites" as inherently corrupt and intransigent (Castaño 2018). Mudde (2004) illustrates this by showing how populists build the notion of "pure people" in contrast to the "corrupt elite". Kossow (2019: 4) continues this idea by arguing that when looking at cases of populism around the world, corruption indeed emerges as a key element in the rhetoric and communication of populist candidates.

Another risk is that the centralization of power and policy decisions in the leader's figure diminishes the effectiveness of checks and balances, even within the public administration. The very contributions and the essential role of this type of leadership – even if we are willing to accept that at some point they could have accomplished the strengthening of democracy – populism transforms the leader and his inner core of supporters into largely unaccountable elements (Balderacchi 2023: 218).

In the same way as with policymaking, populism seeks to shift anti-corruption efforts from a "liberal democracy" perspective to a "direct democracy" one. This displaces out-of-the-window accountability, i.e., measures such as vertical and horizontal oversight, professional auditing, collaboration with civil society and international watchdog organizations, etc., with discourses that frame corruption as a matter of morality, as a "perversion" of public service that can be amended by enforcing the principles of the people's movement. This is the idea of the morally superior group that is true to the people's interest, as they are the only ones that share the identity, sense of belonging, values, or even tragedies, as Kossow (2019) suggests.

As argued by Curini (2018), the promise of addressing corruption has become a common theme in the electoral promises of populist movements, enormously appealing to the discontent of voters who feel aggravated by the abuses of the political establishment. However, in political moralization, corruption is weaponized as an argument that can be used to derail the campaign and career of politicians who are claimed to be involved in corruption schemes.

Before discussing how the Overton Window model helps understand the political discourses built around anti-corruption policies in Mexico during AMLO's administration, it is essential to disclose that, for this chapter's purposes, we are focusing only on the political discourse, not on whether it materializes in policies. Our point is that discourses and narratives by themselves can reflect and influence the tolerance and acceptance of ideas and beliefs. This paradox is linked to the three conceptual lenses proposed by the editors of this book. Our chapter is focused on the "contestation lens", which shows how much anti-corruption is wrapped up in systems of unjust power and how politics plays out arbitrarily and is re-interpreted in this fashion, thus repudiating the normative approaches, such as the one based on more technical analysis.

Narrative Discourses, Change, and Legitimacy

The Overton Window of Political Possibilities is a model to understand the political reasoning behind choosing specific ideas and using them to win elections. Therefore, the model can serve as a guideline to understand and analyze the subsequent implementation of policies (Mackinack Center for Public Policy 2019; Pritchett 2023). "The core concept is that politicians are limited in what policy ideas they can support – they generally only pursue policies that are widely accepted throughout society as legitimate policy options" (Mackinack Center for Public Policy 2019). By framing the ideas considered acceptable in political discourse, the model maps the boundaries between what is deemed radical, acceptable, or unthinkable at any given time. As mentioned earlier, the range of ideas upon which the window can be placed is defined by the dominant ideological narrative; however, the window can play a vital role in understanding the ongoing policy discussions and the trajectory of reshaped ideological discourses.

The model is pertinent and valuable as populist discourses embrace different ideological positions, sometimes incoherently, the notion of the Overton Window serves to trace the paradoxes in the discourse, showing the demagogic nature of the political narratives in populism. It can also show how a populist context mobilizes ideas more practically and speedily, as populists have a considerable amount of power and flexibility in their positions to adapt to the necessities and feelings of their audience (Mendilow 2021). The model is not concerned with how political narratives are created but with why politicians will not support a particular policy. They will only support policies they believe will *not* compromise their election chances (Mackinack Center for Public Policy 2019).

The ongoing contestation of narratives means that the Overton Window can expand or shrink the number of ideas politicians can endorse without risking their electoral support. Of course, these shifts can be influenced by misleading information that becomes relevant enough to sway people's beliefs (Mackinack Center for Public Policy 2019; Pritchett 2023).

Changes of Discourse during AMLO's Administration

In this third section, we will analyze the discursive changes in anti-corruption policies and strategies in Mexico. It focuses on the period from the creation of the National Anti-corruption System (NAS) in 2015 to the presidential elections of June 2024. This period represents a significant turning point in the country's fight against corruption. First, the NAS marked a milestone in institutionalizing anti-corruption efforts. Then, the administration of Andrés Manuel López Obrador (AMLO) introduced a new populist narrative that redefined both the perception of and strategies to combat corruption, emphasizing austerity in terms of budget cutbacks, centralization of procurement procedures, and confrontation with political elites.

The discussion on fighting corruption has been marked by a struggle between promises of change and the challenges of implementing reforms. AMLO has prioritized combating corruption but has faced criticism for the lack of tangible results, as different surveys displayed (Vargas 2023). We will analyze speeches, official documents, and news articles to understand the core beliefs of key political figures during this period.

The analysis will focus on reviewing different discourses to identify prominent trends in anti-corruption policies. It will pay particular attention to the differences between the proposals during the creation of the NAS and those promoted during AMLO's administration. The analysis will also examine how the previously unacceptable approaches gained legitimacy and support within the official discourse, particularly in the context of the populist anti-corruption policy.

After corruption scandals, such as the one involving the *Casa Blanca* in 2016, which involved the former president, Enrique Peña Nieto, and a public contractor that was awarded substantial public contracts and generated pressure from citizens, the government led by Enrique Peña Nieto (2012 to 2018), decided to show its commitment to addressing the problem (Rincón 2018). As a result, it was decided to reinstitute the Ministry of Public Function, in charge of the discipline and sanctions to public servants of the federal executive power, which had been closed during that government's tenure in 2013 (Arellano-Gault 2020). However, this proposal faced widespread criticism from opposition parties, the press, and civil society organizations. This was because the secretariat was under the executive branch's control, and the secretary was known to be close to the president himself (Bureaugard 2015). Skepticism and criticism focused on concerns about the agency's potential lack of independence, neutrality, and impartiality. While Peña Nieto's decision to shut down the Ministry can be considered populist, the fact that actually, he was sensitive to the public opinion position against the decision and did not label them as traitors proves he is not a populist.

In response to constant pressure, the Peña Nieto administration proposed the establishment of an anti-corruption agency to investigate acts of corruption (Monsivais-Carrillo 2019). The proposal addressed the need for an independent entity with technical and legal expertise to handle complex corruption cases involving public officials and private individuals. The agency was expected to operate impartially and independently from the executive branch, and to rebuild citizen confidence in the justice system and the government's commitment to transparency and accountability.

However, the proposal faced skepticism from opposition parties at that moment. The right-wing party *Partido Acción Nacional* (PAN) and the left-wing parties *Movimiento Regeneración Nacional* (Morena) and *Partido de la Revolución Democrática* (PRD) questioned the relevance of an agency that the ruling party, *Partido de la Revolución Institucional* (PRI), could potentially influence (Arellano-Gault 2020; Nieto 2020). Furthermore, Mexico's history of impunity raised concerns about the willingness to tackle corruption, especially in cases involving high-profile individuals or those with close ties to power (Rodriguez et al. 2015).

In December 2015, PRI, the party in power, established a political pact with PAN and PRD named "The Pact for Mexico," in which one of the agreements was the design of an anti-corruption policy (Rodriguez et al. 2015; Transparencia Mexicana 2016). PAN presented a new proposal with six points, including the creation of the National Anticorruption System, a

Citizen Committee for Public Ethics, the strengthening of the Minister of Public Function (SFP), and the creation of a National Council on the matter, among others (Rodriguez et al. 2015). This even represented a change in the political system, as the three parties with assumably different ideologies were negotiating and unifying to achieve policy outcomes on a myriad of topics.

An alternative idea was to create a network of public organizations collaborating in an institutional framework under citizen oversight to prevent the concentration and abuse of power and address institutional distrust (Palifka et al. 2021). This was proposed by various social actors and gained legitimacy among relevant actors also in the public policy sector (Monsivais-Carrillo 2019; Nieto 2020; Transparencia Mexicana 2016).

The NAS was therefore designed to collaborate with non-governmental organizations, academia, and the government (Palifka et al. 2021). NAS consists of various organizations working together to identify, prevent, and sanction acts of corruption. The system includes a Coordinating Committee and Civic Participation Committee to pursue public and citizen interests. It has been replicated in local and state governments to create anti-corruption systems at different levels (Sistema Nacional Anticorruption [SNA], n.d).

The rationale behind NAS was based on the need for power distribution through establishing a governance network in which collaboration was necessary and substantive and in which the specialization of technical functions was fundamental, i.e., the organizations in charge of auditing must be experts. The courts and prosecutors' offices had to be dedicated to processing investigations through information gathered through internal and external controls (Arellano-Gault 2020). Moreover, NAS made a distinction between identification, investigation, prevention, and sanctioning processes. Additionally, the NAS pursues a decentralization logic, seeking the transfer and development of capacities of local and municipal governments (Palifka et al. 2021). All of the above was a way to shield the system from the possibility of capture, manipulation, or dismantling, which were the main concerns of the political actors at that time.

From 2015 to 2017, the National Anti-Corruption System (NAS) received attention and resources from political figures. However, corruption remained a significant issue on the public agenda. New corruption cases, such as the *Estafa Maestra*, an investigation that revealed a corrupt network in which different actors from PRI were involved in the embezzlement of more than 9 billion pesos, were uncovered by a team of auditors and independent journalists (Corona 2017; Hernandez 2017; Redacción Animal Político 2017). Additionally, there were notable instances of favoritism and nepotism. Several supplementary laws and legislative reforms were enacted to support the NAS operations, including the *General Law of Administrative Responsibilities*, the *Organic Law of the Federal Court of Administrative Justice*, and the *General Law of Transparency and Access to Public Information*.

However, in 2018, establishing the NAS was not concluded because the Senate had not appointed the anti-corruption prosecutor, and the local congresses had not yet finished harmonizing their regulatory frameworks (Bohorquez 2018). Thus, there was a change in the discourse, where Peña Nieto's government had reduced its interest in backing the NAS (Nieto 2020).

In contrast, citizens continued to see this as one of the principal debts of his administration that was about to end in the 2018 National Survey of Quality and Trust in Government (INEGI 2019); corruption was chosen as the second major problem. At the same time, the then-candidate of Morena, the only significant party that did not join the Pact for Mexico, AMLO, used the anti-corruption discourse as one of his main banners during the campaign, highlighting the constant cases of abuses involving the administration of PRI and the PAN's previous governments. Thus, during his campaign, the term *PRIAN* was coined to show the similarity of both parties and their shared characteristics: corrupt, unscrupulous, and uninterested in the social demands of the working and peasant classes.

Mainly, social weariness with corruption and the indolence of Peña Nieto's administration led to a landslide victory for the Morena party in the 2018 presidential elections. AMLO won with 53% of the vote and over 30 million votes (Torreblanca et al. 2018). AMLO's discourse was oriented towards characterizing and explaining the central causes of the main public problems under an easy-to-use yet ambiguous and straightforward explanation: neoliberalism as the root of the main problems afflicting the people of Mexico. For example, in the president's speeches, he characterized neoliberals as unethical people who are indifferent, distant from the Mexican people, and have personal interests that contradict those of the nation and people (Rojas-Salazar 2020).

In his inauguration speech, AMLO stated that the "hallmark of neoliberalism is corruption" and "privatization has in Mexico been synonymous with corruption" (2019). Likewise, the National Government Plan of his administration mentioned that "the most destructive and pernicious characteristic of the Mexican neoliberals was the widespread corruption that has become a regular administrative practice. Corruption has been the main inhibitor of economic growth" (Presidencia de la República 2019). These rhetorics are widely studied by Morris (2021), showing the differences and similarities between the left and right populist leaders.

AMLO's discourse was instrumentalized from a populist logic, where "the neoliberal" and "the people" were constructed according to the president's needs and movement. Partisan interests shaped the categories, simplifying reality and disregarding central aspects such as professionalization, expertise, and the importance of dissent. The presidential rhetoric under AMLO's administration highlighted the importance of corruption and anti-corruption efforts championed by his government (López Obrador 2018, 2019, 2023a,

2023b, 2023c, 2023d). Likewise, austerity was considered a highly effective alternative to reduce corruption, so much so that the Federal Law of Republican Austerity recognized in its Article 4 that republican austerity is the policy

> that public entities [...] are obliged to abide by in accordance with their legal order, to combat social inequality, corruption, greed, and waste of national assets and resources, administering resources with efficiency, effectiveness, economy, transparency, and honesty to meet the objectives for which they are intended.
>
> *(Cámara de Diputados del H. Congreso del Unión 2019)*

"Republican austerity" is tied to the perception of corruption. According to Secretaría de Función Pública [SFP] (2019a, 2019b, 2019c), government austerity in Mexico aims to depart from the neoliberal austerity that negatively impacts social rights. The discourse was shifted to a discourse where austerity is advocated as a centralization and simplification of the problem, and to the need for concentration of power (Sandoval 2023). The president's supposed will and example were presented as tools.

Another relevant point was that in 2021, Morena's power in both chambers was enhanced as Morena, with its allied political parties, gained the majority in both chambers. Thus, the *Partido del Trabajo* (PT) and *Partido Verde Nacional* (PVEM) were essential to extend AMLO's power to control the legislative power and promote the policies that he wanted. In those mid-term elections, the opposition parties, PRI, PAN, and PRD, formed a coalition with poor results, as they were parties from the center, right, and left.

With a new position of power, the rhetoric did not change. Republican austerity and the criticism of the "expensive and redundant NAS" remained the same, and AMLO claimed that the responsibilities of those organizations were already performed by the executive power (Arellano-Gault and Rojas-Salazar 2021). Therefore, during this period, the NAS experienced a considerable reduction in its available resources (Instituto Mexicano para la Competitividad [IMCO] 2023). At the same time, some of its member organizations, such as the INAI, an independent public body in charge of transparency of public information, were openly questioned and boycotted since the Senate had not yet appointed the counselors.

AMLO and Morena supported the dismantling of independent public bodies such as INAI, NAS, and the election oversight agency (National Electoral Institute). The rationale behind this political discourse was to dismantle them as they "served the elites" according to the populist rhetoric of these reform proposals, as he argued: "It doesn't matter if it exists or no... whether they are appointed or not, what are they good for? They are good for nothing". (López Obrador 2023e). At the same time, the proposals were based on giving these responsibilities and tasks to the executive power controlled by Morena.

Claudia Sheinbaum, Morena's presidential winner of the 2024 elections, also presented her anti-corruption plan during her campaign, where she stated that the intention was to dismantle the NAS and to create a new anti-corruption agency that will depend on the executive branch (Corral 2024). This means discarding the incipient institutional advances and returning to a proposal initially questioned and discarded by several political factions, among which was AMLO and most of the party members who were part of the opposition at that time. Additionally, Sheinbaum continued with the discourse oriented to eliminate the autonomous agencies, especially INAI, repeating the same reasons AMLO has argued (Sarabia 2024), promising that the executive can carry out its functions, even if the reason behind the creation of INAI was part of the reforms to tackle down the high opacity of the Mexican governments prior to its creation. In this sense, aspects such as political will, loyalty, decorum, and centralization of power are highlighted under the mandate of the president and the party in power (Arellano-Gault and Rojas-Salazar 2021).

At the same time, the AMLO administration has not shown any progress in reducing corruption. On the contrary, corruption scandals persist involving people from the ruling party and close to the president, such as in the cases of SEGALMEX, and in conflicts of interest in the assignment of contracts for the mega infrastructure projects of this administration (Casar and Cejudo 2024; Mexicanos contra la Corrupción e Impunidad [MCCI] 2024, 2023, 2022, 2021). This indicates there have been changes in the discourse but not in reality. Equally, corruption cases and data on people's experiences and perceptions of corruption have not been reduced (INEGI 2021, 2023; Transparency International 2025). Still, the election results show that Morena enjoys high legitimacy.

Discursive Changes: Testing the Overton Window?

The Overton Window helps to understand how ideas or policy proposals can move from being unthinkable to becoming acceptable and, ultimately, mainstream policy. By linking this tool to a discursive analysis of Mexico's anti-corruption policies, it can be observed that, in the period between the creation of the National Anti-Corruption System (NAS) in 2015 and the 2024 presidential elections, the anti-corruption discourse has shifted significantly within the Overton Window. In this period, the fight against corruption has gone from being a citizen demand and a marginal issue in political discourse for the political actors in power to one of the main banners of political campaigns and the government in office, especially under AMLO, and then to be minimized again by Sheinbaum in her campaign.

The first significant change within the Overton Window occurred in 2015 with the creation of the NAS. At that time, Mexican society was in a state of outrage following the *Casa Blanca* scandal, which allowed an idea previously considered radical – to create an autonomous institutional network to directly fight corruption; while it is true that other institutions already exist, none of them were directly created to address corruption as their main issue – to move to the center of the Window, i.e., it became acceptable and eventually implemented (Arellano-Gault 2020). This creation responded to social demands for greater transparency and accountability and was made possible by a broad political consensus. NAS was seen as a technical and complex solution involving multiple actors, contrasting the previous top-down approach, which was highly criticized as symbolic in the past.

AMLO's arrival to the presidency in 2018 introduced a new populist narrative that transformed the Overton Window. His anti-corruption discourse focused on austerity and eliminating "neoliberalism" as the root of the country's problems, including corruption. In doing so, AMLO moved the debate toward a more simplified conception of corruption, where morality and the centralization of power in a substantial figure were positioned as the solution, conveying the message that he and his political party were the saviours, the moral keepers, and the ones that were honest and true to the people, against the corrupted neoliberals – the morally defeated serving the elites and foreigners (Rojas-Salazar 2020). Ideas that in previous years might have been considered unacceptable – such as the weakening of autonomous bodies and the concentration of power in the Executive – moved to the center of the window under this new discourse, gradually becoming more accepted in the political debate.

While some policies were created under AMLO's government, such as a program of disclosures by all public officials of assets and conflicts of interest; the strengthening of OIC (inspector generals) and the number of internal audits; the increase in administrative sanctions; whistleblower programs; integrity in business programs under the Ministry of Public Function (Ballesteros 2024). Nevertheless, the fact that it is under an Executive ministry in a government that was reluctant to share information reduces the credibility and trustworthiness of the results of these actions (Unidad de Investigación Aplicada MCCI 2023; Zavala 2024). Moreover, Ballesteros (2024) revamps the discourse of corruption as a problem related to neoliberalism, blaming the institutionalization on specific political actors who are opposition members, suggesting again a higher moral stance from the party in power.

This change from a collaborative, technical, and specialized process to another based on a populist discourse where political will is the center of the anti-corruption policy was not without its critics. Civil society organizations and academic sectors have pointed out that while AMLO's anti-corruption rhetoric has been effective politically, it has not produced the expected tangible results in reducing corruption. The lack of independence of specific institutions, such as the anti-corruption prosecutor, and the dismantling of bodies, such as the INAI, are seen as setbacks compared to the decentralized and collaborative model of the NAS (Casar and Cejudo 2023). However, these changes have gained public support thanks to the austerity narrative and confrontation with elites, allowing previously unthinkable ideas – such as proposing the dismantling of the Executive Office of the NAS – again to enter the public debate in the 2024 elections.

Finally, it can be argued that the Overton Window illustrates how anti-corruption discourse in Mexico evolved from more technical and decentralized proposals, at least with the creation of NAS and the strengthening of INAI, among other institutions, to more populist and centralized narratives, such as concentrating power under the Executive power, disregarding in the process other actors, such as NGOs and think tanks. While this chapter does not compare the discourses between Peña Nieto and AMLO, the fact that after some actions, Peña Nieto received backlash, which caused changes and corrections. At the same time, AMLO's government defended all its policies under a discourse that labeled its opposition as neoliberals, traitors of the nation, and enemies of the people, showing some differences in the rhetoric.

This movement reflects the tensions between professionalization and simplification of the corruption problem. While the NAS promoted a technical and specialized approach, AMLO's administration has moved the debate towards a vision in which political will and morality are sufficient to fight corruption. Looking ahead to Claudia Sheinbaum's new administration in 2024, anti-corruption proposals continue to shift within the Overton Window as a centralizing and simplified approach persists. Sheinbaum's administration announced in October 2024 a new anti-corruption ministry, the Anti-corruption and Good Government Minister (Presidencia de la República 2024), which will guide and support the NAS. Yet, the institutional functions and relations between both organizations are not precise. Moreover, the new president confirmed the dismantling of INAI among other independent oversight bodies.

Final Remarks

During the studied period, we observed a significant shift in how corruption is perceived and confronted, from an institutional and technical approach with the NAS to a more centralized and simplified one under AMLO. This discursive change is based on the populist narrative that identifies corruption as a product of neoliberalism. It proposes that its eradication depends on the

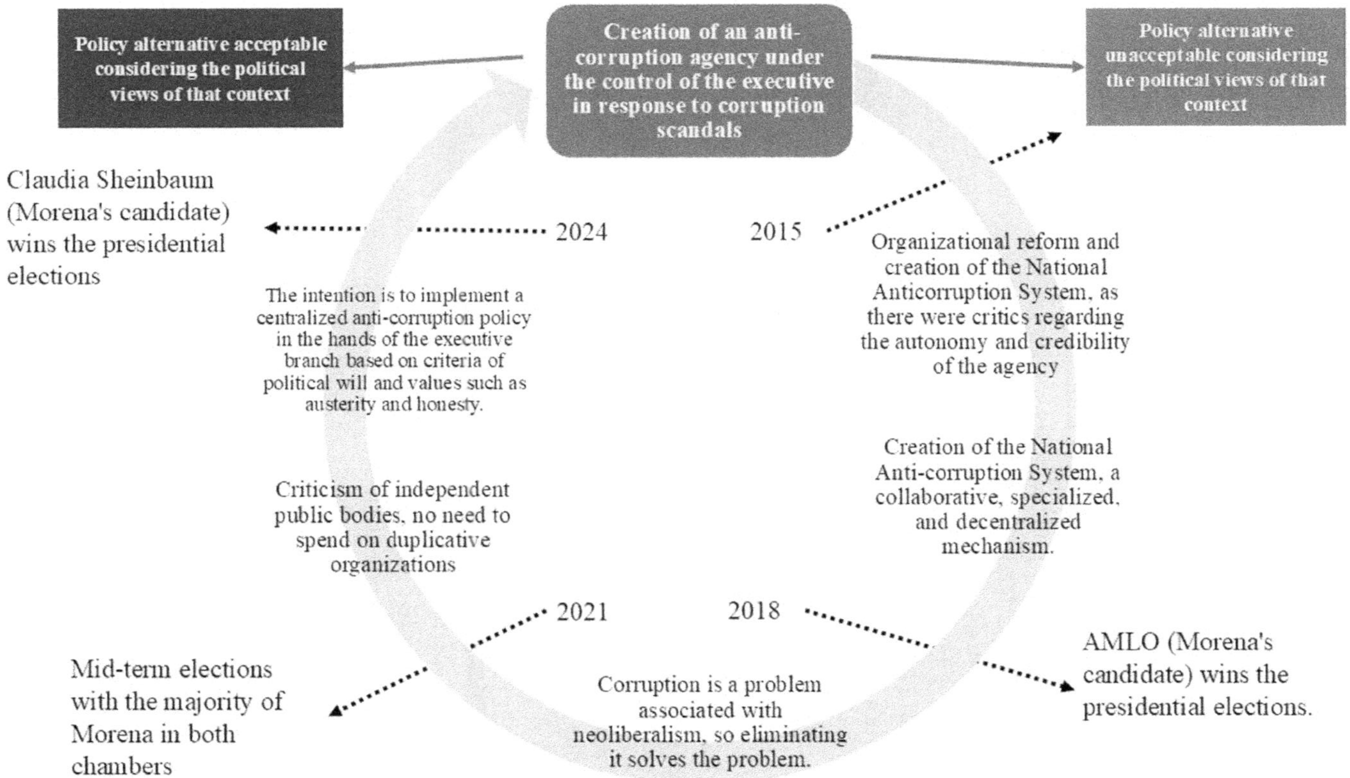

FIGURE 2.1 Overton Window of the anti-corruption policy discourse in Mexico from 2015 to 2024.

Source: Author's own compilation

leader's political will and republican austerity measures rather than on the construction of solid and autonomous institutions.

Using the Overton Window model demonstrates that discourses related to the centralization of power have changed considerably. To illustrate this, the proposal of an anti-corruption agency reflects the return to an initiative that was initially questioned: the anti-corruption agency. Initially, this initiative was criticized as there were suspicions of political capture. However, for the new populist regime, that is not a fear but a typical element in public institutions that "serve the will of the people". Therefore, an idea that was unacceptable eight years ago, in the current conditions, is legitimate enough to be implemented. Even if some political actors, civil society, and members of academia do not share the feasibility and appropriateness of the anti-corruption agency, the populist regime has enough power and acceptance to implement it. The results, viability, and consequences of creating a new organization, throwing away eight years of institutional knowledge, and organizational learning are not a concern, as this action is a statement, a symbolic element.

This chapter offers a good illustration of how anti-corruption policies should be critically reviewed and how, as with any other policy, anti-corruption requires the participation of actors different from the ones in the government. A pre-condition to trust in an anti-corruption is that it is open to include different groups' interests, views, and concerns, which might sound basic. However, one lesson from these discordant times and the world is that we should never overlook the basics. Ideas change, and legitimacy is built on the simplest emotions and feelings. Thus, putting back the public in anti-corruption policy is a must. Populist regimes game with this idea of representativeness, but it should be contested. A consensus could be something good, but it actually is an early alarm.

Finally, this analysis is linked to the paradox posed by the analytical lens of abuse of anti-corruption for power purposes. Our analysis shows how AMLO's government has used corruption to attack and delegitimize its political adversaries and protect its political allies. The "abuse lens" can be broken down into two dimensions. On the one hand, it is weaponizing, where anti-corruption is used as a weapon against opponents, reducing their legitimacy, silencing critics, and forcing the exile or imprisonment of critical figures. On the other hand, we find self-restraint, which implies strategic self-restraint not to act against the regime's allies, providing impunity. This phenomenon is not exclusive to Mexico; countries such as Argentina, Hungary, El Salvador, and other nations with populist governments show a similar pattern in discursive and practical corruption management.

References

Arellano-Gault, D. (2020). *Corruption in Latin America*. New York: Routledge.

Arellano-Gault, D. (2021). Respuesta al ataque populista a la administración pública. Estado Abierto. *Revista sobre el Estado, la Administración y las Políticas Públicas*, 4(3), 109–120.

Arellano-Gault, D., and Rojas-Salazar, G. (2021). Dealing with the "original contradiction" in fighting corruption in countries with systemic corruption: A critique of the cases of Brazil and Mexico and their multiorganizational strategies. In Pozsgai-Alvarez, J. (Ed.). *The Politics of Anti-Corruption Agencies in Latin America*. New York: Routledge.

Balderacchi, C. (2023). Populism and democracy: An analysis of the outcomes of populism. *Revista de Derecho Uninorte*, 59, pp. 204–224. Retrieved in: https://doi.org/10.14482/dere.59.340.325.

Bauer, M. W. (2023). Public administration under populist rule: Standing up against democratic backsliding. *International Journal of Public Administration*, 1–13.

Bauer, M. W., and Becker, S. (2020). Democratic backsliding, populism, and public administration. *Perspectives on Public Management and Governance*, 3(1), 19–31.

Bauer, M. W., Peters, B. G., Pierre, J., Yesilkagit, K., and Becker, S. (Eds.). (2021). *Democratic Backsliding and Public Administration: How Populists in Government Transform State Bureaucracies*. New York: Cambridge University Press.

Bohorquez, E. (2018). Por un Sistema Nacional Anticorrupción 2.0. *Letras Libres*. Retrieved in: https://letraslibres.com/revista/por-un-sistema-nacional-anticorrupcion-2-0

Bureaugard, L. (2015). Un zar anticorrupción ligado al poder en México. El País. Retrieved in: https://elpais.com/internacional/2015/02/05/actualidad/1423172524_532282.html

Busby, E., Doyle, D., Hawkins, K. A., and Wiesehomeier, N. (2018). Activating populist attitudes: The role of corruption. In Hawkins, K. A., Carlin, R. E., Littvay, L. and Kaltwasser, C. R. (Eds.). *The Ideational Approach to Populism: Concept, Theory, and Analysis*. New York, NY: Routledge.

Cámara de Diputados del H. Congreso de la Unión. (2019). Ley Federal de Austeridad Republicana. *Diario Oficial de la Federación*. Retrieved in: https://www.dof.gob.mx/nota_detalle.php?codigo=5575115andfecha=19/11/2019

Casar, M. A., and Cejudo, G. (2023). Anatomía de la Corrupción (4ª ed.). *Mexicanos Contra la Corrupción y la Impunidad*. Retrieved in: https://contralacorrupcion.mx/anatomia-de-la-corrupcion-cuarta-edicion/

Castaño, P. (2018). Populism and democracy. *International Journal of Sociology*, 76(4), 113. Available at: https://doi.org/10.3989/ris.2018.76.4.18.089.

Cheeseman, N., and Peiffer, C. (2024). Opening the door to anti-system leaders? Anti-corruption campaigns and the global rise of populism. *European Journal of Political Research*.

Collin, K. (2019). Populist and authoritarian referendums: The role of direct democracy in democratic deconsolidation. *Brookings policy brief*, Democracy and Disorder.

Corona, L. (2017). Gobierno federal, acusado de desviar casi 8,000 mdp entre 2013–2014. *Expansión*. Retrieved in: https://expansion.mx/nacional/2017/09/05/gobierno-federal-acusado-de-desviar-casi-8-000-mdp-entre-2013-2014

Corral, J. (2024). El plan anticorrupción de Claudia Sheinbaum. *El País*. Retrieved in: https://elpais.com/mexico/opinion/2024-04-11/el-plan-anticorrupcion-de-claudia-sheinbaum.html

Curini, L. (2018). *Corruption, Ideology, and Populism*. Cham: Springer International Publishing. Available at: https://doi.org/10.1007/978-3-319-56735-8.

Dussauge-Laguna, M. I. (2022). The promises and perils of populism for democratic policymaking: The case of Mexico. *Policy Sciences*, 55(4), 777–803. Available at: https://doi.org/10.1007/s11077-022-09469-z.

Engler, S. (2020). "Fighting corruption" or "fighting the corrupt elite"? Politicizing corruption within and beyond the populist divide. *Democratization*, 27(4), 643–661.

Groza, T., ānd Groza, E. (2017). Populism – A factory of myths. *Journal for the Study of Religions and Ideologies*, 16(48), 147–152.

Hernandez, M. (2017). Universidades públicas demuestran maestría en desvíos por más de 7,000 millones de pesos. *Huff. Post*. Retrieved in: https://web.archive.org/web/20180118064527/http://www.huffingtonpost.com.mx/2017/03/09/universidades-publicas-demuestran-maestria-en-desvios-por-mas-de_a_21876544

INEGI (2021). *Encuesta Nacional de Calidad e Impacto Gubernamental (ENCIG) 2021*. INEGI. Retrieved in: https://www.inegi.org.mx/programas/encig/2021/

Instituto Nacional de Estadística y Geografía [INEGI]. (2019). *Encuesta Nacional de Calidad e Impacto Gubernamental (ENCIG) 2019*. INEGI. Retrieved in: https://www.inegi.org.mx/programas/encig/2019/

INEGI (2023). *Encuesta Nacional de Calidad e Impacto Gubernamental (ENCIG) 2023*. INEGI. Retrieved in: https://www.inegi.org.mx/programas/encig/2021/

Jancsics, D. (2024). *Sociology of Corruption: Patterns of Illegal Association in Hungary*. Ithaca: Cornell University Press.

Kossow, N. (2019). Populism and corruption. Transparency international anti-corruption helpdesk answer. Transparency International.

Kubbe, I., and Loli, M. (2020). Corruption and populism: The linkage. In Mungiu-Pippidi, A. and Heywood, P. M. (Eds.). A *Research Agenda for Studies of Corruption* (pp. 118–130). Edward Elgar Publishing.

López Obrador, A. M. (2019). *Carta a todos los servidores públicos del gobierno de México*. Retrieved in: https://presidente.gob.mx/wp-content/uploads/2019/10/22-10-2019-CARTA-A-TODOS-LOS-SERVIDORES-PUBLICOS-DEL-GOBIERNO-DE-MEXICO.pdf

López Obrador, A. M. (2018). *Discurso del Lic. Andrés Manuel López Obrador durante su Toma de Posesión como Presidente de los Estados Unidos Mexicanos*. Gobierno de México. Retrieved in: https://www.gob.mx/presidencia/es/articulos/discurso-del-lic-andres-manuel-lopez-obrador-durante-su-toma-de-posesion-como-presidente-de-los-estados-unidos-mexicanos-331219

López Obrador, A. M. (2023a). *Conferencia de prensa matutina 16 de marzo 2023*. Retrieved in: https://youtu.be/Cqjp1LnPCfs

López Obrador, A. M. (2023b). *Conferencia de prensa matutina 18 de abril 2023*. Retrieved in: https://youtu.be/H6TpOzlaYZc

López Obrador, A. M. (2023c). *Conferencia de prensa matutina 28 de abril 2023*. Retrieved in: https://youtu.be/HaHmvaINjq8

López Obrador, A. M. (2023d). *Conferencia de prensa matutina 29 de junio 2023*. Retrieved in: https://youtu.be/3bNRkdTFUTo

López Obrador, A. M. (2023e). *Crecimiento económico mejora aprobación del pueblo a la 4T*. Retrieved in: https://www.youtube.com/watch?v=m-clvnxR5EY

Mackinack Center for Public Policy. (2019). *The Overton Window*. Retrieved in: https://www.mackinac.org/OvertonWindow (Accessed: 15 September 2024).
Mendilow, J. (2021). Introduction to populism and corruption. In *Populism and Corruption* (pp. 1–35). Edward Elgar Publishing.
Mény, Y., and Surel, Y. (2002). The constitutive ambiguity of populism. In *Democracies and the Populist Challenge* (pp. 1–21). London: Palgrave Macmillan UK.
Mexicanos contra la Corrupción y la Impunidad [MCCI]. (2021). Anuario de la corrupción 2020. MCCI. Retrieved in: https://contralacorrupcion.mx/anuario-de-la-corrupcion-2020/
Mexicanos contra la Corrupción y la Impunidad [MCCI]. (2022). Anuario de la corrupción 2021. MCCI. Retrieved in: https://contralacorrupcion.mx/anuario-corrupcion-2021/
Mexicanos contra la Corrupción y la Impunidad [MCCI]. (2023). Anuario de la corrupción 2022. MCCI. Retrieved in: https://contralacorrupcion.mx/anuario-de-la-corrupcion-2022/
Mexicanos contra la Corrupción y la Impunidad [MCCI]. (2024). Anuario de la corrupción 2023. MCCI. Retrieved in: https://contralacorrupcion.mx/anuario-de-la-corrupcion-2023/
Mohrenberg, S., Huber, R. A., and Freyburg, T. (2021). Love at first sight? Populist attitudes and support for direct democracy. *Party Politics*, 27(3), 528–539.
Monsivais-Carrillo, A. (2019). Innovación institucional para la rendición de cuentas: el Sistema Nacional Anticorrupción en México. *Íconos*, (65), 51–69.
Morris, S. D. (2021). *Corruption and Anti-Corruption from the Left and Right in the Americas* (Issue Brief No. 07.20.21). Rice University's Baker Institute for Public Policy. https://doi.org/10.25613/61ZB-RW45
Morris, S. D. (2022). *The Corruption Dilemma: Controlling the Power of the Powerful*. Lynne Rienner Publishers.
Moynihan, D. P. (2022). Public management for populists: Trump's schedule F executive order and the future of the civil service. *Public Administration Review*, 82(1), 174–178.
Mudde, C. (2004). The populist zeitgeist. *Government and Opposition*, 39(4), 541–563.
Mudde, C., and Kaltwasser, C. R. (2017). *Populism: A Very Short Introduction*. New York: Oxford University Press.
Müller, J. (2019). False flags: The myth of nationalist resurgence. *Foreign Affairs*, 98(2), 35–41.
Nieto, F. (2020). El legado del "sexenio de la corrupción": los retos del sistema nacional anticorrupción. *Foro Internacional*, 60(2), 683–715. Epub 14 de agosto de 2020. https://doi.org/10.24201/fi.v60i2.2736
Palifka, B. J., de los Ángeles Estrada, M., and González, I. V. G. (2021). Mexico's national. In *The Politics of Anti-Corruption Agencies in Latin America* (pp. 134–154). Routledge.
Peters, B. G., and Pierre, J. (2020). A typology of populism: Understanding the different forms of populism and their implications. *Democratization*, 27(6), 928–946.
Presidencia de la República. (2019). Plan Nacional de Desarrollo 2019–2024. *Diario Oficial de la Federación*. Retrieved in: https://www.dof.gob.mx/nota_detalle.php?codigo=5565599andfecha=12/07/2019

Presidencia de la República. (2024). Decreto por el que se reforman, adicionan y derogan diversas disposiciones de la Ley Orgánica de la Administración Pública Federal. *Diario Oficial de la Federación.* https://www.dof.gob.mx/nota_detalle.php?codigo=5744005&fecha=28/11/2024

Pritchett, L. (2023). The political acceptability of time limited labor mobility: Five levers opening the overton window. *Public Affairs Quarterly*, 37(3), 284–306.

Redacción Animal Político. (2017). Así inició la investigación de "La Estafa Maestra". *Animal Político.* Retrieved in: https://www.animalpolitico.com/2017/09/asi-inicio-la-investigacion-laestafamaestra

Retamozo, M. (2014). Populism in Latin America: From theory to political analysis. Discourse, subject and inclusion in the Argentine case. *Colombia Internacional*, 82, 221–258. Available at: https://doi.org/10.7440/colombiaint82.2014.09.

Rincón, S. (2018). Mexicanos piden investigar a Peña Nieto y a su esposa, pero el sistema anticorrupción no está listo. *Univisión.* Retrieved in: https://www.univision.com/noticias/mexicanos-piden-investigar-a-pena-nieto-y-a-su-esposa-pero-el-sistema-anticorrupcion-no-esta-listo

Rodríguez, S., Rosagel, S., Sánchez, M., ānd Martínez, D. (2015). La explicación de la SFP sobre las casas no convence ni a los viejos amigos de EPN: PRD y PAN. *Expansión.* Retrieved in: https://www.sinembargo.mx/22-08-2015/1459034

Rojas-Salazar, G. (2020). Análisis discursivo del combate a la corrupción: la 4T no es muy distinta al neoliberalismo. *Nexos.* Retrieved in: https://anticorrupcion.nexos.com.mx/analisis-discursivo-del-combate-a-la-corrupcion-la-4t-no-es-muy-distinta-al-neoliberalismo/

Sandoval, I. E. (2023). Institucionalización vs burocratización en el combate a la corrupción en México. *Gestión y Política Pública*, 32(2), 29–59.

Sarabia, D. (2024). Claudia Sheinbaum: La transparencia no requiere grandes organismos. *Animal Político.* Retrieved in: https://animalpolitico.com/elecciones-2024/presidencia/claudia-sheinbaum-transparencia-no-requiere-grandes-organismos

Secretaría de la Función Pública [SFP]. (2019a). *COMUNICADO 052: Austeridad republicana es eliminar gastos excesivos y canalizar recursos para los más necesitados: Función Pública.* Retrieved in: https://www.gob.mx/sfp/prensa/que-si-y-que-no-202116?idiom=es

SFP. (2019b). *COMUNICADO 042: Ley de Austeridad Republicana, clave para eliminar derroches y ampliar derechos fundamentales: IESB.* Retrieved in: https://www.gob.mx/buengobierno/prensa/ley-de-austeridad-republicana-clave-para-eliminar-derroches-y-ampliar-derechos-fundamentales-iesb; https://www.gob.mx/sfp/prensa/ley-de-austeridad-republicana-clave-para-eliminar-derroches-y-ampliar-derechos-fundamentales-iesb?idiom=es

SFP. (2019c). *COMUNICADO 116: La peor herencia del neoliberalismo es la corrupción, afirma ante diputados la secretaria Irma Sandoval.* Retrieved in: https://www.gob.mx/buengobierno/galerias/la-peor-herencia-del-neoliberalismo-es-la-corrupcion-afirma-ante-diputados-la-secretaria-irma-sandoval-231348; https://www.gob.mx/sfp/prensa/la-peor-herencia-del-neoliberalismo-es-la-corrupcion-afirma-ante-diputados-la-secretaria-irma-sandoval-225142?idiom=es

Sistema Nacional Anticorrupción (SNA) (n.d.). ¿Quiénes Somos? *SNA Website.* Retrieved in: https://www.sna.org.mx/quienes-somos/

Stanley, B. (2008). The thin ideology of populism. *Journal of Political Ideologies*, 13(1), 95–110.

Torreblanca, C., Muñoz, M., and Merino, J. (2018). ¿Cómo ganó AMLO? Breve historia gráfica de la migración electoral más grande en la historia democrática de México. *Nexos*. Retrieved in: https://datos.nexos.com.mx/como-gano-amlo-breve-historia-grafica-de-la-migracion-electoral-mas-grande-en-la-historia-democratica-de-mexico/

Transparencia Mexicana. (2016). Historia de una reforma: SNA, #3de3 y #Ley3de3. Transparencia Internacional. Retrieved in: https://www.tm.org.mx/reformasna/

Transparency International. (2025). Corruption Perceptions Index 2024: Corruption fuels environmental crime across the Americas. *Transparency International*. Retrieved in: https://www.transparency.org/en/press/2024-corruption-perceptions-index-corruption-fuels-environmental-crime-across-the-americas

Unidad de Investigación Aplicada MCCI. (2023). Sin otros datos: El legado de la política de transparencia de AMLO y el abandono de la información pública. *Mexicanos Contra la Corrupción y la Impunidad*. Retrieved in: https://contralacorrupcion.mx/sin-otros-datos-el-legado-de-la-politica-de-transparencia-de-amlo-y-el-abandono-de-la-informacion-publica/

Vargas, O. (2023). ¿Gobierno de AMLO corrupto? Así lo perciben los mexicanos, según encuesta. *Infobae*. Retrieved in: https://www.infobae.com/mexico/2023/12/27/gobierno-de-amlo-corrupto-asi-lo-perciben-los-mexicanos-segun-encuesta/

Zaslove, A., Geurkink, B., Jacobs, K., and Akkerman, A. (2021). Power to the people? Populism, democracy, and political participation: A citizen's perspective. *West European Politics*, 44(4), 727–751.

Zavala, D. (2024). La opacidad marca las obras emblemáticas del gobierno de AMLO. *Obras Expansión*. Retrieved in: https://obras.expansion.mx/infraestructura/2024/10/07/transparencia-gobierno-amlo-grandes-obras

3

ANTI-CORRUPTION IN POST-BREXIT BRITAIN

Rebecca Dobson Phillips

Introduction

This chapter examines what happened to the anti-corruption norms that govern Britain in the post-Brexit period, with a particular focus on the anti-corruption governance regime (Barrington 2024) and the set of institutions that govern the conduct of politicians.[1] It argues that these anti-corruption norms and institutions were subject to significant contestation amid the political discord that accompanied Brexit. This contestation threatened to undermine the integrity of established anti-corruption norms. However, by placing corruption on the political mainstage it also provoked a deeper collective reflection on the character and prevalence of corruption in British society, and on the appropriateness of the norms and institutions by which it is controlled. The chapter does not make any substantive claims about corruption as a decisive factor in either the 2016 European Union Membership Referendum (EU Referendum) or in the negotiated withdrawal process that followed (for such analyses see McGaughey 2018; Pasculli 2019). While evidence certainly exists of concerning practices in Referendum campaigning (e.g., Electoral Commission 2018; Information Commissioner 2018; DCMSC 2018) and questionable political manoeuvres in the subsequent negotiations (e.g. Bowcott 2018),[2] making broad-based claims about the corruption "of Brexit" risks oversimplification and confusing a messy kind of politics and strained governance system with a much more intangible but inherently damaging phenomenon: the corruption of politics itself. A sole focus on Brexit and the character of the politics that it elicited also overlooks the critical insight that Brexit was embedded in and an expression of a whole range of political and social discontents, including

DOI: 10.4324/9781003531920-5

perceptions and experiences of political corruption that existed prior to the EU Referendum.

Britain has long claimed a privileged global position as a country with relatively low levels of corruption (e.g., Raab 2021; Barrington 2016). However, this notion has been at odds with public perceptions (Transparency International 2016), empirical cases, and an increasing number of academic analyses (Hodgkinson 1997; Whyte 2015; Barrington 2021). Indeed, sustained critiques of the ways in which corruption is measured globally (Galtung 2006; Andersson and Heywood 2009; Hough 2017), have also put into question many of the assumptions governing ideas about where in the world corruption is most prevalent and damaging. This has spurred a reconsideration of the character, extent and impact of corruption in mature democracies, and increased awareness that corruption in Western contexts is more concerning than had been readily acknowledged (Cockcroft and Wegener 2016; Whyte 2015; Johnston 2005, 2014; Maciel and De Sousa 2017). Indeed, recent efforts to quantify state capture—rather than traditional transactional forms of corruption—show Britain and countries like it to be at much greater risk of corruption than previously thought (Kaufmann 2024, 17).

Another knock to the confident positioning of Britain as a global anti-corruption leader is recent work critiquing the focus on corruption at the national level (Heywood 2017). This has led to a much more nuanced understanding of the transnational and networked nature of corruption globally and corruption at the sub-national level. For Britain, this has implications for considering corruption in the devolved nations and local authorities, as well as the role of the City of London as a financial centre and facilitator of corruption (e.g., Heathershaw *et al.* 2021). Indeed, recent years have witnessed increased concerns about Britain's role in global networks of corruption and the harm this can inflict both on far-flung shores and on domestic politics and the economy. Studies of corruption—including this chapter—still primarily take a national focus, but this fails to account for the often-globalised and localised nature of corruption and the limitations inherent in nationally bounded anti-corruption institutions and policies to control it. Recent work has begun to unveil some of the ways in which British institutions and society intersect with global corruption (e.g., House of Commons 2016); indeed, Transparency International UK, has long acknowledged "Britain's role in corruption overseas, and corruption in global sectors critical to international security and development" (TI-UK 2021).

It is in this context of evolving ideas about the presence and role of corruption and anti-corruption in Britain that this chapter unfolds. It argues that the discord inherent in the post-Brexit context created an environment in which rule-breaking became commonplace amongst the political leadership. This ignited a heightened awareness about the presence, extent, and nature of corruption in British institutions—an awareness that was long overdue—and a contestation of the norms that govern the UK's anti-corruption regimes. This contestation then provided space for the emergence of a range of new ideas (both progressive and regressive) about how anti-corruption in Britain should and could be practised.

The chapter proceeds as follows. Section 2 introduces norm theory and explains how it provides a useful analytical framework for examining how "shared understandings" about corruption and anti-corruption are constructed and adapt through contestation in times of crisis or discord. Section 3 describes how the political discord experienced in the wake of Brexit stalled the establishment of the anti-corruption governance regime, which as a nascent set of anti-corruption norms was vulnerable when crisis hit. Section 4 moves to the more established anti-corruption norms governing the conduct of politicians. It examines how these norms came under severe attack, leading to a visible contestation over how they should be applied and their justification in the post-Brexit context. Section 5 reflects on the longer-term impacts of this contestation on the sustainability and appropriateness of existing anti-corruption norms and institutions. It suggests that while there has been a significant increase in perceptions of corruption and a decrease in levels of trust in politics, there are already signs of positive and proactive responses and opportunities to engage with more innovative and participatory forms of anti-corruption governance.

Discord, Contestation, and (Anti-)Corruption Norms

A key claim of this volume is that discordance, understood as instability, unpredictability, and disagreement, makes corruption more difficult to address and that new kinds of anti-corruption approaches might be required to meet the challenges that arise in a discordant world (Jackson *et al.* 2026). This chapter argues that the political discord that accompanied Brexit—the EU Referendum and the political context it created—provides a rich context for examining this broader claim. Furthermore, it suggests that the post-Brexit context not only challenged the effectiveness of Britain's anti-corruption architecture but provided the opportunity to contest the legitimacy of these institutions and reshape ideas about the meaning of anti-corruption itself. This claim is embedded in a conceptual framework that does not see corruption or anti-corruption as static phenomena or as a rigid set of practices or processes that can be objectively identified and observed. On the contrary, it understands the norms that govern these phenomena—our "shared understandings" about them (Niemann and Schillinger 2016)—to be politically and socially constructed, and as such contingent and inherently subject to contestation (Wiener 2014).

This is not a novel claim: the changing nature of the ways in which corruption is understood, and anti-corruption is practised, has been particularly well illustrated by historians (Kroeze 2016; Kroeze *et al.* 2017; Knights 2016, 2019, 2021; Buchan and Hill 2014). Political theorists have also shown how ideas about corruption are shaped by the political process and what is understood as its legitimate role and aims (Philp 1997; Williams 1999); and that as these views on politics change, so too will our "shared understandings" of corruption and anti-corruption (Dobson Phillips 2024). However, the underlying mechanisms for this change are often hidden from view. Much of the literature on defining corruption—including the author's own work (Dobson Phillips *et al.* 2025)—focuses on "pinning down" the concept of corruption instead of identifying, tracing, or explaining how it is contested in different forums and changes over time and context. This is where recent work on norms can be applied to understand how corruption and anti-corruption both are conceptualised and practised, and how contestation can act as a mechanism by which these norms adapt and change.

Norms can be usefully understood as "shared understandings", which are intersubjective and internalised to the point of rarely being questioned (Niemann and Schillinger 2016). This perspective has informed the corruption and anti-corruption literature in two ways. First, norms are increasingly recognised as important in explaining why corruption occurs in context and why it is difficult to identify and combat. Kubbe *et al.* (2024, 436) emphasise that as unwritten rules, norms are particularly difficult to shift and can undermine anti-corruption programming if the norms driving corrupt behaviour are not identified, understood, and addressed. Second, norms have provided critical purchase for examining how ideas about corruption and anti-corruption are contingent and shaped by the distributions of power in the contexts where they arise. Katzarova's (2018) work shows how the global anti-corruption norm was "constructed as a problem" through contestation, with the Global North's claim to a limited single actor, *quid pro quo* form of corruption winning out over the more expansive Global South perspective on corruption as "the use of politics for private (corporate) gain" (Katzarova 2018, 303). A common theme in both these approaches is that once formed, norms are theorised as being relatively "stable"; contestation occurs at the point of norm emergence, but once these norms are accepted, and even more so once they are internalised, the contestation surrounding them all but disappears (Finnemore and Sikkink 1998).

This idea of norms as accepted and internalised—in effect uncontested by those that practise them—means that norm theory finds it difficult to explain change (Niemann and Schillinger 2016, 30). However, recent work on norm contestation argues that contestation is not limited to the process by which norms emerge or are constructed but is inherent in them even when they are broadly accepted and internalised (Wiener 2014). This contestation is not always plain but can become visible and arise in certain contexts and interactions. For example, Niemann and Schillinger (2016, 40) identify three points at which contestation over norms emerge and become visible and subject to change: historical contingency that leads to "changes in social practice", which also leads to change in norms over time; norms moving beyond the original contexts that gave them meaning; and crisis. Each of these points at which contestation can arise and reshape norms is familiar in the corruption literature, particularly in the challenge of fixing global norms about corruption and anti-corruption in local contexts. However, the focus of this chapter is on what happens to anti-corruption norms in times of crisis: how are ideas about corruption and anti-corruption contested and reshaped in contexts of discord? And what can we learn about this from the post-Brexit context in Britain?

A further insight of value from norm theory is that contrary to common fears about contestation and engaging with alternative views being necessarily corrosive of a norm (e.g., Hough 2017, 34; Heywood 2017, 28), contestation can have positive and "democratic" force, which implies that it is both unavoidable and *potentially* normatively good, rather than always a destructive force (Wolff and Zimmermann 2016, 534). Niemann and Schillinger (2016, 36) suggest that the destructive or productive nature of contestation depends upon the focus of that contestation—it is non-disruptive if it focuses on the application of the norm, but more fundamental contestation aimed at the justification of the norm itself can pose greater challenges to sustaining it. However, as explored in the analysis below, attempts at contesting the underlying justification for a norm are not always successful: they can meet with an even more powerful counter-contest, either in the moment or over the long term. Indeed, attempts to contest the justification for a norm—particularly one deeply embedded in the normative framework—can potentially serve to strengthen it.

Discord and the Anti-Corruption Agenda

There is no doubt that the UK's EU Referendum in June 2016 was a disruptive moment in British history, and one which exposed fault lines in a society that had hitherto been regarded by many as relatively untouched by political spectacle. The discord that accompanied the vote and the UK's negotiated withdrawal from the European Union placed a unique set of demands upon British institutions (Haddon 2019) and revealed divides and tensions within British society that had previously been ignored or at least underestimated (Goodwin and Heath 2016; Sorace and Hobolt 2021). In the wake of Brexit, Britain navigated three general elections, deployed six prime ministers to the helm,[3] and weathered not only the political storm that ensued, but a range of intersecting pressures on its governance capacity and legitimacy, including, not least, the COVID-19 pandemic.

The Referendum threw a whole range of issues up into the air, but there were few at the time who considered the possible implications for anti-corruption policy when they eventually came to land (exceptions include Barrington 2016; Corruption Watch UK 2016; Dobson 2016; Hough 2016).[4] These contributions were primarily concerned with the negative implications of Brexit on the ability of the state to control corruption. Some were more concerned with the economy and private sector relations, while others concentrated on the political realm. Robert Barrington (2016), the then-Executive Director of Transparency International UK,[5] outlined 12 concerns related to the upheaval and possible discord that would ensue in the post-Brexit context, including the risk that at a time of economic downturn and searching for new international partners, the UK's anti-corruption standards would decline. Barrington's main concern was that Brexit would distract from anti-corruption activities, with government failing to pass necessary legislation because of the legislative backlogs and find itself making alliances and trade deals with riskier global counterparts. Similar concerns were raised by Corruption Watch UK (2016),[6] which also focused on the strength of influence business could have on the Brexit negotiations, and the resource constraints that would be placed on anti-corruption institutions, such as the Serious Fraud Office, which could stymie the development of further anti-corruption architecture. Hough (2016) also raised concerns about anti-corruption slipping off the political agenda; and stressed the role of leadership in setting the tone for future developments.

The focus on the potential damage Brexit might wreak on the anti-corruption agenda was an understandable preoccupation for anti-corruption campaigners and academics at the time. Britain was in the middle of an *anti-corruption moment*, and in the preceding years much had changed in legislative, regulatory, and rhetorical terms. Indeed, in the decade prior to the Referendum, the UK government had positioned itself as a global leader on anti-corruption reform, and had set about constructing what Barrington (2024, 174) describes as an "anti-corruption governance" regime. In effect, a set of broad anti-corruption norms was in a phase of emergence—still contested but increasingly accepted as necessary considering the growing awareness of corruption risks in and around the British state.

Reforms began with the then-Labour government establishing the role of Anti-corruption Champion in 2006 and sponsoring the Bribery Act 2010, which is widely regarded as some of the "strictest legislation internationally on bribery".[7] However, the regime was further bolstered by the Coalition government (Conservative and Liberal Democrat), which took power after the General Election in 2010, and the subsequent Conservative government led by David Cameron continued this focus on domestic anti-corruption reform. Indeed, Cameron made several key commitments to developing Britain's anti-corruption norms and institutions and fostering its reputation as a global anti-corruption leader.

- At the 2013 G8 meeting in Lough Erne, the government announced new rules on the transparency of company ownership (beneficial ownership) and urged other governments to do the same (HM Treasury 2013).
- In 2014, the government's first Anti-corruption Plan was published with strong claims about the threat of corruption to the UK's "national security, economic prosperity and international reputation", and plans for the creation of the Inter-Ministerial Group on Anti-corruption and a Joint Anti-corruption Unit (JACU) to coordinate action (HM Government 2014).
- The government hosted an Anti-corruption Summit in 2016, which included 50 heads of country delegations; five representatives of overseas territories and crown dependencies; and 61 representatives of national and international organisations.[8]
- In 2017, Theresa May's government published the UK's first Anti-corruption Strategy 2017-2022 and JACU was tasked with coordinating action across government (HM Government 2017).

The development of this anti-corruption governance regime over a decade and across four different government administrations is impressive. However, it also proved fragile and limited in its scope for addressing the corruption problems that would emerge in the post-Brexit context. At the time of writing in June 2025, this anti-corruption governance regime has been significantly eroded. The Anti-corruption Champion's role has progressively lost its standing and power: initially appointed as a Cabinet Minister, the role passed to lesser ministerial positions until being effectively vacated in June 2022 when MP John Penrose resigned due to allegations that the prime minister had broken the Ministerial Code (Mason 2022). Since 2022 there has been increasing pressure on government to fill this post, with the UK Anti-corruption Coalition writing directly to Prime Minister Keir Starmer in the first days of his government emphasising the Champion's critical role in "delivering oversight and coordination of a cross-government anti-corruption strategy" (Davies Teka and Townsend 2024). Despite previous appointments being made within a month of taking office, it took four months for Starmer to appoint Margaret Hodge as his champion on 9 December 2024. Hodge is a senior politician with a strong track-record, but as a member of the Lords and not a Cabinet Minister it is unclear how the post will function in terms of its access to and influence on government.[9]

The post-Brexit context has also seen a significant delay in the publication of an updated Anti-corruption Strategy, which was due to be published in 2022. While the Anti-corruption Plan and Strategy 2017-22 can be seen as partial successes—updates on Strategy progress were published up until the end of

2021—no post-2022 Strategy has been forthcoming, despite significant efforts from civil servants to make that happen, repeated commitments from government that it would be published imminently and vocal calls from civil society to do so (Hawley 2024a). Even the UK's flagship legislation, the Bribery Act, has led to limited success in terms of convictions. This may simply signal a lack of criminal activity, but as Hicks (2021, 7) highlights political will may also be a challenge: he identifies "no resources at all … devoted to domestic corruption; there are no targets, no performance measurement, no lead agency, no training, and no specific staff allocated to this crime type". This may be set to change with the establishment of a new Domestic Corruption Unit being piloted by the City of London police, announced in early December 2024 (Hawley 2024b). There has also been some legislative progress, including on economic crime and corporate transparency,[10] which has begun to address the threat of "dirty money" in the UK's economy. However, this has been seen as a necessary reaction to the Russian threat following the invasion of Ukraine rather than a proactive commitment to anti-corruption progress.[11]

Fears that meaningful progress on anti-corruption would stall post-Brexit have come to pass, even if Brexit itself cannot necessarily be slated as the sole cause of the inertia. In the discord and distraction of other policy priorities, it was easy—and perhaps even natural—for government to draw back from its promotion of this new agenda. However, although not yet forthcoming, the rhetorical promise of a new anti-corruption strategy and the continued pressure on government by civil society to produce one, suggests that the discord of Brexit has not entirely quashed this emerging set of anti-corruption norms.

Contestation Over Standards in Public Life

While there were expressed concerns about the resilience of the emerging anti-corruption agenda during the discord of Brexit, what was less predicted and less predictable in 2016 was the effect this would have on what in Britain are called "standards in public life". These standards effectively describe the anti-corruption norms and institutions that govern the conduct of public officials. These norms were the site of much greater overt contestation post-Brexit, and this contest found its most vociferous expression in the political realm. Significantly, this contestation was not limited to the application of norms or the institutions designed to uphold them. Instead, the breach of these norms by senior members of government led to a deeper and potentially more disruptive contestation over the justification for these norms and their place in British public life.

The Committee on Standards in Public Life (CSPL) was established in 1994 by the then-Prime Minister John Major in response to the Cash for Questions scandal, which revealed that MPs had accepted cash donations in exchange for asking questions in the House of Commons (Guardian 1999).

Its task was to "examine current concerns about standards of conduct of all holders of public office", and to advise the prime minister on how to ensure the "highest standards of propriety in public life".[12] The CSPL's first report outlined the Seven Principles of Public Life, which became known colloquially as the Nolan Principles, and went on to inspire a similar codification of standards around the world (Dávid-Barrett 2015). These Nolan Principles—selflessness, integrity, objectivity, accountability, openness, honesty, and leadership—establish a foundation for the norms of behaviour expected of British public officials, including members of parliament. They have proven both durable and popular. Research conducted for the CSPL in 2021 found not only that the public were strongly in favour of a clear ethical framework for public officials with 75% agreeing that ethical standards are important for effective government (Deltapoll 2021, 7); but that the Nolan Principles specifically resonate with diverse communities across Britain and reflect their expectations of both elected and appointed office holders (CSPL 2021, 33).

There are several institutions that govern the conduct of Ministers and Members of Parliament (MPs), and all are guided by the Nolan Principles (for more detail on these institutions see Dobson Phillips 2020). The system is largely self-regulating, in the sense that there is no independent external body responsible for overseeing politicians' conduct.[13] This has long been a contentious issue, but claims about the constitutional sovereignty of Parliament have tended to drown out calls for reform. Two parts of this self-regulated system are examined below—the Ministerial Code, and the MPs Code of Conduct—as the norms and institutions surrounding them were highly contested in the political discord post-Brexit.

Anti-Corruption Norms and the Ministerial Code

The Ministerial Code sets out the standard of conduct expected of government ministers. The Code is published by the prime minister and is liable to frequent updates: it has been updated seven times since 2010. The prime minister is also responsible for adjudicating on the implementation of the Code and has the final say on any breaches. An independent adviser assists the prime minister in this role and is expected to investigate alleged breaches and provide impartial advice; although until November 2024, the adviser had no right to initiate investigations without the prior consent of the prime minister (Baker *et al.* 2024). In the post-Brexit context, there were a litany of norm and rule breaches, with significant concerns raised that those in breach of the Ministerial Code were not seen to face the normal or expected consequences (Elgot 2022a). These breaches involved those in the highest positions of power, including Prime Minister Boris Johnson, who ultimately became the first sitting prime minister to be punished for breaking the law (Woodcock 2022).

As a result, the treatment of the Ministerial Code became a hot-potato topic and led to the resignation of two independent advisers. In 2020, Home Secretary Priti Patel was investigated for bullying. The then-Independent Adviser Sir Alex Allen found her to have breached the Code, but Johnson, as prime minister, disagreed and resolved to keep Patel in post. This move by Johnson was seen to "fatally undermine the Ministerial Code", because it implied that prime ministers were free to subjectively interpret its meaning for political or personal advantage (Haddon 2020). While this had always been "technically" the case, the convention (or norm) had been for the prime minister to take the advice of the independent adviser seriously; failing to do so breached this established norm. The fallout from this was huge. Sir Allen, who had served as independent adviser since 2011 resigned his post in protest;[14] and the Chair of the CSPL, Lord Evans, stated that this raised "serious questions about the effectiveness of the current arrangements" and committed to looking into them "urgently", which he did in the *Standards Matter 2* review published the following year (CSPL 2021).

In June 2022, a second independent adviser resigned his post following the Partygate Affair, for which Johnson was fined by police, and criticised for flouting the Nolan Principles and breaking his own Ministerial Code. Lord Geidt's resignation letter included the claim that his advice had been sought on deliberately breaching the Code and argued that "a deliberate breach, or even an intention to do so, would be to suspend the provisions of the Code to suit a political end" (BBC News 2022). Again, it appeared that the Code was to be compromised for political advantage. Less than a month later, the Johnson administration collapsed in scandal (Amos 2022), without having appointed a successor to Geidt. Indeed, the Liz Truss government, which followed, also failed to appoint an independent adviser and it was left to the next Prime Minister, Rishi Sunak, to fill the role in late December 2022 with the appointment of Sir Laurie Magnus (Durrant and McAlary 2024). It was observed at the time that the role was so toxic, and the government so unwilling to enhance the powers of the adviser, that a series of potential candidates had refused to take the role (Elgot 2022b). This left five months in which the prime minister was without an ethics adviser at all. One consequence of this was that at the end of 2022, Transparency International UK identified 40 potential breaches of the Ministerial Code in the previous five years that had not been investigated (TI-UK 2022).

It was not just in the application of the norms associated with the Ministerial Code that there was a contestation over norms, however. In May 2022 a revised Code was issued by Johnson, which caused a storm of controversy as the prime minister was "accused of changing ministerial code to 'save his skin'" (Mason and Allegretti 2022). The main complaint was that while under investigation for misleading Parliament—a clear breach of the Ministerial Code—Johnson had taken the opportunity to re-write the

Code to his benefit. Three changes were significant: a change in sanctions for breaches of the Code, as ministers would no longer be expected to resign in all instances but could instead apologise or temporarily lose their pay; the removal of references to the Nolan Principles from the foreword, which were instead relegated to an appendix; and a change in the tone of the Code, reasserting the prime minister's ultimate authority. The first of these changes was the focus of much ire, as it was interpreted as an attempt by Johnson to avoid penalties for his own behaviour. The defence offered for this re-write was that it was intended to implement a recommendation made by the CSPL in the *Standards Matter* 2 report a year earlier and would not have shielded Johnson from the allegations against him, as "knowingly misleading parliament" still carried the expectation of resignation (Durrant 2022).

However, the timing of the re-write and the way it was presented failed to provide any reassurance that the norms expected of public office would be upheld by the Code or the prime minister. Other recommendations of the *Standards Matter 2* report such as empowering the independent adviser to initiate investigations were not implemented. The Chair of the CSPL, Lord Evans, referred to the new Code as "lacking in ambition" and insufficient for easing the "suspicion about the way in which the Ministerial Code is administered" (Evans 2022). However, most concerning was the belligerent tone with which the Code was delivered, and the exclusion of the Nolan Principles, which were interpreted as conveying the clear message that government should enjoy impunity from outsider oversight and questioning once elected (Durrant 2022). As events were soon overtaken by the Pincher affair, which brought down the Johnson government about a month later (Amos 2022), it is impossible to know how Johnson as prime minister would have responded to the Privileges Committee's finding that he had misled Parliament and breached his own Code (Committee of Privileges 2023). What we do know is that fears were ignited that the Code and its norms no longer held sway over the conduct of ministers, and that the trust imbued in the norm of ministerial self-regulation was under severe threat.

Anti-Corruption Norms and the Code of Conduct for MPs

Members of Parliament (MPs) are also broadly self-regulating when it comes to their conduct, but with some provisos. They are governed by a Code of Conduct, which is based on the Nolan Principles, but the Commissioner for Standards responsible for investigating breaches of the Code is appointed from outside the House. When severe breaches of the Code are identified, the matter is referred to the Committee on Standards, which includes seven MPs from different parties and seven lay members of the public. The Committee reaches a conclusion on the breach in question and recommends sanctions to the House of Commons to vote upon. In this manner, the process integrates independence in the Commissioner, political balance and a public perspective in the Commission, and ultimate accountability in the decision-making of Parliament.

In the case of Owen Paterson MP, the whole system of governing standards of MP conduct threatened to collapse. Paterson was a Conservative backbencher who took advantage of the freedom MPs are given to take second jobs. Paterson had been paid to advise two companies—healthcare firm Randox and food manufacturer Lynn's Country Foods—and the *Guardian* newspaper obtained documents suggesting that he had used his position as an MP to lobby government departments on their behalf (Evans *et al.* 2019). This prompted an investigation by the Commissioner for Standards, which concluded that Paterson had been involved in an "egregious case of paid advocacy", and the Committee on Standards further recommended that in line with previous similar cases Paterson should be suspended from the House of Commons for a period of 30 sitting days (Committee on Standards 2021, 48). The Committee brought its report to the House of Commons in the expectation that, as on all previous occasions, its recommendations would be approved without a vote. However, instead the government tabled an amendment that expressed "concerns about potential defects in the standards system", and proposed setting up a Select Committee to review the case against Paterson, the broader system of standards and specifically to consider whether its procedures were in line with natural justice.[15] The justification for the amendment articulated by Jacob Rees-Mogg in the House of Commons mirrored Paterson's own complaints that the investigation was biased and did not comply with natural justice. In particular, he claimed he had not had the opportunity to defend himself, although the Committee report detailed how Paterson had been given "extensive opportunities to provide evidence and to respond fully to the allegations against him" (Committee on Standards 2021, 35).

Although the amendment passed, supported by the government whip, it took only a day for the government to backtrack and Paterson to resign amidst a media storm of indignation and as opposition parties refused to sit on the new Select Committee. While many acknowledged that the standards regime might need reform, how the government had sought to reform it was highly controversial (Durrant 2021); not least because the proposed Select Committee had fewer safeguards and even less independence than the system it was tasked with reviewing (Dobson Phillips 2021). This move was interpreted by many as an underhand attempt by the government to simultaneously protect one of its own (Paterson was a staunch supporter of Brexit) and weaken the authority of the Committee on Standards at a time when serious questions were starting to be asked about COVID-19 contracts (Mason and Davies 2021; Dobson Phillips 2021). In an unusual turn for British politics, which prefers to use the term "sleaze" to describe political misdemeanours, people across the political spectrum began to use "corruption" to characterise not only Paterson's behaviour—Chris Bryant chair of the Committee on Standards called it a "corrupt practice" (BBC News 2021)—but also the actions of the government, which were described by former Conservative Prime Minister John Major as "politically corrupt" (Parker 2021) and by Labour Leader Sir Keir Starmer as a case of "corruption" (Starmer 2021). The prime minister's own adviser Lord Evans, chair of the CSPL, described the amendment as an "extraordinary proposal … deeply at odds with the best traditions of British democracy" (Booth 2021).

The Paterson episode can be interpreted as a high-stakes contest to the established norms governing the conduct of MPs in the House of Commons. Ultimately, the contest failed when the government was forced to walk back its plans. However, it did illustrate the vulnerability of the self-regulated system safeguarding standards in public life to attempted manipulation, particularly when government power and interests are at stake.

From Contestation to Innovation

There is no doubt that the post-Brexit period was one of significant discord, which provided the context for contestation not only over the nascent anti-corruption governance regime, but also over the well-established norms of political conduct. In one perspective, this contestation can be viewed as part of a process of sustained erosion of standards and norms. Indeed, much of the discourse on the period—and Johnson's administration in particular—highlights its negative impact on standards of conduct and the development of the anti-corruption governance regime.

In blunt terms, we can observe a government in 2016 that was perceived to place anti-corruption high on its agenda and was supported by a relatively friendly anti-corruption civil society. Indeed, at the time of the Referendum, Robert Barrington, Chief Executive of Transparency International UK (TI-UK) wrote that:

> The current government has said and done more about tackling corruption than any other UK administration since the second world war.
>
> *(Barrington 2016)*

But, a mere five years later in 2021, Barrington's view had made a full about-turn as he suggested:

> There is more corruption and corruption risk in and around this government than any British government since 1945.
>
> *(Barrington 2021)*

This change in perception is stark, but it aligns with evidence of more general shifts in perceptions of corruption and declining trust in state institutions in Britain. There has been a profound change in the way Britain is perceived both in the international arena and by its own public. Its position on the Corruption Perceptions Index (CPI), which scores countries on levels of perceived corruption in the public sector, has taken a huge hit. In January 2024, Britain received its lowest ever score of 71/100, falling from a high of 81/100 in 2016. Transparency International, the compiler of the CPI, explained the fall due to a "rise in concern over political corruption risks, including cronyism, patronage and the diversion of public funds" (TI-UK 2024). A poll from September 2023 found that 53% of voters agreed with the statement that Rishi Sunak's government was "institutionally corrupt" (Bienkov 2023); and polling from early 2024 found that 66% of voters believed UK politics was becoming more corrupt, while 80% believed that some or all of the main parties are corrupt or untrustworthy (UKACC 2024). These figures are in line with the long-running British Social Attitudes survey that found "record low" levels of trust in Britain's system of governance in June 2024, with 45% of respondents stating that they "almost never" trust governments of any party to place the needs of the nation above the interests of their own political party (Curtice *et al.* 2024, 4).

This evident decline in trust in British political institutions and increase in perceptions of corruption is certainly significant, but it is not necessarily defining. The contestation over anti-corruption norms in the post-Brexit context was inevitably going to spark public concern about the erosion of standards, but it has also sparked public debate about the long-ignored problem of corruption in British institutions. In the post-Brexit context, it is no longer possible to be complacent about matters of British institutional integrity or the sufficiency of the anti-corruption norms in place to always hold their ground. As Pasculli (2019, 214) has aptly commented, this period has "eradicate[ed] the delusion that UK institutions are exempt from corruption". In other words, the contestation ignited by the turmoil post-Brexit could prove productive in terms of the development of anti-corruption norms in the long run. Indeed, the new Prime Minister, Keir Starmer, committed at the outset of the 2024 general election campaign to put "country first, party second" in a direct reference to combating the public's distrust in British politics (BBC News 2024).

The government is yet—in mid-2025—to deliver its long-awaited Anti-corruption Strategy, but when it does, it will be difficult to justify delivering one without a strong focus on domestic corruption and political institutions. The previous framework had resisted integrating the conduct of politicians and other public officials into the broader anti-corruption governance framework. Indeed, the 2014 Anti-corruption Plan dedicated a mere page and a half to Parliament, with a relatively weak commitment made to "supporting the Parliamentary authorities to put in place proportionate controls to address corruption risks and ensure public confidence" (HM Government 2014, 28). While the 2017 Strategy failed to mention Parliament or politicians at all, except in the limited reference to corruption risks surrounding local level elections (HM Government 2017). It's unlikely similar omissions will be tolerated this time round, but the long gestation of the strategy suggests that there is considerable contestation at the heart of government about what it should include. The previous government had signalled that a new strategy would include provisions on money laundering, scaling up anti-corruption enforcement and strengthening the UK's institutional integrity, including the resilience of democratic institutions (HM Government 2023; Hawley 2024a), but it remains unclear whether the new government will necessarily follow suit.

Commitments made by the prime minister and other senior members of his Cabinet prior to the 2024 general election signal that they are planning to respond to the previous government's integrity failings. In direct response to the Paterson case, Starmer pledged to introduce a "truly independent anti-corruption and anti-cronyism commission" (Starmer 2021). In the run-up to the general election, Angela Rayner, the deputy prime minister, framed her plans for an ethics and integrity commission as a response to the suspicion and mistrust surrounding the Ministerial Code. She stated that the Commission would "[end] the current situation in which the Prime Minister is the judge and jury on every case of ministerial misconduct" (Rayner 2024). While the response is not fully developed, there are some encouraging signs. In June 2025, the Public Administration and Constitutional Affairs Committee launched an inquiry into "Propriety, ethics and the wider standards landscape in the UK". It is currently collecting evidence on how the government can best meet its commitments to propriety and ethics in government, including the form a new Ethics and Integrity Commission would take, its relationship with other ethics bodies and the power it should be granted.[16]

Whether or not more ambitious plans will be realised, including the proposal of creating an overarching anti-corruption commission, only time will tell, but the space for making such claims and proposing far-reaching ideas about how to reform the system has certainly broadened in recent years. Dávid-Barrett (2022, 2) has reflected on the ways in which the Paterson case re-opened previously closed debates on the propriety of MPs taking second jobs while working as constituency representatives; as well as the increasing scepticism about the ability of Parliament to effectively self-regulate. Indeed, the contestation of recent years has arguably spurred some creative ideas for new anti-corruption norms and institutions; including restructuring power at the top when it comes to the regulation of ethics. For example, the Brown Commission Report (2022, 132) recommended improving integrity by introducing citizens' juries to oversee the "operation of the system and issue an annual report on the standards followed by ministers and MPs".[17] While there are already lay members of the public appointed to balance the view of politicians on the Committee on Standards, a citizens' jury of randomly selected members of the public with powers to adjudicate on the conduct of politicians would be a truly radical shift in power. This kind of innovation is in line with debates around "deep democratisation" as an anti-corruption approach (Johnston 2014) and connects to other work that explores the potential of deliberative forms of democracy to ameliorate some of the legitimacy gaps in the British political system (e.g., the Constitution Unit's work on citizens' assemblies).[18]

Finally, a much livelier and better organised civil society pushing for reform and holding government to account can also be observed in the post-Brexit context. In 2019, in parallel to the paralysis of government, 18 anti-corruption civil society organisations came together to create the UK Anti-corruption Coalition (UKACC).[19] While previously functioning as a small and relatively fragmented group, their combined strength and experience are increasingly recognised in policy-making spaces. The force of the coalition as a "norm entrepreneur", with the ability to promote new anti-corruption norms attuned to the changing political and ethical landscape, is yet to be fully tested. However, its recommendations for change are ambitious and it has begun to stake its claim as a real force for pushing and contesting the norms in a range of important areas of public life, including lobbying, MPs' second jobs, the revolving door, money in politics, and Britain's role in global corruption networks (UKACC Manifesto 2019; UKACC Agenda 2024).

Conclusion

The raging storm of Brexit caught British politics and politicians at sea. There were huge fears for the integrity of the political ship, as the discord that ensued jostled and tested its institutions in ways it had not previously encountered. The development of the anti-corruption governance regime did falter; and the established norms governing the conduct of public officials were contested and did fall short. But ultimately Britain did not find itself shipwrecked with an unrecognisable politics, or with a complete breakdown in the anti-corruption norms surrounding its public institutions—even if that outcome was at points a significant risk. A much less dramatic, but perhaps more compelling narrative is one that sees the British system, weathered by the Brexit storm and the accompanying crisis of COVID-19, disabused of the illusion that it is exempt from the problem of corruption. In this story, which continues beyond the pages of this chapter, there is potential for further "democratic" contestation and deliberation over the anti-corruption norms that should govern the conduct of Britain's public institutions, including their appropriate relationship with the private sector and their duty of accountability to the British people.

Notes

1. The term post-Brexit incorporates the EU Referendum, the negotiating process that followed it, and the Britain that survives its membership with the EU.
2. This refers to the following case: https://www.supremecourt.uk/cases/uksc-2019-0192
3. Prime Minister David Cameron resigned on 13 July 2016; Prime Minister Theresa May resigned on 24 July 2019; Prime Minister Boris Johnson resigned on 6 September 2022; Prime Minister Liz Truss resigned on 25 October 2022; Prime Minister Rishi Sunak's Conservative government lost the General Election to Keir Starmer's Labour Party on 4 July 2024.
4. For the sake of transparency, it is important to note that all the authors listed here are in some way professionally connected to the author. The UK's anti-corruption ecosystem is small and somewhat insular; see CSC and Joffe Trust (2020) for analysis.
5. Robert Barrington is currently Professor of Anti-corruption Practice at the Centre for the Study of Corruption at the University of Sussex.
6. Corruption Watch UK is no longer in operation, but Susan Hawley, its former policy director, established Spotlight on Corruption after its closure in 2022.
7. See: https://www.transparency.org.uk/bribery-act
8. See: https://www.gov.uk/government/publications/anti-corruption-summit-attendance-list
9. Thanks to Professor Robert Barrington for this insight.
10. For example, the Economic Crime and Corporate Transparency Bill 2023.
11. See: https://www.transparency.org.uk/corruption-and-uk/Stop%20the%20flow%20of%20dirty%20money
12. The terms of reference for the CSPL can be found here: https://www.gov.uk/government/organisations/the-committee-on-standards-in-public-life/about/terms-ofreference
13. An exception to this rule is the relatively newly established Independent Parliamentary Standards Authority (IPSA), which regulates MPs' salaries, pensions, business costs, and expenses.
14. https://www.gov.uk/government/news/statement-from-sir-alex-allan
15. See: https://commonsbusiness.parliament.uk/document/51267/html#_idTextAnchor004
16. See: https://committees.parliament.uk/call-for-evidence/3674
17. The Brown Commission was led by former Prime Minister Gordon Brown. The Report, "A new Britain: Renewing our democracy and rebuilding our economy. Report of the Commission on UK's Future" was published by the Labour Party.
18. See: https://www.ucl.ac.uk/constitution-unit/research-areas/deliberative-democracy
19. For transparency, it is important to note that the author's research group—the Centre for the Study of Corruption—is one of the 18 members of this coalition.

References

Amos, O. 2022. "Boris Johnson resigns: Five things that led to the PM's downfall", BBC News, 7 July. https://www.bbc.co.uk/news/uk-politics-62070422

Andersson, S. and Heywood, P. M. 2009. “The politics of perception: Use and abuse of transparency international’s approach to measuring corruption”, *Political Studies* 57(4): 746–767.

Baker, F., McAlary, P., Savur, S. and Durrant, T. 2024. “Keir Starmer’s ministerial code”, Institute for Government, 6 November. https://www.instituteforgovernment.org.uk/explainer/keir-starmer-ministerial-code

Barrington, R. 2016. “What does Brexit mean for the UK’s fight against corruption?”, TI-UK Blog. https://www.transparency.org.uk/what-does-brexit-mean-uk-s-fight-against-corruption

Barrington, R. 2021. “There is more corruption and corruption risk in and around this government than any British government since 1945”, LSE Blog, 25 November. https://blogs.lse.ac.uk/politicsandpolicy/government-corruption/

Barrington, R. 2024. “The governance of corruption in the UK”, in Rotberg, R. and Hampson, F. O. (eds), *Grand Corruption: Curbing Kleptocracy Globally.* Routledge.

BBC News. 2021. “Owen Paterson: Anger as Tory MP avoids suspension in rule shake-up”, 3 November. https://www.bbc.co.uk/news/uk-politics-59154221?at_medium=RSS&at_campaign=KARANGA

BBC News. 2022. “In full: Lord Geidt’s resignation letter and Boris Johnson’s reply”, 16 June. https://www.bbc.co.uk/news/uk-politics-61824796

BBC News. 2024. “‘Country first, party second’- Starmer sets out vision”, 27 May. https://www.bbc.co.uk/news/videos/c2jj44k808lo

Bienkov, A. 2023. “Rishi Sunak’s government is ‘Institutionally Corrupt’ say voters”, Byline Times, 1 September. https://bylinetimes.com/2023/09/01/rishi-sunak-government-institutionally-corrupt-poll-voters/

Booth, R. 2021. “Standards chair attacks Tory efforts to dismantle anti-sleaze system”, Guardian, 4 November. https://www.theguardian.com/politics/2021/nov/04/standards-committee-chair-attacks-tory-dismantling-anti-sleaze-system

Bowcott, O. 2018. “‘Corrupt’ vote leave campaign undermines Brexit vote, court told”, Guardian, 7 December. https://www.theguardian.com/politics/2018/dec/07/corrupt-vote-leave-campaign-undermines-brexit-vote-court-told

Brown, G. 2022. “A new Britain: Renewing our democracy and rebuilding our economy. Report of the Commission on UK’s Future”, Labour Party. https://labour.org.uk/wp-content/uploads/2022/12/Commission-on-the-UKs-Future.pdf

Buchan, B. and Hill, L. 2014. *An Intellectual History of Corruption.* Palgrave.

Cockcroft, L. and Wegener, A.-C. 2016. *Unmasked: Corruption in the West.* I.B. Tauris.

Committee of Privileges. 2023. “Matter referred on 21 April 2022 (conduct of Rt Hon Boris Johnson): Final Report”. https://publications.parliament.uk/pa/cm5803/cmselect/cmprivi/564/report.html

Committee on Standards. 2021. “Mr Owen Paterson third report of session 2021–22”. London: House of Commons. https://committees.parliament.uk/publications/7644/documents/79907/default/

Corruption Watch UK. 2016. “Brexit: What next for the anti-corruption movement in the UK?”, UNCAC Coalition Blog. https://uncaccoalition.org/brexit-what-next-for-the-anti-corruption-movement-in-the-uk/

CSPL. 2021. *Upholding Standards in Public Life: Final Report of the Standard Matter 2 Review.* Committee on Standards in Public Life.

Curtice, J., Montagu, I. and Sivathasan, C. 2024. "Damaged politics? The impact of the 2019–24 Parliament on political trust and confidence". National Centre for Social Research. https://natcen.ac.uk/sites/default/files/2024-06/BSA%2041%20Damaged%20Politics.pdf

Dávid-Barrett, E. 2015. "Nolan's legacy. Regulating parliamentary conduct in democratising Europe", *Parliamentary Affairs* 68(3): 514–532.

Dávid-Barrett, E. 2022. "Shirking self-regulation? Parliamentary standards in the UK", *Public Integrity*: 1–12. https://doi.org/10.1080/10999922.2022.2075632

Davies Teka, R. and Townsend, T. 2024. "Our letter to the new PM: Appoint the Anti-Corruption Champion". London: UKACC. https://www.ukanticorruptioncoalition.org/work/our-letter-to-the-new-pm-appoint-the-anti-corruption-champion

Deltapoll. 2021. "A research report from Deltapoll for the committee on standards in public life". https://assets.publishing.service.gov.uk/media/617bfac9d3bf7f56080b1c62/Deltapoll_Research_Report.pdf

Dobson, R. 2016. "Something is Rotten: Brexit and its consequences for (anti-) corruption in the UK", Centre for the Study of Corruption Blog.

Dobson Phillips, R. 2020. *Standards Landscape: A Mapping Exercise.* CSPL.

Dobson Phillips, R. 2021. "Owen Paterson saga sees government integrity called into question", The Conversation, 4 November. https://theconversation.com/owen-paterson-saga-sees-government-integrity-called-into-question-171154

Dobson Phillips, R. 2024. Climates of corruption. PhD Thesis, University of Sussex, UK.

Dobson Phillips, R., Dávid-Barrett, E. and Barrington, R. 2025. "Defining corruption in context", *Perspectives on Politics*: 1-15. https://doi.org/10.1017/S153759272400286X

Durrant, T. 2021. "Owen Paterson vote reinforces the need for truly independent standards regulators", Institute for Government, 3 November. https://www.instituteforgovernment.org.uk/article/comment/owen-paterson-vote-reinforces-need-truly-independent-standards-regulators

Durrant, T. 2022. "The new ministerial code fails again to improve standards", Institute for Government, 30 May. https://www.instituteforgovernment.org.uk/article/comment/new-ministerial-code-fails-again-improve-standards

Durrant, T. and McAlary, P. 2024 (2021). "Independent adviser on ministerial standards", Institute for Government, 10 May. https://www.instituteforgovernment.org.uk/explainer/independent-adviser-ministerial-interests

Electoral Commission. 2018. "Report of an investigation in respect of vote leave limited, Mr Darren Grimes, BeLeave, veterans for Britain". https://www.electoralcommission.org.uk/political-registration-and-regulation/our-enforcement-work/investigations/investigation-vote-leave-ltd-mr-darren-grimes-beleave-and-veterans-britain

Elgot, J. 2022a. "Forty potential ministerial code breaches never investigated, report reveals", Guardian, 2 December. https://www.theguardian.com/world/2022/dec/01/forty-potential-ministerial-code-breaches-never-investigated-report-reveals

Elgot, J. 2022b. "Candidates snub Sunak's ethics adviser role left vacant for five months", Guardian, 28 November. https://www.theguardian.com/politics/2022/nov/28/candidates-snub-sunak-ethics-adviser-role-left-vacant-for-five-months

Evans, J. 2022. "The government should go beyond a 'low level of ambition' on the Ministerial Code", CSPL Blog, 1 June. https://cspl.blog.gov.uk/2022/06/01/the-government-should-go-beyond-a-low-level-of-ambition-on-the-ministerial-code/

Evans, R., Lawrence, F. and Pegg, D. 2019. "Revealed: Owen Paterson lobbied for firms he was paid to advise" Guardian, 30 September. https://www.theguardian.com/politics/2019/sep/30/revealed-owen-paterson-lobbied-for-firms-he-was-paid-to-advise

Finnemore, M. and Sikkink, K. 1998. "International norm dynamics and political change", *International Organization* 52(4): 887–917.

Galtung. 2006. "Measuring the immeasurable", in Sampford, C., Shacklock, A. and Galtung, F. (eds), *Measuring Corruption*. Routledge.

Goodwin, M. and Heath, O. 2016. "Brexit vote explained: Poverty, low skills and lack of opportunities". Rowntree Foundation. https://www.jrf.org.uk/public-attitudes/brexit-vote-explained-poverty-low-skills-and-lack-of-opportunities

Guardian. 1999. "How the scandal unfolded", Guardian, 22 December. https://www.theguardian.com/uk/1999/dec/22/hamiltonvalfayed

Haddon, C. 2019. "The Brexit battle is fundamentally changing the constitution", Institute for Government, 2 September. https://www.instituteforgovernment.org.uk/article/comment/brexit-battle-fundamentally-changing-constitution

Haddon, C. 2020. "The handling of the Priti Patel bullying inquiry has fatally undermined the Ministerial Code", Institute for Government, 20 November. https://www.instituteforgovernment.org.uk/article/comment/handling-priti-patel-bullying-inquiry-has-fatally-undermined-ministerial-code

Hawley, S. 2024a. "Will the UK's new anti-corruption strategy be a paper tiger or slay the dragon?", Spotlight on Corruption Blog. https://www.spotlightcorruption.org/the-uks-new-anti-corruption-strategy/

Hawley, S. 2024b. "No more turning a blind eye: Spotlight welcomes new Domestic Corruption Unit", Spotlight on Corruption Blog. https://www.spotlightcorruption.org/welcome-new-domestic-corruption-unit/

Heathershaw, J., Cooley, A., Mayne, T., Michel, C., Prelec, T., Sharman, J. and Soares de Oliveira, R. 2021. The UK's kleptocracy problem: How servicing post-Soviet elites weakens the rule of law. Chatham House.

Heywood, P. M. 2017. "Rethinking corruption: Hocus-pocus, locus and focus", *Slavonic and East European Review* 95(1): 21–48.

Hicks, T. 2021. "Why are there so few domestic corruption cases in the UK?", CSC Working Paper No.9. https://www.sussex.ac.uk/webteam/gateway/file.php?name=domestic-corruption-in-the-uk-2021-no9.pdf&site=405

HM Government. 2014. UK Anti-Corruption Plan. London: Crown. https://assets.publishing.service.gov.uk/media/5a7eaccfed915d74e33f1b59/UKantiCorruptionPlan.pdf

HM Government. 2017. United Kingdom Anti-Corruption Strategy 2017–22. London: Crown. https://assets.publishing.service.gov.uk/media/5a829eb7e5274a2e87dc21f0/6_3323_Anti-Corruption_Strategy_WEB.pdf

HM Government. 2023. "Integrated Review Refresh 2023 responding to a more contested and volatile world". https://assets.publishing.service.gov.uk/media/641d72f45155a2000c6ad5d5/11857435_NS_IR_Refresh_2023_Supply_AllPages_Revision_7_WEB_PDF.pdf

HM Treasury. 2013. “G8 2013: New rules to bring unprecedented transparency on company ownership”, Press Release, 15 June. https://www.gov.uk/government/news/g8-2013-new-rules-to-bring-unprecedented-transparency-on-company-ownership

Hodgkinson, P. 1997. “The sociology of corruption: Some themes and issues”, *Sociology* 31(1): 17–35.

Hough, D. 2016. “Anti-corruption after Brexit: What is left of David Cameron’s legacy?” LSE Blog, 25 July. https://blogs.lse.ac.uk/europpblog/2016/07/25/anti-corruption-after-brexit/

Hough, D. 2017. *Analysing Corruption*. Agenda.

House of Commons, Digital, Culture, Media and Sport Committee (DCMSC). 2018. *Disinformation and ‘Fake News’: Interim Report*. HoC.

House of Commons, International Development Committee. 2016. *Tackling Corruption Overseas*. HoC.

Information Commissioner’s Office. 2018. Investigation into the use of data analytics in political campaigns: Investigation update. ICO. https://ico.org.uk/media/action-weve-taken/2260271/investigation-into-the-use-of-data-analytics-in-political-campaigns-final-20181105.pdf

Jackson, D., Amundsen, I. and Williams, D.A. 2026. *Anti-Corruption in a Discordant World: Contestation, Abuse and Innovation*. Routledge.

Johnston, M. 2005. *Syndromes of Corruption: Wealth, Power and Democracy*. Cambridge University Press.

Johnston, M. 2014. *Corruption, Contention and Reform: The Power of Deep Democratisation*. Cambridge University Press.

Katzarova, E. 2018. “From global problems to international norms: What does the social construction of a global corruption problem tell us about the emergence of an international anti-corruption norm”, *Crime, Law and Social Change* 70(3): 299–313.

Kaufmann, D. 2024. “State capture matters: Considerations and empirics toward a worldwide measure”, Results for Development. https://r4d.org/resources/state-capture-index/

Knights, M. 2016. “Old corruption: What British history can tell us about corruption today”. Transparency International UK.

Knights, M. 2019. “The history of corruption and the benefits of an historical approach”, in Ellis, J. (ed), *Corruption, Social Sciences and the Law: Exploration across the Disciplines*. Routledge.

Knights, M. 2021. *Trust and Distrust Corruption in Office in Britain and its Empire, 1600–1850*. Oxford University Press.

Kroeze, R. 2016. “The rediscovery of corruption in Western democracies”, in Mendilow, J. and Peleg, I. (eds), *Corruption and Government Legitimacy*. Lexington Books.

Kroeze, R., Vitória, A. and Geltner, G. (eds). 2017. *Anti-corruption in History: From Antiquity to the Modern Era*. Oxford University Press.

Kubbe, I., Baez-Camargo, C. and Scharbatke-Church, C. 2024. “Corruption and social norms: A new arrow in the quiver”, *Annual Review of Political Science* 27(4): 423–444.

Maciel, G. G. and de Sousa, L. 2017. “Legal corruption and dissatisfaction with democracy in the European Union”, *Social Indicators Research*: 1–22.

Mason, R. 2022. "Boris Johnson's former anti-corruption tsar calls for urgent lobbying reform", Guardian, 12 June. https://www.theguardian.com/politics/2022/jun/12/boris-johnson-former-anti-corruption-tsar-john-penrose-calls-for-urgent-lobbying-reform

Mason, R. and Allegretti, A. 2022. "Boris Johnson accused of changing ministerial code to 'save his skin'", Guardian, 27 May. https://www.theguardian.com/politics/2022/may/27/boris-johnson-changes-ministerial-code-to-remove-need-to-resign-over-breaches

Mason, R. and Davies, H. 2021. "Is worry over future inquiries driving PM to change watchdog?", Guardian, 4 November. https://www.theguardian.com/politics/2021/nov/04/is-worry-over-future-inquiries-driving-pm-to-change-watchdog

McGaughey, E. 2018. "Could Brexit be void?", *King's Law Journal* 29(3): 331–343.

Niemann, H. and Schillinger, H. 2016. "Contestation 'all the way down'? The grammar of contestation in norm research", *Review of International Studies* 43(1): 29–49.

Parker, G. 2021. "John Major attacks 'politically corrupt' Johnson government", Financial Times, 6 November. https://www.ft.com/content/1b4003fa-b179-4063-bfcb-2ee224b7a3fc

Pasculli, L. 2019. "Seeds of systemic corruption in post-Brexit UK", *Journal of Financial Crime* 26(3): 706–718.

Philp, M. 1997. "Defining political corruption", *Political Studies* 45 (3): 436–462.

Raab, D. 2021. "A global leader in the fight against corruption: Foreign Secretary statement to General Assembly". https://www.gov.uk/government/speeches/a-global-leader-in-the-fight-against-corruption-foreign-secretary-statement-to-general-assembly

Rayner, A. 2024. "Keynote speech: Angela Rayner MP, Labour's Deputy Leader". Institute for Government, 13 July. https://www.instituteforgovernment.org.uk/event/angela-rayner

Sorace, M. and Hobolt, S. B. 2021. "A tale of two peoples: Motivated reasoning in the aftermath of the Brexit Vote", *Political Science Research and Methods* 9(4): 675–692.

Starmer, K. 2021. "Let's call out the Tories' behaviour for what it is: Corruption", Guardian, 3 November. https://www.theguardian.com/commentisfree/2021/nov/03/call-out-tories-corruption-conservative-owen-paterson-keir-starmer

TI-UK. 2021. "Stopping corruption, promoting integrity: Transparency international UK strategy 2021–30". London: TI-UK.

TI-UK. 2022. "Analysis finds dozens of potential Ministerial Code breaches were not investigated". Press Release, 2 December. https://www.transparency.org.uk/uk-politics-potential-ministerial-code-breaches

TI-UK. 2024. "Concerns of corruption at all-time high as UK falls to its lowest ever score on global Corruption Perceptions Index". Press Release, 30 January. https://www.transparency.org.uk/concerns-corruption-all-time-high-uk-falls-its-lowest-ever-score-global-corruption-perceptions-index

Transparency International. 2016. People and corruption: Europe and Central Asia. Berlin: TI.

UKACC. 2019. Fighting Corruption. A Manifesto. London: UKACC.

UKACC. 2024. Time to ramp up the fight against corruption: An anti-corruption agenda for the 2024 government. UKACC.

Whyte, D. 2015. *How Corrupt is Britain?*. Pluto Press.
Wiener, A. 2014. *A Theory of Contestation*. Springer.
Williams, R. 1999. "New concepts for old?", *Third World Quarterly* 20: 503–513.
Wolff, J. and Zimmermann, L. 2016. "Between banyans and battle scenes: Liberal norms, contestation, and the limits of critique", *Review of International Studies* 42(3): 513–534.
Woodcock, A. 2022. "Boris Johnson resists calls to quit after becoming first UK prime minister to be punished for breaking law", *The Independent,* 12 April. https://www.independent.co.uk/news/uk/politics/boris-johnson-sunak-partygate-fines-b2056339.html

4

TEN YEARS LATER, IT'S NO MORE

Unraveling the Threads of All-Out Contestation to Operation Car Wash

Guilherme France and Guilherme Siqueira

No anti-corruption probe in recent history has inspired as much hope and enthusiasm among practitioners, activists, and scholars as the *Operação Lava Jato* (Operation Car Wash) in Brazil. The operation was initially hailed as a groundbreaking success—a large, democratic nation overcoming entrenched corruption through robust law enforcement efforts, anchored in a strong institutional framework and supported by successful international cooperation. It appeared to set a new global standard for tackling corruption at the highest levels of government and business.

However, only a few years later, the initial enthusiasm gave way to widespread disillusionment. The operation became mired in controversy, with its key figures discredited, many of its convictions overturned, and the implicated political leaders re-entering national politics. The once-praised legal and institutional framework that supported the operation has suffered setback after setback, leaving behind a sense of disappointment about what was once considered a historic step forward in the fight against corruption. Instead of reforms to address the root causes of the corruption schemes revealed by investigations, Brazil has ushered back in old practices under poorly disguised new facades (Viapiana, 2022; Vieira and Miranda, 2024).

This chapter seeks to contribute to the understanding of Operation Car Wash's dramatic rise and, especially, its fall. We aim to disentangle what we call the 'threads of contestation' to Car Wash—the various arguments and narratives employed by its critics to challenge the operation's legitimacy, merits, and consequences. We use the metaphor of 'threads' because each line of criticism is independent—one can be valid without relying on the validity of another—yet these threads are often deeply interwoven in practice. For each thread, we also identify a domestic and an international dimension.

DOI: 10.4324/9781003531920-6

Our analysis reconstructs these threads of contestation through qualitative analysis of primary data, including media reports, opinion polls, editorials, public statements by key stakeholders, legislation discussed and/or enacted by Congress and judicial files and decisions. We avoid taking a stance on whether these criticisms are justified or plausible. Instead, our goal is to present the critiques themselves, and their origins, without endorsing or contesting them.

The Rise and Fall of Operation Car Wash

In its early years—particularly between 2014 and 2016—Operation Car Wash was incredibly popular among Brazilians, who saw in it the end of impunity for a discredited corrupt political class and a disfavored business elite (Ipsos, 2017). The operation also garnered international praise, hailed as a success story in the global fight against corruption (Transparency International, 2016). However, by the time Car Wash was shut down in 2021, while a majority of the population still supported the anti-corruption investigation (Poder360, 2021), among the political and judicial elites the tide had shifted with widespread criticism of its key figures, numerous convictions overturned (Marzullo and Altino, 2024), the rehabilitation of political actors (IstoÉ, 2023) and the revision of penalties imposed on implicated companies (Landim, 2023). Structurally, key legal and institutional provisions that had enabled the operation came under attack (OECD, 2022).

The Rise (2014–2018)

Operation Car Wash began in March 2014 as a relatively minor investigation into money laundering at a Car Wash station in Brasília, the country's capital city. However, what started as a localized effort quickly escalated into one of the most significant anti-corruption probes in modern history. Spearheaded by the Federal Police and a task force of federal prosecutors based in Curitiba, a city in the south of Brazil, the operation uncovered a web of corruption centered on Petrobras, Brazil's state-controlled oil company. Investigations revealed that Petrobras executives received large payments from construction companies, with portions of these funds funneled to politicians and political parties—including the governing *Partido dos Trabalhadores* (Workers Party, PT)—to finance election campaigns, cement alliances, and enrich those involved. As the operation expanded, it further exposed corruption in state-owned enterprises and public institutions, both at the federal and state levels. The probe also expanded internationally, as some companies admitted to similar practices in other Latin American and African countries, often involving offshore centers to launder illicit funds.

The early years of the investigation were marked by a series of high-profile arrests and convictions, largely enabled through plea bargains and leniency agreements. Introduced in Brazil's legal framework less than a year before the operation began, these instruments proved highly effective by incentivizing corporate executives and political figures to cooperate in exchange for reduced sentences. This rapid evidence-gathering allowed prosecutors to expand the probe to include some of Brazil's largest companies, especially in the construction sector.

Throughout this period, Operation Car Wash drew support from two key sources. First, it garnered widespread backing from the Brazilian public. The unveiling of systemic political corruption led many Brazilians to view the operation as a bold and necessary step toward accountability (Jornal Nacional, 2019), with major media outlets lending strong support. Second, a series of crucial Supreme Court rulings bolstered the operation: centralizing most cases in Curitiba, endorsing plea bargains and leniency agreements, and authorizing the execution of sentences even with pending appeals. These decisions provided the judicial backing that enabled the probe's rapid expansion.

Though Operation Car Wash sent shockwaves throughout Brazil's entire political system, a particularly significant blow was dealt to the Workers' Party, which had held the presidency since 2003—first under Luiz Inácio Lula da Silva and, later, Dilma Rousseff. The public outrage generated by Car Wash's revelations played a key role in the political crisis that culminated in Rousseff's controversial impeachment in 2016 (Datafolha, 2015). In 2018, former President Lula was convicted on corruption charges, imprisoned, and barred from running in that year's presidential elections, marking a watershed moment in the operation's political impact.

The 'rise' of Operation Car Wash, then, was characterized by its forward momentum, strong judicial backing, overwhelming public support, and wide-reaching political consequences. By 2018, it had become a symbol of the fight against corruption, both in Brazil and internationally.

The Fall (2019–2021)

In October 2018, Jair Bolsonaro was elected president, defeating Fernando Haddad, a former São Paulo mayor from PT, selected to replace Lula after he was barred from running. Bolsonaro—a far-right candidate known for his outspoken authoritarian leanings—marked a turning point for Operation Car Wash.

Most political observers linked Bolsonaro's rise to Car Wash, although the nature and extent of that association would remain controversial. Some argued that the probe weakened the political establishment by targeting high-profile figures and fueling an anti-establishment narrative that benefited Bolsonaro, who offered only cursory support for the operation and few anti-corruption proposals. Others contended that his election was not a byproduct, but an intended consequence of Car Wash.

This association became unequivocal when, days after the election, the president-elect announced that Judge Sérgio Moro—who had tried the cases in Curitiba and was the operation's most prominent figure—would serve as his Minister of Justice.

In mid-2019, public perception of the operation took another hit with the release of the 'Vaza Jato' [Car Wash Leaks] (Mortari, 2019).[1] Leaked messages—illegally obtained by a hacker—from Deltan Dallagnol, the Operation's chief prosecutor, suggested close coordination between the judge and the prosecution, casting further doubt on the impartiality of the investigations.

This period not only saw declining public support but also a noticeable shift in the Supreme Court's stance toward Car Wash (Fernandes and Santana, 2020). Starting in 2019, a series of rulings dealt blows to the probe, curtailing its scope or weakening widely used instruments. In March, the Court determined that criminal corruption and money laundering cases related to illegal campaign contributions should be tried by electoral courts, rather than by the specialized federal criminal courts (Supremo Tribunal Federal, 2019). This decision removed hundreds of high-profile cases from the Operation's reach and overturned prior convictions. In November, the Court declared unconstitutional the enforcement of prison sentences while appeals were pending—reversing its 2016 decision and leading to the release of former President Lula, whose cases were still under review.

Operation Car Wash also faced setbacks in the legal and institutional framework that supported its success. On the legal front, Congress passed laws designed to weaken prosecutorial power. The Abuse of Authority Act from 2019, for example, was widely seen as a way to gain leverage over prosecutors, prompting criticism from the OECD (OECD, 2019). Reforms to the legislation on civil and administrative liability of public officials further limited the ability to hold corrupt officials accountable (Transparência Internacional-Brasil, 2022). Other measures, such as Law n. 13964/2019, narrowed the scope of plea deals and added hurdles for the admissibility of evidence. On the institutional front, the Bolsonaro administration weakened law-enforcement independence. For instance, while since Lula all presidents had selected the head of the Prosecutor's Office from a shortlist provided by the association of prosecutors, Bolsonaro ignored the shortlist, choosing a name seen as largely sympathetic to his administration.

By 2021, Car Wash had lost much of its momentum. In February 2021, nearly seven years after its inception, the Car Wash Task Force in Curitiba was discontinued, signaling the end of the operation, with the investigations and trials in course being redistributed within the Public Prosecutors Office. Once hailed as a model for anti-corruption efforts, the operation was mired in controversy, its credibility undermined by accusations of political bias, ethical violations, and judicial overreach. While some legal victories persisted, the operation no longer held the same sway in Brazil's political landscape, and many of its earlier gains were reversed or overshadowed by subsequent developments.

The Multiple Threads of an All-Out Contestation

Contestation refers to the different ways in which claims to legitimacy are called into question by other social and political actors, who ultimately try to persuade relevant audiences that the actions being contested fail the test of justification as put forward not only by the law enforcement agents responsible for leading the operation, but also by other stakeholders who sought to support it, for different reasons, including politicians and the media.

By examining public manifestations, political speeches, media editorials, among other archival data, we propose, in this section, to organize such narratives into four different 'threads of contestation' that, we suggest, constitute the core of the backlash against Car Wash:

a) the contestation of the actors, that is, narratives that contest the legitimacy of the actors involved in the operation, particularly of law enforcement agents;
b) the contestation of the means, that is, narratives that challenge the instruments used by law enforcement to carry out the investigation;
c) the contestation of the cause, that is, narratives that bring into question the merits of an 'anti-corruption' effort in the first place;
d) the contestation of the consequences, that is, narratives that highlight the alleged harms caused by the anti-corruption probe.

Each thread of contestation consists not of a single narrative, but rather of a collection of narratives. The narratives grouped under each thread, however, share a focal point of Operation Car Wash that is called into question to undermine its claim to legitimacy. As will be discussed below, there are multiple narratives as to what the motivation behind the actions of Sergio Moro and Deltan Dallagnol, the two central figures of Operation Car Wash, was. What is common between these narratives, however, is how they cast doubt on the legitimacy of the Operation.

By disentangling these threads, we treat them as autonomous insofar as the validity of each of them is not contingent on the validity of the others; in reality, however, they rarely appear in isolation, as it is much more common for them to arise interwoven in the various critical manifestations against Operation Car Wash. Hence the need for disentangling. This also allows for an improved understanding of who and what drives each thread and if and how they are similar to contestation efforts in other countries.

Our analysis shows how each of these threads can be understood as having both a domestic and an international dimension. While the domestic components are deeply rooted in Brazil's specific context, the international components reflect broader concerns about the influence of international actors and global anti-corruption frameworks on the country's political and economic landscape. We summarize the central dimension of each thread in Table 4.1, below.

The different threads of contestation can be connected to the different forms of operationalizing contestation, as presented in the introduction of this book. The contestation of the means is, by definition, about *how* the anti-corruption agenda and policies are articulated domestically. While a lot of the attention to '*re-interpretations*' has been directed at the policy disputes at the legislative and executive branches of national governments, this case study demonstrates that there is also dispute over how anti-corruption tools are actually implemented by law enforcement. The role of the Brazilian Supreme Court, as it will be demonstrated below, also demonstrates that judicial institutions can become the *locus* for disputes over policy, not just over concrete cases.

On the other hand, contestation over the cause of anti-corruption articulates a *repudiation* of the anti-corruption agenda more broadly. Likewise, the contestation of the consequences is more likely to lead to discussions and disputes about the priorities of anti-corruption efforts, a matter of *resistance*. The international components of all threads do articulate, on some level, criticisms of the liberal political agenda that permeates the anti-corruption agenda. Through different paths and underscoring distinct elements of the Operation Car Wash inner workings, they highlight how foreign actors, especially the United States, played a defining role in its emergence and rise to prominence.

To some level, though not necessarily explicitly, these threads challenge the 'technical' nature of anti-corruption policies, noting that they can and have been used to advance foreign policy and economic goals of foreign actors, either through attacks against Brazil's biggest multinational companies or through interference in the domestic political scene. While criticisms of the anti-corruption agenda for its Western/liberal undertones are not new, the Brazil case demonstrates how elements of this agenda have been directly targeted to undermine its entire legitimacy.

Unraveling the Threads of an All-Out Contestation

In this section of the chapter, all four threads of contestation—contestation of the actors, contestation of the means, contestation of the cause, and contestation of the consequences—are presented along with evidence of their domestic and international dimensions.

TABLE 4.1 Summary of threads of contestation

Thread of contestation	Domestic dimension	International dimension
Contestation of the actors	The actors (mostly prosecutors and judges) were not legitimate because they had ulterior political motives for carrying out the investigation	Prosecutors and judges acted as proxies for foreign powers
Contestation of the means	The investigations deployed methods that violated defense prerogatives and the presumption of innocence and, therefore, did not meet due process standards	The investigations made use of 'imported' legal mechanisms, often incompatible with Brazilian legal framework
Contestation of the cause	The investigation treated legitimate political processes as being corrupt, leading to a 'criminalization of politics'	The anti-corruption movement reflects an US-eurocentric view of political processes, disregarding the complex realities of other institutional contexts
Contestation of the consequences	Car Wash resulted in serious harm to Brazilian economy and to its political system, regardless of any merits of the investigation	The negative consequences of Car Wash were not merely a byproduct of the investigation, but a calculated effort by foreign powers (particularly the US) to undermine Brazilian sovereignty

Source: Author's own compilation

Contestation of the Actors

As Operation Car Wash expanded across multiple jurisdictions in Brazil and abroad, it increasingly relied on the collaboration of hundreds of authorities—prosecutors, judges, police, tax agents. Yet, public attention remained focused on two key figures in Curitiba: Sérgio Moro, the federal judge overseeing the investigations and trials, and Deltan Dallagnol, the federal prosecutor coordinating the task force.

Except for Moro's earlier involvement in trying a high-profile corruption case, both men were largely unknown before Car Wash. However, in a country with a widespread perception of impunity (Da Ros and Taylor, 2022), the investigation's rapid progress made them household names (Cifuentes, 2014).

Their newfound notoriety brought intense public scrutiny, and much of the contestation of Operation Car Wash began to focus on the legitimacy of its leadership.

Criticism of the legitimacy of the actors took various forms, but the central argument was that the investigators and judges had ulterior motives. Three primary accusations surfaced: (i) political bias; (ii) personal ambition, within the domestic dimension; and (iii) foreign influence, within the international dimension. Though these accusations often overlap, each merits separate examination.

Political Bias

A frequent criticism of Operation Car Wash was its alleged political bias, specifically targeting the Workers' Party. Critics argued that the probe was less a genuine anti-corruption effort than a deliberate strategy to weaken or dismantle the PT.

In its early stages, PT leaders—mindful of the public's support for anti-corruption efforts—maintained a neutral stance and even expressed tentative support for the investigation, emphasizing that its success was rooted in the anti-corruption measures enacted during their tenure. In November 2014, for example, shortly after the arrest of top executives from major construction firms, President Dilma Rousseff stated that Operation Car Wash 'could change Brazil forever... by ending impunity,' hailing it as 'the first effective anti-corruption investigation in Brazil targeting both public and private sectors' (G1, 2014).

As the investigation progressed, however, the narrative that Car Wash was politically motivated and disproportionately targeted PT gained traction. Supporters of this view pointed to the damage inflicted on the party, particularly (i) Car Wash's role in fueling public support for Rousseff's impeachment (Rousseff, 2019), despite little evidence of her personal involvement in corruption,[2] and (ii) the conviction and imprisonment of former President Lula, who was barred from running in the 2018 presidential election, despite being the frontrunner (Partido dos Trabalhadores, 2024).

Several episodes were cited as clear evidence of political bias. Two key decisions made by Moro in March 2016, during the impeachment hearings, were particularly controversial. On March 4th, Moro authorized law enforcement agents to coercively bring in Lula for questioning, a departure from the standard of inviting voluntary testimony. Days later, President Rousseff appointed Lula as a minister, effectively shielding him from Moro's jurisdiction since investigations of ministers fall under the Supreme Court.

On the day before Lula was to be sworn in, Moro publicly released wiretap recordings of conversations between Lula and Rousseff, suggesting that the appointment was intended to protect him from Car Wash. The release sparked public outrage, and Lula's appointment was suspended shortly thereafter. Both decisions were later criticized by the Supreme Court; in June 2016, Justice Teori Zavascki ruled that some of the wiretaps were illegal and admonished Moro for making them public. In 2018, the Supreme Court further ruled coercive depositions to be unconstitutional in a case brought forward by PT.

These decisions formed the backbone of Lula's complaint to the United Nations Human Rights Committee in July 2016, where he argued that he was being persecuted by Car Wash (Consultor Jurídico, 2016).

Through 2017 and 2018, as investigations involving the Workers' Party gained visibility, culminating in Lula's imprisonment and exclusion from the presidential race, public perception of Operation Car Wash progressively deteriorated. Ipsos polls show that in July 2017, 74% of respondents believed Car Wash was investigating all political parties; by August 2018, this figure had dropped to 46%, and approval of Judge Moro's work declined from 64% to 41%.

Despite this decline, significant public support remained: in August 2018, 80% of respondents agreed that Car Wash should 'continue investigations until the end, even if it brings political instability,' and 69% believed it was strengthening democracy (Ipsos, 2019).

However, in 2019 two major developments further eroded public confidence. First, Moro's decision to join President Bolsonaro's government—after effectively sidelining Bolsonaro's main electoral rival—fueled suspicions of political bias, even among some supporters (Folha de S. Paulo, 2018). Second, the Car Wash Leaks revealed messages suggesting that Moro had blurred the line between judge and prosecutor, further undermining the investigation's credibility, a concern compounded by the fact that both figures publicly supported Bolsonaro against Lula in the 2022 run-off.

Personal Ambition

A second line of criticism contended that Moro and Dallagnol exploited Car Wash to advance their personal ambitions.

As the probe gained national and international attention, speculation grew that Moro harbored political ambitions. In a June 2017 poll, Moro appeared with 14% of the declared votes for president, second only to former President Lula (Bilenky and Marques, 2017). Although Moro consistently denied any intention of running, his decision to join Bolsonaro's government in 2018 was widely seen as evidence of latent ambitions. Early 2019 reports suggested that Moro's acceptance to join the administration was partly motivated by hopes of a Supreme Court nomination (Marreiro, 2019), a claim made by Bolsonaro himself after Moro left the government in 2020 (Venaglia, 2020).

Dallagnol faced similar accusations. His increasing popularity led to frequent, well-paid speaking engagements (Ferreira et al., 2019), prompting critics to argue that he was profiting from the operation's success. These criticisms intensified in 2021 when reports revealed that prosecutors in the Car Wash task force in Curitiba were receiving additional per diems for working outside their official headquarters, despite having been based in Curitiba for several years. Dallagnol was among three individuals sanctioned by the Federal Court of Audit in 2022 for authorizing these payments, although that decision was subsequently annulled by a federal judge (Landim, 2024).

Dallagnol's electoral ambitions also drew criticism (Martins and Neves, 2019). After resigning from the Federal Prosecutor's Office, he ran for office and was elected in 2022 as a congressman, though he later lost his mandate by a decision of the Superior Electoral Court.[3] During his term, Dallagnol aligned himself with members of the opposition to Lula's government.

However, the most significant controversy surrounding Dallagnol concerned the destination of the assets recovered through Car Wash. A 2022 report from the Federal Prosecutor's Office noted that the operation recovered 25 billion reais (approximately US$ 5 billion) in seized assets, fines, and settlements. The use of these funds sparked significant debate, particularly regarding proposals to create a foundation to manage a portion of the penalties Petrobras was to pay US authorities for FCPA violations. One agreement between the US DOJ and Brazilian prosecutors allowed 80% of the US$ 850 million in penalties to be paid in Brazil and counted towards total penalties, while another agreement between Petrobras and the MPF envisioned investing half of the US$ 682 million in projects to strengthen anti-corruption efforts. Controversies arose with evidence that Dallagnol and other prosecutors had planned for the creation of a foundation to manage these funds—sardonically dubbed the 'Dallagnol Foundation' by a Supreme Court Justice (Migalhas, 2023)—a move criticized as an overreach of prosecutorial power and ultimately blocked by the Supreme Court.

Foreign Interests

Finally, critics of Operation Car Wash have sometimes suggested that its key figures were advancing the interests of foreign powers—particularly the United States—portraying Moro and Dallagnol as proxies for U.S. influence, contributing to a geopolitical strategy designed to weaken Brazil's autonomy.

A widely circulated claim was that Moro had been 'trained' by U.S. authorities to execute Car Wash (Giovanaz, 2017). This accusation gained visibility after a 2016 interview with philosopher Marilena Chauí, who suggested that Moro had been trained by the FBI (Folha de S. Paulo, 2016). The claim focused on his participation in events related to U.S. anti-money laundering and counterterrorism measures. Notably, in 2007, Moro participated in the International Visitor Leadership Program, funded by the U.S. State Department, during which he visited law enforcement agencies combating money laundering; in 2009, he also attended a seminar under Projeto Pontes [Bridges Project], an initiative by the U.S. embassy in Brazil to promote bilateral law enforcement training.

Critics argued that Moro's participation in U.S.-funded programs was part of a larger pattern of foreign interference, in particular—a broader U.S. strategy to curb the growth of Brazilian companies—such as Petrobras and Odebrecht—that could threaten U.S. economic and geopolitical interests. According to this narrative, Car Wash was not merely a Brazilian anti-corruption effort but rather a tool used to advance U.S. strategic goals in Latin America (Fernandes, 2020).[4]

Contestation of the Means

One of the most contested aspects of Operation Car Wash was not the individuals involved but the legal tactics employed throughout the investigation. Critics argued that these methods jeopardized the integrity of the Brazilian legal system, raising concerns over practices like plea deals and coercive depositions, as well as accusations that the investigation was theatricalized to manipulate public opinion.[5]

A central critique focused on the use of plea deals and leniency agreements—relatively new tools in Brazil at the time—that allowed defendants to negotiate reduced sentences in exchange for cooperation. While these agreements helped prosecutors to gather evidence quickly, critics contended that they were applied coercively and unethically (Folha de S. Paulo, 2015). Defendants were often held in pre-trial detention for extended periods, with the implicit threat of prolonged imprisonment being used as leverage for cooperation (Moraes, 2015). This practice was criticized as a violation of basic rights, effectively turning plea bargaining into a coercive tool rather than a legitimate legal procedure.

The leniency agreements were also criticized for being excessively harsh. Their terms were deemed 'overly prejudicial' to companies and the penalties imposed were said to impair the companies' ability to continue operating (Supremo Tribunal Federal, 2023).

Another highly criticized practice was the use of coercive depositions, whereby defendants were forcibly brought in for questioning without a prior invitation to testify. Although such depositions were routinely used by Brazilian law enforcement officials, their extensive use in Car Wash was viewed as excessive and unjustified, further damaging the operation's reputation. In 2016, the coercive deposition of former President Lula was widely criticized by legal scholars and politicians (Jornal Nacional, 2016). The practice was declared unconstitutional by the Supreme Court in 2018 by a 6-5 majority.

One additional source of controversy stemmed from the investigation of lawyers and law firms. In particular, the wiretapping of telephones at the law firm representing Mr. Lula—allegedly unintended by prosecutors—was widely criticized, and those tapings were later destroyed (Barbosa, 2018). Lawyers and bar associations contended that Car Wash repeatedly violated attorneys' professional prerogatives (Nunes, 2019).

A further criticism revolved around the 'spectacularization' of Operation Car Wash. Anticipating resistance from political elites, prosecutors and judges adopted a highly publicized approach, using press conferences and public statements to rally public support. It is often noted that, in 2004, Moro wrote a paper on Italy's Mani Pulite Operation in which he acknowledged that media exposure—including publicizing arrests—played a crucial role in the investigation's success:

> The publicity given to the investigations had the salutary effect of alerting potential investigators about the increase in the mass of information in the hands of judges, leading to new confessions and collaborations. Most importantly: it guaranteed public opinion support for judicial proceedings, preventing public figures under investigation from obstructing the work of magistrates, which, as seen, was indeed attempted.
>
> *(Moro, 2004: 59 [translation by the authors])*

Critics argued that this approach created a media circus around the investigation, building an image of guilt before legal proceedings were complete. For instance, details from plea deals were often publicized before accusations had been thoroughly investigated or corroborated, undermining the presumption of innocence. This tactic was especially controversial when it coincided with key political moments. During the 2018 presidential election, details from a plea deal involving Antonio Palocci—a former finance minister under Lula—were released a week before voting, prompting accusations that the move was intended to damage the Workers Party's electoral prospects. In other cases, such as allegations of bribe demands by former president Temer, plea deal details were illegally leaked to the press, further fueling suspicions about the operation's methods, although the source of these leaks remained unclear (G1, 2017).

Supreme Court Justice Gilmar Mendes frequently expressed concerns over prosecutorial excesses, criticizing practices like coercive depositions and the 'spectacularization' of the investigation through press conferences and selective leaks.

Attorneys also played a key role in voicing these criticisms, mobilizing in public debates and legal forums to protest against Car Wash's methods. In January 2016, over one hundred attorneys published an open letter denouncing the operation's tactics (Migalhas, 2016), accusing it of creating a 'regime of episodic suppression of rights and guarantees' by systematically violating defendants' rights—including the presumption of innocence, the right to a defense, and judicial impartiality.

Prominent figures in Operation Car Wash also engaged in legislative debates, drawing criticism for both their policy positions and methods. In 2015, prosecutors introduced a legislative package titled '10 Measures against Corruption' and launched a nationwide campaign to rally public support. Critics argued that the proposals focused excessively on punitive aspects and weakened human rights and due process guarantees. As voting on these proposals in the House of Representatives turned sideways for prosecutors, with the approval of the Abuse of Authority bill, they threatened to collectively resign in case the bill was turned into law.

Finally, the methods used in Operation Car Wash were not only criticized on legal grounds but also from an international perspective. The introduction of plea deals and leniency agreements in 2013 was seen by some as importing foreign legal concepts, particularly from the United States. Critics argued that these instruments, long employed in the U.S., were ill-suited to Brazil's legal and institutional framework, representing a form of legal imperialism that undermined the country's traditions of justice and due process.

One frequently used legal tool of the Operation Car Wash that brings together the domestic and international critiques is international judicial cooperation. While Brazilian law enforcement has a history of collaborating with foreign counterparts, during Car Wash this cooperation intensified dramatically (Giacomet Júnior, 2018). However, the close connections between Brazilian and foreign—especially U.S.—law enforcement agents soon raised concerns, as critics alleged these contacts bypassed established protocol requiring cooperation to go through the Ministry of Justice (Consultor Jurídico, 2018). The Car Wash Leaks further bolstered this contestation by revealing additional contacts between Dallagnol's team and foreign prosecutors. Leaked messages showed that, in 2015, Brazilian prosecutors hosted a delegation of U.S. officials—mostly from the FBI and the Department of Justice (DOJ)—to discuss ongoing investigations, a meeting reportedly held without the participation of Brazil's Ministry of Justice, which is legally responsible for such cooperation (Viana et al., 2020).

Multi-jurisdictional settlements that involved Brazilian prosecutors and foreign agencies, such as the one signed by Odebrecht and Braskem with U.S. and Swiss authorities, were initially not questioned for their international nature. Criticism arose with the Petrobras settlement, primarily over the destination of the penalties, as discussed elsewhere in this chapter. However, in 2023, Supreme Court Justice Toffoli annulled all evidence from the Odebrecht leniency agreement based on (later disproved) arguments that it had been obtained through informal channels (Arbex, 2023).

Some critics have traced a line between the Wikileaks disclosures and the beginning of the Car Wash investigations. They noted that the National Security Agency's documents leaked by Edward Snowden mentioned Petrobras—a widely reported revelation (G1, 2013)—, and posited that compromising information about the company was fed to Moro and other law enforcement agents to spark investigations that would harm Petrobras' prospects (Miranda, 2016).

Lula's lawyers combined domestic and international critiques by applying the concept of lawfare—defined as the 'strategic use of the Law to delegitimize, damage or annihilate an opponent' (Zanin et al., 2023)—to the investigations against the former president. They argued that the legislative reforms in Brazil that produced the aforementioned means were the result of foreign interference—namely, U.S.-led and OECD-backed pressure—to incorporate U.S. legal provisions, such as plea bargains and leniency agreements. According to this view, the lawfare against Lula was motivated by geopolitical interests in Brazil's recently discovered pre-salt oil reserves. One of these lawyers, Cristiano Zanin, was appointed by Lula to the Supreme Court in 2023.

In some cases, contestation the means and the actors intertwine. For example, a widely disseminated investigative piece in Le Monde from April 2021 (Estrada and Bourcier, 2021) connected Mr Moro's personal and professional journey to Brazil's changing legal landscape. The article noted that international, mostly US-originated pressures pushed Brazil to enact FCPA-inspired legislation, culminating in the 2013 Anticorruption Law, which introduced leniency agreement provisions. According to the piece, Moro, a judge trained by the US Embassy in Brazil, was an ideal candidate to employ these new tools to gather evidence. The authors also argued that the push for FCPA-inspired legislation was intended to protect US-based multinationals and, in Brazil's case, to curb Brazil's geopolitical influence in Latin America and Africa.

Contestation of the Cause

A substantive thread of contestation around Operation Car Wash centers on the legitimacy of its anti-corruption goals. Critics argue that the operation mischaracterized elements of the natural workings of the political system. According to this perspective, while there might have been illegal activities uncovered by Car Wash, many actions that the operation framed as corrupt were, in fact, part of the standard political processes—albeit imperfect ones—rather than examples of outright criminal behavior.

The core argument is that Operation Car Wash exaggerated the extent to which corruption was entrenched in Brazil's political system. For instance, campaign financing was a focus of investigations and even officially registered contributions were argued to be bribes received by candidates in some cases (Carneiro and Falcão, 2017; Flores, 2017). Even in cases where companies failed to disclose these payments according to electoral laws, this failure did not necessarily constitute bribes, for some critics. This led to an attempted reaction by Congress to set rules distinguishing acts of corruption from legitimate efforts to defend the interests of certain economic sectors (Gama et al., 2017). In the end, the Supreme Court banned corporate donations, and the reaction of the political class has been to increase public funding for political parties and electoral campaigns.

Similarly, Car Wash scrutinized the role of Brazilian politicians in advancing the interests of national companies abroad, portraying these actions as part of a corrupt *modus operandi*. However, some have argued that this is a legitimate and necessary part of a politician's duties and that the actions of Brazilian officials working to secure favorable contracts for companies like Odebrecht abroad were wrongly classified as corrupt practices, when in reality, such actions are typical of what politicians around the world do to support their country's economic interests (Jiménez, 2015). The very nature of politics, which often involves negotiations and the exchange of favors, was criminalized by Car Wash in a way that distorted its reality.

This argument reflects a deeper critique about the limitations of anti-corruption movements when applied to complex political realities like those in Brazil. Car Wash's approach to tackling corruption, according to this line of thought, ignored the practical and often unavoidable intricacies of political deal-making, misinterpreting what many see as necessary evils of the political process as evidence of systemic corruption.

Once again, this critique of Operation Car Wash had an important international dimension. According to this view, the anti-corruption movement itself has a U.S.-centric, imperialistic flavor, exporting a narrow definition of corruption that may be suited to developed economies but fails to account for the political complexities of countries like Brazil. The argument is that the concepts of corruption and acceptable political behavior that underpinned Operation Car Wash were largely influenced by legal and political norms from the United States and other developed nations, rather than being adapted to the realities of emerging economies.

This international critique goes beyond Operation Car Wash itself, tapping into larger concerns about how global anti-corruption norms are shaped and who they benefit. In this view, the growing global focus on anti-corruption, while seemingly virtuous, often reflects the priorities of developed economies, which use anti-corruption initiatives to discipline and weaken political actors in emerging markets. In Brazil, this translated into the prosecution of activities that are often accepted in political systems around the world—such as campaign financing and the promotion of national industries—but that were reframed as part of a corrupt network in Car Wash's investigations.

Contestation of the Consequences

One common thread of contestation surrounding Operation Car Wash focuses on its negative consequences. Critics argue that regardless of its original intent—whether a genuine effort to combat corruption or not—Car Wash ultimately caused more harm than good. This criticism unfolds along two main lines: economic and political consequences.

Economic Consequences

On the economic front, critics contend that Operation Car Wash inflicted significant damage to Brazil's economy, resulting in lost productivity and job cuts. To bolster their claims, they often cite a few widely circulated figures. For instance, a 2021 study by the Department of Statistics and Socioeconomic Studies of the Labour Movement (DIEESE, 2021) suggests that Car Wash cost Brazil 4.4 million jobs and 3.6% of its GDP between 2014 and 2017—with R$ 47.6 billion in taxes left uncollected and wages declining by R$ 85.6 billion. Another popular claim is that in 2015 alone, Car Wash had a negative impact of 2.5% on Brazil's GDP, a figure originating from a consultancy firm's study (Costas, 2015).

Despite the fact that neither study has been peer-reviewed and both offer limited methodological transparency, these figures have become widely disseminated. They are frequently cited in the media—including recent publications by the government-controlled news agency Agencia Brasil (Máximo, 2024)—and have been embraced by politicians. Notably, Lula has cited these numbers on multiple occasions (Consultor Jurídico, 2020), and political parties have used them in judicial proceedings aimed at vacating all leniency agreements signed by companies implicated in the Operation Car Wash investigations (Supremo Tribunal Federal, 2023).

Building on these macroeconomic estimates, critics also point to the tangible impact on key industrial sectors—particularly on the petrochemical and construction industries, both deeply entangled in the corruption schemes revealed by Car Wash. Petrobras, the state-controlled oil giant, and Braskem, a major petrochemical company, were central to many of the corruption allegations. As investigations unfolded, these companies—and many others connected to them—became embroiled in massive legal battles, fines, and sanctions, ultimately freezing operations and investments.

The construction sector, dominated by companies such as Odebrecht, suffered severe setbacks. Responsible for major infrastructure projects across Brazil and Latin America, these companies found their ongoing and planned investments effectively paralyzed. With companies barred from bidding on public contracts and weakened by legal liabilities and a loss of investor confidence, infrastructure projects came to a standstill. This paralysis had ripple effects throughout the economy, arguably contributing to a slowdown in growth and a significant loss of jobs.

Political Consequences

On the political front, critics argue that Operation Car Wash destabilized Brazil's young democracy by significantly weakening some of its most important political institutions. The operation's focus on high-ranking politicians, especially those from the Workers' Party, contributed to a growing sense of disillusionment with the political establishment as a whole. While Car Wash initially received widespread public support for its anti-corruption efforts, it gradually fostered an anti-establishment sentiment that many argue paved the way for the rise of Jair Bolsonaro, a far-right candidate who capitalized on the public's frustration with traditional parties and the perceived corruption of the ruling class, and paid only lip service to the anti-corruption agenda.

By implicating a majority of political parties and a substantial portion of Brazil's political elite, the operation contributed to a broader delegitimization of the country's political system. At one point, Odebrecht executives mentioned 415 politicians, from 26 political parties (VEJA, 2017). The fact that most of the individuals mentioned were not prosecuted or convicted due to insufficient evidence beyond plea bargains further strengthens impressions that these accusations contributed more to discrediting the political class than to holding corrupt individuals accountable (Fellet, 2017). Critics contend that this anti-establishment wave weakened democratic institutions and gave rise to populist forces that prioritized confrontation over consensus-building.

The economic and political consequences of Operation Car Wash were not seen by all critics as merely unintended side effects. A common internationally-oriented critique posits that these consequences were in fact deliberate—serving the interests of developed economies, particularly the United States. This view asserts that Car Wash was not simply a domestic anti-corruption operation but part of a broader geopolitical strategy to undermine Brazil's rising global influence.

One version of this narrative centers around Brazil's oil reserves in the pre-salt layer, vast offshore oil fields that were expected to play a key role in the country's economic future. Critics argue that Operation Car Wash, by crippling Petrobras, prevented Brazil from fully exploiting this resource, thereby serving the interests of foreign oil companies and governments (Poder360, 2021). According to this narrative, the United States had a vested interest in ensuring that Petrobras did not emerge as a dominant player in the global oil market.

Another (related) version of the geopolitical critique focuses on Brazil's construction industry (Brasil 247, 2022), particularly the international reach of companies like Odebrecht, known as 'national champions,' that served to reassert the country's political influence in Latin America and Africa. By targeting these firms, critics argue, Car Wash helped eliminate Brazil's competitive edge in the global construction market, opening the door for foreign firms to fill the void left by the collapse of Brazilian companies. These industries, which had become increasingly successful abroad, were seen as a threat to established players in developed countries, and Car Wash is viewed as a means of neutralizing that threat.

Finally, some critics argue that Operation Car Wash was part of a broader effort to oust the PT government, which had a long history of anti-U.S. policies and a commitment to a more independent foreign policy. By weakening the PT and contributing to the rise of Bolsonaro—a candidate that this narrative portrays as more aligned with U.S. interests—Car Wash is seen as part of a geopolitical strategy to bring Brazil closer to the Western fold.

Resonance of Contestation Threads in Institutional Spaces

From our analysis, it seems clear that the thread centered around the *means* used in Operation Car Wash was the first to successfully penetrate these institutional spaces. The early responses to Car Wash took the form of efforts to constrain the means available to investigators, often justified by concerns over prosecutorial overreach. These efforts materialized in the form of petitions and appeals filed by the lawyers of individuals and companies under investigation.

The contestation of the means was key in prompting the series of Supreme Court rulings that, particularly after 2019, dealt significant blows to the Operation, such as the decision to remove cases about illegal campaign contributions from the scope of Car Wash and the decision that sentences could not be executed until all appeals had been exhausted. These rulings collectively signaled that the Court had begun to align itself with the criticism that Car Wash's methods violated due process.

In 2019, Moro's entry into politics and the Car Wash Leaks fueled the thread of contestation centered on the legitimacy of the actors, and this was incorporated in Supreme Court rulings. In 2021, in a clear endorsement of the 'ulterior motives' claim, after Lula's conviction had already been overturned on the grounds of lack of jurisdiction, the Supreme Court issued a separate ruling, stating that Moro had not acted impartially in the case. By 2023, the contestation of the actors reached new heights with Justice Toffoli's ruling that all evidence stemming from Odebrecht's leniency agreement was illegal, which included a strongly worded opinion in which Justice Toffoli heavily criticized the methods used by Car Wash prosecutors and described the investigation as a politically motivated effort to bring down Lula and other political figures. Toffoli's decision incorporated elements of multiple contestation threads, accusing Car Wash of violating due process and engaging in a 'cover-up of anti-corruption' to achieve political ends.

While the threads of contestation focused on the means and actors were successful in penetrating institutional spaces, the other threads—those focused on the legitimacy of the cause and the consequences of Car Wash—did not find the same level of resonance. Although some aspects of these threads were occasionally referenced in judicial decisions such as Justice Toffoli's claim in his 2023 decision that Car Wash 'destroyed national technologies, companies, jobs and public and private assets'—they were generally less central to the institutional backlash against Car Wash.

Interestingly, the international dimensions of the contestation threads received little to no acknowledgment in formal institutional spaces. While critics often pointed to foreign influence as part of their critique of Car Wash, these arguments rarely surfaced in official decisions or statements.

Conclusion

Taking seriously the contestation of anticorruption efforts is long overdue. Acknowledging contestation does not mean endorsing it uncritically but rather recognizing, as noted in this book's introduction, that anticorruption is a 'policy arena wrapped up in systems of unequal power, of personal and group interests, of bargaining, and of matters of social justice and basic social values.'

While we refrained from judging the merits of the arguments used to challenge the operation, we are also mindful that those charged with corruption will invariably seek to delegitimize anti-corruption efforts. Considering the relevance of such arguments does not mean that they should justify interrupting investigations or even changing their course. It does, however, mean that we should begin considering how, 25 years after the OECD Anti-Bribery Convention came into force, the classical tenets of anti-corruption enforcement may need some adjustments considering the current state of world affairs, if for nothing else than to provide antidotes against these criticisms.

Given that 'sand' has replaced 'grease' as the paradigm for corruption's economic impact, it has become an article of faith for anti-corruption practitioners to say that their work will, despite some minor initial disruption, lead to improved business relations which will (re)form on a more efficient basis. Are these traditional prescriptions valid for developed and developing economies alike? Do they still hold in the face of increased economic and commercial protectionism from some of the former champions of globalization?

The OECD Anti-Bribery Convention enshrined the principle that considerations of national economic interests should not influence anti-corruption enforcement (art. 5). However, understanding the economic impacts of anti-corruption efforts could prove valuable, especially as evidence mounts on the impact of these actions on citizens' socioeconomic well-being. Are there different law enforcement alternatives to combating impunity while mitigating the economic impact

One should not discount the additional risks in contexts of deep polarization where any disruption may fuel the deep discontent about economic opportunities that serve as fuel for populist leaders well adept at weaponizing anti-corruption tools and policies against their enemies.

These discussions have direct policy implications. For example, what is the tradeoff between wholesale economic impact of fines and penalties applied to companies and the deterrent aspect of these penalties for future wrongdoing? Could leadership removal or equity restructuring be more effective tools with fewer economic repercussions?

Similarly, foreign policy motivations and repercussions of anti-corruption enforcement have received little scholarly attention. Under the apparent risk of validating somewhat fringe arguments about the 'politicization' of anti-corruption enforcement, some prefer to ignore them. Much like the economic aspects, wouldn't it be better to fully consider them and discuss policy alternatives in terms of possible trade-offs?

Contestation of anticorruption efforts has often been dismissed as thinly veiled attempts to shield economic and political actors from accountability. However, it is time to take them seriously. Addressing contestation does not mean assuming that all criticisms are valid or even well-intentioned. It does mean recognizing that anticorruption must ground its legitimacy in more than the 'badness' of corruption—it must bolster the legitimacy of its actors, its instruments, and its processes.

Notes

1. 'Vaza Jato' is a play-on-words combining 'Lava Jato' (Car Wash in Portuguese) and 'vazamento' (leaks, in Portuguese). The term was widely used by the press when referring to the leaked messages initially reported by *The Intercept Brasil.*
2. Although President Rousseff was charged with corruption in 2017, the charge was later dropped by the Federal Prosecutor's Office, which admitted there was not sufficient evidence, as Rousseff was acquitted (Oliveria, 2019).
3. The controversial decision to revoke Mr. Dallagnol's mandate was based on the fact that he had resigned from his position as prosecutor while there were pending investigations about prosecutorial misconduct. These investigations, had they resulted in sanctions, would have deemed him ineligible. The court considered that his resignation was a way to circumvent those sanctions (Azevedo, 2023).
4. In 2019, in an interview from prison, former President Lula stated: 'I have no doubt... that everything that's happened in connection with Operation Car Wash has been to prevent Lula from running for president. Nowadays I'm certain of this, the same way that I'm certain that the US Department of Justice is behind this' (Greenwald, 2019).

5. There is little dispute that the Car Wash task force deployed 'an aggressive, relentless, and unorthodox prosecutorial strategy' (Gonzalez-Ocantos, 2023: 65), which was deemed a significant reason for the investigation to gain momentum. There has been a significant scholarly debate about the use made by the operation of legal instruments both old and new, such as pre-trial detentions, leniency agreements, plea bargaining, among others.

References

Arbex, T. (2023) 'Lava Jato formalizou cooperação internacional um ano após leniência com Odebrecht, aponta documento de ministério', *CNN Brasil*, 13 September. Available at: https://www.cnnbrasil.com.br/politica/lava-jato-formalizou-cooperacao-internacional-um-ano-apos-leniencia-com-odebrecht-aponta-documento-de-ministerio/ (Accessed: 18 October 2024).Azevedo, V. (2023) 'Câmara confirma decisão do TSE e declara perda de mandato de Deltan', Folha de S. Paulo, 6 June. Available at: https://www1.folha.uol.com.br/poder/2023/06/camara-confirma-decisao-do-tse-e-declara-perda-de-mandato-de-deltan.shtml (Accessed: 7 December 2024).

Barbosa, B. (2018) 'Justiça manda destruir grampos de escritório de advogados de Lula', *UOL*, 14 March. Available at: https://noticias.uol.com.br/politica/eleicoes/2018/noticias/2018/03/14/justica-manda-destruir-grampos-de-escritorio-de-advogados-de-lula.htm (Accessed: 18 October 2024).

Bilenky, T. and Marques, J. (2017) 'Lula lidera, e 2° lugar tem empate de Bolsonaro e Marina, diz Datafolha', *Folha de S. Paulo*, 26 June. Available at: https://www1.folha.uol.com.br/poder/2017/06/1895987-lula-lidera-e-2-lugar-tem-empate-de-bolsonaro-e-marina-diz-datafolha.shtml (Accessed: 18 October 2024).

Brasil 247 (2022) 'Objetivo da Lava Jato era destruir a engenharia brasileira, diz Pezão à TV 247', 7 May. Available at: https://www.brasil247.com/economia/objetivo-da-lava-jato-era-destruir-a-engenharia-brasileira-diz-pezao-a-tv-247-u9z4h757 (Accessed: 18 October 2024).

Carneiro, L. and Falcão, M. (2017) '2ª Turma do STF: Doação eleitoral pode maquiar propina', *JOTA*, 7 March. Available at: https://www.jota.info/justica/2a-turma-do-stf-doacao-eleitoral-pode-maquiar-propina (Accessed: 18 October 2024).

Cifuentes, P. (2014) 'Sergio Moro: O juiz que sacode o Brasil', *El País Brasil*, 26 November. Available at: https://brasil.elpais.com/brasil/2014/11/26/politica/1417013006_508980.html (Accessed: 18 October 2024).

Consultor Jurídico (2020) 'Lava Jato deu prejuízo de R$ 142 bi ao país, diz Lula', 8 February. Available at: https://www.conjur.com.br/2020-fev-08/lava-jato-deu-prejuizo-142-bi-pais-lula/ (Accessed: 18 October 2024).

Consultor Jurídico (2016) 'Leia a íntegra da petição de Lula à ONU questionando atuação de Sergio Moro', 1 August. Available at: https://www.conjur.com.br/2016-ago-01/leia-integra-peticao-lula-onu-questionando-sergio-moro/ (Accessed: 18 October 2024).

Consultor Jurídico (2018) 'Lula tenta anular sentença apontando parceria ilegal entre MPF e FBI', 16 March. Available at: https://www.conjur.com.br/2018-mar-16/lula-anular-sentenca-apontando-parceria-ilegal-entre-mpf-fbi/ (Accessed: 18 October 2024).

Costas, R. (2015) 'Sem Lava Jato, recessão poderia ser 3 vezes menor, dizem consultorias', G1, 2 December. Available at: https://g1.globo.com/economia/noticia/2015/12/sem-lava-jato-recessao-poderia-ser-3-vezes-menor-dizem-consultorias.html (Accessed: 18 October 2024).

Da Ros, L. and Taylor, M. (2022) *Brazilian Politics on Trial: Corruption and Reform Under Democracy*. Boulder: Lynne Rienner Publishers. https://doi.org/10.1515/9781955055192.

Datafolha (2015) 'Por Lava Jato, maioria quer abertura de processo contra Dilma Rousseff', 13 April. Available at: https://datafolha.folha.uol.com.br/opiniaopublica/2015/04/1615897-por-lava-jato-maioria-quer-abertura-de-processo-contra-dilma-rousseff.shtml (Accessed: 18 October 2024).

DIEESE (2021) 'Implicações Econômicas Intersetoriais da Operação Lava Jato', 16 March. Available at: https://www.dieese.org.br/outraspublicacoes/2021/impactosLavaJatoEconomia.pdf (Accessed: 18 October 2024).

Estrada, G. and Bourcier, N. (2021) 'Au Brésil, une opération anticorruption aux méthodes contestables', *Le Monde*, 9 April. Available at: https://www.lemonde.fr/international/article/2021/04/09/au-bresil-une-operation-anticorruption-aux-methodes-contestables_6076204_3210.html (Accessed: 18 October 2024).

Fellet, J. (2017) 'Após dois anos, só 5 dos 47 políticos investigados em 1ª lista de Janot no STF viraram réus', *BBC News Brasil*, 13 April. Available at: https://www.bbc.com/portuguese/brasil-39573351 (Accessed: 18 October 2024).

Fernandes, D. F. and Santana, T. B. (2020) Discursos sobre a corrupção nas votações do Supremo Tribunal Federal (2015–2017). *Revista Brasileira de Direito Processual Penal*, 6(3), 1345–1387. https://doi.org/10.22197/rbdpp.v6i3.432.

Fernandes, F. A. (2020) *Geopolítica da Intervenção: a verdadeira história da Lava Jato*. 2nd ed. São Paulo: Geração Editorial.

Ferreira et al. (2019) 'Deltan montou plano para lucrar com fama da Lava Jato, apontam mensagens', *Folha de S. Paulo*, 14 July. Available at: https://www1.folha.uol.com.br/poder/2019/07/deltan-montou-plano-para-lucrar-com-fama-da-lava-jato-apontam-mensagens.shtml (Accessed: 18 October 2024).

Flores, P. (2017) 'O que é e como funciona a prática do "caixa 3"', *Nexo*, 27 December. Available at: https://www.nexojornal.com.br/expresso/2017/12/27/o-que-e-como-funciona-a-pratica-do-caixa-3 (Accessed: 18 October 2024).

Folha de S. Paulo (2018) 'A guinada do juiz', 1 November. Available at: https://www1.folha.uol.com.br/opiniao/2018/11/a-guinada-do-juiz.shtml (Accessed: 18 October 2024).

Folha de S. Paulo (2016) 'Marilena Chaui diz que Moro foi treinado por FBI para Lava Jato', 4 July. Available at: https://www1.folha.uol.com.br/poder/2016/07/1788553-marilena-chaui-diz-que-moro-foi-treinado-por-fbi-para-lava-jato.shtml (Accessed: 18 October 2024).

Folha de S. Paulo (2015) 'Editorial: Delação aprovada', 4 January. Available at: https://www1.folha.uol.com.br/opiniao/2015/01/1570126-editorial-delacao-aprovada.shtml (Accessed: 18 October 2024).

G1 (2017) 'Janot pedirá abertura de investigação para apurar vazamento da delação de ex-diretor da Odebrecht', 10 December. Available at: https://g1.globo.com/politica/operacao-lava-jato/noticia/janot-pedira-abertura-de-investigacao-para-apurar-vazamento-da-delacao-de-ex-diretor-da-odebrecht.ghtml (Accessed: 18 October 2024).

G1 (2014) 'Dilma defende Petrobras e diz que o que deve ser condenado são as pessoas', 16 November. Available at: https://g1.globo.com/politica/operacao-lava-jato/noticia/2014/11/dilma-defende-petrobras-e-diz-que-o-que-deve-ser-condenado-sao-pessoas.html (Accessed: 18 October 2024).

G1 (2013) 'Petrobras foi alvo de espionagem de agência dos EUA, aponta documento', 8 September. Available at: https://g1.globo.com/politica/noticia/2013/09/petrobras-foi-alvo-de-espionagem-de-agencia-dos-eua-aponta-documento.html (Accessed: 18 October 2024).

Gama et al. (2017) 'Base e oposição tentam blindar doações e dificultar condenações', *Folha de S. Paulo*, 14 March. Available at: https://www1.folha.uol.com.br/poder/2017/03/1866216-base-e-oposicao-tentam-blindar-doacoes-e-dificultar-condenacoes.shtml (Accessed: 18 October 2024).

Giacomet Júnior, I. (2018) 'Quatro anos de Operação Lava Jato: desempenho da cooperação jurídica internacional', *Cooperação em Pauta*, April. Available at: https://www.gov.br/mj/pt-br/assuntos/sua-protecao/lavagem-de-dinheiro/drci/publicacoes/cooperacao-em-pauta/2018/cooperacao-em-pauta-n38.pdf (Accessed: 18 October 2024).

Giovanaz, D. (2017) 'Agente da CIA, treinado pelo FBI: Um raio-X da relação Moro-EUA', *Brasil de Fato*, 5 June. Available at: https://www.brasildefatopr.com.br/2017/06/05/agente-da-cia-treinado-pelo-fbi-um-raio-x-da-relacao-moro-eua (Accessed: 18 October 2024).

Gonzalez-Ocantos, E.A., Chirinos, P.M., Pavão, N. and Hidalgo, V.B. (2023) *Prosecutors, Voters and the Criminalization of Corruption in Latin America: The Case of Lava Jato.* Cambridge Studies in Law and Society. Cambridge: Cambridge University Press.

Greenwald, G. (2019) 'Interview with Brazil's ex-President Lula from prison', *The Intercept*, 22 May. Available at: https://theintercept.com/2019/05/22/lula-brazil-ex-president-prison-interview/ (Accessed: 7 December 2024).

Ipsos (2019) Pulso Brasil – Lava-Jato. Available at: https://www.ipsos.com/pt-br/lava-jato-e-opiniao-publica (Accessed: 7 December 2024).

Ipsos (2017) 'Pulso Brasil – Operação Lava Jato'. Available at: https://www.ipsos.com/sites/default/files/2017-05/Lava_Jato_Ipsos_Pulso_Brasil.pdf (Accessed: 18 October 2024).

IstoÉ (2023) 'José Dirceu, Cunha e outros condenados na Lava Jato planejam retorno à política após absolvições', 23 May. Available at: https://istoe.com.br/jose-dirceu-cunha-e-outros-condenados-na-lava-jato-planejam-retorno-a-politica-apos-absolvicoes/ (Accessed: 18 October 2024).

Jiménez, C. (2015) 'Miguel Jorge: "Clinton também fez lobby por empresas dos EUA no Brasil"', *El País Brasil*, 30 September. Available at: https://brasil.elpais.com/brasil/2015/09/30/politica/1443579012_196676.html (Accessed: 18 October 2024).

Jornal Nacional (2019) 'Pesquisa Datafolha mostra forte apoio à Lava Jato', 13 December. Available at: https://g1.globo.com/jornal-nacional/noticia/2019/12/13/pesquisa-datafolha-mostra-forte-apoio-a-lava-jato.ghtml (Accessed: 18 October 2024).

Jornal Naciona (2016) 'Condução coercitiva de Lula provoca polêmica nos meios jurídicos', 5 March. Available at: https://g1.globo.com/jornal-nacional/noticia

/2016/03/conducao-coercitiva-de-lula-provoca-polemica-nos-meios-juridicos.html (Accessed: 18 October 2024).

Landim, R. (2024) 'TRF-4 anula condenação de Dallagnol para ressarcir diárias da Lava Jato', UOL, 26 September. Available at: https://noticias.uol.com.br/colunas/raquel-landim/2024/09/26/trf-4-anula-condenacao-de-dallagnol-para-ressarcir-diarias-da-lava-jato.htm?cmpid (Accessed: 7 December 2024).

Landim, R. (2023) 'Com decisão de Mendonça, sobe para 10 o número de empresas da Lava Jato com multas suspensas', *CNN Brasil*, 27 April. Available at: https://www.cnnbrasil.com.br/blogs/sem-blogueiro/politica/com-decisao-de-mendonca-sobe-para-10-o-numero-de-empresas-da-lava-jato-com-multas-suspensas/ (Accessed: 18 October 2024).

Marreiro, F. (2019) 'Próxima vaga do STF é de Sérgio Moro, o "compromisso" público de Bolsonaro', *El País Brasil*, 13 May. Available at: https://brasil.elpais.com/brasil/2019/05/12/politica/1557677235_562717.html (Accessed: 18 October 2024).

Martins, R. and Neves, R. (2019) 'Deltan queria usar fama da Lava Jato para se eleger senador, revelam mensagens', *The Intercept Brasil*, 3 September. Available at: https://www.intercept.com.br/2019/09/03/deltan-senado-candidato/ (Accessed: 18 October 2024).

Marzullo, L. and Altino, L. (2024) 'Dez anos depois, anulações e absolvições já favoreceram mais de 60 réus da Lava-Jato', *O Globo*, 9 March. Available at: https://oglobo.globo.com/politica/noticia/2024/03/09/dez-anos-depois-anulacoes-e-absolvicoes-ja-favoreceram-mais-de-60-reus-da-lava-jato.ghtml (Accessed: 18 October 2024).

Máximo, W. (2024) 'Lava Jato destruiu 4,4 milhões de empregos, aponta estudo', *Agência Brasil*, 17 March. Available at: https://agenciabrasil.ebc.com.br/economia/noticia/2024-03/lava-jato-destruiu-444-milhoes-de-empregos-aponta-estudo (Accessed: 18 October 2024).

Migalhas (2023) 'Gilmar diz que fundação Dallagnol "não se tratava de clube de freiras"', 8 May. Available at: https://www.migalhas.com.br/quentes/406920/gilmar-diz-que-fundacao-dallagnol-nao-se-tratava-de-clube-de-freiras (Accessed: 18 October 2024).

Migalhas (2016) 'Advogados repudiam supressão de direitos e garantias na Lava Jato', 15 January. Available at: https://www.migalhas.com.br/quentes/232571/advogados-repudiam-supressao-de-direitos-e-garantias-na-lava-jato (Accessed: 18 October 2024).

Miranda, E. (2016) 'Moniz Bandeira: Moro e Janot atuam com os Estados Unidos contra o Brasil', *Jornal do Brasil*, 3 December. Available at: https://www.jb.com.br/pais/noticias/2016/12/03/moniz-bandeira-moro-e-janot-atuam-com-os-estados-unidos-contra-o-brasil/ (Accessed: 18 October 2024).

Moraes, C. (2015) 'As delações premiadas da Lava Jato provocam uma guerra entre juízes e advogados', *El País Brasil*, 8 August. Available at: https://brasil.elpais.com/brasil/2015/08/07/politica/1438977328_141841.html (Accessed: 18 October 2024).

Moro, S.F. (2004) Considerações sobre a Operação Mani Pulite. *Revista CEJ (Brasília)*, 26, 56–62.

Mortari, M. (2019) 'Para 40%, Lava Jato cometeu excessos e parte das decisões deve ser revista', *InfoMoney*, 15 October. Available at: https://www.infomoney.com

.br/politica/para-40-lava-jato-cometeu-excessos-e-parte-das-decisoes-deve-ser-revista/ (Accessed: 18 October 2024).

Nunes, W. (2019) 'OAB classifica como grave o relato da defesa de Lula sobre grampo de advogados', *Folha de S. Paulo*, 7 June. Available at: https://www1.folha.uol.com.br/poder/2019/06/oab-classifica-como-grave-o-relato-da-defesa-de-lula-sobre-grampo-de-advogados.shtml (Accessed: 18 October 2024).

OECD (2019) Abuse of authority provisions adopted by the Senate raise concerns over Brazil's capacity to ensure independence of prosecutors and judges in fighting corruption. Available at: https://web-archive.oecd.org/2019-07-01/524615-abuse-of-authority-provisions-adopted-by-the-senate-raise-concerns-over-brazil-s-capacity-to-ensure-independence-of-prosecutors-and-judges-in-fighting-corruption.htm (Accessed: 18 October 2024).

OECD (2022) Implementing the OECD anti-bribery convention: Phase 4 report – Brazil. Available at: https://www.oecd.org/en/publications/implementing-the-oecd-anti-bribery-convention-phase-4-report-brazil_fd55d063-en.html (Accessed: 18 October 2024).

Oliveria, M. (2019) 'Justiça do DF absolve Lula, Dilma, Palocci, Mantega e Vaccari no 'Quadrilhão do PT'', *G1*, 4 December. Available at: https://g1.globo.com/politica/noticia/2019/12/04/justica-do-df-absolve-lula-dilma-palocci-mantega-e-vaccari-no-quadrilhao-do-pt.ghtml (Accessed: 18 October 2024).

Partido dos Trabalhadores (2024) 'A perseguição política, jurídica e midiática a Lula'. Available at: https://pt.org.br/a-perseguicao-politica-juridica-e-midiatica-a-lula/page/2/ (Accessed: 18 October 2024).

Poder360 (2021) 'Em 1ª pesquisa após fim de força-tarefa, 80% dizem apoiar Operação Lava Jato', 12 February. Available at: https://www.poder360.com.br/lava-jato/em-1a-pesquisa-apos-fim-de-forca-tarefa-80-dizem-apoiar-operacao-lava-jato/ (Accessed: 18 October 2024).

Rousseff, D. (2019) 'A Lava Jato foi decisiva para o golpe de 2016', *Carta Capital*, 15 September. Available at: https://www.cartacapital.com.br/opiniao/dilma-rousseff-a-lava-jato-foi-decisiva-para-o-golpe-de-2016/ (Accessed: 18 October 2024).

Supremo Tribunal Federal (2023) 'Partidos pedem a suspensão de pagamentos de acordos de leniência da Lava Jato', 30 March. Available at: https://portal.stf.jus.br/noticias/verNoticiaDetalhe.asp?idConteudo=504928&ori=1 (Accessed: 18 October 2024).

Supremo Tribunal Federal (2019) 'Plenário do STF reafirma competência da Justiça Eleitoral para julgar crimes comuns conexos a delitos eleitorais', 14 March. Available at: https://portal.stf.jus.br/noticias/verNoticiaDetalhe.asp?idConteudo=405834 (Accessed: 18 October 2024).

Transparency International (2016) 'Brazil's carwash task force wins transparency international anti-corruption award', 3 December. Available at: https://www.transparency.org/en/press/brazils-carwash-task-force-wins-transparency-international-anti-corruption (Accessed: 18 October 2024).

Venaglia, G. (2020) 'Presidente diz que Moro pediu indicação ao STF', *CNN Brasil*, 24 April. Available at: https://www.cnnbrasil.com.br/politica/presidente-diz-que-moro-pediu-indicacao-ao-stf/ (Accessed: 18 October 2024).

VEJA (2017) 'Odebrecht: delatores citaram 415 políticos de 26 partidos', 17 April. Available at: https://veja.abril.com.br/brasil/odebrecht-delatores-citaram-415-politicos-de-26-partidos (Accessed: 18 October 2024).

Viana et al. (2020) 'Como a Lava Jato escondeu do governo federal visita do FBI e procuradores americanos', *Agência Pública*, 12 March. Available at: https://apublica.org/2020/03/como-a-lava-jato-escondeu-do-governo-federal-visita-do-fbi-e-procuradores-americanos/ (Accessed: 18 October 2024).

Viapiana, T. (2022) 'Brazil's 'Secret Budget': What will happen to the vote-buying scheme in Congress when Lula takes power?', Brazil Reports, 5 December. Available at: https://www.brazilreports.com/brazils-secret-budget-what-will-happen-to-the-vote-buying-scheme-in-congress-when-lula-takes-power/3312/ (Accessed: 18 October 2024).

Vieira, J. and Miranda, L. (2024) 'When corruption strikes back: How congress reverses anti-corruption reforms in Brazil', in Odilla, F. and Tsimonis, K. (eds.) *Corruption and Anti-Corruption Upside Down. Political Corruption and Governance.* Cham: Palgrave Macmillan, 145–164. https://doi.org/10.1007/978-3-031-66032-0_11.

Zanin, C., Martins, V. and Valim, R. 2023. *Lawfare: uma introdução.* São Paulo: Ed. Contracorrente.

5

ADAPTING ANTI-CORRUPTION TO A DISCORDANT WORLD

The Missed Opportunity of Monitoring, Evaluation, and Learning

Thomas Shipley

In this period of increased self-reflection in the corruption field, one point of agreement is that there is a lack of evidence regarding how best to combat corruption and prevent unintended harms (Johnsøn, Taxell and Zaum, 2012; Marquette and Peiffer, 2020). That wide evidence gaps persist, despite large-scale investments of resources into anti-corruption initiatives over the last three decades, is in itself a failure. International aid organisations and their partners, which play a critical role in shaping and delivering an anti-corruption agenda in low and middle-income countries, have received particular criticism in this regard. Different experts have criticised these organisations for repeating tired formulas, proposing "magic bullet solutions", and failing to learn from mistakes (Johnston, 2005; Heywood, 2018; Mason, 2021). Continued investment in the absence of demonstrable success gives fuel to Sampson's critique of the field as a self-serving industry of "moral entrepreneurs" who must be "seen to be doing something rather than asking: is what we are doing any good?" (Sampson, 2010, p.278).

The lack of evidence is all the more troubling because organisations across the international development sector have invested in Monitoring, Evaluation and Learning (MEL) systems. The stated aims of these systems are ensuring accountability to stakeholders for results, while simultaneously promoting learning to improve programming. The learning gathered through MEL systems ought to be a valuable source of empirical evidence for understanding "what works" when implementing anti-corruption measures and simultaneously highlighting innovative approaches. In leading academic analyses of corruption, however, including major theoretical contributions and systemic mappings of evidence, evaluation evidence barely features. This raises the

DOI: 10.4324/9781003531920-7

question of whether a source of evidence has been overlooked, or alternatively, whether there are problems with the quality and/or communication of this research which have limited its value.

In deconstructing anti-corruption practice, this chapter synthesises research undertaken by the author on the operation of MEL systems in the aid sector. The chapter begins by tracing how MEL became an established practice in the sector and what it can offer to debates around anti-corruption effectiveness. The analysis then turns to a critical examination of current MEL practice in this field. While there are a small number of practitioner guides on how to evaluate anti-corruption interventions (Johnsøn and Søreide, 2013; Trapnell, 2015; Wathne, 2022), there has been negligible analysis to date of the evidence actually produced through evaluation. Drawing on structured analysis of 91 published evaluations of anti-corruption portfolios and programmes and interviews with 50 practitioners in the sector, the chapter analyses the quality of existing evaluation evidence and the uses to which this is put.

The analysis ultimately casts doubt on whether MEL systems are fulfilling their twin goals of supporting accountability and learning. MEL in its current form more often functions as a mechanism reinforcing dominant modes of thinking in anti-corruption instead of providing independent challenge and space for debate. The concluding section considers the acute dilemmas created by global discordance for the aid sector and the role MEL might play in adapting anti-corruption to these realities.

The Emergence of MEL in International Development

Evaluation is an unusual discipline because it is undertaken across many spheres of public policy but equally has its own distinct literature (for introductions to key debates in evaluation see Fox, Grimm and Caldeira, 2016; Mark, Greene and Shaw, 2006). The chapter employs the following widely cited definition of evaluation as:

> A type of disciplined inquiry undertaken to determine the value (merit and/or worth) of some entity – the evaluand – such as a treatment, program, facility, performance and the like – in order to improve or refine the evaluand (formative evaluation) or to assess its impact (summative evaluation).
>
> *(Lincoln and Guba, 1986, p.550)*

The definition captures key goals of evaluation, notably its practical orientation – the aim is to apply research to improve activities – while the emphasis on disciplined inquiry further denotes that evaluation should follow high standards of research. Evaluation additionally aspires to a position of impartiality even while this can be challenging to maintain in practice and represents a tension running through all evaluative work (Mark, Greene and Shaw,

2006, p.5). Monitoring typically goes hand in hand with evaluation and is understood here as the ongoing collection of information to both inform decision-making as an activity unfolds and to provide part of the evidence base for evaluation.

Organisations across the sector bundle monitoring and evaluation with learning such that MEL has become part of the lexicon of the aid sector, even if the learning component is often weakly defined. Organisational learning can take place at different levels (for instance at the headquarters or field level) and take varying forms. Yanguas (2021, pp.4–5) distinguishes between operational learning (the processes by which knowledge influences the delivery cycle) and strategic learning (the processes by which knowledge influences the objectives, structures and processes that govern the design and implementation of activities). Knowledge can derive from various sources external and internal to the organisation but, crucially, by linking monitoring and evaluation to learning, organisations are committing to learning from reviews of their own operational experience. It is this channel for learning which is under scrutiny here.

While the roots of evaluation practice can be traced back to the 1960s and 1970s and the adoption of New Public Management[1] approaches to public administration in the United States (Mark, Greene and Shaw, 2006, pp.9–10), MEL systems assumed a more prominent position within international aid organisations and partners from the 2000s onwards. This was the period during which results-based management took hold as an agenda in the sector amid pressure from domestic publics for more accountability around aid spending (Eyben, 2015). International institutions reinforcing these ways of working were also established. The Organisation for Economic Co-operation and Development – Development Assistance Committee (OECD-DAC) created a committee on Managing for Development Results in 2003 and a focus on results became one of the five principles of the Paris Declaration on Aid Effectiveness (2005). The OECD-DAC's coverage criteria for evaluation, namely relevance, coherence, effectiveness, efficiency, impact and sustainability (first published in 1991 and last revised in 2019), have in effect become a normative standard against which development organisations evaluate their programming (OECD-DAC, 2019).

This background is important to the analysis which follows because it shows how MEL systems became institutionalised at international aid organisations as an accountability function (Raimondo, 2018, p.30). Evaluation was subsumed into a wider agenda emphasising evidence and results premised on rationalist ideas that evaluation can objectively produce evidence to inform programming for the better. Reflecting this history and the influence of sub-fields in international development, particularly health and education, a hierarchy of evaluation research designs and methods also emerged at this time. There are conventions which still prevail in many domains of the aid sector which designate experimental designs (i.e. a research design involving randomisation to compare effects across groups) accompanied by quantitative methods as the "gold standard" (Network of Networks for Impact Evaluation (NONIE), 2009).

The term "impact evaluation" was originally born from these conventions and can be defined as an evaluation which assesses "the causal effects of a programme, measuring what net change can be attributed to it", usually requiring the establishment of a counterfactual (Johnsøn and Søreide, 2013, p.10). Many organisations distinguish "impact evaluation" from "performance or programme evaluation", which is presented as a less rigorous review of whether a programme has achieved its objectives (United States Agency for International Development (USAID), 2022).

Several leading thinkers on evaluation have nonetheless pushed back against this prevailing hierarchy, questioning the feasibility and utility of experimental designs in ways which are especially relevant for evaluating complex activities like anti-corruption programmes (Aston et al., 2022; Schwandt, 2019). Corruption has been labelled as a "wicked problem" (Heywood, 2019), i.e. a problem which is "enduring and bewildering", comprised of "multiple, interacting causal factors", and where stakeholder groups have different perspectives on the solutions (Schwandt and Gates, 2021, pp.118–119, referencing Ritel and Webber, 1973). In consequence, assessing impact in anti-corruption programmes – where outcomes are hard to observe and measure, will be contested, and are shaped by various political, economic and socio-cultural contextual factors – rarely lends itself well to randomisation. If experimental evaluation designs strip out context and instead focus on "average treatment effects" (White, 2009), it must further be questioned whether they will yield the types of information the corruption field needs. Practitioners need to understand how and why outcomes were achieved in a given context and what aspects of the strategy were successful or not, for instance how reforms were timed, sequenced and framed politically (on strategic choices in anti-corruption see Heywood and Pyman, 2024). These are the types of questions which should be at the centre of the "what works" debate for anti-corruption rather than simply choices of intervention types.

Philosophical and methodological debates in the evaluation field have spurred experts to propose alternative evaluative research designs which have promise for understanding the dynamic change processes which surround anti-corruption programmes. Aston et al. (2022) draw a distinction between the "counterfactual logic" behind experimental designs and evaluation designs based on a "generative logic" of causation, seeing the latter as "chiefly concerned with the 'causes of effects', that is, necessary and/or sufficient conditions for a given outcome" (Aston et al., 2022, p.39).

These designs are often based around small-n case studies, developed through mixed methods, and provide critical analysis of a Theory of Change (ToC) – an "articulation of how and why a given intervention will lead to specific change" (Stein and Valters, 2012, p.1). Examples include contribution analysis, an approach to systematically test the plausibility of claims that a programme has contributed to specific outcomes; outcome harvesting, an evaluative approach in which evaluators, grant makers, and/or programme managers and staff identify, formulate, verify, analyse and interpret "outcomes" in programming contexts; and realist evaluation, which develops hypotheses around context-mechanism-outcome statements that can be synthesised and aggregated into middle-range theories around how programmes are working (for summaries of designs see Aston et al., 2022; Better Evaluation, 2024).

In sum, there have been recent innovations in the evaluation field which have the potential to help organisations implementing anti-corruption measures grapple with the challenges involved in assessing the impact of their work, while also testing the assumptions guiding their dominant modes of programming. The extent to which these ideas have permeated practice is the issue to which the chapter now turns.

MEL and Anti-Corruption in Practice

To explore how evaluation systems function in practice, the author employed two main methods: first, undertaking a structured review of the quality of published evaluation reports of anti-corruption programmes and portfolios, and second, conducting fifty semi-structured interviews with a range of experts including evaluators, evaluation commissioners, programme officers, funders, and evaluands (the subjects of evaluation) to gather perspectives on practice. The primary purpose of the interviews was to examine how leading organisations in this field use evaluation research and the extent to which MEL systems are supporting organisational goals related to accountability and learning.

Evaluation Quality

The compilation of a database of published evaluation research brings together a source of empirical evidence which has been largely ignored to date by academics interested in questions of anti-corruption effectiveness.[2] The 91 evaluation reports making up the database were published by 11 aid agencies and civil society organisations (CSOs) between 2010 and 2023 and cover 33 different types of anti-corruption interventions. The analysis was organised around a new framework for assessing evaluation quality in anti-corruption work which included 21 data points covering both the portfolio/programme set-up – principally whether a ToC was in place and the organisation collected baseline and monitoring information – and the evaluation itself. On the second component, the review considered criteria related to evaluation design, methods, internal and external validity, measurement of outcomes, and responsiveness to gender and intersectionality, among other factors.

The analysis has acknowledged limitations, most importantly stemming from the reliance on published information. Organisations may withhold unfavourable or poor-quality evaluations, and some information relevant to scoring criteria may not be public. As many organisations in the field either do not publish or do not commission evaluations, the database is additionally weighted towards four organisations (Transparency International-Secretariat (TI-Sec), USAID, the United Nations Development Programme, and the United Nations Office on Drugs and Crime). To create a manageable database, the research also only incorporates programmes with explicit aims of addressing corruption, with the consequence that more indirect forms of programming may be under-represented. However, overall, the breadth of interventions and organisations covered allows for some key observations about the standard of evaluative work across this field.

While there are exceptions, the review points to generalised problems with the quality of evaluations of anti-corruption programming. Many of the issues start with programme design. For only a fifth of the programmes evaluated was there clear evidence of a ToC in place at the outset and therefore in most cases evaluators did not have a basis against which to test the programme's original assumptions and expected pathways to change. A clear majority of the evaluations also failed to incorporate baseline or monitoring information gathered by the programme.

When programmes used numeric indicators to assess performance, these were often unsuitable for tracking change at the level at which an intervention operates; for instance, a country-level index such as the Corruption Perceptions Index was used to monitor the impact of an intervention targeting a particular sector, geography or policy area. As a result, many anti-corruption programmes were poorly placed to optimise an evaluation process.

On the evaluations themselves, the principal issues can be broken down into problems of design, depth of analysis, and validity (internal and external). On design, three quarters of the evaluations did not have a structured research design, instead providing synthesis of document reviews and interview comments against the OECD-DAC criteria. Only one evaluation used an experimental design – confirmation of the practical problems involved in using this form of research for anti-corruption interventions – while there has been limited uptake of the designs based on generative logic described above. Therefore, while organisations consistently *ask* challenging questions around the impact and effects of their activities, evaluations are not usually designed in a way which would allow them to authoritatively answer these questions. The focus is usually internal management aspects of programmes rather than detailed analysis of their external effects.

It is a common mantra that anti-corruption reforms need to be understood in context, but this is a clear weakness in existing evaluative work. Just over half of the evaluations reviewed did not incorporate any contextual analysis.

Where this is presented, it is often high-level and not used to situate analysis around the intervention. A typical example would be for the evaluation to include a short description of the country context but not analysis of specific corruption problems, the drivers of those problems, and the actors involved.

The lack of contextual analysis further reduces confidence in the validity of findings as a reader is less able to judge whether the evaluation represents an authentic account of the intervention. While evaluations generally include details on the methodology followed and their information sources, attribution of information is a weakness for many. The level of evidence to support a conclusion is often not clear, and evaluations also rarely acknowledge conflicting perspectives on outcomes. If the information sources are unclear, this begs the question of whose perspective is being presented through evaluation, and whether there has truly been an attempt to consult and solicit challenges from stakeholders beyond those directly involved in the activities. External validity is equally a weakness. Evaluations rarely consider whether findings might have relevance to other comparable settings, reducing the potential for lesson learning across the field.

The analysis finally reveals structural constraints around evaluation processes which contribute to the weaknesses set out. The median timeframe given to evaluators to complete their work is three months – not a lot of time to understand a complex programme and produce independent analysis. Evaluation also usually only starts at the end of a programme's lifespan. There is a logic to this in that to fully understand its contribution a programme needs to be finished, but this means many opportunities for applying learning during the programme have passed.

There are exceptions in the database of evaluations which, usually following a theory-based design, advance understanding of how certain types of anti-corruption intervention have worked, including donor support to anti-corruption agencies and advocacy by CSOs (Kirch, Neumann and Russel, 2021; Johnsøn et al., 2016). The inherent difficulties in evaluating anti-corruption work should also not be underestimated. Nevertheless, evaluations are often formulaic and insufficiently analytical, suggesting there are problems with how MEL systems are operating in this field. Evaluation is not typically being used to interrogate the mental models underpinning how international aid organisations and their partners undertake anti-corruption programmes.

Use of Evaluation Research

To complement the review of evaluation quality, the next phase of analysis explored how organisations in this field use evaluation research and the functions it serves. Use is a major concern in the evaluation literature, driven by the widespread belief that evaluation research is often under-used or "misused" (Weiss, 1998; Patton, 1997).

There are different prospective users of evaluation, from decision-makers within aid organisations to funders, programme partners, and wider groups of intended beneficiaries. Use further takes various forms, including instrumental uses (the conventional view that evaluation will inform operational or strategic learning around programming), conceptual uses (building individual and organisational understanding of issues), and more problematic symbolic forms of use. An example of the latter would involve evaluation evidence being used disingenuously to legitimise a pre-determined approach.

Use should be analysed within an organisational context (Dahler-Larsen, 2012; Højlund, 2014; Raimondo, 2018) and this case-based research focused on three organisations – the Foreign, Commonwealth and Development Office (FCDO) (formerly the Department for International Development (DFID)), TI-Sec and USAID – and the evaluation structures these organisations had in place between 2010 and 2023. These organisations were selected as they have all undertaken significant levels of anti-corruption programming but also exhibit some variance in the structures of their MEL systems and the quality of the evaluation evidence produced which provides a basis for analytical comparison.[3]

Table 5.1 on the following page summarises findings on evaluation use at these three organisations alongside key features of their evaluation systems during the period under review. Notwithstanding some variations in approach, there were common patterns in use across all three organisations. At the central level, evaluation was peripheral to strategic decision-making on organisational approaches to anti-corruption. There were a multitude of factors influencing an organisation's overall approach to programming, most significantly the direction set by funders or political authorities, but the consistent view from key informants at all three organisations was that evaluation evidence rarely influenced decision-making at this level. Where publicly available, strategy documents published by these organisations did not reference lessons gleaned from evaluations (TI, 2021; USAID, 2022).

The picture at the programme level, where there might be more potential for use given the operational orientation of most evaluations, was more mixed. Non-use of evaluation research appeared to be the most common outcome at all three organisations, with interviewees citing multiple constraints to use, most frequently the timing of evaluation (it often occurred at too late a point to influence decision-making); poor perceptions of the evidence, either due to quality issues or the belief that the evaluation had not offered significant new insights; or other operational or political factors dominating decision-making and, in effect overriding any potential use of evidence. Where interviewees did describe instrumental forms of use, this was most commonly in support of operational learning. Interviewees gave examples of programmes changing their implementation approach in response to an evaluation or adding new components to an existing programme. The most important conditions

TABLE 5.1 Comparison of MEL systems at three anti-corruption organisations (2010–2023)

Key aspects of the MEL system		TI	USAID	FCDO
Timing and initial impetus for adoption of a MEL system		• 2010 onwards. • Pressure from donors to better demonstrate results.	• Origins in the 1990s with a big push on evaluation from 2010/11. • Cross-party support for stronger performance management measures in aid delivery.	• Origins in the late 1990s but significant investment from 2010 onwards. • 2010–2015 Conservative-led government emphasising results-based management in aid delivery.
System structure	Organisation of responsibilities	• Small central team with moderate oversight of all Secretariat-commissioned evaluations.	• Decentralised to regional and country offices. • Small central team provided limited technical inputs and occasionally commissioned evaluation centrally.	• Decentralised to country offices. • Small central team but broader evaluation cadre of trained professionals. • Additional independent external evaluation body (the Independent Commission for Aid Impact).
	Frequency of evaluation	• Frequent but dependent on individual donor requirements.	• Formalised requirements for evaluation based on monetary and reporting thresholds but fluctuation in enforcement of rules.	• Infrequent and ad hoc (4 evaluations in the dataset). • Evaluation gap for anti-corruption. • Compulsory Programme Completion Reviews as alternatives to evaluation.
	Evaluators	• External. • Individual consultants or small firms.	• External. • Large consulting firms.	• External. • Mix of large and small consulting firms.

(Continued)

TABLE 5.1 (Continued)

Key aspects of the MEL system		TI	USAID	FCDO
Evaluation quality		• Average score of 0.19 across core indicators of evaluation quality. • Negligible use of structured designs and Theory of Change (ToC).	• Average score of 0.21 across core indicators of evaluation quality. • Limited use of structured designs and Theory of Change (ToC). • Stronger scores on measurement and monitoring.	• Average score of 0.53 across core indicators of evaluation quality. • Theory-based evaluation designs. • Some variation in quality of individual reports.
Predominant forms of evaluation use	Headquarters-level	• Negligible evidence of influence on strategy and overarching approaches to programmes.	• Negligible evidence of influence on strategy and overarching approaches to programmes.	• Negligible evidence of influence on strategy and overarching approaches to programmes.
	Field-level	• Limited evidence of engagement with and use of evaluation research. • Some instrumental and justificatory uses of mid-term evaluations.	• Evidence of engagement with evaluation with mixed purposes: symbolic uses appeared more dominant; some examples of conflict; non-use. • Instrumental and symbolic uses of mid-term evaluations.	• Evidence of engagement with evaluation with mixed purposes: instrumental and symbolic uses but also non-use.
Principal practical constraints to evaluation supporting learning		• Budgets and timeframes imposed by donors. • Limited institutionalisation of evaluation across the organisation. • Staff capacity and skills.	• Predominance of performance management metrics over independent evaluation. • Staff capacity and skills. • Contractor defensiveness. • Political swings with major impacts on funding for anti-corruption work.	• Complexity, length and timing of evaluation processes. • Infrequency of evaluation. • Political swings with major impacts on funding for anti-corruption work.

Source: Author's PhD research based on reviews of public policies, procedures and strategy documents and interviews with professionals connected to these organisations.

needed for operational learning to take place were typically engagement by senior influential individuals; the timing of the evaluation (mid-term evaluations and evaluations ahead of follow-on programmes saw the most engagement); and higher quality evaluation driven by evaluators with expertise in both evaluation and anti-corruption.

As Table 5.1 illustrates, there were however some differences across these organisations. TI-Sec, working in a context in which donors have exercised strong influence over the formation and operation of its MEL systems, has consistently struggled to institutionalise MEL practice in secretariat-led programmes. Notwithstanding different initiatives by MEL specialists to promote the practice, interviewees internal and external to the organisation, as well as a review commissioned by the organisation (Firetail, 2020), support the view that evaluation processes have not played a significant role in shaping TI-Sec's approach to programming. This is despite evaluation becoming a frequent and routine practice. The organisation also scores lowest of the three for evaluation quality.

FCDO (and its predecessor entity DFID) in contrast scores highest on quality and has shown more openness to using theory-based evaluation designs, in part driven by a decision to develop an evaluation cadre of trained professionals across the organisation. It also takes a much more selective approach to evaluating, which has supported instrumental use in some cases where the conditions noted aligned. It nonetheless exhibits an evaluation gap – the number of published evaluations is minimal compared to its level of anti-corruption programming. Internal reviews (known as Programme Completion Reviews) to some extent provide a substitute, but evaluation avoidance additionally appears to be a strategy at the organisation. More complex evaluation designs at FCDO have also not necessarily translated into use, with some interviewees involved noting that the length of these processes was a major impediment to the practical application of findings.

The forms of learning identified across all three organisations additionally have limitations. In theories of organisational learning a common distinction is made between single and double-loop learning. The former represents a learning response based on an existing set of values, beliefs, and norms, while the latter is a learning response which also entails questioning underlying values and assumptions (Rogers and Williams, 2006, p.78). The aforementioned focus of evaluation on operational implementation means that double-loop learning through evaluation is unlikely, even if there were the organisational appetite for it. The types of uses identified show evaluation findings being assimilated into existing frames of understanding rather than being used to fundamentally question whether an approach is the right one to pursue in the first place.

Equally, it needs to be considered which audiences are learning through evaluation. Interviewee comments showed it was the exception rather than the norm for evaluation processes in this field to be truly participatory in the sense of engaging intended beneficiaries (e.g. programme partners such as CSOs, government agencies or citizens) in the design and use of an evaluation. Evaluation processes often extract information from these groups without necessarily providing much information in return, while the space for debate of ideas is often limited due to power imbalances between implementers and intended beneficiaries. The primary audience for findings was instead usually internal management, the donor (in the case of TI), or political decision-makers (in the case of FCDO and USAID), showing that evaluation was principally directed in service of upward accountability.

At the field level at all organisations, the research further uncovered examples of problematic uses of evaluation. Interviewees gave varied examples of the ways in which evaluation processes were manipulated, including positive bias in the selection of activities to be evaluated; the creation of unreasonable practical constraints to evaluation (i.e. limited budget and time); controlling the data collection process, such as by managing access to interviewees; putting pressure on evaluators; and the misrepresentation of findings.

There were also examples of evaluations being purposively commissioned to provide legitimising arguments for decisions already made. While present at all three organisations, this theme came through strongest at USAID, where the contractor-based delivery model for anti-corruption programming greatly accentuated the stakes around evaluation. Contractors were strongly incentivised to secure positive evaluation because of the financial implications from losing or gaining other work. FCDO has a similar operational model, but the infrequency of evaluation means those dynamics likely play out principally through its Programme Completion Review (PCR) process. The various forms of use observed altogether reflect the fact that evaluation is a zone of contention where organisational power dynamics shape the formation, interpretation and use of findings.

Understanding Evaluation Systems

The analysis has illustrated issues with the quality of evaluation evidence produced by aid organisations and partners implementing anti-corruption measures and, regardless of the standard of evaluative work, three important organisations in this field were often not using this evidence in the ways they nominally intended. This is a paradox that needs explanation – why is it that organisations are continuing to invest in MEL systems despite seemingly limited returns?

To answer this question, the evaluation literature offers several alternative theoretical frameworks. The conventional view on how evaluation systems function is premised on the concept of what Dahler-Larsen (2012) stylises as the “rational organisation”. Influenced by Weberian ideals of modern bureaucracy, this perspective sees organisations as geared towards meeting performance goals, with evaluation part of the structures put in place to ensure they do so efficiently. This is how MEL is presented in organisational policy documents – it will produce evidence which will be applied to improve outcomes from programmes. Where this does not occur, this can be rationalised as a consequence of practical issues in the process of translating evidence into practice, such as issues with communication or presentation of evidence. While this function of MEL is widely promoted by organisations, the empirical evidence presented does not bear it out in this field at least – MEL systems rarely fulfil this function in practice.

Another way of understanding evaluation systems is through the principal-agent theoretical lens, a model familiar to corruption scholars which offers explanations for some of the contradictions observed in MEL systems (Martens, 2002; Picciotto, 2016). In the aid sector, there are multiple layers of principal-agent relationships – the principal can be theorised as the taxpaying public and/or their elected representatives who delegate the task of managing development programmes to an administrative agency. That agency in turn also delegates authority to its staff, contractors and partners. In this framing the purpose of MEL is to redress information asymmetries between these layers and enable principals to more closely monitor the work of agents. At the same time, because the same agents manage these systems, there are risks that those agents will manipulate evaluation processes in ways that promote their individual interests over those of the organisation. The careerist programme manager who orchestrates a positive evaluation of a failing programme would be an archetypal example.

The principal-agent framework provides a route to understanding dysfunction in evaluation systems but, grounded in rationalist assumptions around individual behaviour, does not account for the full range of norms or broader structural forces influencing how MEL systems operate. Other evaluation theorists have alternatively drawn on normative institutionalist theory to analyse MEL systems (Dahler-Larsen, 2012; Raimondo, 2018; Højlund, 2014). These writers regard the functioning of evaluation systems as "symptom of cultural and political patterns" rather than the culmination of individual choices (Dahler-Larsen, 2012, p.21). Institutions in this framing would encompass both formal organisational structures and processes for evaluation and then the norms and beliefs which guide the actions of key actors in MEL systems. The rules which determine behaviour are constituted of these formal and informal elements, and normative institutionalism provides its strongest insights when looking at the interplay between the two.

Based on her research at the World Bank, Raimondo (2018, p.35) maps four main influences on MEL systems at international organisations, as replicated below.

There are elements here which stand out as especially relevant for understanding the patterns observed in MEL systems at the three anti-corruption organisations. From the external environment, power politics and the political role of RBME are critical. All three organisations operate in an unstable political climate where funding cuts are common. In the last five years there have been dramatic changes in funding and operational structures under different political administrations in the UK and US which have had knock-on effects across the whole aid sector.[4] TI-Sec for its part has seen changes to funding mechanisms which restrict its freedom of action and increase its financial vulnerability – the proportion of unrestricted funding (money not tied to specific programmes) has fallen from highs of 40% in 2006 to 17% in 2022 (TI, 2022).

Organisational insecurity greatly limits the political feasibility of the type of self-critical assessment nominally expected through MEL. Each organisation has its own "political authorising environment", a constellation of gatekeepers which control "the funding, the mandate, and the very survival of public agencies" (Honig, 2018, p.41). In his work on development administrations, Honig (2018) has shown how organisational pressure to respond to expectations of authorisers encourages the adoption of bureaucratic processes which stifle innovation. Top-down evaluation can form part of these structures, outwardly demonstrating results to authorisers, but not necessarily helping an organisation to achieve its objectives.

If evaluation is seen as externally imposed by authorisers, it has important effects on internal perceptions of its function. A recurrent theme in interviews was evaluation being perceived principally as a compliance and/or box-ticking function to meet donor requirements as opposed to a mechanism supporting lesson learning. At all three case study organisations, the initial impetus for establishing MEL systems came from external authorisers (see Table 5.1), which can cement these types of attitudes towards the function over the long-term (Højlund, 2014). For Raimondo (2018), the logical outcome for MEL systems is "loose coupling", a concept developed in the sociological institutionalist literature to describe detachment between organisational rules and reality. Loose coupling is apparent in the performative role for evaluation described at anti-corruption organisations – systems which are going through the motions often without significantly influencing organisational direction. Raimondo (2018, p.36) describes loose coupling as a "coping mechanism" for organisations "when facing cacophonic demands from a heterogenous environment, while retaining stability in some core organisational values and processes".

This framework explains predominant practices around MEL systems, but this does not preclude there being exceptions to norms in specific evaluation processes. Self-interest is not the sole motivating factor determining how individuals engage with MEL. In the aid sector, values have a strong

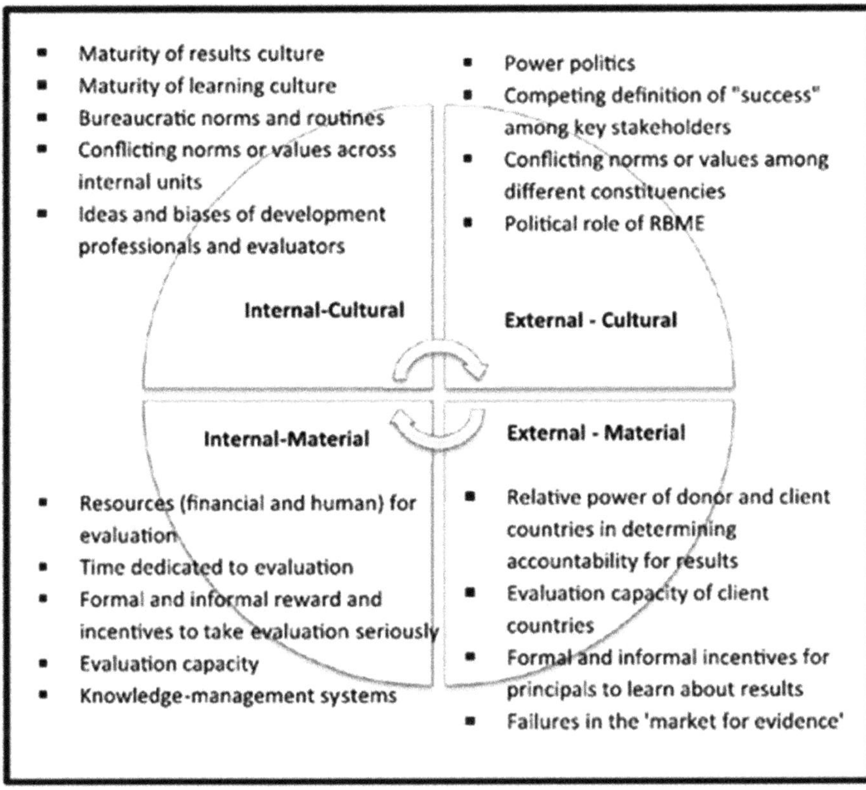

FIGURE 5.1 Raimondo's framework of MEL systems.

Source: Raimondo, E. (2018) "The power and dysfunctions of evaluation systems in international organizations", Evaluation, 24 (1), pp.35.

influence on behaviour and may pull individuals in conflicting directions. Depending on the maturity of the learning culture, many individuals will respond positively to internal logics promoting values of self-scrutiny and learning as a route to achieving the organisation's developmental objectives. On the other hand, belief in the core mission may lead some to be less willing to question their ideas and biases – a criticism which has been made of anti-corruption practitioners fixated on the moral imperative of addressing corruption over engaging with the practical challenges (Sampson, 2010). Normative institutionalism consequently shows that while the structural constraints on MEL systems are considerable, individuals can still shape practice in ways which affect engagement with MEL systems and the quality of the work produced.

Innovation in MEL

A better understanding of constraints around MEL systems has led academics working on evaluation to propose alternatives to established evaluation models. Schwandt sees sufficient evolution in thinking to speak of the emergence of "post-normal evaluation", comprising evaluative approaches which are much more willing to consider uncertainty and a "plurality of perspectives in value determination", than the project-driven, rationalist modernisation project to which MEL has to date been attached (Schwandt, 2019, p.317). Schwandt and Gates, for instance have argued that evaluating interventions to address complex social problems requires:

> expanding beyond a point-in time judgement "how did we do?" based on chosen criteria, to an ongoing learning process among all stakeholders bringing together data and values to change a state of affairs, innovate and adapt.
>
> *(Schwandt and Gates, 2021, p.XIV)*

They draw a distinction between evaluation which is *purposive*, assessing whether the goals fixed by an intervention in advance have been met, and *purposeful* evaluation, where goals are recognised as changeable and negotiable, with the evaluator mediating between different stakeholder perspectives on how actions ought to be adapted (Schwandt and Gates, 2021, p.122). Patton's earlier work on "developmental evaluation" envisages a similar reconfigured role for the evaluator. He starts from the premise that in complex systems outcomes are often "unpredictable, uncontrollable and unknowable" in advance (Patton, 2011, p.8). Rather than simply "validating effective practices and options", Patton instead sees the role of the evaluator as to:

> identify and document initial conditions, monitor, provide ongoing rapid feedback, track incremental actions and decisions, and facilitate regular reflective practice about what is developing.
>
> *(Patton, 2011, pp.109–110)*

There are some signs of these ideas permeating anti-corruption work and parallel activities in the governance field, albeit on a small scale. The Open Government Partnership (OGP), for example published findings from a developmental evaluation in 2022, where the aim was to provide real-time information from five national contexts to support adaptation in the organisation's work on beneficial ownership, open contracting and civic engagement. The evaluation culminated by presenting different options for strengthening the open government movement (Dyer, Hutchings and Jones, 2022).

Accountability Lab, a CSO promoting integrity and civic participation in governance, is an example of an organisation taking a more innovative approach to MEL. Organised as a "global translocal network", MEL is a central element integrated into the organisation's ways of working. The organisation holds monthly learning calls where country teams share reflections on effective approaches to building engagement with their programmes. Priority is also given to talking about failure at what have been labelled internally as "fail fairs". Attention to MEL has partly been driven by necessity – many of the organisation's ideas, such as its Integrity Idol campaign to celebrate leaders in anti-corruption, had not previously been attempted, and the organisation needed intelligence gathered through MEL to refine its approach (Interview with staff member).

It is notable that for these two organisations the MEL approaches adopted were supported initially at least by foundation donors (the Hewlett Foundation and Open Society Foundation (OSF) alongside DFID/FCDO for the OGP and OSF for Accountability Lab), funders with more political freedom to promote innovation in MEL. Luminate, a philanthropic foundation which has previously supported open government and anti-corruption CSOs as part of its wider work on democracy and human rights, is another foundation changing its approach. In its 2022–2027 organisational strategy Luminate moved away from key performance indicators to a hypothesis-based MEL framework. Instead of reporting against pre-determined targets, partners are asked to develop learning questions and collect evidence on an ongoing basis to confirm or identify flaws in hypotheses (Bertermann, 2023).

While this approach shows promise, like the other examples, this is a new initiative where time and further research are needed to understand how well it ultimately supports the organisation and its partners to achieve their objectives. Even while many individuals at bilateral and multilateral aid agencies recognise the value of these ideas, it is more difficult to deliver reforms in MEL practice at larger organisations managing demands from political authorisers. Case-based research focussed on DFID/FCDO and the World Bank has shown how initiatives on adaptive management have struggled to deliver sustained changes in organisational practice beyond immediate project teams, a consequence of the structural and political constraints facing these organisations (Yanguas, 2021).

Conclusion – Facing the Headwinds

For aid organisations and partners implementing anti-corruption programmes, global discordance presents an enormous set of challenges. Dramatic reductions in aid funding at the start of 2025 presented an existential threat for some organisations, while severely constraining the operations of others. Discordance also challenges the normative assumptions on which anti-corruption interventions promoted in the aid sector are premised, namely that there is broad-based support for democracy and an intrinsic relationship between democracy and better governance. De-democratisation and increased acceptance of corruption at home raise questions on the levels of domestic support for the good governance agenda promoted globally by aid agencies – there is potentially a growing disconnect between the values of aid agency staff and those of their funders, the taxpaying public. Where democratic values are contested at home, this clearly undermines the credibility of aid organisations promoting good governance elsewhere. Credibility in aid-recipient countries is further diminished by inconsistency between aid and foreign policy – technical assistance on good governance means little if donors simultaneously legitimise authoritarian partners for geopolitical and/ or economic reasons.

Meanwhile, strengthened authoritarianism in aid-recipient countries endangers non-state partners and carries the real risk of anti-corruption institutions supported by aid organisations being employed in support of autocratic goals. Authoritarian states can deliver apparent successes on some dimensions of the anti-corruption agenda – for instance, meeting measurable targets in prosecuting bureaucratic corruption – while at the same time entrenching abusive and inequitable power structures organised through corruption. Well-intentioned aid organisations risk being manipulated if they are not politically astute and if they focus too much on meeting surface-level targets.

Facing these headwinds, it can be easy to overlook MEL, especially if regarded as an operational burden. It can alternatively be seen as an approach which can help organisations make sense of a changing world and their role within it. This requires explicitly scrutinising Theories of Change which today only implicitly guide dominant ways of doing anti-corruption programming and developing these organisations' own "Theories of Action" – theory on the distinct role the organisation can fulfil within wider change processes (Green, 2016, p.236).

These are long-recognised ideas, but they have proven difficult to achieve in practice on account of the political constraints facing organisations in the aid sector. In this context of global discordance, donors need to scrutinise much more closely where and how they work on anti-corruption. Re-considering how anti-corruption measures are framed to publics at home and abroad – for instance, emphasising core economic and social benefits alongside ethical arguments – is critical to building resilience around this agenda, and ultimately helping organisations better defend their work against harmful counter narratives.

This chapter has shed new light on MEL systems, which, while intended to support organisational adaptation and learning, instead more often reinforce the status quo in anti-corruption programming. There is limited evidence of

MEL systems supporting learning goals at three organisations that have played key roles in this field, while the wide-ranging quality issues with evaluation across the field cast doubt on whether the evidence produced should indeed be used in this way. MEL systems are currently put in service of requirements for upwards accountability, but the analysis has revealed how this is a flawed form of accountability. MEL systems nominally provide transparency around results but have, in reality largely been controlled in a way that does not seriously scrutinise assumptions, allow for contention from diverse perspectives, nor expose potential failings. As currently organised, they are not well placed to facilitate the adaptation needed to respond to the challenges of discordance.

While the politics of evaluation require realism about the prospects of sustained organisational reform on MEL, steps can be taken to improve practice. Aid organisations delivering anti-corruption measures should make more use of complexity-responsive evaluative designs. Basic methodological problems with evaluation quality can be improved through stronger quality assurance and peer review processes. Organisations should also strongly consider structural changes to MEL systems. Ideas on re-casting the role of the evaluator to surface value as opposed to making fixed judgements have promise for improving understanding of impact in this space (Honig, 2022; Schwandt and Gates, 2021). The disconnection of academics working on corruption from evaluative processes should further be redressed. Notwithstanding flaws and pressures, evaluation has been neglected as a route to building evidence on anti-corruption effectiveness in a way which is informed by the operational and political realities of delivering these types of measures.

Discordance demands that aid organisations and partners accept that there is more uncertainty and risk around outcomes and evaluate for organisational respect of recognised principles of importance for anti-corruption work – local ownership, political astuteness, openness about success and failure and adaptability. MEL can support these shifts, but it requires the corruption field to engage much more seriously with it as a practice.

Notes

1. NPM is commonly understood as the replication of managerial practices from the private sector into the public administration including privatisation, competition between service providers, performance management, and emphasis on cost efficiencies (Hood, 1991).
2. This chapter incorporates a synthesis of findings on evaluation quality for anti-corruption work. For the full analysis along with illustrative examples and a list of all evaluations reviewed see Shipley (2024).
3. Each evaluation was given simple numeric scores for ten core indicators of quality where weak = 0, fair = 0.5, and strong = 1. An average was then calculated for the ten indicators. The averages for the three organisations were TI-Sec (0.19),

USAID (0.21) and DFID/FCDO (0.53). Note for TI the review only covered evaluations published by the secretariat and not individual chapters.

4. This chapter was finalised in early 2025 at a time of significant uncertainty around the status of USAID and the future of aid spending by the US.

Bibliography

Aston, T., Roche, C., Schaaf, M. and Cant, S. (2022) 'Monitoring and evaluation for thinking and working politically', *Evaluation*, 28(1), pp. 36–57.Bertermann, K. (2023) 'Embedding systems thinking in daily learning', ITAD. Available at: https://www.itad.com/article/embedding-systems-thinking-in-daily-learning/ (Accessed: 25 August 2024).

Better Evaluation, https://www.betterevaluation.org/ (Accessed: 25 August 2024).

Dahler-Larsen, P. (2012) *The evaluation society*. Stanford: Stanford University Press.

Dyer, K., Hutchings, C. and Jones, E. (2022) *Independent evaluation of OGP*. Open Government Partnership. Available at: https://www.opengovpartnership.org/documents/independent-evaluation-of-ogp/ (Accessed: 25 August 2024).

Eyben, R. (2015) 'Uncovering the politics of evidence and results', in Eyben, R., Guijt, I., Roche, C. and Shutt, C. (eds) *The politics of evidence and results in international development. Playing the game to change the rules?* Rugby: Practical Action Publishing.

Firetail (2020) *Evaluation of the action grant*. TI. Available at: https://files.transparencycdn.org/images/TI-Action-Grant-Evaluation-Findings-Report.pdf (Accessed: 25 August 2024).

Fox, C., Grimm, R. and Caldeira, R. (2016) *An introduction to evaluation*. London: Sage Publications.

Goetz, A. and Jenkins, R. (2004) *Reinventing accountability: Making democracy work for human development*. London: Palgrave Macmillan.

Green, D. (2016) *How change happens*. Oxford: Oxford University Press.

Heywood, P. (2018) 'Combating corruption in the twenty-first century: New approaches', *Daedalus*, 147(3), pp. 83–97.

Heywood, P. (2019) 'Episode 7: Paul Heywood on which questions to ask to gain new insights into the wicked problem of corruption', Kickback: The global anti-corruption podcast. Available at: https://soundcloud.com/kickback-gap/7-episode-paul-heywood (Accessed: 25 August 2024).

Heywood, P. and Pyman, M. (2024) *Sector-based action against corruption. A guide for organisations and professionals*. Cham: Palgrave Macmillan.

Højlund, S. (2014) 'Evaluation use in the organizational context – Changing focus to improve theory', *Evaluation*, 20(1), pp. 26–43.

Honig, D. (2018) *Navigation by judgement: Why and when top down management of foreign aid doesn't work*. New York: Oxford University Press.

Honig, D. (2022) Evaluation at a watershed: Actions and shifting paradigms for challenging times. Presentation at the 14th European Evaluation Society Biennial Conference, Copenhagen, Denmark, 6 – 10 June 2022. Available at: https://www.dropbox.com/sh/f23p97n25slnf8a/AABWTjToN7RupOvVnmLA7wlza/Video%20Recordings%20-%20EES%20Conference%202022/honig_The%20Power%20and%20Peril%20of%20the%20Evaliators%20Gaze.mp4?dl=0 (Accessed: 25 August 2024).

Hood, C. (1991) 'A public management for all seasons?' *Public Administration*, 69(1), pp. 3–19.

Johnsøn, J., Aiko, R., Messick, R., Mwombela, S., Schütte, S. and Sengu, H. (2016) *Evaluation of the strengthening tanzania's anti-corruption action programme*. DFID. Available at: https://www.gov.uk/government/publications/evaluation-on-strengthening-tanzanias-anti-corruption-action-staca-programme (Accessed: 25 August 2024).

Johnsøn, J. and Søreide, T. (2013) Methods for learning what works and why in anti-corruption. An introduction to evaluation methods for practitioners. U4 Issue 2013(8). U4 Anti-Corruption Resource Centre. Available at: https://www.u4.no/publications/methods-for-learning-what-works-and-why-in-anti-corruption-an-introduction-to-evaluation-methods-for-practitioners (Accessed: 25 August 2024).

Johnsøn, J., Taxell, N. and Zaum, D. (2012) Mapping evidence gaps in anti-corruption: Assessing the state of the operationally relevant evidence on donors' actions and approaches to reducing corruption. U4 Issue 2012 (7). U4 Anti-Corruption Resource Centre. Available at: https://www.u4.no/publications/mapping-evidence-gaps-in-anti-corruption-assessing-the-state-of-the-operationally-relevant-evidence-on-donors-actions-and-approaches-to-reducing-corruption (Accessed: 25 August 2024).

Johnston, M. (2005) *Syndromes of corruption: Wealth, power and democracy*. Cambridge: Cambridge University Press.

Kirch, E., Neumann, L. and Russel, H. (2021) *Evaluation of the transparency international accountable mining programme*. Available at: https://files.transparencycdn.org/images/TI_AMP_Evaluation2021_Report.pdf (Accessed: 25 August 2024).

Lincoln, Y. and Guba, E. (1986) 'Research, evaluation and policy analysis: Heuristics and disciplined inquiry', *Policy Studies Review*, 5(3), pp. 546–565.

Mark, M., Greene, J. and Shaw, I. (2006) 'The evaluation of policies, programs and practices', in Shaw, I., Greene, J. and Mark, M. (eds.) *The Sage handbook of evaluation*. London: Sage Publications.

Marquette, H. and Peiffer, C. (2020) Why a corruption functionality framework? Anti-Corruption Evidence Research Programme. Available at: https://ace.globalintegrity.org/interactive-framework/ (Accessed: 25 August 2024).

Martens, B. (2002) 'Introduction', in Martens, B., Mummert, W., Murrell, P. and Seabright, P. (eds.) *The institutional economics of foreign aid*. Cambridge: Cambridge University Press.

Mason, P. (2021) *Reassessing donor performance in anti-corruption*. U4 Anti-Corruption Resource Centre. Available at: https://www.u4.no/publications/reassessing-donor-performance-in-anti-corruption (Accessed: 25 August 2024).

NONIE (2009) Impact evaluations and development. Available at: https://documents.worldbank.org/en/publication/documents-reports/documentdetail/411821468313779505/impact-evaluations-and-development-nonie-guidance-on-impact-evaluation (Accessed: 25 August 2024).

OECD (2019) *Better criteria for better evaluation. Revised evaluation criteria definitions and principles for use*. Available at: https://www.oecd.org/en/publications/better-criteria-for-better-evaluation_15a9c26b-en.html (Accessed: 25 August 2024).

Patton, M. (1997) *Utilization-focus evaluation: The new century text.* London: Sage Publications.

Patton, M. (2011) *Developmental evaluation: Applying complexity concepts to enhance innovation and use.* New York: Guildford Press.

Picciotto, R. (2016) 'Evaluation and bureaucracy: The tricky rectangle', *Evaluation*, 22(4), pp. 424–434.

Raimondo, E. (2018) 'The power and dysfunctions of evaluation systems in international organizations', *Evaluation*, 24(1), pp. 26–41.

Rogers, P. and Williams, B. (2006) 'Evaluation for practice improvement and organizational learning', in Shaw, I., Greene, J. and Mark, M. (eds.) *The Sage handbook of evaluation.* London: Sage Publications.

Sampson, S. (2010) 'The anti-corruption industry: From movement to institution', *Global Crime*, 1(2), pp. 261–278.

Schwandt, T. (2019) 'Post-normal evaluation?' *Evaluation*, 25(3), pp. 317–329.

Schwandt, T. and Gates, E. (2021) *Evaluating and valuing in social research.* New York: The Guildford Press.

Shipley, T. (2024) *Evaluating anti-corruption interventions: The state of practice.* U4 Issue 2024 (4). U4 Anti-Corruption Resource Centre. Available at: https://www.u4.no/publications/evaluating-anti-corruption-interventions-the-state-of-practice (Accessed: 25 August 2024).

Stein, D. and Valters, C. (2012) *Understanding theory of change in international development: A review of existing knowledge.* DFID. Available at: https://www.gov.uk/research-for-development-outputs/understanding-theory-of-change-in-international-development-a-review-of-existing-knowledge (Accessed: 25 August 2024).

TI (2021) *Holding power to account: A global strategy against corruption 2021 – 2030.* Available at: https://www.transparency.org/en/publications/holding-power-to-account-a-global-strategy-against-corruption-2021-2030 (Accessed: 25 August 2024).

TI (2022) *Financial statements for the year ended December 2022.* Available at: https://files.transparencycdn.org/images/2022-Financial-Statements.pdf (Accessed: 25 August 2024).

Trapnell, S. (2015) *A user's guide to measuring corruption and anti-corruption.* Global Integrity and UNDP. Available at: https://www.undp.org/sites/g/files/zskgke326/files/publications/Users-Guide-Measuring-Corruption-Anticorruption.pdf (Accessed: 25 August 2024).

USAID (2022) *Anti-corruption policy.* Available at: https://www.usaid.gov/sites/default/files/2022-12/USAID-Anti-Corruption-Policy.pdf (Accessed: 25 August 2024).

Wathne, C. (2022) *Effectively evaluating anti-corruption interventions.* U4 Anti-Corruption Resource Centre. Available at: https://www.u4.no/publications/effectively-evaluating-anti-corruption-interventions#:~:text=Evaluation%20methodology%20must%20consider%20the,and%20the%20likelihood%20of%20unintended (Accessed: 25 August 2024).

Weiss, C. (1998) 'Have we learning anything new about the use of evaluation?', *American Journal of Evaluation*, 19(1), pp. 23–33.

White, H. (2009) *Theory-based impact evaluation: Principles and practice.* International Initiative for Impact Evaluation, Working Paper 3. Available at:

https://www.3ieimpact.org/sites/default/files/2017-11/Working_Paper_3.pdf (Accessed: 25 August 2024).

Yanguas, P. (2021) *What have we learned about learning? Unpacking the relationship between knowledge and organisational change in development agencies.* Deutsches Institut für Entwicklungspolitik. Discussion Paper, No. 9/2021. Available at: https://doi.org/10.23661/dp9.2021 (Accessed: 25 August 2024).

PART III

Abuse

6

DEMOCRACY DEFERRED

The Executive Presidential System and Abuse of Anti-Corruption in Sri Lanka

Ramesh Ramasamy and Hasan Muhammad Baniamin

The Struggle

Sri Lanka has seen high levels of corruption for decades, which is not an exception but rather an indication of institutionalized corruption in the governance structure and an entrenched culture in everyday life. When the governance institutions are corrupt, it reflects in society as well, with citizens believing there is no reason to be honest and incorrupt.

According to the IMF, "corruption issues have persisted in Sri Lanka despite almost 50 years of anticorruption efforts" (IMF 2023: 21). Public institutions are tainted with endemic corruption, and Sri Lankan citizens have been paying the price for both political and administrative/bureaucratic corruption, not least since the introduction of the executive presidential system. The introduction of the executive presidential system in 1978 was at the core of the governance failure in Sri Lanka, leading both to systemic corruption and autocratic rule (Uyangoda 2020, Fernando 2014). In 2022, Sri Lanka was listed as a bankrupt country, leading to an economic crisis and political instability (Gamage and Ul Haque 2024).

Against this backdrop, the IMF published its *Governance Diagnostic Report* in September 2023, urging the government of Sri Lanka to build robust measures to fight against corruption as a key condition to further financial support (IMF 2023: 25). The report underscored that a culture of impunity regarding official corruption existed in Sri Lanka, raising concerns that officials would continue to enjoy impunity for their misconduct (ibid.: 11). Therefore, the demand for robust anti-corruption increased and peaked in the popular protests known as the *Aragalaya/porattam* ("The Struggle"). A series of mass protests that began in March 2022 and culminated with the

DOI: 10.4324/9781003531920-9

storming and occupation of the Presidential Palace and the resignation of President Gotabaya Rajapaksa in July 2022.

In the wake of the IMF recommendations, the then President Ranil Wickremesinghe took two crucial steps to fight corruption. One was the enactment of *Anti-Corruption Legislation* in 2023; the other was the formulation of a *National Anti-Corruption Strategy* for 2025–2029. Although the IMF recommended that the government also adopt a mechanism to appoint independent members of the anti-corruption commission to enhance transparency, accountability, and integrity, this did not happen.

The National Anti-Corruption Strategy highlighted expanded powers of the Auditor General and the anti-corruption commission (the *Commission to Investigate Allegations of Bribery or Corruption*, CIABOC). It also emphasized transparency in the state's procurement policies and mandated the disclosure of state procurement information exceeding one billion rupees, along with requiring public disclosure of tax exemptions for all companies. While these strategies appeared promising, their impact hinged on effective implementation. This raises the question of why Sri Lanka's anti-corruption drives often failed in execution, and why such measures continued to be short-lived.

We will claim that Sri Lanka's anti-corruption drives produced futile results because of the vested interests of political and business elites, and these vested interests were deeply entrenched in how governance institutions operated. In our view, the explanation for the failure of the battle against corruption was this domination of an elite with vested interests, a domination expressed by the executive presidential system and its authoritarian elements, i.e., power abuse including the abuse of anti-corruption.

This chapter aims to explore the impact of the executive presidential system on the abuse of anti-corruption initiatives in Sri Lanka. We are drawing on a large volume of data collected from different sources such as the Auditor General, the Attorney General, the CIABOC, and Transparency International, as well as other reports and articles on corruption published by both the government of Sri Lanka, civil society organizations, and the media. We also interviewed eight former civil servants who held high-ranking positions, two civil society anti-corruption activists, and two political leaders who have persistently advocated for anti-corruption. They all requested us to keep their names anonymous.

Sri Lanka's Executive Presidency

The *United National Party* (UNP), led by Mr. Jayewardene, gained power by securing five-sixths of the parliamentary seats at the general election held in 1977, and he enacted a new constitution, which was one of the UNP's key election promises (Wickramaratne 2015). Thus, Sri Lanka adopted its second Republican Constitution in 1978, which introduced a powerful executive presidency (Senaratne 2019: 626). It was a radical shift from a hitherto practiced parliamentary form of government to a semi-presidential system, and it was the most significant change to Sri Lanka's political architecture since its independence in 1948 (Wickramaratne 2015, Venugopal 2015). Moreover, a distinctly developmentalist rationale inspired it – it was considered that an executive presidency with unfettered power was crucial for economic development (Venugopal 2015: 671). Horowitz (1980) argued that its principal purpose was to create a political executive with a fixed term that would permit the incumbent to make unpopular decisions.

Venugopal (2015: 674) claims that Sri Lanka's executive presidency was born out of an elite impulse to create a more stable, centralized, and authoritarian political structure that would overcome and reverse the negative economic effects of populist electoral democracy. Political elites anticipated that it would help revive economic growth under a market-driven development regime. In reality, the executive presidency has not met this objective; rather, it led the country into bankruptcy, competitive authoritarianism, and endemic corruption. As argued by several scholars, executive presidency remains a key factor for the current debacle (Uyangoda 2022, Fernando 2011, Perera 2022, Welikala 2020).

Senaratne (2019: 626) notes that by fusing the roles of Head of Government and Head of State, the 1978 Constitution creates an extremely powerful president. Elected for a period of five years, the President can run for office twice and he is directly elected by the people of Sri Lanka. Thus, there are two separate elections, for president and for parliament, and the president has unfettered powers regarding the appointment and removal of the Prime Minister, appointing a Cabinet of Ministers, and as per the original constitution, there was no limit to the number of ministers he can appoint (all members of the Cabinet have to be Members of Parliament, though). Yet, the number of Cabinet Ministers has been limited to 30 under the 21st amendment to the constitution (Article 47 of the 1978 Constitution).

As per the original constitution, the president has total immunity, and it was further strengthened in the 18th and 20th amendments to the constitution, and this extends even to executive action (Senaratne 2019: 626). According to the original constitution as well as the 18th and 20th amendments to the constitution, the president can appoint any person he desires to the high-ranking posts of the state, such as the Chief Justice, judges of the superior courts, the Attorney General and the Inspector General of Police, Ambassadors, secretaries to the ministries, heads of government institutions and public companies, and so on. The president also appoints members to nine important independent commissions (see Chapter 7, Articles 33, 33A, 34, and 35 of the 1978 Constitution).

These powers were somewhat restricted with the introduction of a Constitutional Council by the 19th Amendment to the Constitution in

2015. Yet, it should be mentioned that the idea of the Constitutional Council first came into existence under the 17th Amendment to the constitution of 1978 and the council could not carry out its tasks as anticipated due to visible political unwillingness. The council that was set up under the 19th Amendment was entrusted with the powers to make *recommendations* to the president on higher-ranking appointments, such as Auditor General, Attorney General, Police Chief, and Ombudsman (Senaratne 2019, Wickramaratne 2015). Former Justice Chandradasa Nanayakkara (2021) argues that the 19th Amendment reduced the scope and purview of presidential immunity by permitting any citizen to challenge an executive action of the president by way of fundamental rights application under Article 126 of the Constitution.

Yet, the 20th Amendment to the Constitution restored full and unfettered legal immunity to the president and removed the provisions relating to the institution of legal proceedings in respect of presidential executive action by way of fundamental right application. He further argued that there should be constitutional checks and balances that could restrain excesses and abuses that could result from unbridled presidential immunity. In a democracy, presidential immunity should be clearly defined and limited to ensure accountability, as unfettered immunity could lead to a culture of impunity.

According to the original constitution of 1978, not even a fundamental rights application can be filed and maintained against the President of Sri Lanka. In view of the immunity of the president, this is paralleled elsewhere only in dictatorships and monarchies. The president is, in fact, above the law, as warned when the executive presidency was first introduced (Wickramaratne 2015: 929). Colvin R. de Silva, a prominent left politician who drafted the First Republican Constitution of Sri Lanka, described the system of government under the 1978 Constitution as a "constitutional presidential dictatorship dressed in the raiment of a parliamentary democracy" (cited in Sunday Times 2014).

The executive presidency in Sri Lanka became one of the strongest presidential systems in the "democratic" world (see Wickramaratne 2015: 929). Since the 1990s, several attempts were made to reform this executive presidency (like in the 17th (2001) and 19th (2015) Amendments), but they did not produce any meaningful results as they did not change the fundamental balance of power. The executive presidents manufactured a majority in the parliament through coalition politics, patronage distribution, buying MPs for money, intimidations, abductions, extortion, and various other forms of power abuse: unethical and extra-judicial means (Uyangoda 2022).

Also, the executive presidents aggravated racism by mobilizing Sinhala-Buddhist majoritarianism – all of which helped Mahinda Rajapaksa and his younger brother Gotabaya Rajapaksa to win the presidential elections by a large margin in 2010 and in 2020, respectively (DeVotta 2021, 2024). As a result, they both were able to amend the constitution with the overwhelming support of the legislature to strengthen their authoritarian power hold and to disregard all the checks imposed in the 17th and 19th Amendments (Ramasamy 2024). Some tend to argue that corruption existed even before the executive presidential system was introduced, but it became much worse after 1978 not only because of the executive presidential system but also because of the open market system or liberalization, and its attendant consumerist culture (Abeyagoonasekera 2023). In contrast, DeVotta (2024) claims that ethnocracy led to masking corruption and nepotism and eventually legitimized a *kakistocracy*. He defines kakistocracy as a government comprised of subpar and crooked leaders. He puts forth that the executive presidential system effectively supported ethnocracy in Sri Lanka, because the country at large kept rewarding political entrepreneurs who marginalized minorities and thereby undermined the national interests.

Given the key features of this executive presidency, Sri Lanka's governance system falls within the definition of *competitive authoritarianism*, as formulated by Levitsky and Way (2002: 53):

> In competitive authoritarian regimes, formal democratic institutions are widely viewed as the principal means of obtaining and exercising political authority, namely periodical elections. Incumbents violate those rules so often and to such an extent, however, that the regime fails to meet conventional minimum standards for democracy.

Centralization of Power and Abuse of Anti-Corruption

Despite a large volume of scholarship on corruption in general, there have been very few empirical studies of how anti-corruption has been abused by ruling elites. As argued by Amundsen and Jackson (2021), the abuse of anti-corruption is closely related to de-democratization. Illiberal and de-democratizing leaders can hijack and weaponize anti-corruption measures as an element in their power grabs. According to Jackson, Williams, and Amundsen in the introduction chapter of this volume, the abuse of anti-corruption is usually one element in a broader set of power abuse, which typically includes repressive legislation, the politicization of the judiciary and the state bureaucracy, media restrictions, manipulation of elections, disinformation, intimidation, threats, and violence.

Existing scholarship vindicates that opposition forces can be targeted by the ruling party and ruling elite by weaponizing anti-corruption initiatives. Opposition parties, civil society, and the media can be subjected to close scrutiny, intimidation, and, at times, violence – leveraging illiberal laws, policies, and institutions under the guise of anti-corruption (Zhu and Zhang 2017, Sberna and Vannucci 2013). We have seen how illiberal governments have imposed excessive controls on civil society and the media and how the registration and renewal of media institutions have become a weapon to stifle the former to silence them or prevent them from exposing corruption-related news to the public (Mukherji and Zarhani 2023, Kuris 2015). We have also seen civil society organizations, opposition parties, and politicians, as well as media outlets and journalists, being harassed by police and charged with financial fraud and corruption (Sberna and Vannucci 2013, Ojo et al. 2019). For instance, Ojo et al. (2019) notes that in Nigeria, the president has used the three government anti-corruption agencies as state-coercive tools to intimidate political opponents and rivals. In China, we have seen such weaponization in China's Central Commission for Discipline Inspection, which political leaders have used against their opponents (Quah 2015). Weaponizing anti-corruption institutions seems also to be the case in several South Asian countries (Sangita et al. 2024, Baniamin and Jamil 2018).

Politicizing public institutions has been another effective tool in the process of weaponizing and abusing anti-corruption. Illiberal and populist leaders can manipulate watchdogs, law enforcement, and regulatory agencies to serve their narrow political and economic interests (Kuris 2015). Sberna and Vannucci (2013: 570) argue that illiberal leaders disregard the idea of meritocracy and foster clientelism in appointing persons to high-ranking government positions, and that the substitution of merit-based criteria by political criteria in the selection, retention, promotion, rewarding, and disciplining became the rule of the game in Italy.

Amundsen and Jackson (2021: 12) argue that this pattern not only reduces democratic controls but also secures impunity for the perpetrators. This seems to be the case in many South Asian countries where executive or illiberal leaders have dismantled and abused independent institutions for narrow political gains. Importantly, the politicization of anti-corruption not only impairs the implementation of anti-corruption policies but also undermines democratic stability. Personalization of anti-corruption and judicial activism, and protection of suspected politicians have derailed effective anti-corruption (Sberna and Vannucci 2013: 566). Zhu and Zhang (2017: 1188) hypothesize that the politicization of anti-corruption is the most intense when power transitions occur. They argue that party leaders have the greatest incentive and capacity to politicize anti-corruption when aimed at weakening their predecessors' political networks and patrons, when they aim at securing their hold on power by weakening their opponents.

Impunity is also granted by the executive to protect the government and its supporters (Ojo et al. 2019), and we have seen examples of new anti-corruption institutions created to retaliate against political opponents. As Amundsen and Jackson (2021) note, one element in the democratic backsliding we have seen in so many countries is to change the rules of the game through constitutional and legal reforms to cement illiberal leaders' hold on power – through electoral fraud, buying publicity, influencing media, buying opposition party members, bribing key institutions, and functionaries – all of which makes the removal of illiberal leaders extremely difficult. Evidence suggests that many anti-corruption efforts have ultimately become entangled in the very corrupt networks that they were meant to fight (Mungiu-Pippidi 2016, Persson et al. 2010, Shah 2007). Yet, overall, there has been limited scholarship on abuse of anti-corruption institutions and measures in general and South Asia specifically. In this context, the chapter seeks to contribute to the existing scholarship on the abuse of anti-corruption under the presidential form of government, taking Sri Lanka as a case in point.

Abuse of Anti-Corruption in Sri Lanka

Our argument is that this long list of possible and actual abuses of anti-corruption is also a conceptual framework that can be used to aptly capture the Sri Lankan case. In our view, the battle against corruption in Sri Lanka has been unsuccessful largely due to the executive presidential system and its authoritarian tendencies, including the abuse of anti-corruption. Sri Lanka's anti-corruption drives have produced futile results as the institutions of governance are deeply entrenched in the vested interests of political and business elites. The government in power tends to use state resources to fund their own parties' political campaigns and to co-opt important businesses and other key groups, while harassing opponents with regulatory retaliation, tax inspections, and other punitive measures.

Protecting Political Allies

In Sri Lanka, governments of all parties have claimed that they want to tackle corruption. This has led to a series of high-profile, top-down campaigns involving new legislation, the introduction of new institutions, and ultimately some high-profile court cases (Herath et al. 2019). Despite initial enthusiasm amongst much of the Sri Lankan population, these attempts' success has been minimal thus far. Therefore, Sri Lankan citizens are unlikely to trust the government's promises of anti-corruption. Although anti-corruption agencies initiate investigations shortly after a new government comes into power, such investigations get stuck due to class interests, partisan politics, and various forms of abuses (Ramasamy and Vinayagathasan 2023).

Whether it is the ruling or opposition party, in most cases, politicians tend to share a common class, interests, values, social background, and caste, and they try to protect each other when they are subjected to legal scrutiny. There seems to be an unwritten agreement among politicians to protect them at a time of crisis – because ruling party members do expect protection when they are in opposition (Marsoof 1999). As discussed in the conceptual framework, this seems to be a common pattern in many developing countries (e.g., India, Bangladesh, Nepal).

In Sri Lanka, like other developing countries, representative democracy is controlled by a small and powerful political class to serve their own interests so that they have the understanding to protect each other when they face legal consequences for wrongdoings (Uyangoda 2022). In some instances, only higher-ranking civil servants are being arrested for corruption charges, whereas politicians get immunity from the executive. It is argued that the over-centralization of powers in the hands of the executive has dismantled anti-corruption agencies and other watchdog institutions for narrow political gains (Abeyagoonasekera 2023).

Almost every government of Sri Lanka has come to power on an anti-corruption platform. In 2015, Sri Lankan voters voted for a government popularly known as the "Good Governance Government", which aimed to eliminate corruption and the political dynasty of Mahinda Rajapaksa. This government change became a reality because of the anti-corruption rhetoric at a time when Rajapaksa was extremely powerful and quite popular (Gunatilake 2024). The "good governance" government took certain measures to control corruption, like the establishment of the *Financial Crime Investigation Division* (FCID), in addition to the existing anti-corruption commission CIABOC, and a couple of Presidential Commissions to investigate large-scale political corruption of the previous Rajapaksa government. This sparked a glimmer of hope among Sri Lankans on the government's willingness and commitment to fight corruption.

Yes, it failed to prosecute and punish corrupt leaders of the previous government. Another former civil servant who held high-profile positions in the government stated that

> *anti-corruption measures did not yield any result in convicting corrupt leaders and officials in the court of law, which in turn gave a clear message that anti-corruption was merely a rhetoric tool to satisfy the supporters of the government. It has some effect, however, in punishing political opponents.*

For instance, during the 'good governance' government, the main political opponents of President Maithripala Sirisena continuously underwent investigations over corruption charges, and occasionally they were arrested and remanded.

In October 2015, the *Presidential Commission of Inquiry to Investigate and Inquire into Serious Acts of Fraud, Corruption, and Abuse of Power, State Resources, and Privileges* (PRECIFAC) summoned former President Mahinda Rajapaksa for questioning. The previous month, in September 2015, an investigative team visited Rajapaksa's residence and recorded a statement regarding a petition received by PRECIFAC. The petition alleged that the state-owned television network, ITN, had incurred a loss of Sri Lankan Rs. 200 million (approximately 670,000 USD) due to the non-payment of outstanding dues by Rajapaksa for airing his presidential campaign advertisements during the January 2015 election (Colombo Telegraph 2015). This incident received extensive media coverage and sparked significant public attention.

It is argued, however, that these anti-corruption initiatives were nothing but media reporting and hot news in a media culture that is hungry for sensational and speculative content, and that the questioning of Rajapaksa by the anti-corruption commission was more "hot" news for Sri Lankans. This seems to be a pattern – that people are satisfied as long as "investigations" are seen to be going on. Ruling party supporters seemed to trust the government when inquiries into previous rulers were mentioned in the media and exposed to the public.

Controlling corruption was the major theme of the "good governance" government, but things have not improved much. In fact, corruption increased under this government, and the perpetrators went free (Gunatilake 2024). For instance, the most significant insider trading scandal at the Central Bank of Sri Lanka, known as the "central bank bond scam", took place in February 2015, inflicting a more than 11 million USD loss to the nation – the largest known sum lost in political corruption since Sri Lanka gained independence. One of the respondents stated that "*a presidential commission was set up to investigate the scam, and the finance minister and a few others were remanded a couple of times, but eventually, the case was cleared up with political support*". The governor of the Central Bank, the finance minister, and eight others were then accused and subsequently acquitted by the Sri Lankan judiciary (Economy Next 2021, Abeyagoonasekera 2023). A governor even did not appear in court despite the arrest warrant. Thus, without proper investigation, higher political office bearers or their financiers were never sentenced for corruption.

During the interview, a respondent who was a former civil servant explained that

> Lalith Weeratunga, a high-profile civil servant who served as the Secretary to former President Mahinda Rajapaksa was convicted of corruption in 2017 under the good governance government. Weeratunga was convicted of diverting Sri Lankan Rs 600 million from the Telecommunication Regulatory Commission (TRC) to fund Rajapaksa's election campaign. He was sentenced to three years in jail and fined Sri Lankan Rs 2 million (more than 2 million USD). He was also asked to pay 50 million rupees in damages to the TRC.

The High Court accepted that Weeratunga himself did not directly benefit from the transaction, but it amounted to a criminal misappropriation of public funds and a violation of laws relating to the TRC, which he chaired (Economy Next 2017).

The first accused in the case was the then TRC Director General Anusha Palpita who tried to wash his hands by blaming Weeratunga for ordering the transfer of money from the TRC to an account at the Presidential Secretariat. Interestingly, the court of law or anti-corruption commission did not attempt to recover from Rajapaksa, the ultimate beneficiary of the criminal misappropriation, of the 600 million rupees. It is worth mentioning that the case against Lalith Weeratunga was one of the first to be filed after Maithripala Sirisena defeated Rajapaksa at the January 2015 presidential election. The incident was widely viewed as an attempt to retaliate against the Rajapaksas. Nevertheless, after Mahinda Rajapaksa's younger brother Gotabaya Rajapaksa became the president, the Court of Appeal acquitted Weeratunga and Palpita from all charges, and they were released in 2020. The Judge stated that the two defendants in the case were senior public servants and that the analysis of the evidence and documents presented did not reveal any evidence that they had misused public finance (Farzan 2020).

Following the judgment, a dozen ministers and deputies who were discontent with the coalition government and planning to quit the government were shocked to learn of this incident, and they suddenly became silent. Because almost all members of the then government had some investigation or court case pending against them. The message from the High Court decision was that anyone was at risk of having legal action accelerated against them. This implies that the president could influence the judiciary to suppress both opposition and ruling party politicians who tend to disrupt and criticize the government. Former President Mahinda Rajapaksa effectively used this strategy to control the opposition and his own party members with the support of his younger brother Basil Rajapaksa.

This case vindicates two important points. The first is that President Sirisena did not initiate any serious investigations against Rajapaksas and powerful ministers of the then government since they belong to the same class, and they have played the same politics together for decades – they both are from the same party. Thus, to satisfy the general public, he took up this case against the Secretary to the president. This explicates how the corrupt political class is protected by the executive – cases filed against some ministers, including Rajapaksas' sons, were cleared up once President Gotabaya assumed office. In such a situation, the judiciary is under the pressure of the executive, and it becomes extremely vulnerable to blatant political manipulation. There were also instances where the executive made higher judicial appointments in line with partisan politics, anticipating judicial support and protection for extra-legal acts and corruption charges (ICG 2009). The second point is that the executive president uses his power to control or silence those who act against or criticize the government's policies and decisions while being in the government.

During the interview, a retired civil servant stated that the COPE committee found critical allegations in relation to the so-called mega road development project *Maga Neguma* which was carried out under the direct control of Mahinda Rajapaksas' brother Basil Rajapaksa. They did not even submit their accounts to the Auditor General, and produced letters from the Attorney General's department to support their argument that the COPE has no powers to probe them. As such, under the Rajapaksas' rule, Sri Lanka was a state in transition from a flawed democracy into competitive authoritarianism. Thus, they institutionalized and normalized corruption and abused the anti-corruption institutions and made oversight or watchdog institutions toothless. It could be argued that corruption was an instrument exercised with impunity by the executive presidents in general and the Rajapaksas in particular to enhance their power within the parliament and society at large.

In a recent television program (November 2024), former Auditor General Gamini Wijesinghe (2015–2019) made it clear that there is no political will to investigate and prosecute perpetrators involved in large-scale political corruption. He further went on to say that the role of the Auditor General Department is to provide an independent review of the public financial management, performance, and accountability of the public institutions, and to report to parliament for further actions in relation to financial fraud, mismanagement, corruption, etc. Yet, in most instances, the reports and investigations did not move beyond the parliament. The former Auditor General highlighted seven reports on large-scale corruption cases that were sent to the parliament, but nothing happened. The parliamentarians took no action basically because politicians were involved. Instead, they took all possible opportunities to prevent legal actions, with the full support of the executive president (Wijesinghe on Sirasa TV 2024).

State Capture

In Sri Lanka's authoritarian "Executive Presidency" model, when exercised by Mahinda Rajapaksa and Gotabaya Rajapaksa, corruption shifted towards a monopolistic corruption structure, centralizing on their family, cronies, and the military, and Sri Lanka's powerful elites have supported the model (Abeyagoonasekera 2023: 1433). Rajapaksa rule held Sri Lankans hostage to state extraction, as 70% of the national budget was controlled in five ministries with four Rajapaksa brothers in executive positions (Al Jazeera 2010).

The executive presidential system has provided an opportunity for big businesses to engage in large-scale corruption in state-sponsored investments, development projects, and procurement, and to evade tax. Large-scale development projects have been given to allies of the president and his party members – to such an extent that observers have been talking about "state capture", which "prevents public institutions from fulfilling its mandate and neutralizes internal and external checks on such systems" (Parakrama 2023). Ostensibly, it is possible to argue that the executive presidential system in Sri Lanka created the avenue for state capture and kleptocracy – a powerful group with the support of the executive president with undue influence in state affairs. Theoretically, state capture operates in three ways: it influences the formation of law and policy, it influences the implementation of policy, and it disables the accountability institutions, thus paving the way to usher in a kleptocratic regime (Dávid-Barrett 2023).

In Sri Lanka, individuals representing corporate companies, big business, and underworld groups have been donating large sums of money to the leading political parties and candidates. Though this has been a general pattern across the world, the executive presidential system has aggravated this tendency in Sri Lanka, leading to kleptocracy. In most cases, political parties and candidates are aware of their donors and use these funds for election campaigns. Some of these donations come from the black money of drug traffickers, casino kings, illicit businesses, and individuals who benefit from politicians through tax evasion, unlawful business licenses, and other illegal or unethical practices (Jeyanathan 2014). These donations allow economically powerful groups and individuals to influence government policies, laws, and programs, aiming to expand their wealth and protect their vested interests (Seneviratne 2014). Examples include securing permits, receiving tax evasions, or exerting undue influence over the allocation of public resources, such as public works contracts, to name a few. These donations also put the government under pressure from businesses – all of which inherently involve malpractices and corruption. A former senior civil servant stated that

> As a cabinet appointed Procurement Committee Chairman, I have observed that in procurement Technical Evaluation Reports are not prepared in time; in some cases, they are purposely delayed leaving room for so called emergency procurement; they are vague leaving room for interpretations; and they are prepared to suit identified suppliers.
>
> *(Maliyadde 2023)*

Debilitating Oversight Institutions

The CIABOC only plays a low-key role in the investigation processes due to the influence of the executive president (personal communication, August 2024), and citizens' trust in anti-corruption institutions is extremely low due to excessive political control, manipulation, lack of autonomy, institutional weaknesses, lack of infrastructure facilities, etc. (Governance and Trust Survey 2020). Anti-corruption authorities can be divided into "watchdog" and "guard dog" agencies, based on the strength of their investigative powers. These institutions have powers to enforce laws, prosecute persons involved in corruption, and initiate programs to prevent corruption (Kuris 2015). In our interviews, former civil servants stated that the watchdog institutions, including the anti-corruption commission, became weak largely because of politically motivated appointments and the patron-client relationship in appointing officials to high-profile positions.

In Sri Lanka, the independence of watchdog institutions has systematically been distorted by the executive for political gains, to protect corrupt leaders of the ruling government. Although civil society organizations and anti-corruption activists make complaints to the Anti-Corruption Commission and the Criminal Investigation Department, response to such complaints remains extremely unsatisfactory owing to political interference (Herath et al. 2019).

In 2010, in his second term after his sweeping victory following the end of the civil war, President Mahinda Rajapaksa repealed the 17th Amendment of the Constitution, which limited the president's power to appoint people to key positions, and replaced it with the 18th Amendment, which further empowered the president in terms of powers and functions. With this, Sri Lanka's executive presidential system has very limited safeguards against abuse of power (Perera 2011, Edrisinha and Jayakoday 2011), which has led to democratic backsliding and institutional decay. This echoes what Wrong (2009: 181) describes as a country "where presidents have done their best to centralise power, altering constitutions, winning over the army and emasculating the judiciary, [and] the notion that key decisions can be taken without their approval is laughable".

In 2015, the 19th Amendment to the Constitution came into force, and this amendment was considered to be a very progressive and democratic reform, under which nine independent commissions were set up, including an Election Commission and a Commission to Investigate Allegations of Bribery or Corruption, and a National Procurement Commission. The 19th Amendment also removed the president's direct and sole discretion in appointing persons to high positions. It also curtailed the powers of the president to dissolve the parliament until four and a half years of its tenure. The Amendment also introduced the long-awaited Right to Information (RTI) Act as a means to foster a culture of accountability and transparency in governance, and it was widely believed that the RTI would help the fight against corruption (Ramasamy 2020, Gomez 2019).

Yet, neither the 19th Amendment nor the RTI Act helped to reduce corruption in Sri Lanka. The measures failed to prevent politicized appointments to important public institutions, including the watchdog institutions and the anti-corruption commission (Gunatilleke and de Mel 2015). No international comparative statistics on corruption, like the *Corruption Perception Index* of TI and the *Control of Corruption* indicator of the World Bank, reported any improvements after 2016.

In 2019, there was a regime change in Sri Lanka, and an authoritarian leader, Gotabaya Rajapaksa, became the president, and his party got a clear majority in the parliamentary election in 2020. With the view to concentrate more power in the hands of the presidency, he passed the draconian 20th Amendment to the Constitution, which was a bombshell to Sri Lanka's democracy (Ramasamy 2024). It provided unfettered and unchecked powers to the president and effectively dismantled all autonomy of governance institutions – the institutions of oversight and control, the judiciary, and the parliament became subservient to the executive and served the interests of the president (Uyangoda 2020, Fonseka and Dissanayake 2020).

The military also came to play a stronger role in civil administration, as they got high-profile positions in the government, including permanent secretaries to the ministry, Director General of the anti-corruption commission, and so forth, leading to an irreversible impact on governance institutions (Ramasamy 2024, Fonseka and Dissanayake 2020). Furthermore, civil society organizations came under severe scrutiny and surveillance, subjected to interrogation and intimidation (Fonseka and Ranasinghe 2020).

It is against this backdrop that the people of Sri Lanka took to the streets in 2022 amidst an unfolding economic crisis, fuel shortages, power cuts, and shortages of essential commodities. Sri Lankan citizens finally understood the fact that authoritarian rule meant misgovernance, mismanagement of the economy, politically motivated nominations, and more importantly: large-scale political corruption that resulted in the country's bankruptcy in 2022 (Silva and Ramasamy 2023). Sri Lankan citizens, for the first time in history, came to the streets to oust a powerful president, demanding a clean government, accountability and anti-corruption, and peoples' participation in governance (CPA 2023, Biyanwila 2023). The protest not only ousted a corrupt leader and his family but also led people to understand the entrenchment of corruption and its destructive impact on socio-economic welfare, economic growth, accountable governance, and development. During this period, social media was full of anti-corruption discussions and debates, and there were discussions on how to bring stolen money back to Sri Lanka as well.

Paralyzing the Anti-Corruption Commission

In the past, every executive president tried their level best to control the CIABOC by all possible means, including appointment, removal, and resource allocation, among many others. As discussed elsewhere in this chapter, executive presidents used corruption effectively to secure a majority support base within and outside the parliament and government so that, in reality, they had little or no interest at all in empowering the CIABOC despite anti-corruption rhetoric during the election campaigns. As such, the members of the CIABOC were appointed directly by the president without any transparent scrutiny of the appointees. This compromised and dismantled the integrity of the commission as a whole. Members of the commission were very loyal to the president in retaining their positions; therefore, complaints in relation to large-scale corruption were put under the carpet (Maliyadde 2023).

Furthermore, the CIABOC does not have its own investigators; it borrows serving police officers from the Police Department to serve as investigators. The CIABOC also has no disclosed internal integrity checks on its officials or investigators. There is no guarantee of security of tenure of its chief executive officer (Director General), or any investigators released from the police. The president held the power to remove the Director General and any investigators and to halt investigations, even at the peak of an important investigation (Transparency International 2008). As such, the 18th Amendment gave the president uncontrollable power to directly and indirectly interfere with an investigation of bribery or corruption against powerful individuals.

Although the anti-corruption commission is viewed as an independent commission under the 19th Amendment to the Constitution and again under the 21st Amendment, it continues to encounter various challenges in terms of powers, functions, investigations, and resources (physical, human, and financial). Currently, some 250 positions have not been filled (personal communication, September 2024). Furthermore, executive control remains a key factor that precludes the independent functioning of the commission. For instance, in February 2008, the president (by his Secretary) removed the Director General of the commission, without giving any reason publicly (Transparency International 2008). This unilateral removal of the Director General led to an institutional crisis within the commission. The worst consequence of the whole episode was the bad precedent created, which continues to date. Sri Lanka is a party to the United Nations *Convention against Corruption* and the regional anti-corruption initiative called the *OECD-ADB Anti-Corruption Initiative*, under which Sri Lanka is required to strengthen the independence of the anti-corruption commission, but this was blatantly broken. The unilateral removal of the Director General was also perceived by the public as interference by the executive in the independence of the Commission (personal communication, July 2024).

As demonstrated above, the independent operation of the CIABOC was challenged from its inception. Since the establishment of the commission, there have been long delays in appointing commission members and the Director General, with instances of vacancies filled only after two to three years, which crippled the functioning of the commission. These were deliberate acts of the executive to delay or prevent investigations over corruption.

Conclusion

This chapter endeavored to explore the abuse of anti-corruption under Sri Lanka's executive presidential system and found that Sri Lanka created an executive authoritarianism, leading to de-democratization, power abuse, institutional debilitation, and eventually to endemic corruption. The democratic backsliding had been visible since the introduction of the executive presidency. Recent economic and political bankruptcy is a direct result of institutionalized corruption triggered by the executive presidential system.

Anti-corruption has been a popular slogan in Sri Lanka, but it has usually been framed in an anti-establishment and anti-government rhetoric, with the consequence that it has produced no meaningful results. Instead, anti-corruption has been an effective tool to delegitimize and stifle anti-government forces (opposition political parties, media, civil society, pressure groups, community leaders), dismantling the institutional systems of checks and balances, changing the rules of the game (constitution), politicizing the entire state bureaucracy, and enabling state capture by the presidency and its cronies. Since the executive president remains above the law with legal impunity, he/she is empowered to intrude into the affairs of any institution, including law enforcement, watchdogs, and the institutions of control and oversight. Until and unless there are strong checks and balances on the powers and functions of the executive president, it is highly unlikely that the abuse of anti-corruption will be prevented in Sri Lanka.

However, the general elections of 2024 brought in a renewed hope for anti-corruption with the election of new President Anura Kumara Dissanayaka (AKD) and his party. The entire election campaign of AKD and his party, the *National People's Power*, was based on an anti-corruption platform and on promises to deliver the demands of a clean and incorruptible government – which was also the key demand of the 2022 popular uprising. In the past, AKD actively campaigned to abolish the executive presidency, and he seems to have understood the negative consequences of this system. Thus, reforming the executive presidential system with effective checks and balances is likely to be helpful, but, as argued by many, only the abolition of the executive presidential system as such will be necessary to effectively implement anti-corruption.

References

Abeyagoonasekera, A. (2023). Sri Lanka's political-economic crisis; corruption, abuse of power and economic crime. *Journal of Financial Crime*, 30(6), 1432–1443.

Al Jazeera (2010). *Profile: Mahinda Rajapaksa*. 19 November 2010 (www.aljazeera.com/news/2010/11/19/profile-mahinda-rajapaksa/).

Amundsen, I. and D. Jackson (2021). *Rethinking anti-corruption in de-democratising regimes*. Bergen: Chr. Michelsen Institute (U4 Issue 2021: 5).

Baniamin, H. M. and I. Jamil (2018). Dynamics of corruption and citizens' trust in anti-corruption agencies in three South Asian countries. *Public Organization Review*, 18, 381–398.

Biyanwila, S. J. (2023). *Debt crisis and popular social protest in Sri Lanka: Citizenship, development and democracy Within global North–South dynamics.* Emerald Publishing Limited.

Colombo Telegraph (2015). *Instead of summoning Rajapaksa before PRECIFAC, commission members visited his residence.* 23 September 2014 (www.colombotelegraph.com/index.php/instead-of-summoning-rajapaksa-before-precifac-commission-members-visited-his-residence/).

CPA (2023): *A brief analysis of Aragalaya.* Colombo, May 2023, Centre for Policy Alternatives (CPA) (www.cpalanka.org/a-brief-analysis-of-the-aragalaya/).

Dávid-Barrett, E. (2023). State capture and development: A conceptual framework. *Journal of International Relations and Development*, 26(2), 224–244.

DeVotta, N. (2021). Sri Lanka: The return to ethnocracy. *Journal of Democracy*, 32(1), 96–110.

DeVotta, N. (2024). Sri Lanka in 2024: Political realignment and the road ahead. *South Asian Voices*, 16 December 2024 (https://southasianvoices.org/pol-m-sl-r-sri-lanka-2024-12-16-2024/).

Dhal, S., Singh, N., and Nasrullah, A. M. (Eds.) (2024). Mapping Governance Innovations: Perspectives from South Asia. India: Routledge.

Economy Next (2017). *The fallout from Sri Lanka jailing Lalith Weeratunga.* 11 September 2017 (https://economynext.com/the-fallout-from-sri-lanka-jailing-lalith-weeratunga-8309/).

Economy Next (2021). *Sri Lanka bond scam: Former finance minister, others cleared of 11 out of 22 charges.* 6 December 2021 (https://economynext.com/sri-lanka-bond-scam-former-finance-minister-others-cleared-of-11-out-of-22-charges-88539/).

Edrisinha, R. and A. Jayakoday (2011). *The eighteenth amendment to the constitution: Substance and process.* Colombo, March 2011, Centre for Policy Alternatives (CPA).

Farzan, Z. (2020). Lalith Weeratunga and Anusha Palpita acquitted in Sil Cloth case. *News 1st*, 9 November 2020 (www.newsfirst.lk/2020/11/19/lalith-weeratunga-and-anusha-palpita-acquitted-in-sil-cloth-case).

Fernando, B. (2011). *Gyges' ring: The 1978 constitution of Sri Lanka.* Hong Kong: Asian Human Rights Commission, resources.

Fernando, B. (2014). *Sri Lanka: A system of governance based on a failed idea.* Asian Human Rights Commission, news, 28 July 2014 (http://www.humanrights.asia/news/ahrc-news/AHRC-ART-062-2014/).

Fonseka, B. and K. Ranasinghe (2020). Sri Lanka's accelerated democratic decay amidst a pandemic. In Pradeep Peiris (ed.) *Is the cure worse than the disease?* Colombo, August 2020, Centre for Policy Alternatives (CPA).

Fonseka, B. and U. Dissanayake (2020). *Sri Lanka's recent political challenges and prospects for the future.* Colombo, March 2020, Centre for Policy Alternatives (CPA).

Gamage, R. and M. S. Ul Haque (2024). *Sri Lanka's 2022 debt default crisis: Geopolitics and foreign policy developments.* Institute of South Asian Studies (ISAS), *ISAS Insights*, 23 April 2024 (www.isas.nus.edu.sg/papers/sri-lankas-2022-debt-default-crisis-geopolitics-and-foreign-policy-developments/).

Gomez, M. (2019). The right to information and transformative development outcomes. *Law and Development Review*, 12(3), 837–864.

Gunatilleke, G., and de Mel, N. (2015, June). *19th amendment: The wins, the losses and the In- betweens.* Colombo: Verite Research.

Gunatilake, H. M. (2024). *Economic and social costs of corruption: Can Sri Lanka survive without eliminating corruption?* Centre for Poverty Analysis, 5 September 2024 (https://www.cepa.lk/blog/economic-and-social-costs-of-corruption-can-sri-lanka-survive-without-eliminating-corruption/).

Herath, D., J. Lindberg and C. Orjuela (2019). Swimming upstream: Fighting systemic corruption in Sri Lanka. *Contemporary South Asia*, 27(2), 259–272.

Horowitz, D. (1980). *Coup theories and officers' motives: Sri Lanka in comparative perspective.* Princeton, NJ: Princeton University Press.

ICG (2009). *Sri Lanka's judiciary: Politicised courts, compromised rights.* International Crisis Group (ICG), Report 172/Asia, 30 June 2009.

IMF (2023). *Sri Lanka: Technical assistance report – Governance Diagnostic Assessment.* Washington, International Monetary Fund (IMF), 30 September 2023 (www.imf.org/en/Publications/CR/Issues/2023/09/29/Sri-Lanka-Technical-Assistance-Report-Governance-Diagnostic-Assessment-539804).

Ishtiaq, J. (2020). Governance and Trust Survey 2. The data are available via email at: Ishtiaq. Jamil@uib.no.

Jeyanathan, A. B. (2014). Black money rears its ugly head. *The Sunday Times*, 14 December 2014 (www.sundaytimes.lk/141214/sunday-times-2/black-money-rears-its-ugly-head-132274.html).

Kuris, G. (2015). Watchdogs or guard dogs: Do anti-corruption agencies need strong teeth? *Policy and Society*, 34(2), 125–135.

Levitsky, S. and L. A. Way (2002). Elections without democracy: The rise of competitive authoritarianism. *Journal of Democracy*, 13(2), 51–65.

Maliyadde, C. (2023). Anti corruption bill nets small fish while sharks swim free. *Groundviews*, 7 October 2023 (https://groundviews.org/2023/07/10/anti-corruption-bill-nets-small-fish-while-sharks-swim-free/).

Marsoof, S. (1999). Sri Lanka: Prosecutions of bribery and corruption. *Journal of Financial Crime*, 6(3), 287–290.

Mukherji, R. and S. H. Zarhani (2023). India's democracy: The competitive authoritarian propensity? *Pacific Affairs*, 96(4), 747–768.

Mungiu-Pippidi, A. (2016). For a new generation of objective indicators in governance and corruption studies. *European Journal on Criminal Policy and Research*, 22, 363–367.

Nanayakkara, C. (2021). In a democracy, presidential immunity should be clearly defined and limited. *Daily Mirror*, 5 January 2021 (www.dailymirror.lk/opinion/In-a-democracy-presidential-immunity-should-be-clearly-defined-and-limited/172-203118).

Ojo, E. M., V. Prusa and I. Amundsen (2019). *Congenitally conjoined and inseparable: Politics and corruption in Nigeria.* In Inge Amundsen (ed.) *Political corruption in Africa. Extraction and power preservation.* Cheltenham: Edward Elgar Publications.

Parakrama, A. (2023). *Civil society governance diagnostic report.* Colombo: Transparency International Sri Lanka Chapter.

Perera, B. (2022). Of men and the "Ruling Ring": Destructive resilience of Sri Lanka's executive presidency. *University of Colombo Review*, 3(2), 19–40.

Perera, J. (2011). A More centralised state after war. *Strategic Analysis*, 35(2), 194–198.

Persson, A., B. Rothstein and J. Teorell (2010). *The failure of anti-corruption policies: A theoretical mischaracterization of the problem.* University of Gothenburg QoM Working Paper Series 2010:19, June 2010.

Quah, J. S. (2015). Evaluating the effectiveness of anti-corruption agencies in five Asian countries: A comparative analysis. *Asian Education and Development Studies*, 4(1), 143–159.

Ramasamy, R. (2020). Governance and administration in Sri Lanka: Trends, tensions, and prospects. *Public Administration and Policy*, 23(2), 187–198.

Ramasamy, R. (2024). Constitutional amendments, institutional tensions (Crisis), and governance quality in Sri Lanka. In S. Dhal, N. Singh and A. M. Nasrullah (eds.) *Mapping governance innovations.* Routledge India, pp. 210–230.

Ramasamy, R. and T. Vinayagathasan (2023). The impact of corruption, rule of law, accountability, and government expenditure on government effectiveness: Evidence from Sri Lanka. *Journal of Asian and African Studies*, 59(6), 1843–1866.

Sberna, S. and A. Vannucci (2013). "It's the politics, stupid!". The politicization of anti-corruption in Italy. *Crime, Law and Social Change*, 60, 565–593.

Senaratne, K. (2019). The executive and the constitutional reforms process in Sri Lanka. *The Round Table*, 108(6), 625–638.

Seneviratne, T. (2014). *Black money vs public resources.* The Sunday Time, 14 December, 2014. (https://www.sundaytimes.lk/141214/sunday-times-2/black-money-rears-its-ugly-head-132274.html).

Shah (2007). Tailoring the fight against corruption to country circumstances. In A. Shah (ed.) *Performance accountability and combating corruption.* Washington D.C.: World Bank, pp. 233–254.

Silva, K.T. and Ramasamy, R. (2023). *Popular protest (Aragalaya), repression and future of democracy in Sri Lanka.* Kandy: Institute of Social Development.

Sirasa TV (2024). *Mawatha.* Sirasa TV, 10 October 2024 (Available on YouTube: www.youtube.com/watch?v=jkmuY8783iU).

Sunday Times (2014). *Remembering Colvin and his prophetic words on the executive presidency.* By Jayampathy Wickramaratne, 23 January 2014 (www.sundaytimes.lk/140223/sunday-times-2/remembering-colvin-and-his-prophetic-words-on-the-executive-presidency-86471.html).

Transparency International (2008). Transfer of the director general of the commission to investigate allegations of bribery or corruption. *Urgent position paper*, 28 February 2008. Colombo: Transparency International Sri Lanka.

Uyangoda, J. (2020). 20th amendment: End to Sri Lanka's democracy: Shouldn't it be resisted? *EconomyNext*, 20 September 2020 (https://economynext.com/20th-amendment-end-to-sri-lankas-democracy-shouldnt-it-be-resisted-uyangoda-74054/).

Uyangoda, J. (2022). Sri Lanka: Decoding political messages from the citizens. *Daily Mirror*, 9 May 2022 (www.dailymirror.lk/opinion/Decoding-political-messages-from-the-citizens/172-236535).

Venugopal, R. (2015). Democracy, development and the executive presidency in Sri Lanka. *Third World Quarterly*, 36(4), 670–690.

Welikala, A. (2020). *The return of Sri Lanka's imperial presidency: The twentieth amendment to the constitution bill.* Constitutionnet. 8 September 2020 (https://constitutionnet.org/news/return-sri-lankas-imperial-presidency-twentieth-amendment-constitution-bill).

Wickramaratne, J. (2015). The executive presidency: A left perspective. In Asanga Welikala (ed.) *Reforming Sri Lankan presidentialism: Provenance, problems and prospects*, vol. 2. Colombo: Centre for Policy Alternatives.

Wrong, M. (2009). *It's our turn to eat: The story of a Kenyan Whistleblower*. London: Fourth Estate Publishing.

Zhu, J. and Zhang, D. (2017). Weapons of the powerful: Authoritarian elite competition and politicized anticorruption in China. *Comparative Political Studies*, 50(9), 1186–1220.

7

ARE WE ALL THIEVES?

Countering the State's Strategic Absence with Superficial Anti-Corruption Measures in Mongolia's Coal-Gate

Bayar Dashpurev

Introduction

'Mine-golia' is another moniker for Mongolia, capturing the fact that the country's economic and political affairs are highly affected by the mining sector (Bulag 2009, Lander 2019). Mongolia exemplifies a mining regime where the economy and broader society are deeply dependent on mineral extraction, particularly coal, gold, copper, and iron ore. Despite its rich natural resources, Mongolia's trade is dominated by a single buyer—China—limiting its role in the global minerals market to border transactions. This dependency makes Mongolia's economy highly sensitive to global price fluctuations, creating significant uncertainty. As a result, there is an urgent push within the extractive sector to maximize resource exploitation whenever market conditions are favorable.

In such resource frontier contexts, states often simplify or erase complexity to facilitate resource extraction (Tsing 2003, Cons and Eilenberg 2019). In Mongolia, the mining industry's clout means the state opts to be strategically absent from the sector: it deliberately steps back from its monitoring and regulation role, allowing the mining industry and local people to negotiate expected social and economic benefits on their own (Hatcher 2015, Lander et al. 2021, Hatcher and Lander 2023). The recent 'coal theft' case has revealed hitherto hidden crises in the minerals sector, forcing the state to re-engage (Dashpurev 2024). 5.2 million tons of coking coal from Erdenes Tavan Tolgoi (ETT), the state-owned enterprise, was stolen and smuggled into China (Ahearn and Munkherdene 2023, Dierkes 2023, Dashpurev 2024). This case of 'coal theft' or resource looting has been explained by ruling party leaders with reference to the nation's widespread corruption over the

DOI: 10.4324/9781003531920-10

last 30 years. As a result, the government of Mongolia responded by pursuing strategies ostensibly aimed at strengthening its presence to address mineral theft. This created a paradox, however. On the one hand, the state prefers a minimal presence at the local level so that the industry enjoys greater economic returns; on the other, to penalize theft, the state had to enforce rules in resource-rich regions.

Rather than reverse its strategic absence policy and enhance its presence through enforcing key legislation, however, the state mobilized superficial anti-corruption measures to announce its presence in the extractives sector at the local level. This detour, where the state's presence was asserted by exploiting anti-corruption measures to punish theft, ironically stemmed from the state's own failure to establish meaningful communication and collaboration in local settings. Consequently, its anti-corruption measures were inherently open to abuse. This dynamic shaped the application of the state's anti-corruption measures, creating opportunities for political abuse and selective prosecution. This chapter focuses, therefore, on how superficial anti-corruption measures aimed at addressing the state's strategic absence in the minerals sector led to abuses and long-term negative outcomes.

The chapter examines the relationship between theft and corruption in Mongolia's minerals sector, with a particular focus on the 'coal theft' case. While recognizing corruption as a significant facet of this case, the chapter argues that corruption was not the primary facilitator of theft. Instead, it argues that the state's deliberate strategic absence in overseeing the minerals supply chain created the conditions for widespread theft. The state then strategically mobilized theft as a narrative device to broaden corruption investigations, particularly targeting non-state actors. The chapter further explores the possibility that some instances of theft could represent resistance against inequitable resource extraction. However, the state's anti-corruption measures functioned as a coercive method to suppress this resistance and enforce discipline throughout the minerals supply chain. Although anti-corruption measures did lead to increased accountability and transparency in the mineral supply chain, boosted minerals production, and even penalized some instances of theft, their superficial nature, and abusive enforcement rendered temporarily any positive outcomes. This approach depended on the production and reproduction of anti-corruption abuse by branding everyone associated with the case as a thief. However, framing all involved as thieves created an impracticable enforcement scenario, and thus only some were selectively prosecuted i.e., potential rivals.

The chapter is grounded in three sets of data: ethnographic fieldwork, legal case analysis, and observation of the political process surrounding the coal theft case. The author conducted five months of fieldwork in the South Gobi province of Mongolia, home to the nation's largest mining operations, including the Erdenes Tavan Tolgoi coal company at the center of the 'coal theft' case. The chapter begins by investigating the relationship between corruption and theft to establish a theoretical framework for analyzing anti-corruption measures in a mining regime. The chapter then summarizes the coal theft case, highlighting key events and the socio-legal challenges encountered during investigation and prosecution. It then turns to how the Mongolian state mobilized superficial anti-corruption measures to address theft in the minerals sector, exploring the outcomes of these measures. The chapter shows how the state's efforts to correct previous shortcomings through anti-corruption led to negative consequences in Mongolia's mineral sector. Finally, the chapter draws on the 'coal theft' case to ask what kinds of anti-corruption strategies are needed to tackle this and similar cases in a discordant world.

Theft, Corruption, and Regimes

Theft typically occurs in the absence of rules and institutions, whereas corruption often stems from the abuse of rules and institutions for private gain. However, the two can also coexist, with corruption facilitating theft by weakening institutions, or theft emerging as a reaction to corrupt systems. This section explores the interrelationships between corruption and theft in different regimes, highlighting the contrasting dynamics between the two. It examines why theft and corruption often coexist and argues that anti-corruption measures aimed at addressing theft can, paradoxically, lead to further abuse rather than effective anti-corruption outcomes.

At a theoretical level, corruption requires the presence of an active, functional, and operational state, regardless of whether it operates under a rule-of-law or rule-by-law system (Robbins 2000). The relationship between regimes and corruption has predominantly been examined through ideologically driven perspectives, and corruption control systems are typically categorized as autocratic, democratic, or hybrid (Carothers 2022). For instance, democratic control of corruption relies on institutions that decentralize power across various bodies, ensuring they keep each other in check. This approach requires rules and laws that limit power, increase public participation in government decisions, and enhance governmental transparency (Johnston 2014, Lindstedt and Naurin 2010, Mungiu-Pippidi 2013). In contrast, autocratic corruption control centralizes power, enforces top-down authority, and often relies on regime propaganda to maintain discipline (Carothers 2022, Quah 2017, Zhu and Zhang 2017). Hybrid control systems, meanwhile, combine elements of both democratic and autocratic approaches, either leveraging quasi-democratic institutions or temporarily centralizing political power to control and curb corruption (Carothers 2002, Diamond 2002, Levitsky and Way 2002).

Scholars have often celebrated democratic approaches to corruption control over authoritarian and hybrid models, arguing that the latter are more prone to politicization and the abuse of anti-corruption measures (Mungiu-Pippidi 2015). However, some studies highlight exceptions where authoritarian and even hybrid regimes have successfully curbed some forms of corruption. Carothers, for instance, has argued that authoritarian regimes curb corruption more frequently—and sometimes more effectively—than is widely acknowledged. In his study of twenty-five significant anti-corruption efforts by authoritarian regimes since 1950, he found that in at least nine cases, corruption was significantly reduced nationwide, resulting in political and economic benefits (Carothers 2022). Successful authoritarian anti-corruption reforms typically involve an ambitious leader using personal power to disrupt the state's corrupt equilibrium by centralizing authority, imposing top-down control, and employing regime propaganda (Carothers 2022). Such authoritarian anti-corruption efforts are evident in Mongolia's two larger neighbors, the People's Republic of China and the Russian Federation. Xi Jinping's wide-ranging anti-corruption campaign is sometimes celebrated as a success, but both his and Vladimir Putin's campaigns have involved the abuse of anti-corruption, being used to silence political rivals and consolidate power (Pavlova 2020, Zhu and Zhang 2017, Carothers 2022).

In different regimes, corruption does not simply arise from a lack of rules and institutions. It also stems from the misuse, weak enforcement, or exploitation of these structures for personal or political gain, regardless of regime type. As De Sardan argued, corruption does not arise from a lack of state involvement in managing natural resources but from the very process of building and operating a state apparatus (De Sardan 1999). Paul Robbins further supports this argument with evidence from India, asserting that corruption functions as an institution in its own right, rather than as a consequence of their absence (Robbins 2000). According to Robbins, in Latwara, as in other Indian regions, corruption transforms fair resource management practices into inequitable systems by establishing and maintaining institutions that rely on strong networks of cooperation between elites and officials. Thus, corruption thrives not due to the absence of rules and institutions, but because of their manipulation and exploitation for private interests.

Theft is often associated with weak regime conditions, such as ineffective institutions, political instability, lack of territorial control, and widespread corruption (Addison and Roe 2024). For example, a case study comparing Brazil nut theft in Pando, Bolivia, and the adjacent State of Acre, Brazil, highlights several factors that contribute to higher theft rates in Pando (Duchelle et al. 2011). These include differences in the timing and process of formally recognizing property rights. In Pando, communities only recently emerged from a struggle with private estate owners to have their customary property rights recognized by government. This research suggests that the more recent, top-down process of formalizing communal tenure in Pando may have led to greater insecurity over property rights and, consequently, a higher incidence of theft. In this context, theft occurred due to the delayed and incomplete recognition of property rights over resources, underscoring that theft is likely to arise where effective rules and institutions are absent.

Moreover, theft also carries contrasting interpretations, especially in the context of colonialism and resistance studies. Theft can be seen as a form of everyday resistance by ordinary people to challenge and limit the power of rulers (Johansson and Vinthagen 2016, Scott 2016). Within the context of settler colonialism, as Robert Nichols argued, theft and property share a recursive relationship rather than a linear one, meaning that the establishment of property rights and the act of taking it are intertwined, making theft a form of property (Nichols 2018). These contrasting views illustrate that theft can result from either the absence of rules and institutions or as a reaction to them. Depending on the context, theft may be seen as an immoral and illegal act or, alternatively, as a form of justified resistance and claim to legal rights.

Theft and corruption often reinforce each other. While corruption involves abuse of power by individuals in institutions, theft typically occurs outside institutional frameworks. However, the two phenomena are not mutually exclusive. Corruption weakens rules and institutions, creating an environment where theft can thrive. Both theft and corruption exploit resources for personal gain, making them morally and legally objectionable behaviors. These conceptual interrelationships between theft and corruption further clarify how both are produced. Theft can be seen as an immoral or illegal behavior that exists outside formal rules and institutions, or it can emerge as a form of resistance to corrupt systems or broader political dynamics. Corruption, on the other hand, occurs when legal frameworks that formalize authority over resources are manipulated and reshaped along lines of class, caste, and gender, resulting in specific ecologies governed by rules formed through extralegal exchanges (Robbins 2000). These dynamics illustrate how theft and corruption are deeply intertwined, with corruption often creating the conditions that allow theft to flourish.

Regimes typically respond to corruption and theft by either penalizing or, in some cases, tolerating them. These responses can evolve sequentially, influenced by various socio-political factors such as the need to maintain control, public pressure, economic instability, shifting alliances, or international scrutiny. Consequently, regimes often perceive corruption and theft as interconnected illegal behaviors, assuming that one drives the other. As a result, they tend to prioritize anti-corruption policies aimed at deterring, disciplining, and penalizing both. Even in cases where theft and corruption lack a direct causal link, regimes may overlook theft as a significant issue, believing that strengthening anti-corruption will inherently reduce theft.

This logic has a crucial flaw, as it assumes that the presence of rules and institutions—whether weak or strong—determines the relationship between theft and corruption. However, when regimes strategically design or promote the absence of rules and institutions in specific places or sectors, the interaction between theft and corruption may shift. In such cases, theft does not emerge as a reaction to a corrupt system, broader political dynamics, or as illegal behavior outside legitimate frameworks. Instead, theft is normalized as a legitimate economic activity, while corruption is constructed as a coercive intervention executed by regimes to extract, secure, and enhance rent.

Regimes strategically design and promote legal and institutional absence in several ways. First, undermining the process of establishing rules and institutions; second, containing legitimate grievances related to recognizing rules and institutions; or third, suppressing the enforcement of rules and institutions. In resource frontier contexts, the distinction between legal and illegal is exacerbated, and the line between what is lawful and unlawful is often reduced to mere interpretation. As a result, theft becomes rampant and may even be viewed as a legitimate economic activity.

The irony is that the state's deliberate absence enables theft. Subsequently, the state may exploit this theft as a narrative device to mobilize anti-corruption measures that ultimately serve a political machine. In practice, these performative anti-corruption mechanisms, in turn, become tools for political leaders or elites to secure rents, precisely because establishing effective rules and institutions, and reasserting state presence, is far costlier and time-consuming than simply pushing anti-corruption campaigns. This dynamic is evident in Mongolia's coal theft case, where the government implemented policies ostensibly to strengthen efforts to address theft and corruption. However, these efforts failed to introduce effective rules and institutions in the mineral sector or re-establish the state's presence at the local level.

The 'Coal Theft' Case: Measures and Outcomes

Mongolia's minerals sector has long been plagued by widespread theft and corruption. While these issues were commonly discussed, evidence and public exposure were often lacking. In recent years, however, the country has been rocked by a series of high-profile corruption scandals, including the Erdenet mining case, the Ulaanbaatar Railroad, Development Bank, Educational Fund, and Green Bus controversies. In response, the government launched a public campaign against corruption, framing it as a battle against former allies and political rivals. Government leaders positioned themselves as whistleblowers, claiming to expose a vast network of corruption in the mining and finance sectors, and in government and law enforcement. But the handling of the coal theft case in particular served as a blueprint for the government's consolidation of power. By tightening control over the nation's key economic sector and silencing opposition in the guise of tackling corruption, the government effectively strengthened its position.

The 'Coal Theft' Case

The coal theft scandal erupted in late December 2023 when it was alleged that vast quantities of coking coal from Erdenes Tavan Tolgoi (ETT), Mongolia's state-owned mining company, were illegally exported to China without proper registration or recordkeeping (Dashpurev 2024). Thousands of protesters gathered in front of the parliament building, demanding the identification and punishment of those involved (Dierkes 2023). The case was quickly politicized, with conflicting reports circulating about the amount of coal, its value, and the parties implicated (Dashpurev 2024, Ahearn and Munkherdene 2023). This complexity stems from the fact that the 'coal theft' was not merely a criminal act but a multi-faceted socio-legal case involving various actors. Indeed, the 'coal theft' case can be broken down into several interconnected acts, each with broader social, political, and legal implications.

The coal theft case encompasses a range of illegal activities. First was the theft of 5.2 million tons of coking coal, which was exported to China without proper recordkeeping. Second, the undervaluation of coal prices in sales and barter exchanges, which resulted in significant revenue losses. When Erdenes Tavan Tolgoi (ETT) used coal to settle debts with its developers, operating companies, subcontractors, and others, the coal was valued below market price, causing further financial damage. Third, the case involves disproportionate transport costs, with the government alleging that transportation companies colluded to inflate prices between the Tsagaan Khad interim border point and the Gants Mod border in Inner Mongolia, China. Fourth, the case includes unlawful tendering procedures for selecting operating companies, subcontractors, and procurement services. Fifth, the coal theft case highlights corrupt hiring practices, where social connections, rather than merit, determined employment. The coal theft case is not merely an instance of theft; therefore, it involves embezzlement, tax evasion, corruption, money laundering, unlawful enrichment, and other illicit activities.

The case also involved a wide range of actors, from the CEO of Erdenes Tavan Tolgoi (ETT) to truck drivers, and from local officials to members of parliament (Batchimig 2023). For example, several truck drivers have been prosecuted for bribing government officials and forging documents as part of the coal theft scheme (2023b). Moreover, numerous local government officials, border militia personnel, customs officers, and inspectors are under investigation and face prosecution in connection with the case.[1] The case has not only penalized lower- and mid-level officials but has also led to the suspension or removal of several MPs, including Ayursaikhan Tumurbaatar, Bat-Erdene Dashdemberel, and Munkhbat Jamyan, due to their involvement in the scandal. Of these, Gankhuyag Battulga, CEO of ETT, Ayursaikhan Tumurbaatar, a parliament member from 2016–2020, and eleven others holding key positions in ETT and its subcontracting companies, were charged with unlawful enrichment, money laundering, and corruption.[2]

The 'coal theft' case also underscores the critical complexities and ambiguities plaguing Mongolia's minerals governance. Beyond the theft itself, the incident exposed a web of issues related to exploitation, transportation, finance, exports, and development projects. The involvement of a wide range of actors further compounded complexity. Moreover, the case has revealed the sector's chronic problems of incoherent information, insufficient data, and poor recordkeeping. These issues are exacerbated by the state's policy of treating the minerals sector and its associated development as strategic, shielding them from external review. Such opacity hinders effective intervention, analysis, evaluation, and resolution. Instead of addressing the root causes of these complexities, the state opted to focus primarily on performative anti-corruption measures. These efforts failed to address the underlying systemic issues that contributed to the case, however.

The Anti-Corruption Measures

Various governance indices suggest a crisis in Mongolia's governance overall, though not necessarily in its natural resource sectors (Project 2023, Borders 2024, Institute 2024, International 2023b). Since 2015, Transparency International has consistently reported worsening corruption, with Mongolia ranking 121st out of 180 countries (International 2023a). By contrast, the Natural Resource Governance Institute (NRGI) has categorized the country's resource governance as 'satisfactory' (NRGI 2021). Although these sources appear contradictory, the data reflect the ambiguity and failure inherent in the resource governance of Mongolia.

While the CPI shows worsening conditions, NRGI acknowledges gaps and limitations in resource governance which are plagued by ambiguity and a lack of reliable data. NRGI has, indeed, recommended that the Erdenes Mongol company (the parent company of the Erdenes Tavan Tolgoi and loci of the 'coal theft' case) improve transparency through enhanced disclosure and reporting. The institute calls for more detailed information on production and sales data, the company's relationships with subsidiaries, and the use of revenues for quasi-fiscal spending (NRGI 2021). Yet, the government labeled the 'coal theft' case solely as a corruption issue, exclusively attributing it to individual misconduct and immoral behavior. Rather than recognizing it as partly a failure of resource governance, the government has focused predominantly on strengthening anti-corruption measures aimed at disciplining, penalizing, and reforming only certain aspects of the minerals sector.

The most crucial measure was the appointment of the 'Büren Erkht Tölöölögch,'—BET (the sovereign representative). This official is temporarily appointed by the central government into state-owned enterprises to manage operations and to assist the government in curbing corruption. Since 2016, the government has increasingly promoted the BET measure to address corruption and inefficiency within state-owned enterprises. In the ETT's context, the Ulsyn Ikh Khural (the Parliament of Mongolia) approved and adopted several resolutions to establish a state of emergency (Ontsgoi deglem) within ETT and appointed Ganbat Jigjid as BET (Legalinfo 2022, Legalinfo 2023b, Legalinfo 2023a). This appointment led to the exposure of critical information, including confidential off-take agreements, revenue losses, and inefficiencies in ETT's management.

The second measure involved amending criminal laws and adopting the third national anti-corruption plan. In response to the 'coal theft' scandal, the government revised both the penal code and the criminal procedure law, intensifying criminal charges and extending the statute of limitations for corruption crimes. For instance, the amendments stipulated that no pardons or excuses would be granted to individuals indicted for corruption.[3] Additionally, fines were no longer considered an acceptable sentence for bribery offenses, and the imprisonment terms were extended from the previous range of 6 months to 2 years, to a stricter range of 2 to 8 years.[4] Alongside these legal reforms, the government announced the year 2024 as an anti-corruption year and introduced a new anti-corruption plan, which they claim incorporates democratic measures recommended by Transparency International, including greater accountability, transparency, and inclusiveness (Toves 2023, Darambazar 2023).

The third major response to the 'coal theft' case was the government's decision to open multiple criminal investigations and indict various individuals and corporate entities (Mongolia March 14, 2023, Batchimig 2023). Notably, charges were brought against Gankhuyag Battulga, Ayursaikhan Tumurbaatar, and 11 others for offenses such as unlawful enrichment, money laundering, and accepting bribes. In addition to these high-profile cases, many others—including truck drivers, inspectors, border militia personnel, and local politicians—were also investigated and prosecuted in connection with the 'coal theft' scandal. Beyond the criminal prosecutions, other political and legal measures were taken. Several MPs were suspended, state officials were removed from their positions, and political parties pledged not to nominate individuals associated with the scandal for the 2024 parliamentary elections.

Another strategic response to the 'coal theft' case was a parliamentary public hearing (2023a). The public hearing took place over two separate sessions, lasting a total of ten days at the end of 2024. The parliamentary committee summoned 175 individuals to appear and broadcast the hearings to the public. Enkhbayar Battömör, MP and the minister of justice at the time of the hearing, made a statement, declaring that 15 inspectors had examined the expansive set of documents and substantial number of people's involvement in the case: 698 coal sale agreements, 943 procurement contracts, over

10 thousand bank transactions, 2.5 million border crossings, and 217,629 people's affiliations with the Erdenes Tavan Tolgoi company (Battömör, November 27, 2023). This hearing revealed the loss of 5.2 million tons of coking coal from the Erdenes Tavan Tolgoi company, highlighting the company's mismanagement, the state's governance failures, and the involvement of a wide range of actors.

The Outcomes

The government's anti-corruption measures produced some positive results in Mongolia's minerals sector. A key outcome has been a substantial increase in coal exports. This boost is widely attributed to the government's mobilization of anti-corruption measures and the subsequent improvements in transparency and management in the sector. The government reported a 112% rise in coal exports in 2023 compared to the previous year.[5] This upward trend continued in the first half of 2024, with exports growing by 37% compared to the same period ending in June 2023.[6] A significant portion of this increase is attributed to Erdenes Tavan Tolgoi (ETT), which has accounted for nearly half of the country's coal production and exports (Chung 2019). In addition to this boost in production and exports, the government introduced greater transparency in ETT's operations. Previously confidential off-take contracts, coal sale agreements, and subcontracting arrangements were disclosed for public review. Furthermore, coal sales are now conducted through public auctions on the Mongolian Stock Exchange, a move designed to enhance transparency in Mongolia's minerals sector.

Anti-corruption measures in response to the 'coal theft' case have undoubtedly had a profound impact on Mongolia's minerals sector. The prosecution, public labeling, and removal of numerous government officials created a strong deterrent against corrupt practices. Moreover, these efforts led to the adoption of significant legislation and policies aimed at penalizing and reducing corruption in the sector. However, a crucial question remains: Are these measures truly effective and genuine in addressing the root causes of corruption behind the case?

Theft, Anti-Corruption Campaign, and Implications

In the 'coal theft' case, should the primary concern be the theft of 5.2 million tons of coking coal, or the underlying corruption that facilitated the theft? The Mongolian government diagnosed the coal theft as primarily a corruption problem, framing it as an issue driven by corrupt actors. The government argues that pursuing anti-corruption measures will also help penalize theft itself. Although, as noted above, some positive outcomes are observed, I argue these measures are more symbolic than substantive and are temporary in nature. In some cases, they can be characterized as abusive forms of anti-corruption.

The main argument I put forward is that theft, not corruption, is the primary issue. As the coal theft case shows, the state's strategic absence in the minerals sector and resource-rich regions facilitated large-scale resource looting. The deliberate weakening and neglect of rules and institutions by the state allowed this theft to occur; indeed, it turned it into a major economic activity. Theft offers a clearer explanation for the ambiguities in the 'coal theft' case, more so than corruption. In other words, theft explains why the government struggled to prosecute culprits, as it implicated a wide range of actors colluding in the theft. The investigation extended beyond state officials to include non-state actors such as truck drivers, trucking companies, subcontractors, and their employers. This challenge was amplified by the sheer number of people involved, leading the government to adopt a guilt-by-association approach, labeling nearly everyone as complicit in the theft. This tactic reshaped public perceptions, framed as a potentially dangerous collective narrative that 'everyone was corrupt'.

However, when prosecuting officials involved in the cases, the state often charged them with unlawful enrichment instead of accepting bribes. For non-state actors, the charges typically focused on giving bribes to officials without targeting the officials who demanded bribes or abused their positions. For instance, Ayursaikhan T., Gankhuyag B., and 11 others were charged with unlawful enrichment, not for taking bribes. Truck drivers were charged with giving bribes and forging official documents. While unlawful enrichment and giving bribes are technically corruption crimes under the criminal code, these charges do not fully capture the essence of corruption, where those in authority exploit their positions and authority for personal gain. Moreover, despite indications that the coal theft case involved tax evasion and embezzlement, no individuals were charged with these crimes. This highlights the government's attempt to frame the coal theft case as a corruption issue and its reliance on anti-corruption measures to address it.

Theft also better explains why the government lacks coherent, adequate, and reliable information. In the coal theft case, the government failed to track essential details such as how much coal was involved, what type of coal was exported, how it was exported, and who was responsible. This failure wasn't due to the complexity of the minerals supply chain but because key information was missing, poorly recorded, or even lost (Battömör 27. November. 2023). Such poor recordkeeping in the nation's strategic sector reveals that the government has not established the basic rules, institutions, and oversight mechanisms needed to properly account for the commodity. This clear absence of the state in the minerals sector allowed theft to become widespread. While corruption may have played a role, the root problem lies in the government's failure to establish a robust system for accounting and managing the nation's mineral resources, including coal.

A salient question is whether the government's anti-corruption measures in reaction to the coal theft were effective. Since the coal theft case, the government has mobilized several anti-corruption measures, as discussed in the previous section, such as appointing a BET, amending criminal and criminal procedure laws, adopting the national anti-corruption plan, prosecuting high-ranking officials and non-state actors, and organizing a public hearing. The government argues these measures have been successful, pointing to increased coal exports, the disclosure of confidential information, and the prosecution of many actors. However, these anti-corruption measures appear more cosmetic than substantive.

For instance, the appointment of BET, a practice similar to China's 'paratrooper' officials, was a clear and concrete violation of Mongolia's legal framework. Despite this, the government not only continued this practice but extended it to the local Tavan Tolgoi company, where ownership of the company is allocated to the local government and private investors. This undermined the rule of law and blurred the lines between state and private interests. This was underscored by the recent news that Ganbat Jigjid, the BET in ETT, received 1.2 billion Mongolian Tugrik as a bonus, highlighting the importance of personal ties over meaningful reform.[7] While the government publicly emphasized pursuing transparency in the mineral sector by disclosing confidential agreements, its actions contradicted this in practice. The government failed to hold open court proceedings for the high-ranking official implicated, and entire court sessions were conducted closed to the public and media. Additionally, the public hearing on the case excluded the very individuals accused of wrongdoing, and a dedicated webpage for sharing evidence was taken offline.[8] These actions demonstrate a lack of commitment to due process, genuine reform, and accountability.

The government's claim that increased coal production and revenues are solely due to anti-corruption efforts is an oversimplification. While these measures likely played a role, global market dynamics have probably had a more significant impact. During the time of the coal theft case, there was a surge in international demand for coal, driving up prices to record highs (IEA 2023, IEA July 2024). The price of coal per ton reached as much as US$ 400, which impacted Mongolia's coal production and the revenues generated from it (IEA, July 2024). However, the disparity between the increase in production (112%) and revenue (37%) suggests that other factors, such as pricing fluctuations and potential inefficiencies, are influencing the sector's performance. Looking ahead, coal production is expected to remain stable, but revenues may decline. This fluctuation is driven by changes in global market prices, not by Mongolia's anti-corruption measures.

The government's anti-corruption measures, such as appointing a BET, prosecuting high-ranking officials, amending criminal laws, and adopting an anti-corruption plan, were temporary and rather superficial reforms. Rather than addressing the underlying systemic issue of strategic state absence, these actions were primarily aimed at maintaining control over resource rents. As a result, theft continues to be a pervasive problem, and anti-corruption campaigns serve as a façade to obscure the government's failure to implement more meaningful reforms.

The 'coal theft' case reveals how the absence of effective governance, masked by anti-corruption rhetoric, fosters further exploitation rather than addressing the systemic issues in minerals sectors. Anti-corruption measures implemented in response to Mongolia's 'coal theft' case—where 5.2 million tons of coking coal were stolen from the state-owned company Erdenes Tavan Tolgoi (ETT)—were largely political maneuvers. These measures served as tools for internal political factions vying for control over the nation's key mineral resources, rather than genuine efforts to reform the extractive industry or enhance accountability. The state's strategic absence from the mineral sector is continued via these anti-corruption measures, while these measures become tools to extract and secure rents from minerals while perpetuating political manipulation and abuse.

Conclusion

The 'coal theft' case provides valuable insights into the application of anti-corruption measures in the context of mining. Where the political economy is heavily reliant on resource extraction, the effectiveness, and nature of anti-corruption measures are particularly influenced by this dependency. Despite having abundant natural resources, states often lack significant control over the broader mineral supply chain and are, ironically, highly vulnerable to global market fluctuations. This dynamic—where the economy and politics are heavily dependent on extractive activities yet there is a lack of meaningful control over broader conditions—defines the political and economic system, known as the 'mining regime'.

Mining regimes have often pursued strategies that are set apart from environmental, social, and cultural issues, as well as from conflicts between local communities and mining companies. These regimes prioritize policies focused on extracting, securing, and enhancing revenue from resource exploitation. This deliberate non-involvement is referred to as the state's 'strategic absence,' where governments intentionally refrain from enforcing crucial environmental and social protection laws, only intervening to protect and secure its rent-seeking interests. This strategic absence is not just about distancing from and avoiding the enforcement of legislation, undermining institutions, and suppressing local authorities. It also creates a resource frontier-like environment, where the landscape is continuously made and remade ambiguous, blurring the lines between what is legal and illegal.

The coal theft case is a striking example of the consequences of Mongolia's strategic absence in its minerals sector and resource-rich regions. The government's role has been not only one of neglect—failing to introduce effective rules and institutions—but also one of active discouragement, deliberately undermining any recognition or enforcement of such frameworks. This has blurred the lines between what is legal and illegal, fostering illicit activities like theft. In these regions, the boundaries between legitimate business, theft, and even corruption are blurred and indistinct. As a result, corruption and theft are often conflated.

The theft of 5.2 tons of coal occurred as a direct result of the state's deliberate policy of minimal presence in the mineral sector. Rather than addressing the underlying issues, the government opted to respond with superficial anti-corruption measures such as appointing a BET, prosecuting a few people, holding public hearings, reforming a few rules, and so forth. The state's strategic absence not only facilitated theft but exacerbated it, creating an environment where anti-corruption measures were used selectively, leading to further abuses. This approach perpetuated rather than dismantled a cycle of corruption and theft. To truly address these issues, a shift in strategy is needed—one that goes beyond surface-level measures and tackles the systemic issues at the heart of the mining regime. Effective anti-corruption efforts must involve genuine enforcement of environmental and social protection laws, a commitment to transparency, and the establishment of institutions that hold all actors equally accountable. Only by addressing the root causes of theft in the state's absence from the sector can we hope to break the cycle of exploitation and corruption that defines the current regime.

Notes

1. The Judicial Council of Mongolia published at least a dozen criminal cases related to coal theft that were tried in the Khanbogd soum first-instance criminal court between March 2024 and May 2025. These cases resulted in the sentencing of numerous government officials—particularly from the border militia and customs office—for corruption-related offenses, as recorded in the court's decision database.
2. The case is currently pending before the appellate criminal court of Mongolia. Although the lower court has rendered its decision, the proceedings were conducted in a closed session, with no public or media access. Consequently, the only available information relates to the sentencing of the defendants. Reports indicate that Gankhuyag received a sentence of 5.9 years imprisonment, while Ayursaikhan was sentenced to 3 years, both for unlawful enrichment, and 11 others were subjected to monetary fines.
3. Criminal Law of Mongolia. 2015. Art 6.14.2. as amended 16 December 2023.

4. Criminal Law of Mongolia. 2015. Art 22.4.1. as amended 16 December 2023.
5. National Statistics Office of Mongolia (the year 2022: the year 2023). www.1212.mn. It was reported that Mongolia exported 31,821,600 million tonnes of coal to China, while in 2023, this increased significantly to 69,612,500 tonnes.
6. National Statistics Office of Mongolia (June 2023: June 2024). www.1212.mn. By June 2024, Mongolia had already exported 40,620,570 million tonnes of coal to China, compared to 29,519,900 million tonnes in June 2023.
7. Tegshbayar Darambazar, a Mongolian financial crimes compliance consultant, recently criticized Ganbat Jigjid, BET and Executive Director of Erdenes Tavan Tolgoi (ETT), for receiving a 1.2 billion Mongolian Tugrik bonus, despite the government's efforts to reduce state expenses. Her interview with Ödriin Sonin was reportedly altered by ETT and removed from DNN.mn's website. When she reposted it on Time.mn, it was taken down again. The original article about the bonus can be found on www.gogo.mn (https://gogo.mn/r/wl035) and the removed interview on time.mn (https://time.mn/vqt.html).
8. The website www.songsgol.mn was created to share critical information, assist government officials in communicating with the public, facilitate public hearings, and preserve data for future studies related to the 'coal theft' case. However, the site was taken down without any explanation.

References

2023a.The Parliament of Mongolia (Mongol Ulsyn Ikh Khural). Coal Public Hearing (Nüürsnii Sonsgol). 04 December 2023. www.sonsgol.mn. Judicial Council of Mongolia, 2023b. U.D., M.D., J.D., and others v. the State of Mongolia. Khanbogd soum Criminal Court of the First Instance.

Addison, T. and Roe, A. 2024. *Extractive industries: Addressing transparency, corruption, and theft*, WIDER Working Paper.

Ahearn, A. and Munkherdene, G. 2023. Coal smuggling trains the Mongolian public's eye on systemic corruption, East Asia Forum. https://eastasiaforum.org/2023/04/17/coal-smuggling-trains-the-mongolian-publics-eye-on-systemic-corruption/.

Batchimig, M. 2023. Criminal charges were filed against seven parliament members relating to the 'coal theft' case. www.Ikon.mn.

Battömör, E. 27 November 2023. The parliamentary public hearing relating to the 'coal theft' case. www.sonsgol.mn.

Borders, R. W. 2024. World Press freedom index 2024. https://rsf.org/en/country/mongolia.

Bulag, U. E. 2009. Mongolia in 2008: From Mongolia to Mine-golia. *Asian Survey*, 49, 129–134.

Carothers, C. 2022. Taking authoritarian anti-corruption reform seriously. *Perspectives on Politics*, 20, 69–85.

Carothers, T. 2002. The end of the transition paradigm. *Journal of Democracy*, 13, 5–21.

Chung, J. 2019. The Mineral Industry of Mongolia. *Minerals Yearbook: Area Reports International. Asia and the Pacific. Volume III*, 8.

Cons, J. and Eilenberg, M. 2019. *Frontier assemblages: The emergent politics of resource frontiers in Asia*. John Wiley & Sons.

Darambazar, T. 2023. Guest post: The backbone of the new national anti-corruption strategy will be the praviate sector and civil society. *Mongolia Focus.*

Dashpurev, B. 2024. The 'coal theft'case: Corruption and reform of Mongolia's strategic minerals governance. *U4 Brief.*

De Sardan, J. O. 1999. A moral economy of corruption in Africa? *The Journal of Modern African Studies,* 37, 25–52.

Diamond, L. 2002. Elections without democracy: Thinking about hybrid regimes. *Journal of Democracy,* 13, 21–35.

Dierkes, J. 2023. Mass protests in Mongolia Decry' Coal Mafia,' corruption.

Duchelle, A. E., Cronkleton, P., Kainer, K. A., Guanacoma, G. and Gezan, S. 2011. Resource theft in tropical forest communities: Implications for non-timber management, livelihoods, and conservation. *Ecology and Society,* 16(1): 4.

Hatcher, P. 2015. *Regimes of risk: The World Bank and the transformation of mining in Asia.* Springer.

Hatcher, P. and Lander, J. 2023. Searching for new political spaces: Negotiating citizenship and transnational identities on Mongolia's mining frontier. *Journal of Contemporary Asia,* 53, 311–334.

IEA 2023. Coal 2023 Analysis and forecast to 2026. International Energy Agency.

IEA July 2024. Coal mid-year update July 2024. International Energy Agency.

Institute, V.-D. 2024. Democracy report 2023. *Defiance in the face of autocratization.*

International, T. 2023a. Corruption perception index Mongolia.

International, T. 2023b. Corruption perceptions index 2023.

Johansson, A. and Vinthagen, S. 2016. Dimensions of everyday resistance: An analytical framework. *Critical Sociology,* 42, 417–435.

Johnston, M. 2014. *Corruption, contention and reform: The power of deep democratization.* Cambridge University Press.

Lander, J. 2019. *Transnational law and state transformation: The case of extractive development in Mongolia.* Routledge.

Lander, J., Hatcher, P., Bebbington, D. H., Bebbington, A. and Banks, G. 2021. Troubling the idealised pageantry of extractive conflicts: Comparative insights on authority and claim-making from Papua New Guinea, Mongolia and El Salvador. *World Development,* 140, 105372.

LEGALINFO. 2022. The measures to increase the State's foreign currency reserves. *In:* MONGOLIA, T. G. O. (ed.) *Resolution 362.* Legalinfo.mn: Legalinfo.

LEGALINFO. 2023a. The extension of the emergency status in Erdenes Tavan Tolgoi JSC. *In:* MONGOLIA, T. P. O. (ed.). www.legalinfo.mn.

LEGALINFO. 2023b. The measures taking Erdenes Tavan Tolgoi JSC. *In:* MONGOLIA, T. P. O. (ed.). www.legalinfo.mn.

Levitsky, S. and Way, L. A. 2002. Elections without democracy: The rise of competitive authoritarianism. *Journal of Democracy,* 13, 51–65.

Lindstedt, C. and Naurin, D. 2010. Transparency is not enough: Making transparency effective in reducing corruption. *International Political Science Review,* 31, 301–322.

Mongolia Independent Authority Against Corruption of Mongolia (I. A. A. C. M) 14 March 2023. On the 'Coal Theft' case status. https://iaac.mn/2542/nitem.

Mungiu-pippidi, A. 2013. Controlling corruption through collective action. *Journal of Democracy,* 24, 101–115.

Mungiu-pippidi, A. 2015. *The quest for good governance: How societies develop control of corruption.* Cambridge University Press.
Nichols, R. 2018. Theft is property! The recursive logic of dispossession. *Political Theory,* 46, 3–28.
NRGI 2021. Resource governance index Mongolia. https://resourcegovernance.org/publications/2021-resource-governance-index-mongolia-mining.
Pavlova, E. 2020. Corrupt governance: Self-defeating anti-corruption rhetoric and initiatives in Russia. *New Perspectives,* 28, 205–222.
Project, W. J. 2023. Rule of law index. *Rule of Law Index 2023.*
Quah, J. S. 2017. Learning from Singapore's effective anti-corruption strategy: Policy recommendations for South Korea. *Asian Education and Development Studies,* 6, 17–29.
Robbins, P. 2000. The rotten institution: Corruption in natural resource management. *Political Geography,* 19, 423–443.
Scott, J. C. 2016. *Everyday forms of peasant resistance.* Routledge.
Toves, K. 2023. Q&A: What's next for Mongolia's beneficial ownership transparency and anti-corruption agenda | Results for Development. @results4dev.
Tsing, A. L. 2003. Natural resources and capitalist frontiers. *Economic and Political Weekly,* 5100–5106.
Zhu, J. and Zhang, D. 2017. Weapons of the powerful: Authoritarian elite competition and politicized anti-corruption in China. *Comparative Political Studies,* 50, 1186–1220.

8

"ALL THE KING'S MEN"

Selectivity in the Russian Anti-Corruption Reforms

Alexey Konov

Introduction

In 2017, a high-profile anti-corruption trial took place in Russia. The defendant, Alexey Ulyukaev, recently held the position of Minister of Economic Development and, prior to that, was the First Deputy Minister of Finance and First Deputy Chairman of the Central Bank of Russia. This was the first time a sitting federal minister was charged with a corruption offence. The defendant was accused of extortion by Igor Sechin, the head of Rosneft, one of the largest Russian state-owned enterprises. According to the prosecution, Ulyukaev was caught red-handed: he took a bag from Sechin, in which, upon arrest, cash in the amount of 2 million US dollars was found.

During the court hearings, the defendant and his lawyers stated that the defendant had indeed taken the bag but believed it contained not money but a gift. In his testimony, the defendant explained that he saw nothing unusual in it. When asked whether there had been any other occasions when the Rosneft head had brought him bags or boxes as gifts, the defendant replied that Sechin had visited the ministry two or three times with a bulky bag, and there had always been some present: once, an antique watch, another time, something else (Nikolskaya et al. 2017).

Such a self-revealing statement was surprising for anyone familiar with Russian anti-corruption law. As a minister, i.e., a person holding a public office, the defendant was obliged to comply with anti-corruption standards. One of them was the statutory prohibition on receiving gifts in connection with the performance of official duties. At the time of the defendant's arrest, this prohibition had been in force for over 10 years. The legislation also

DOI: 10.4324/9781003531920-11

contained conflict of interest rules that clearly discouraged the acceptance of gifts from representatives of regulated companies.

Thus, a person accused of corruption readily confessing to systematic violations of anti-corruption legislation was unusual. The defendant was either unaware of anti-corruption rules or did not relate to them and did not realise that they had been applicable to him throughout his entire career in the Government.

In many countries, high-ranking officials routinely fail to comply with anti-corruption restrictions and prohibitions and – sometimes blatantly – disregard the rules that rank-and-file employees are forced to follow. Such cases are widely exposed by the media, anti-corruption NGOs, and activists.[1] However, selective application of anti-corruption legislation has often been mentioned in but has scarcely become the central subject of academic studies (for rare examples see Zhan and Zhu 2023; Nwozor et al. 2020; Sapio 2005).

This chapter seeks to contribute to closing this gap. To do so, it explores the anti-corruption reforms of the 2000s–2010s in Russia from a certain angle. It shows that from the very beginning of the reforms, the new non-criminal anti-corruption provisions were targeted at rank-and-file employees. Top officials were effectively exempt from anti-corruption restrictions and disciplinary sanctions for non-compliance. However, this did not mean they were completely immune from anti-corruption legislation. At least since the 2010s, criminal penalties for corruption have been increasingly applied to high-ranking political appointees. Paradoxically, this might be due not to a commitment to crack down on corruption at the top level, but to a desire to maintain a system based on manipulating elites' access to illegal rents.

Part 1 briefly reviews the history of the latest stage of anti-corruption reforms in Russia. Part 2 demonstrates that the focus on the grassroots level and the difficulty of applying new legislation to high-ranking officials were inherent in its design and institutional infrastructure. Part 3 analyses two data sets that help capture the selective application of certain anti-corruption provisions. Part 4 discusses how and why anti-corruption was present in the world of high-ranking appointees. The Conclusion contains some general findings from the Russian case, which may be useful to enhance the understanding of anti-corruption reforms of recent decades.

The Paradigm Shift

Unlike corruption in Russia, recent Russian anti-corruption reforms have not received much attention in the academic literature. The few existing publications tend to focus on President Medvedev's reforms and often take as the starting point 2008 when the Presidential Anti-Corruption Council was established, the first National Anti-Corruption Plan was issued, and the federal law "On Combating Corruption"[2] was adopted (see, e.g., Black 2013; Holmes 2012; Burger and Gitau 2010).

However, this starting point overlooks important prior reforms. Indeed, the first steps of the reform were made earlier, in 2002–2004, when the following measures were taken:

- for the first time in Russian legal history, conflict of interest rules were introduced for all public servants, conflict of interest legal definition was provided, and ad hoc declaration was put in place;
- anti-corruption restrictions, prohibitions and obligations previously scattered in different legal acts were brought together, including but not limited to asset disclosure rules, prohibitions on direct subordination of close relatives, gift and hospitality rules, ban on entrepreneurship, etc.
- some standards were substantially revised; for example, whereas before public servants had been prohibited from any work other than teaching, research, and other creative work, the new rules allowed outside activities as long as they did not cause a conflict of interest;
- some standards that had never existed in Russia were introduced, such as post-employment rules;
- disciplinary liability for non-compliance with these standards was explicitly provided for, ranging from reprimand to dismissal;
- Conflict of Interest Commissions were established in each government body to provide the employer with recommendations on managing conflicts of interest and sanctioning non-compliance with anti-corruption standards.

Legislative changes that took place from 2008 onwards primarily developed what had been laid down by the reforms of the early 2000s, in particular:

- the statutory asset disclosure procedure was further elaborated and supplemented with the liability for illicit enrichment;
- in addition to Conflict of Interest Commissions, standing Anti-Corruption Units (ACUs) were established in all government bodies to administer compliance procedures and investigate violations of anti-corruption standards;
- liability measures for non-compliance with anti-corruption standards were delineated from disciplinary sanctions and a separate type of dismissal – dismissal with a loss of trust – was introduced. It was prescribed for violating the asset disclosure and conflict of interest rules, as well as breaching prohibitions on entrepreneurship and participation in the governing bodies of organisations;
- a separate department was created in the Prosecutor General's Office to supervise how government bodies complied with the new rules.

These measures should not be regarded as mere legal amendments. They rather signalled a paradigm shift in Russian anti-corruption regulation. Until the early 2000s, in the USSR and then in Russia, combating corruption had been primarily a penal issue. No standards of behaviour were labelled in the law as anti-corruption. Many concepts fundamentally important for corruption prevention, first of all conflict of interest, were completely absent from the public service legislation. There were neither special disciplinary sanctions for corruption offences nor specialised anti-corruption structures in government agencies.

This does not mean that in the early 2000s, Russia switched to non-criminal means in the fight against corruption. Criminal law continued to play a priority role in the anti-corruption infrastructure. However, the reform itself focused mainly not on criminal law but on the "soft" anti-corruption regulation. This approach was fully in line with the recommendations of international organisations.

Gradually, legal innovations began to yield practical results. The number of persons disciplinarily sanctioned annually for non-compliance with anti-corruption standards has reached tens of thousands, and the number of dismissals with a loss of trust has increased from about 130 in 2015 (Soghomonyan 2017) to more than 500 in 2024 (Shashkov 2024). However, these changes did not affect equally all categories of public officials.

Selectivity by Design

In the literature, the problems of anti-corruption reforms are often attributed to the implementation gap. However, in Russia, the reform of the 2000s–2010s was selective by law. From the outset of the reform, it was characterised by peculiarities regarding who was covered by the new standards and to what extent.

Focus on the lower ranks. When the reform started, Russia did not have a framework law on anti-corruption. Thus, anti-corruption standards were enshrined in the Civil Service Act and the Municipal Service Act.[3] However, these laws did not cover the very top ranks of officials: federal ministers, governors, and other federal and regional public office holders.[4] Their activities were regulated by other statutes, which were not supplemented with new anti-corruption provisions. This selective approach was also followed when drafting the Federal Law "On Combating Corruption". In its first version, public office holders were not even mentioned.

Deficient regulation of the senior civil service. In Russia, the right to launch an internal investigation against a public servant and to authorise disciplinary action against him or her has been vested in the appointing authority. For most public servants, this appointing authority was the head of the public body. However, the most senior civil servants – federal deputy ministers, heads of federal agencies and services, high-level military and law enforcement officials – were appointed and dismissed directly by the President or the Government. Thus, a federal minister could not, for example, dismiss his deputy for violating anti-corruption standards; he could only bring up the need to do so. Disciplinary sanctions against presidential and government appointees required a separate procedure, which did not exist.

Reluctant watchdogs. Conflict of Interest Commissions established in each government body were mandated to assist their heads in applying disciplinary sanctions for breach of anti-corruption standards. Some independence safeguards were provided: at least 25% of the Commission members should have been recruited from outside the public body, e.g. from scientific and educational institutions. However, three-quarters of the Commission members were still drawn from the public body employees. Since the Commissions' decisions were made by a majority vote, and independent members did not have the right to veto, the Commissions turned into a "comrades' court". Thus, they were uncomfortable even discussing their peers' behaviour, much less strictly punishing them. They would rather tend to defend agency interests, avoid harsh decisions and be careful about washing dirty linen in public.

Internal non-criminal investigations of anti-corruption standards violations were entrusted to ACUs. However, again, independence was significantly compromised. ACUs were established within HR departments. Plans to subordinate them directly to heads of government bodies never materialised. Obviously, a unit so low in the organisational structure could hardly initiate investigations against high-ranking employees. The unwillingness of government agencies to conduct investigations and impose disciplinary sanctions has been partly remedied by the above-mentioned special department of the General Prosecutor's Office. It was after its interventions that a substantial part of internal investigations was launched. However, the reluctance problem has persisted.

In 2009–2011, anti-corruption standards were mainly extended to public office holders. The Federal Law "On Combating Corruption" was supplemented with a separate article.[5] Relevant norms appeared in the statutes regulating the activities of persons holding public office. The possibility of dismissal of federal and regional public office holders with a loss of trust on the same grounds as public servants was established. However, broadening the scope of reforms did not solve the selectivity issue.

It was decided to duplicate at the top level of the administrative hierarchy the compliance infrastructure initially designed for government bodies. The Presidium of the Presidential Anti-Corruption Council was vested with the powers of the Conflict of Interest Commission with respect to federal public office holders in the executive branch as well as public servants appointed by the President or the Government. The Council has existed since 2008 and initially focused on policymaking. It approved key anti-corruption documents, from draft laws to the most important official guidelines, and monitored the implementation of National Anti-Corruption Plans.

Investigations of possible failure to comply with anti-corruption standards by public office holders and public servants appointed by the President were concluded in the Presidential Administration. They were first entrusted to the Human Resources Directorate and later to the Anti-Corruption Directorate, created in 2013. Similar investigations in relation to public servants appointed by the Government were assigned to the Human Resources Department of the Government Office.

It might have seemed that these measures solved the coverage problems. Unfortunately, this was not the case. Replicating at the top level the approaches applied to rank-and-file employees resulted in the persistence of existing difficulties and the emergence of new ones.

First, the Presidium was too high-level to meet frequently and at short notice. It was chaired by the Head of the Presidential Administration and included heads of national security and law enforcement agencies, several federal ministers, and the heads of some of the most important presidential administration directorates. Thus, it could hardly work with the same intensity as the Conflict of Interest Commissions.

Second, some categories of officials, now subject to the jurisdiction of the Presidium, were equal or superior in terms of formal status or informal influence to many of its members. The need to discuss the behaviour of their high-level colleagues put members of the Presidium in a highly uncomfortable situation, potentially leading to interpersonal and interdepartmental conflicts.

Third, the position of the Presidential Anti-Corruption Directorate was no less controversial. It was just one of more than two dozen structural units within the Presidential Administration. Its head, although appointed by the President, was a public servant, not a public office holder. Unlike the heads of law enforcement agencies responsible for criminal investigations of corruption, the head of the Anti-Corruption Department did not report directly to the President but to the head of its Administration. Under such conditions, the Anti-Corruption Directorate would hardly dare, without prior explicit or implicit instruction from the President, to make probes into the behaviour of public officials, much more high-ranking and influential than the head of this new ACU.

Thus, in Russia, the new anti-corruption norms were rather designed with the lower-ranking employees in mind. At first, this was more evident when public office holders were not covered by the new standards, and there were no accountability procedures for senior public servants. Later, when the law was amended, the anti-corruption standards formally covered everyone, but the procedures were designed in such a way that it was challenging to apply them to top officials.

It is hard to know whether this selectivity was intentional. One possible motivation behind this approach may have been to introduce new tools without engaging in sensitive confrontations with high-level officials. Reformers may have been driven by hopes that once innovative norms were introduced at the grassroots level, they could, over time, be extended to top officials. Part 3 will show that, if such hopes existed, they were futile.

The Zone of Immunity

Giving isolated examples of selective enforcement of anti-corruption legislation may be easy. However, providing convincing evidence of systemic selectivity is much more challenging. The difficulties are not least due to the fact that in many countries – and Russia is no exception – detailed data on penalties for corruption offences, structured by category of offender, are not collected or publicly available. This is particularly true for disciplinary sanctions. To understand whether the new anti-corruption provisions were enforced selectively in Russia and, if so, what the selectivity looked like, this chapter will turn to the unconventional sources not initially intended for monitoring law enforcement practice.

The first one is the public Register of persons dismissed with a loss of trust (hereinafter – the Register).[6] Entered into force in 2018, it was intended to help employers identify candidates previously dismissed for corruption offences, thus preventing the subsequent employment of former officials with tarnished reputations. The Register contains the full name of each offender and, significant for this study, the position from which he or she was dismissed. It provides data on dismissals with a loss of trust of a wide range of public officials, including but not limited to:

- federal public servants appointed by the President or the Government (deputy federal ministers, heads of federal public bodies without ministerial status, a large group of military and law enforcement top officers, heads and deputy heads of certain SOEs),
- regional public office holders (deputy governors, regional ministers).

The Register has certain weaknesses as a source of information. First, it includes data on most but not all high-ranking public officials dismissed with a loss of trust. In particular, the Register does not contain data on federal public office holders, such as federal ministers and governors. To address this shortcoming, the analysis of the Register was supplemented by a manual search for relevant information. Also, data protected by state secrecy is not published, such as those on dismissals of special services employees. Second, it does not contain information about persons dismissed with a loss of trust before 2018, though this type of dismissal was introduced in 2011. Thus, the

Register does not show how the relevant legislation was applied during the first years after its adoption. Third, any record is kept in the Register only for 5 years after a public official is dismissed. Then, all data are deleted, and only the note about when the record was removed remains. Therefore, information on records older than 5 years becomes unavailable.[7]

Analysis of the Register and additional open-source information yields striking results. During the period under review, at the federal level, only one political appointee was dismissed with a loss of trust – the Deputy Minister of Defence in 2024. At the regional level, 3 governors, 2 deputy governors, 14 regional ministers, and other regional public office holders were dismissed with a loss of trust. Thus, during the last 5.5 years, the strictest measure of disciplinary liability for non-compliance with anti-corruption standards has almost never been applied to high-ranking officials at the federal level. The new anti-corruption standards were more present in the lives of regional top officials. However, here, another not-obvious circumstance should be taken into account.

This study examined the circumstances of dismissals of all top officials mentioned in the Register. Since each such dismissal was a notable event, the required information could usually be found in the media. A manual search for relevant news by full name and position of the sanctioned officials showed that the only federal deputy minister mentioned in the Register, as well as all governors and one of two deputy governors, were dismissed with a loss of trust only after criminal proceedings had been initiated against them. With regard to regional ministers and other regional public office holders, opening a criminal case against a public official or his or her close relatives preceded dismissal with a loss of trust in 12 out of 14 cases. These data suggest that the new anti-corruption apparatus of the Russian state that grew in line with international standards was only utilised against high-ranking officials as a form of political convenience. It had no life beyond being instrumentalised as a way to get rid of those who brought themselves into disrepute.

For rank-and-file employees, it is hardly possible to accurately verify what proportion of dismissals with a loss of trust were preceded by criminal prosecution. However, certain data suggest this figure was significantly lower than for top officials. To make this indirect estimate, the records of 330 court proceedings in 2019–2022 were manually collected and analysed, in which public sector employees appealed dismissal with a loss of trust for violating asset disclosure or conflict of interest rules. Related to the criminal cases were 54 (16%) of dismissals. Although not all dismissals with a loss of trust were appealed in court, it can be reasonably assumed that, with regard to rank-and-file officials, disciplinary sanctions stemmed to a much greater extent from violations of anti-corruption standards than from criminal cases and were less used only to get rid of those already caught in crimes.

Further evidence of the selective application of Russian anti-corruption reforms can be found in never-before-analysed press releases on meetings of the Presidium of the Presidential Anti-Corruption Council, which, as noted above, performed the functions of the Conflict of Interest Commission for top officials. A total of 56 such meetings were held between 2010 and 2024. After each meeting, a press release summarising the issues addressed was published on the President's official website.[8] Importantly, for this chapter, the press releases separately mention when the Presidium discussed the behaviour of top officials.

The first such case occurred almost immediately after the Presidium was endowed with new powers. In September 2010, the Presidium considered the results of the verification of the asset and income declaration submitted by a major-general of the Russian Armed Forces and found that the public servant had violated the law's requirements. As a result of the meeting, the perpetrator was dismissed from military service. This fact could create an optimistic mood and give the impression that, despite all the doubts discussed in Part 2 of this chapter, the Presidium would now perform the functions of a commission on a regular basis.

However, further discussions within the Presidium of possible violations of anti-corruption standards by top officials were rare and irregular. Together with the above-mentioned case, probable non-compliance of top officials with anti-corruption provisions was discussed at only 7 meetings out of 56. For almost 7 years (from 2017 to 2024), the Presidium did not address any such matters.[9]

The analysis of the Register and the Presidium materials shows that the system of anti-corruption standards, initially designed for the grassroots level and later extended with significant design flaws to political appointees, never worked for top officials. The probability that their behaviour would be subject to formal collective discussion remained extremely low. Neither federal and regional public office holders nor public servants appointed by the President or the Government have almost never been dismissed with a loss of trust for failing to comply with anti-corruption standards. In the rare cases when this occurred, the dismissal mostly resulted from criminal prosecution. The anti-corruption reform of the 2000s–2010s focused on non-criminal measures did not significantly affect the political and bureaucratic elites.

Paradoxes of Criminal Prosecution

The reluctant application of disciplinary liability to Russian high-level appointees may suggest that they were unofficially protected from *any* anti-corruption measures, including criminal ones. Up to a certain moment, it was indeed so. This is well illustrated by the example of governors.

During Boris Yeltsin's presidency, not a single governor was criminally prosecuted for corruption. The first noticeable shifts in this pattern occurred in 2004–2005, when criminal cases on abuse of office and bribery charges were brought against at least 7 governors. However, only two of those resulted in a guilty verdict, and even then, in one case, the real sentence was replaced by a suspended one by the court of appeal, and in the other, the convicted person was granted amnesty immediately after the sentence was pronounced. The same can be said about other top officials. Sometimes, criminal proceedings were initiated against them, but almost never were they sent to prison.

The situation has changed markedly since 2012. Data collected manually for this study show that between January 2013 and October 2024, at least 2 federal ministers and 3 other heads of federal government bodies; 20 federal deputy ministers and 14 other deputy heads of federal government bodies; 14 governors; and 1 deputy head of a state-owned company were prosecuted or arrested on criminal charges. Deputy governors were prosecuted even more frequently. There were at least 66 such cases during this period.[10] These data suggest that, unlike disciplinary sanctions for non-compliance with anti-corruption standards, criminal liability for corruption was applied to top officials. In addition to this fact, at least two other aspects deserve attention and explanation.

First, when Russian top officials were criminally prosecuted during the period under review, it was overwhelmingly on corruption charges. For example, of all the governors criminally prosecuted, only one – Sergei Furgal – was sent to prison on non-corruption grounds.

Second, somewhat paradoxically, criminal sanctions for corruption were stricter on a privileged group of political appointees than on rank-and-file officials. To grasp this, it is necessary to take a closer look at the thesis of accusatory bias, which has become commonplace in the literature on the application of criminal law in Russia (see, for example, Picci 2024; Solomon 2015; Trochev 2014). Accusatory bias means that the acquittal rate is very low, and at the same time, pretrial screening rarely leads to the withdrawal of charges imposed by prosecutors. At first glance, basic statistics on corruption-related criminal cases support this conclusion. For example, only 1–2.5% of passive bribery cases annually have resulted in acquittals during the last 8 years (Table 8.1). However, the picture is somewhat different if we look at additional indicators.

Indeed, Russian courts rarely acquit defendants, but they use various methods that allow, having found a defendant guilty, not to send him or her to jail. These tools significantly mitigate the accusatory bias. The most common of them is a suspended sentence. The same statistics on passive bribery show that, in general, criminal prosecutions of public officials end in actual imprisonment only slightly more often than in suspended sentences (Table 8.2).

TABLE 8.1 Public officials convicted and acquitted in passive bribery cases.

Year	Convicted	Acquitted
2016	1485 (97.70%)	35 (2.30%)
2017	1184 (98.50%)	18 (1.50%)
2018	1171 (98.32%)	20 (1.70%)
2019	1382 (98.22%)	25 (1.78%)
2020	1052 (97.59%)	26 (2.41%)
2021	1214 (99.18%)	10 (0.82%)
2022	1477 (99.19%)	12 (0.81%)
2023	1786 (99.22%)	14 (0.78%)

Source: Judicial Department under the Supreme Court of the Russian Federation 2016-2023.

TABLE 8.2 Public officials sentenced to imprisonment for passive bribery.

Year	Real imprisonment	Suspended sentence
2016	387 (61.04%)	247 (38.96%)
2017	454 (60.05%)	302 (39.95%)
2018	446 (59.39%)	305 (40.61%)
2019	542 (58.59%)	383 (41.41%)
2020	365 (50.69%)	355 (49.31%)
2021	437 (51.78%)	407 (48.22%)
2022	578 (53.62%)	500 (46.38%)
2023	757 (59.19%)	522 (40.81%)

Source: Judicial Department under the Supreme Court of the Russian Federation 2016-2023.

This has been the case in general, but not for political appointees. Both federal ministers and 2 out of 3 other heads of government bodies were sent to jail (one fled abroad); of the 21 deputy federal ministers and other deputy heads of government bodies whose cases were completed by October 2024, 18 were sentenced to real imprisonment while only 2 to suspended sentences (another one fled abroad); of the 14 governors, 9 went to jail, only 2 received suspended sentences (one case was closed after the statute of limitations expired, and 2 fled abroad). Of the 53 deputy governors whose criminal cases were completed by October 2024, 35 ended up in prison, while only 8 got suspended sentences. Thus, if a political appointee was prosecuted for a corruption offence, real imprisonment was a much more likely prospect for him or her than for a lower-level official.

Notable criminal sanctioning of high-level officials might suggest that the Russian political leadership, once it acquired the necessary administrative capacity in the 2010s, truly decided to actively fight corruption at the top level. If this were so, the selective application of new anti-corruption standards and disciplinary sanctions to political appointees discussed in the previous sections could be seen as a minor issue. The failure to apply the innovative soft mechanisms would be at least partly compensated by the use of traditional tough measures. However, the desire of the Russian political leadership to combat corruption among the "tigers" raises significant doubts. At least some facts suggest that criminal sanctioning of top officials has fulfilled some other functions and was not part of a genuine anti-corruption drive.

First, the Russian authorities have demonstrated reluctance to respond to corruption-related information provided by non-profit organisations and the media. On the contrary, those who have published such materials have often been subjected to reprisals. The activities of Alexei Navalny are the most well known but by no means the only case in point. For example, in 2020–2022, the First Anti-Corruption Media published a series of publications on corruption in the Ministry of Defence, including accusations against Deputy Defence Minister Timur Ivanov.[11] There was no official reaction to these revelations. Ivanov and two other Deputy Defence Ministers, as well as several other high-ranking employees of the ministry, were eventually arrested for corruption, but not until 2024. The First Anti-Corruption Media was recognised as a foreign agent in 2021, unsuccessfully tried to challenge this status in court and was eventually forced to cease its activities.

Second, some remarkable details are revealed when diving into the statistics on the sanctioning of top officials. There are some examples of how numerous arrests and prosecutions for corruption in a government body did not result in any legal sanctions against its head and sometimes had no visible negative consequences for him or her. For example, when the wave of arrests in the Ministry of Defence began in 2024, the Minister was sent to resign but was immediately appointed to the position of Secretary of the Security Council. Much less known, but probably more telling, is the situation in the Ministry of Energy, where four deputy ministers were arrested or prosecuted for corruption in 2023–2024. However, the Minister did not face any sanctions and retained his position. This lack of accountability of leaders for failing to prevent corruption, even among their deputies, hardly proves the desire to eradicate corruption at the top level.

An alternative – less complimentary for the national government – explanation for the active use of criminal sanctions against top officials can be found in the strand of literature that looks at corruption and anti-corruption as tools of governance. Some publications are devoted to autocracies in general (see, for example, Amundsen and Jackson 2021; Kukutschka 2018; Hollyer and Wantchekon 2012). Some speak specifically about Russia under Putin (Szakonyi 2024; Gel'man 2022; Min 2021; Kazyrytski 2020; Pavlova 2020; Pavroz 2017; Ledeneva 2011), including the inheritance of a tradition of corruption as a method of government from imperial and Soviet times (Schulze and Zakharov 2018). A number of publications focus on other post-Soviet countries with or without a comparison with Russia (Duvanova 2023; Huss 2020; Zaloznaya 2015). Some publications discuss differences in the use of corruption as a tool of governance in Russia and other countries (e.g. Picci (2024) compares Russia and Brazil, and Chen (2020) considers Russia and China). The relevant aspect is also considered in relation to other autocracies (see, e.g. Carothers 2022), especially China (see, e.g., Ang 2021; Xi et al. 2018).

This literature suggests that authoritarian leaders may be comfortable with the fact that the real income of top officials and higher layers of the bureaucracy is derived not from law-based monetary remuneration but from bestowed and revocable privileges, the most important of which is the unspoken permission to extract illegal rents. On the one hand, turning a blind eye to how officials provide for themselves makes it possible to solve the complicated problem of the government's competitiveness as an employer. The inability – sometimes centuries old – to ensure decent salaries comparable to those in the private sector is compensated by the prospect of achieving a lavish lifestyle through benefits and corrupt rents (see, e.g., Zhuravleva 2016; Schulze et al. 2016). On the other hand, manipulating access to rents helps secure the loyalty and commitment of political elites as well as of their bureaucratic clientele and the population under their control.

In such a system, the primary type of punishment – not in law, but in practice – is reducing or denying opportunities to extract rents.[12] Its mildest form is a transfer to a less prominent position. The harsher punishment is removal from office on various, but primarily non-compromising, grounds. The harshest and most demonstrative sanction is criminal prosecution, usually resulting in imprisonment and confiscation of assets.

Banishment from elite privilege can come for various "misdeeds". These may involve violating informal rules of extracting illegal rents but often do not even relate to corrupt activities. Sanctions may follow a loss in the behind-the-scenes struggle for influence, the failure to fulfil some critical tasks (e.g., demonstrating economic efficiency, providing the necessary level of electoral support, achieving military objectives, etc.), and, of course, any manifestation of disloyalty to those higher up in the patron-client pyramid, much less to the authoritarian leader. The real reason for punishment is often unflattering to the authorities and, thus, is not named. In the case of criminal prosecution, it is hidden behind the official wording of the accusation.

Using criminal sanctions as the harshest punishment may explain the small share of suspended sentences in the verdicts of top officials. It may be reasonably assumed that the decision to prosecute high-ranking appointees is hardly possible without authorisation – at least informal – at the very top of the administrative hierarchy. It is not always about an autocratic leader personally, but still about highly influential persons. If such authorisation is obtained and the decision is taken to really punish and not intimidate a prosecuted person, no court in an authoritarian state will take the liberty to be lenient. When ordinary employees are prosecuted, there is no high-level authorisation, and the courts enjoy greater freedom.

Criminal sanctions for corruption fit well into this system because they are perfectly functional, convenient and sometimes more familiar for authoritarian leaders. They are functional because, better than any other means, they demonstrate to elites the precariousness of their illicit prosperity and the possibility of an instant deep fall if they incur the wrath of their superiors. This is a stick that complements the carrot of access to rents in securing loyalty and cementing the political system. In addition, the political leadership can thus demonstrate to the public or external counterparts its uncompromising fight against corruption and can sometimes attribute fundamental managerial failures to the dishonesty of individual scapegoats. They are convenient – and even more so than criminal sanctions for other offences – because, given the almost universal involvement of top officials in illegal practices, gathering evidence of their wrongdoing does not pose significant difficulties. In Russia, they are familiar because, at least since the mid-1970s, the prosecution of elite members for corruption, carried out mainly by the intelligence services, has been in the arsenal of Soviet management practices and is well known to the current national leadership.[13]

In contrast, disciplinary sanctions for violating anti-corruption standards in such a system of punishments for top officials are redundant. They require unconventional mechanisms but do not bring anything new in terms of managerial functionality. If a disgraced official needs to be rid of, his or her dismissal does not present legal difficulties for the appointing authority. If such a political appointee is to be punished exemplary, criminal penalties for corruption work better than disciplinary ones.

Criminal prosecution of top officials for corruption is also selective but in a different meaning than the previously discussed selectivity in applying anti-corruption standards. In the case of dismissal with a loss of trust and other disciplinary sanctions, the selectivity was group-based – a whole layer of political appointees was excluded from certain provisions, first on paper and then in practice. In the case of criminal enforcement, selectivity is rather individual. Out of many high-ranking appointees presumably involved in corruption, only a few are prosecuted. And the real reason for their punishment is often not those delinquencies that are voiced in the official verdict.

The literature on corruption and anti-corruption as tools of governance provides a reasonable theoretical framework to explain the patterns of selectivity in the application of anti-corruption measures in Russia. It helps to understand why political and bureaucratic elites have been susceptible to criminal prosecution while enjoying almost complete immunity from soft anti-corruption standards and related disciplinary sanctions. It also cautions against an optimistic interpretation of the statistics on criminal sanctioning of high-level officials. The use of harsh punishments was hardly intended to eradicate corruption at the top level. Rather, anti-corruption turned out to be its opposite and was paradoxically used to maintain the stability of a system based on manipulating access to illicit rents.

What Kind of Anti-Corruption Do We Need in a Discordant World?

The Russian case shows how important it is to lift the veil of legislative activity and seemingly impressive official corruption prosecution figures covering national anti-corruption reforms. This is not easy to do, if only because most countries publish aggregate statistics on sanctions, which obscures how they have been applied to different categories and groups of officials. However, if, as stated in the Introduction of this volume, the aim is to look at anti-corruption as it is and not as it should be, it is necessary to find unconventional data sources and explore the workability of the procedures enshrined in the law. Because such a veil may conceal subtle abuse of anti-corruption tools.

The first level problem is fundamental selectivity: the non-application of certain anti-corruption reforms to specific groups, primarily the political and bureaucratic elites. Importantly, this selectivity often occurs not because of an implementation gap but by design. The reform is meant not for everyone and, therefore, initially applies only to rank-and-file employees. Even when the new norms are later extended to the top level, it is done in such a manner that practical implementation of the envisaged procedures is hardly possible.

In Russia, this happened to anti-corruption standards and relevant compliance infrastructure, which were the core of the reforms of the 2000s–2010s. This prompts the question of whether and how similar preventive mechanisms have actually worked in other countries. Like in Russia, recent anti-corruption reforms worldwide have largely focused on non-criminal measures: asset disclosure, conflict of interest regulation, anti-corruption prohibitions and restrictions. It would be intriguing to examine which layers of public officials have actually been affected by such preventive efforts and whether there has been selectivity in their implementation, similar to Russia's or perhaps different.

The second level problem is probably even more important. When making anti-corruption efforts, national political leadership may be guided by very different rationales than an external observer assessing the successes and failures of reforms. In choosing the measures to use and the categories of officials to target, national decision-makers may be driven not primarily by the usefulness of these measures in reducing corruption but by their effectiveness in taking, consolidating and retaining power. Corruption can also be viewed from the same perspective: whether it ensures the loyalty of elites by manipulating access to illicit rents or harms those in power by preventing their decisions from being implemented.

This can result in unpredictable patterns of selectivity, including the one showcased in this chapter. For example, political leadership may be irritated by corruption and lack of managerial discipline at the middle and lower levels of bureaucracy. As a remedy, familiar criminal law tools may be used along with experimentation with new preventive mechanisms. At the very same time, when dealing with high-ranking officials, the authorities may be tolerant of corruption and actively resort to manipulating access to illegal rents to ensure the loyalty of elites. Elements of the anti-corruption toolkit can still be applied to political appointees. However, they are used not to fight corruption but as a convenient element of the system of formal and informal sanctions for various transgressions against those in power.

When considered from a purely anti-corruption point of view, these patterns may look inconsistent. However, when viewed through the lens of power consolidation, they have a certain logic. The Russian case suggests that the fact that something is being done, even actively, under the anti-corruption banner does not necessarily mean that it is being done to reduce corruption. Thus, to advance the fight against corruption in a discordant world, more attention will have to be paid to understanding the true goals and motivations behind anti-corruption endeavours.

Notes

1. Some recent examples include "Rolexgate" in Peru or US Supreme Court Justice Clarence Thomas' unreported luxury gifts.
2. Federal Law of December 25, 2008 No. 273-FZ "On Combating Corruption".
3. Federal Law of July 27, 2004 No. 79-FZ "On Civil Service of the Russian Federation" and Federal Law of March 2, 2007 No. 25-FZ "On Municipal Service in the Russian Federation".
4. This chapter focuses on public officials in the *executive* branch of government. In Russia, they are divided into several categories: (1) federal, regional and municipal (local) public office holders, and (2) state and municipal (local) public servants.

   Apart from the President, federal public office holders include the Prime Minister, federal ministers, the Prosecutor General, etc. They are mostly appointed and dismissed by the President, following a certain procedure.

   The Governor, the most senior public official at the regional level, is both a federal and a regional public office holder. The Governor can be dismissed by the President.

   Regional public office holders include, among others, deputy governors, heads of regional governments and regional ministers, as well as heads of regional public bodies without ministerial status. They are appointed and dismissed by the governors following a certain procedure.

   The federal public service is exercised in three types of public bodies: ministries, agencies, and services. Ministries are headed by ministers. The most senior public service position in a ministry is a deputy minister. Agencies and services are chaired by heads without ministerial status. Unlike federal ministers, heads of agencies and services are not public office holders but public servants. Deputy ministers, as well as heads of agencies and services and their deputies, are appointed by the President or the Government.

In this chapter, the terms "top officials," "high-ranking officials," and "high-ranking appointees" are used interchangeably to refer to public officials appointed and/or dismissed by the President, the Government, or a governor.

5. Article 12.1, "Restrictions and obligations imposed on persons holding public office of the Russian Federation, public office of the constituent entities of the Russian Federation, and municipal offices".
6. Available at https://gossluzhba.gov.ru/reestr
7. To partially solve this problem, a copy of the Register was made every week starting from 30.01.2024. Thus, the information about 3,316 public officials dismissed from 30.01.2019 to 05.08.2024 was available for the study.
8. The press releases can be found at http://www.kremlin.ru/events/councils/by-council/12
9. In at least 2 of these 7 cases, the Presidium discussed the possibility of authorising high-ranking officials to take up employment after leaving office, i.e., it considered issues unrelated to possible violations of anti-corruption legislation. In one more case, the wording used in the press release – "consideration of the results of inspections conducted by the Presidential Anti-Corruption Directorate" – does not clearly show whether the Presidium performed the functions of the Commission.
10. The relevant articles can be found at https://pasmi.ru/tag/timur-ivanov/?ysclid=m5t0yhr3c5321088511.
11. Existing databases on criminal penalties of Russian top officials for corruption, including the database by the Ruxpert project (https://ruxpert.ru/) used, for example, in Zaloznaya and Reisinger (2025), are obviously incomplete. Therefore, for this chapter, relevant data were collected manually from open sources.
12. In Russia, the indicative informal expression *otluchenije ot kormushki* (separation from the feeding trough) is used.
13. Vladimir Putin began his KGB career in the mid-1970s, precisely at the time when KGB chief Yuri Andropov – unusually for the Soviet Union – began using anti-corruption campaigns to strengthen the KGB's position and advance his rise to power (see, e.g., Duhamel 2010; Clark 1993).

References

Amundsen, I. and Jackson, D. 2021, 'Rethinking anti-corruption in de-democratising regimes'. *U4 Anti-Corruption Resource Centre, Chr. Michelsen Institute, U4 Issue 2021:5.*Ang, Y. Y. 2021, *China's gilded age: The paradox of economic boom and vast corruption.* Cambridge University Press.

Black, J. L. 2013, 'The course of Medvedev's campaigns to curb corruption and encourage modernization'. In: Black, J. L. and Johns, M. (Eds.), *Russia after 2012. From Putin to Medvedev to Putin – Continuity, change, or revolution? (1st edition).* Routledge.

Burger, E. S. and Gitau, R. 2010, 'The Russian anti-corruption campaign: Public relations, politics or substantive change?' Georgetown Law Faculty Working Papers, no. 126.

Carothers, C. 2022, *Corruption control in authoritarian regimes: Lessons from East Asia*. Cambridge University Press.

Chen, C. 2020, 'What is behind anti-corruption? A comparison of Russia and China'. *Communist and Post-Communist Studies*, vol. 53, pp. 155–176.

Clark, W. A. 1993, *Crime and punishment in Soviet Officialdom: Combating corruption in the political elite, 1965–1990 (Contemporary Soviet/Post-Soviet politics) (1st edition)*. Routledge.

Duhamel, L. 2010, *The KGB campaign against corruption in Moscow, 1982–1987 (Russian and East European Studies)*. University of Pittsburgh Press.

Duvanova, D. 2023, *Thieves, opportunists, and autocrats: Building regulatory states in Russia and Kazakhstan*. Oxford University Press.

Gel'man, V. 2022, *The politics of bad governance in contemporary Russia*. University of Michigan Press.

Holmes, L. 2012, 'Corruption in Post-Soviet Russia'. *Global Change, Peace & Security*, vol. 24, no. 2, pp. 235–250.

Hollyer J. R. and Wantchekon, L. 2012, October 10, Corruption in autocracies. Working Paper.

Huss, O. 2020, *How corruption and anti-corruption policies sustain hybrid regimes: Strategies of political domination under Ukraine's presidents in 1994–2014 (Soviet and post-Soviet politics and society)*. ibidem Press.

Kazyrytski, L. 2020, 'Fighting corruption in Russia: Its characteristics and purpose'. *Social & Legal Studies*, vol. 29, no. 3, pp. 421–443.

Kukutschka, R. 2018, 'Anti-corruption strategies for authoritarian states'. *U4 Anti-Corruption Resource Centre, Chr. Michelsen Institute, U4 Helpdesk Answer, no. 2018:7.*

Ledeneva, A. 2011, 'Can Medvedev change sistema? Informal networks and public administration in Russia'. In: Kononenko, V. and Moshes, A. (Eds.), *Russia as a network state*. Palgrave Macmillan.

Min, K. 2021, 'Why does Putin refuse to adopt anti-corruption policies? The impact of the governance strategy on political will'. *Korean Corruption Studies Review*, vol. 26, no. 2, pp. 183–209 [in Korean].

Nikolskaya, P., Lowe, C. and Balmforth, R. 2017, 'Ex-Russian minister says he thought bag with $2 million cash was gift of alcohol'. *Reuters*, 27 November, <https://www.reuters.com/article/world/ex-russian-minister-says-he-thought-bag-with-2-million-cash-was-gift-of-alcohol-idUSKBN1DR218/>.

Nwozor, A., Olanrewaju, J. S., Oshewolo, S. and Ake, M. B. 2020, 'Is Nigeria really fighting to win the anti-corruption war? Presidential body language, "string-puppetting" and selective prosecutions'. *Journal of Financial Crime*, vol. 27, no. 2, pp. 601–617.

Pavlova, E. 2020, 'Corrupt governance: Self-defeating anti-corruption rhetoric and initiatives in Russia. New perspectives'. *Interdisciplinary Journal of Central & East European Politics and International Relations*, vol. 28, no. 2, pp. 205–222.

Pavroz, A. 2017, 'Corruption-oriented model of governance in contemporary Russia'. *Communist and Post-Communist Studies*, vol. 50, no. 2, pp. 145–155.

Picci, L. 2024, *Rethinking corruption: Reasons behind the failure of anti-corruption efforts*. Cambridge University Press.

Sapio, F. 2005, 'Implementing anticorruption in the PRC: Patterns of selectivity'. Working papers in contemporary Asian studies, No. 10, Centre for East and South-East Asian Studies, Lund University.

Schulze, G. G. and Zakharov, N. 2018, 'Corruption in Russia – Historic legacy and systemic nature'. CESifo Working Paper, No. 6864, Center for Economic Studies and ifo Institute (CESifo).

Schulze, G. G., Sjahrir, B. S. and Zakharov, N. 2016, 'Corruption in Russia'. *The Journal of Law and Economics*, vol. 59, no. 1, pp. 135–171.

Shashkov, A. 2024. 'Igor Krasnov: Nado lishat korruptsionerov radosti nazhivy' ['Igor Krasnov: We must deprive corrupt officials of the joy of profit'], *TASS*, 9 December, <https://tass.ru/interviews/22606205> [in Russian].

Soghomonyan, A. 2017, 'V Rossii v skorom vremeni poyavitsya reestr lits, uvolennykh v svyazi s utratoy doveriya' ['A register of persons dismissed with a loss of trust will soon appear in Russia'], *Garant.ru*, 20 June, <https://www.garant.ru/news/1118424/> [in Russian].

Solomon, P. H. 2015, 'Understanding Russia's low rate of acquittal: Pretrial screening and the problem of accusatorial bias'. *Review of Central and East European Law*, vol. 40, pp. 1–30.

Szakonyi, D. 2025, 'Corruption and co-optation in autocracy: Evidence from Russia'. *American Political Science Review*, vol. 119, no. 1, pp. 402–419.

Trochev, A. 2014, 'How judges arrest and acquit: Soviet legacies in postcommunist criminal justice'. In: Beissinger, M. and Kotkin, S. (Eds.), *Historical legacies of communism in Russia and Eastern Europe*. Cambridge University Press.

Xi, T., Yao, Y. and Zhang, Q. 2018, 'Purifying the Leviathan: The anti-corruption campaign and changing governance models in China'. Working Paper, National School of Development Peking University.

Zaloznaya, M. 2015, 'Does authoritarianism breed corruption? Reconsidering the relationship between authoritarian governance and corrupt exchanges in bureaucracies'. *Law & Social Inquiry*, vol. 49, no. 2, pp. 345–376.

Zaloznaya, M. and Reisinger, W. M. 2025, 'A little too little, a little too late: The political impact of Russia's anti-corruption enforcement'. *Laws*, vol. 14, no. 2, p. 20.

Zhan, J. V. and Zhu, J. 2023, 'Policy coordination and selective corruption control in China'. *Policy Studies Journal*, vol. 51, no. 3, pp. 685–702.

Zhuravleva, T. L. 2016, 'Socialnye lgoty, garantii zanyatosti i korrupciya: chto "shtrafuet" byudzhetnikov' ['Social benefits, job security and corruption: What "fines" state employees'], Working Paper, <http://dx.doi.org/10.2139/ssrn.2832819> [in Russian].

PART IV
Innovation

9

CIVIL SOCIETY IN AN ADVERSE ENVIRONMENT

Transparency International Bangladesh

Nurul Huda Sakib, Sahabuddin Ahmed, and Inge Amundsen

A Hostile Environment

In Bangladesh, corruption has been pervasive since independence, under both military and civilian governments. In 2022, Bangladesh ranked as the 12th most corrupt country among the 180 countries of Transparency International (TI)'s *Corruption Perceptions Index* (CPI), and it was predicted to continue at this level for decades (The Business Standard 2023). It has been argued repeatedly that corruption is a major obstacle to economic development, and many believe that removing corruption from Bangladesh will be impossible because almost every sector is infected with the malpractice (Chakravorty 2023: 73). In Bangladesh, corruption is systemic and endemic, deeply woven into the fabric of society, economy, and politics (Mustafa 2024).

It has also been argued that in Bangladesh, like in other developing countries, "culture" is a significant cause of corruption. Sakib (2019a) maintained that when people focus on personal progress, they can easily become part of a traditional practice of corruption. Citizens of Bangladesh are supporting systemic corruption by trying to get hassle-free public or private services and to make some extra money out of their assigned public posts (Sakib 2019a, Chakravorty 2023: 79). At the same time, corruption in Bangladesh has led to an unequal society where a large portion of the population has limited access to services (Iftekharuzzaman 2022).

The government of Bangladesh has taken different anti-corruption initiatives at different times, but most of those efforts have failed due to dysfunctional institutions and the absence of political will to curb corruption. For instance, big businessmen heavily dominate the parliament, giving them the collective power to pass laws that thwart anti-corruption initiatives (Islam

DOI: 10.4324/9781003531920-13

2024, Amundsen 2014). In fact, political leaders have provided security and impunity to the corruptors, due to entrenched patron-client relationships (Islam 2013: 148). The government's *Anti-corruption Commission*, a key institution to combat corruption, has lacked independence and been plagued by internal and external corruption (Daily Star 2019), and is nothing but an isomorphic mimicry (Sakib 2020: 222).

The lack of political will to curb corruption in Bangladesh is noted by many observers. According to Rahman (2021: 1, 3), high-profile political actors are reportedly embroiled in various corruption and embezzlement scandals, and the anti-corruption efforts in Bangladesh have faltered in recent years particularly because they are often politicized.

The link between increasing authoritarianism and the politicization of anti-corruption has been evident in Bangladesh. The (late) government headed by Prime Minister Sheikh Hasina and the ruling party *Awami League* (AL) tightened its grip on power by cracking down on free speech, harassing opposition parties, arresting critics, and censoring the media (Rahman 2021: 3), at the same time as both political and bureaucratic corruption soared. According to Ali Riaz (2020), the government's "anti-corruption drive" fizzled out, with only low-level operatives netted while bigwigs remained untouched.

In this hostile environment, with increasing authoritarianism, politicized government anti-corruption policies and institutions, and a systemic crackdown on civil society and the media, the vacuum was nevertheless filled with various social movements and civil society organizations such as *Transparency International Bangladesh* (TIB). TIB, in particular, made a tremendous effort in fighting corruption in Bangladesh, as well as strengthening people's voice and demand for an efficient, transparent, and accountable system of politics and business (CPSDG 2022).

In this chapter we are focusing on TIB's role as a civil society organization contesting corruption in Bangladesh, and how TIB has survived and managed to operate in an increasingly hostile environment. We are demonstrating how TIB, through a mix of Transparency International standard strategies and some very innovative approaches, has managed to dodge the worst forms of government suppression and continued its work. Most of these strategies have been a continuous balancing act. TIB has even managed to bring out some government institutions to respond positively to its initiatives.

In doing so, we have collected data from sources like reports and studies, newspapers, blog posts, and national and international organizations' websites. Additionally, we have interviewed some key stakeholders to get their views.

Please note, however, that on the 5th of August 2024, the authoritarian Prime Minister of Bangladesh, Sheikh Hasina, and the *Awami League* (AL) government were ousted from power, following weeks of student-led mass protests, known as the *July Revolution* and the *Students–People's Uprising*.

Three days later, an interim government led by Nobel laureate Professor Muhammad Yunus was sworn in. Thus, our story on TIB covers the period prior to the regime change.

The Space for Civil Society

Civil society is composed of voluntary, autonomous institutions that provide an opportunity to voice citizen concerns and to pursue certain goals, such as ensuring good governance or protecting democracy. Landell-Mills (1999) pointed out that civil society can play a crucial role in articulating public concerns and identifying ways to reduce corruption, and added that without considerable public pressure, governments are unlikely to foster the transparency and accountability needed to curb malfeasance by public officials.

According to Ali Riaz (2019), NGOs can fill some of the political vacuum, but at the same time, the backsliding of Bangladesh into a hybrid and increasingly authoritarian regime has restricted how far the anti-corruption activities of civil society and NGOs can go. In Bangladesh, we have seen that civil society groups that criticize the government or pose a threat to its legitimacy are co-opted, politicized, polarized, and/or controlled by the state apparatus (Islam 2023: 60, 61, Tasnim 2017: 99, 102, 119).

Like in other authoritarian countries, a large number of NGOs and civil society organizations in Bangladesh have also been created by the government and ruling party, and these and some others have been working actively to promote the interest of the government, thus purposefully compressing and diverting the scope of dissent.

In Bangladesh, some NGOs have, however, managed to dodge co-optation and control and have been visible and somewhat influential. Some have also been directly involved in promoting good governance and anti-corruption, like TIB, *Shushashoner Jonno Nagorik* (SUJAN, "Citizens for Good Governance"), *Brotee* (a human rights organisation), *Election Working Group* (EWG), and *Centre for Policy Dialogue* (CPD, independent think-tank) (Mollah 2020: 486).

Over many years, TIB has been considered the most successful of the anti-corruption and good governance organizations in Bangladesh. "TIB's activities have significant direct and indirect impacts" (Knox and Yasmin 2007: 5), and

> TIB has played a key role in addressing both the demand and supply sides of corruption in Bangladesh [... and it] has been instrumental in placing corruption on the political agenda and pushing for institutional reforms on the one hand and helping citizens raise their voice against the practice on the other.
>
> *(Khair 2014: 118)*

TI Bangladesh

TIB is an independent, non-partisan, and non-profit organization in Bangladesh dedicated to combating corruption through public awareness and civic engagement. It was established in 1996 and registered under the *NGO Affairs Bureau*. It is the accredited national chapter of *Transparency International* (TI), with which it cooperates, but it operates independently in terms of strategy and program implementation. TIB raises funds from donors aligned with its anti-corruption mission, avoiding any financial contributions that may compromise its independence. Its finances are transparently audited, with funds sourced from a trust fund and donor organizations in the United Kingdom (UK Aid), Switzerland (SDC), the Netherlands (BZ), and Sweden (SIDA) for specific projects.

TIB has approximately 100 members, approved by TIB, who are "individuals of integrity" representing diverse professional identities. In addition, the TIB structure includes a Board of Trustees which is the highest policy-making body, a General Assembly, an Executive Director, an Ombudsperson, a staff of 178 people, and several groups of volunteers. The staff is organized in five divisions (Civic Engagement, Finance and Administration, Management Support Unit, Outreach and Communication, Research and Policy), and 95 of the staff work outside of Dhaka. Among the volunteers, the *Committees of Concerned Citizens* (CCC) operate in 45 areas of the country, and there are 61 *Youth Engagement and Support* (YES) groups (TIB website, updated September 2024).

Research

TIB conducts thorough, evidence-based research, primarily using in-house resources with occasional external expertise, to investigate corruption across public and private sectors and to recommend policies for better governance. TIB's research initiatives include *Diagnostic Studies*, *Monitoring the National Integrity System*, *Citizens' Report Cards*, and *National Household Surveys* (NHS) (TIB website 2024).

Although most research reports, like the *Parliament Watch series*, the *Election Process Tracking*, and the *Integrity in Public Administration* reports, report on government accountability, transparency, and integrity in broad terms, TIB highlights corruption in public institutions and how government officials and public representatives use their positions for personal enrichment (even when TIB does not release any report that may directly or indirectly implicate individuals) (TIB website 2024). TIB has also uncovered monopolistic practices, ethical violations, and the business-politics nexus that sustains corrupt practices, like, for instance, in the TIB report on the private bus transport business (Forhad et al. 2024).

A key initiative of TIB is the household surveys, which measure the corruption households face when accessing services and ranks institutions based on corruption levels. TIB also examines key institutions and strategic areas like appointments, promotions, and disciplinary actions concerning top government officials in the public administration, in the parliament, in roads and highways development projects, etc. (for examples, see TIB 2019a, TIB 2022a, TIB 2024a, TIB 2024b).

All of TIB's publications (research reports, policy briefs, news, press releases, etc.) are published in Bangla language, with most research publications also having a summary in English. By publishing both in the national language and in English, TIB has laid a solid groundwork for knowledge sharing, for engaging citizens, and for influencing government policies.

TIB has also been very explicit in stating the methodology it has been using in its research and data collection. In addition to information checks and cross-checks and a rigorous review process on all research reports, TIB has upheld the principle of always including a detailed description of the adopted methodology (TIB website 2024). This has made it very difficult to question TIB's expertise and to attack TIB's findings. Besides, several hundred academic articles, based on findings from TIB, have been published by local and international scholars.

Advocacy

TIB's advocacy programs aim to engage citizens in anti-corruption efforts, influence government policies, and drive policy reforms. Through meetings, dialogues, news conferences, and media statements, TIB engages policymakers and senior officials. It uses tools like *Policy Briefs*, *Position Papers*, the *Corruption Perception Index* (CPI), and *Concept Notes* in its advocacy efforts. For example, in 2023, TIB criticized the draft *Cyber Security Act* (CSA) as a mere rebranding of the controversial *Digital Security Act* (DSA), urging the government to revise the draft law (see TIB 2023a).

TIB has also provided recommendations during policy discussions, in *Recommendations* and in *Press Releases*, and in press conferences, with some being accepted, like in the *Data Protection Act* of 2023. However, the government has been very selective in adopting TIB's recommendations, favoring those that do not challenge government objectives. TIB's *Policy Briefs* outline strategies to maximize policy outcomes, such as recommending a "zero tolerance on corruption" policy for donor-funded projects (see TIB 2024c: 3). *Concept Notes* are prepared for events like Anti-Corruption Day, Women's Day, and Environment Day, reminding the government (and the public) of the government's commitments under treaties and laws. TIB also releases news and commentaries to contest government malpractice, such as condemning law enforcement's excessive force during the *July Revolution* (see TIB 2024d).

All of this demonstrates that TIB has a very wide focus going beyond a narrow interpretation of the term anti-corruption: TIB is concerned with broad governance issues. This broad approach is also endorsed by the international development agencies that are supporting TIB. The *Swiss Agency for Development* (SDC) for instance, which has been supporting TIB since 2009, states that "with a shrinking civil society space, the importance of having actors such as TIB is becoming even more pertinent", and notes that TIB aims at

> strengthening the governance system bottom-up – by promoting citizens' voice […] to demand for equitable service delivery, accountability and transparency – and top-down – by influencing and improving policies.
>
> *(SDC 2024)*

Citizen Engagement

TIB actively involves Bangladeshis in the fight against corruption through its innovative programs like the *Committees of Concerned Citizens* (CCC) and *Youth Engagement and Support* (YES) groups, *Active Citizen Groups* (ACG), and the *Young Professionals Against Corruption* (YPAC).

TIB operates 45 CCCs across the country, mainly led by the youth. The members of the CCCs are credible and respected members tasked with promoting integrity and challenging corruption at the local level. The YES group consists of students from different universities and colleges, and the ACG groups are local people who are service recipients of different institutions. YPLC is a network of young professionals who were once part of TIB's YES groups, who actively participate in TIB's advocacy and awareness initiatives. The latter three organizations are assisting the CCCs.

These bodies are working to enhance institutional integrity in five sectors: education, health, local government, climate finance governance, and land administration, through evidence-based advocacy and active involvement with relevant actors (TIB 2022b). However, as it requires long-term and meticulous awareness-building campaigns to make local people aware of the negative effects of corruption and to make them aware of their rights, TIB developed the so-called "Road Theatre Shows", where artistes illustrate how corruption takes place and how it directly and indirectly impacts society.

Other initiatives have also been taken to raise awareness and to ensure that a wide range of citizens are participating. Campaigns, seminars, civic gatherings, workshops, webinars, exhibitions, and information rallies have been held. TIB has also been running its flagship *Anti-Corruption Cartoon Competition* every year, which has attracted 3,230 participants since 2006. Similarly, TIB's *National Inter-University Anti-Corruption Debate Competition*, the *Moot Court Competition*, and the *Investigative Journalism Awards* program engage students and young journalists in discussions on governance and corruption, fostering critical thinking and intellectual discourse (TIB 2023b, TIB 2024e). According to their latest annual report (July 2022 to June 2023), TIB claims to have "engaged" 247,995 people in 6,015 events throughout the country (TIB 2022b: 33).

TIB also focuses on empowering people by directly addressing officials of key government service sectors like health, education, local government, land, and environment. For example, events like the *Open Budget Programme* that was organized by Madaripur Municipality in June 2022 promoted direct communication between citizens and officials (TIB 2022c). Public hearings organized by the CCC in Kushtia in November 2023 helped about one hundred complainants have their issues resolved by the *Kushtia Land Office* (TIB 2023c).

TIB's Active Citizens' Groups (ACG) have also been instrumental in improving governance in primary schools and community health clinics at the local level. TIB equips ACG and YES members with the knowledge and tools to monitor technical aspects of local projects, such as road construction, improving oversight on material quality and use.

Technology and media are integral to TIB's transparency efforts. Its website offers access to reports, activities, and data, while the *PACTApp* provides guidance on corruption-related issues, primarily for CCC and YES members. Although TIB has a significant following on social media, the engagement levels remain quite low, as none of their Facebook posts have received more than 1,000 reactions. However, TIB is recognized as a trusted platform for citizens to submit corruption complaints, as TIB forwards these to the relevant government bodies for action.

TIB maintains strong relationships with national and international media outlets, such as *The Daily Star* and *BBC*, ensuring their reports and activities reach a broad audience. Furthermore, TIB actively fosters partnerships and collaborations with organizations like *Article 19* and *Digital Rights* (TIB 2024f).

TIB has also been fostering investigative journalism in Bangladesh with its *Investigative Journalism Awards* programme for the last 25 years. This initiative aims to acknowledge and motivate journalists who play a crucial role in exposing corruption, enhancing transparency, and ensuring accountability of those in power (Financial Express 2024). Furthermore, TIB actively promotes data journalism in Bangladesh by providing training and organizing workshops aimed at university students from journalism departments and members of journalist associations (TIB 2023d).

Youth

As mentioned, TIB has strategically and specifically mobilized young people in Bangladesh on a broader level, with the use of brainstorming activities, competitions, awards, training, and entertainment incorporated into their civic engagement programmes and groups, enabling young people to generate ideas and put them into action. The basis is TIB's *Youth Engagement and Support* (YES) groups and the *Young Professionals Against Corruption* (YPAC). CCC and ACG groups have been trained on how to use social media safely under the strict cyber laws, and this training of the youth on how to navigate and use social media while protecting themselves from potential government harm under the cyber act has been essential.

At the same time, the strategic mobilization of the youth by TIB coincided with several other initiatives taken by young people in Bangladesh to improve their situation. One example is the *Road Safety Movement* that mobilized in 2018 after the death of several students in road accidents (even when it led to little improvement in the road safety situation) (Palma 2024). The youth was already feeling deprived and ignored by the authorities. Most important, however, was the so-called *quota protests.* In June 2024, the government once again suggested reserving a quota of government jobs to the "freedom fighters" of the liberation war – and their families. As students understood this to be another privilege for the ruling party families and a restriction to merit-based jobs, it triggered the massive student protests that eventually led to the regime's downfall.

TIB and the Government

The relationship between TIB and the government has been one of collaboration, mutual criticism, and multiple efforts by the government to restrict,

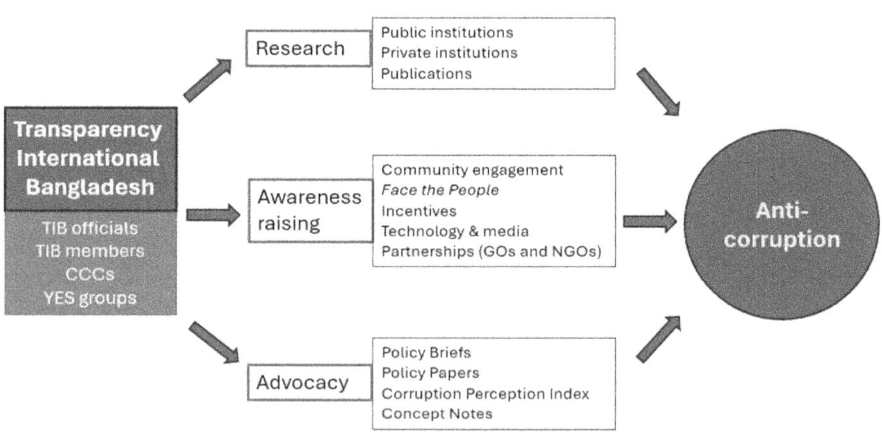

FIGURE 9.1 Anti-corruption techniques of TIB.

Source: Developed by the authors.

control, and curb TIB's activities. The level of democracy and respect for human rights had been declining over several years (Amundsen 2018), and the Gothenburg University V-Dem Institute categorized Bangladesh as an "electoral autocracy" and as an "autocratizing country" (V-Dem 2024: 13, V-Dem 2020: 19, 45). The last general elections, in January 2024, were characterized by observers and foreign governments as very violent and not free and fair (Reuters 2024a). Dissent was stifled, elections were engineered, and political violence, arbitrary arrests, extrajudicial killings, enforced disappearance of opposition figures, and even torture were reported (ASK 2024, Amnesty International 2024).

Cooperation

Nevertheless, TIB was able to criticize the government and to cooperate with some government agencies, especially with some special institutions and at the level of local government, in a process that oscillated for years.

In 2019, TIB established a collaborative framework with the government, cemented by *Memorandums of Understanding* (MoU) with the *Anti-Corruption Commission* (ACC) and the *Information Commission* (TIB 2019b). This laid the groundwork for a multifaceted partnership involving citizen engagement, joint events, knowledge sharing, and capacity building initiatives aimed at fostering a transparent and accountable governance framework in Bangladesh.

One significant aspect of this collaboration is TIB's educational and training initiatives. For example, in June 2024, TIB held a day-long training session on *Basic Research Methodology* for ten senior officials of the ACC, aiming to enhance their capabilities in effectively tackling corruption (TIB 2024g). This training was part of TIB's broader strategy to influence the ACC's operations and policies. To its great achievement, the ACC came to include some of TIB's findings on corruption in its annual reports submitted to the government.

Before these formal collaborations were established, TIB was advocating for and facilitating institutional reforms within the ACC. The *Bureau of Anti-Corruption* (BAC) existed before the ACC, and TIB made a massive effort to establish a reformed ACC. TIB also actively worked to pass the *Anti-Corruption Act* in 2004 by the then government (Sakib 2019b).

Moreover, TIB and the *Information Commission* worked together to promote transparency through the media. TIB successfully negotiated free broadcasting slots for various anti-corruption themed broadcasts on television. This media engagement was supplemented by public events such as the joint organization of an *Information Fair* in Khulna in February 2024, where 27 institutions, including 24 government entities, participated. It served as a platform to educate the public on the *Right to Information* (RTI) Act of 2009 (TIB 2024g).

In the realm of policy formulation, some TIB's contributions have been particularly notable. At the request of the Ministry of Finance, TIB prepared the country's first *Gold Policy*, which was approved in 2018 (Byron 2018). This policy was aimed at preventing gold smuggling and establishing a transparent domestic gold market. More recently, TIB and Article 19 were invited to assist in formulating the draft of the *National Artificial Intelligence* (AI) Policy 2024 (TIB 2024i).

Criticism

TIB has criticized the government not only for corruption, but also for the weaknesses of the government's anti-corruption efforts and institutions. In 2014, for instance, TIB stated in a policy brief that the ACC was "a toothless tiger" that based its filing and withdrawal of cases on political considerations (TIB 2014: 3). TIB thus proposed amendments to the *Anti-Corruption Act* to ensure more independence and less government control over the commission. TIB was also a vocal advocate for granting the ACC increased powers to investigate cases of money laundering and financial fraud (Abdullah 2023).

TIB has actively monitored ACC's work and repeatedly called for reforms to prevent government interference in the commission's investigations and decisions. TIB's continuous pressure led to several debates in parliament and the media about the need for greater autonomy for the ACC, (Reza et al. 2020: 13).

Government Response

As TIB promoted the rule of law, free and fair elections, human rights, accountability, and transparency – and was furthermore a part of the German-based *Transparency International* network, the previous government treated TIB suspiciously as an agent of the West. The government regarded criticism as defamation, misinformation – and treason.

The reaction of the previous government to the research reports, press releases, and commentaries issued by TIB was predominantly negative. All since TI published the first global *Corruption Perceptions Index* (CPI) report in 2001, which identified Bangladesh as being at the top of the list of countries perceived as highly corrupt, the Awami League government said the index was nothing but a "conspiracy" to discredit the party before the elections, which was to be held some months later (Anam 2024).

The publicity apparatus of the ruling party followed up when TIB was formed in 1996, with a "concerted tirade against this newly formed body", claiming undue foreign influence. At the same time, the praise of TIB by the biggest opposition party "knew no bounds" (Anam 2024). The positions flipped to the opposite when the *Bangladesh Nationalist Party* (BNP) came to power. When in power, the BNP refused to accept the CPI score and claimed TIB was an NGO serving a western agenda, whereas the AL in opposition welcomed the CPI and tried to use the narrative of a "top corrupted country" to win the next election (Begum and Sakib 2010: 57-58). Positions then flipped again twice, until the Awami League finally gained the upper hand in 2014 and ruled for the next decade.

The consistent adversarial stance across the different administrations often framed TIB as a proxy for the opposition party. Different governments accused TIB of being an anti-government force, dedicated to harming the image of government. TIB allegedly wanted to destroy the government's authority and legitimacy by fostering a negative perception both domestically and internationally of a government mired in corruption. The government's attitude toward TIB was always hostile and bitter, as the TIB consistently scrutinized the government's activities and presented its findings in different public forums.

An illustrative recent example is the reaction to the TIB report titled *12th National Parliament Election Process Tracking*, which meticulously dissected the election proceedings and revealed "systemic failures that posed a significant threat to the foundations of the country's democracy" (see TIB 2024j). In response, government ministers accused TIB of parroting the views of the opposition party BNP, going as far as labeling it an agent of the opposition (Anam 2024). The Awami League rejected the report as one-sided, anti-government, absurd, and full of nonsense, while the BNP welcomed it, considering it a reflection of public opinion (Jugantor 2024). Awami League General Secretary Obaidul Quader, who was also Minister of Road Transport and Bridges, said in a press conference that the report was one-sided, anti-government, and unrealistic. "They speak in the language that BNP speaks. They are the agents of BNP" (cited in BSS News 2024).

In an interview in June 2024 with *Civicus* (a global civil society alliance), the Executive Director of TIB, Iftekhar Zaman, said that

> Any critical report we or some other CSOs publish is accused of playing into the hands of the political opposition. We are often called "anti-state" or "conspiratorial." The government accuses CSOs, independent journalists and media of misinformation or disinformation, although in the absence of legal definition of these terms, these are interpreted subjectively and used for targeted intimidation and control. Based on these accusations, they have also continued to push for more repressive laws.
>
> *(Civicus 2024)*

In addition to ridicule and allegations of being a destructive proxy for the opposition and foreign interests, the former government also actively used *lawfare* (the use of repressive laws) against civil society in Bangladesh, and these legal maneuvers also included restrictions on TIB.

There were legal barriers to the formation, establishment, and registration of CSOs in Bangladesh (including requirements of a high number of minimum members, a furnished office, a high registration fee, the registration and declaration of any funding from external sources, etc.), as well as barriers to operational activity (the government can suspend activities of a CSO or even cancel its registration for the non-submission of reports to its respective registration authority, and 334 CSOs were canceled for alleged "unlawful activities" – with no right to appeal). CSOs were also subject to government harassment, like frequent inspections, requests for documents, etc. (ICNL 2024).

Two laws in particular, the *Information and Communication Technology* (Amendment) *Act* of 2013 (the ICT Act) and the *Digital Security Act* (DSA) of 2018 were met by massive criticism by national and international human rights organizations and observers for their illiberal content, for restricting the freedom of expression in Bangladesh, and for hindering civil society, the opposition, and the work of journalists.

According to the US Department of State (2024) report on human rights in Bangladesh in 2023, the DSA was increasingly used against speech found on social media, websites, and other digital platforms, including for commentators living outside of the country.

> The DSA, passed ostensibly to reduce cybercrime, provided for sentences of up to life imprisonment for spreading "propaganda" against the Bangladesh Liberation War, the national anthem, or the national flag. Throughout the year the government widely used the DSA against persons criticizing the government. Media and the law minister reported over 7,000 DSA cases pending across the country, with one nongovernmental organization (NGO) reporting police brought cases against 20 children aged 13 to 17 years.
>
> *(US Department of State 2024: 21)*

After this massive international and national criticism of the draconian law, a revised *Cyber Security Act* (CSA) was approved by cabinet in August and by the parliament in September 2023. According to Nadia Rahman, Amnesty International's interim deputy regional director for South Asia, the revised law is not any better, however (Amnesty International 2023). The new law is essentially a rebranded version of its predecessor, the DSA (US Department of State 2024: 22, Rezwan 2023).

Furthermore, the Sheikh Hasina regime also sought to neutralize opponents through strategic manipulation of institutions, where key institutions of oversight and control, like the *Anti-Corruption Commission*, the *Election Commission*, and the *Human Rights Commission* were deeply politicized and made ineffective (Civicus 2024). Real and perceived opposition figures in politics, civil society, and the media were also co-opted (Lorch 2021: 84, Nipaa and Hasan 2023: 95, Sahoo and Chaney 2021: 113).

The most infamous example of the political use of the government's *Anti-Corruption Commission* was in June 2024 when the ACC submitted a charge sheet against Muhammad Yunus and six others of Grameen Telecom for the alleged misappropriation of 252.2 million Bangladeshi Taka (US$ 2 million) of the Grameen Telecom Workers' Profit Participation Fund, and for money laundering. Professor Yunus is the founder of the *Grameen Bank* and a pioneer of microcredit and microfinance (for which he was awarded the Nobel Peace Prize in 2006), and in 2007 he openly considered entering politics by forming a new political party. This idea sparked the ire of Sheikh Hasina, who at the time accused him of "sucking blood from the poor", and in 2011, Hasina's government removed him as head of Grameen Bank, saying that at 73, he had stayed on past the legal retirement age of 60 (Reuters 2024b, Associated Press 2024).

In December 2023, the *CIVICUS Monitor*, which is monitoring the state of civil society and civic freedoms in the world, downgraded Bangladesh's civic space rating from "repressed" to "closed" – the worst category (Civicus 2024).

However, TIB's integrity and the strengths of TIB's research, advocacy, and its wide outreach, coupled with its national and international network and foreign financial backing, prevented the government from threatening TIB in the same way as it did with other critics.

TIB's Survival Strategy

TIB pursued several strategies for survival and for continuing its operations in this hostile environment. Most of these strategies have been a continuous balancing act, because all strategies are met with resistance by some and a risk of resistance.

First of all, TIB avoided direct criticism of individuals within the regime. The entire TI movement refrains from investigating individuals, and TIB was always explicit in this: "TIB is not an investigation agency. It does not investigate individual cases of corruption, nor does it release any report that may directly or indirectly implicate any individual" (TIB website 2024). TIB kept silent whereas others named and shamed people with links to the country's Prime Minister, like for instance in Al Jazeera's Investigative Unit's damning reporting from 2021: *All the Prime Minister's Men* (Al Jazeera 2021).

Massive political corruption, particularly in money laundering, the energy sector, stock market, and tender manipulations (favoritism), the looting of banks in the name of loans, embezzlement, and human trafficking were, reportedly, regular practices in the previous government, and high-profile political actors were reportedly embroiled in endemic corruption and embezzlement. Government ministers, ruling party bigwigs, and businessmen close to the government and the allies of the government were the profiteers of massive political corruption. Crony capitalism appeared as a powerful scenario of the body politic in Bangladesh where politicians, businessmen, and bureaucrats collaborated (Mustafa 2024, Parvez 2024, Rahman 2021, Sakib 2022).

By this restraint, TIB avoided the wrath and repercussions by government insiders and close allies who may otherwise have felt incriminated and may have turned the government's full force against TIB. A focus on the "big fish" could have endangered TIB's operations and even its personnel. The risks involved in exposing cronyism and elite corruption made it difficult for civil society organizations to pursue these targets, in particular in this hostile environment with a complete lack of legal protection. Several of our interviewees confirmed that TIB had chosen to avoid confrontations with individual government officials and rather chosen to go for contests against institutionalized corruption, with "these small storms expected to result in thunder."

Secondly, TIB's ability to engage citizens, and the youth in particular, provided TIB both with credibility, strength, and protection against government crackdowns. With Committees of Concerned Citizens (CCC) all over the country, TIB was very visible, and a violent suppression of the organization would be too costly for the government. An innovative twist was to work at the local level through the CCCs, instead of under the banner of TIB. Due to the general acceptance and respect of the CCC members, the CCCs had a strong standing at the local level. As one TIB official stated,

> The government officials cannot deny the calibre of the CCC members. They are all respected persons and kind of leaders in the society. Therefore, when they visit government officials for collaboration or information, they are hesitant to refuse them. But if we go under the name of TIB, we might be turned down.
>
> *(Personal communication, 9 July 2024)*

Thirdly, TIB pursued cooperation with some local governments and institutions at the lower level of the government hierarchy. As TIB operated in a system where neo-patrimonial dynamics and behaviors overshadow legal-rational principles, the organization was careful not to push lower-level officials to cooperate with TIB. TIB knew that institutional heads would avoid engagement with TIB in order to maintain smooth professional lives. As one TIB official expressed it,

> Literally, the Deputy Secretaries are deputed as a head or deputy director of different public institutions for a few years as an initial for the promotion in the secretariat pyramid. Therefore, they do not want to confront the TIB. They presume, if they pass the tenure without any hazards, their promotion is granted. Then, why will they give floor to the TIB, particularly who are famous for uncovering institutional shortcomings. As a result, our continuous letters to the heads, most of the time, remain unresponsive.
>
> *(Personal communication, 8 July 2024)*

In most cases, the lack of will for cooperation was evident. Stakeholder meetings with TIB, the public, and institutions were often hindered by certain subdepartments and government institutions not sending their representatives, or by plain bureaucratic resistance, leaving proper discussions unachieved.

Thus, TIB used their own network of informal or personal connections to pursue cooperation, knowing that certain officials were sympathetic to TIB's approach and findings, sensitive to the local engagement that TIB mobilized, and interested in addressing the concerns raised by TIB. Despite all the unfavorable comments and claims that TIB's agenda was politically driven, one of our interviewees was of the opinion that

> They are internally positive and externally negative. If they do not counter the findings in public, it will mean accepting their failures to obtain good governance.
>
> *(Personal communication, 8 July 2024)*

Fifth, the fact that TIB was and is fully financed by donors like the United Kingdom, Switzerland, the Netherlands, and Sweden, gave TIB some security although this was at the same time a vulnerability and a point of criticism. It made TIB vulnerable to the insecurity of donor funding and open to criticism in line with the criticism of other donor-dependent NGOs: possible misalignment between the mission of the organization and the interests of its financial backers. However, any introduction of the legal provision as seen in Russia and other anti-Western autocracies that NGOs receiving foreign funding should register as – and include a disclaimer in all their communications – that they are "foreign agents" was never suggested by the Bangladeshi government. In fact, European countries provide significant economic assistance to Bangladesh, and the government has therefore always been careful to maintain good relations with its donors.

Finally, TIB has sought cooperation with the media, both within Bangladesh and beyond. This has provided some protection, at the same time as it has been a double-edged sword because some of the government-controlled and/or government-owned mainstream media tended to present TIB's research findings in a manner that turned the government fiery against TIB. An official of TIB stated that

> Every media house has their own agenda. A few months back, a mainstream newspaper of Bangladesh highlighted a certain portion of our report that does not represent the gist of this report. The key findings of this report were totally ignored. The following day, the government expressed their negative remarks on the credibility of the report.
>
> *(Personal Communication, 8 July 2024)*

Conclusions

In sum, TIB managed well the balancing act of operating and engaging with the (previous) government of Bangladesh, without suffering any major repercussions from this very corrupt and hostile government. In contrast to for instance the human rights organization Odhikar – which saw its funds being frozen, its registration withdrawn, and its founder and director being arrested and charged with "cyber crimes" under the ICT Act for reporting the fact that 61 people were killed by security forces in an operation carried out in May 2013 (HRW 2013) – there are no reports of any violent attacks on individuals TIB leaders.

TIB pursued several strategies to accomplish this, of which the standard TI principle of *not* investigating and naming and blaming individuals was, and is, one of the main precautions. By this restraint, TIB avoided the wrath and repercussions by government insiders.

Furthermore, TIB's rigorous research and data collection methodology made it difficult to question TIB's expertise and findings, and TIB's broad engagement with citizen groups, and youth groups in particular, provided TIB with some protection against government crackdowns. Even autocratic governments need a minimum of popular support to remain in power (and we saw what happened in Bangladesh when this support was gone). TIB's innovative twist in this respect was to work at the local level through the CCCs, instead of under the banner of TIB.

TIB has also pursued cooperation with some local governments and institutions at the lower level of the government hierarchy, even when bureaucrats and politicians have preferred to avoid engagement with TIB to safeguard their positions. By using their network of informal and personal connections and by finding win-win situations, TIB has been able to pursue cooperation and make some officials admit faults and failures and to promise improvements – in public. Furthermore, TIB has sought cooperation with a number of other NGOs and the media, not only for outreach purposes but also for protection.

An assessment of TIB's impact on corruption and governance in Bangladesh is way beyond the purpose of our study of the organization. We have, however, identified two strong success criteria that we will highlight, in addition to the noticeable (obvious) parallel between TIB's deliberate and successful strategy of mobilizing the youth on the one hand, and on the other the fact that the successful 2024 revolution was initiated and led by students and youth.

The first is TIB's engagement of CCCs, ACGs, and YES groups, which was pioneering in terms of public awareness and can serve as a model for the rest of the globe. Secondly, TIB made a reputation of impartiality and professionalism that put it in a unique position to assist the interim government in reducing the economic and politically destructive forces of corruption and thereby in laying the groundwork for the necessary improvements in democracy and governance that the Bangladeshis called for by ousting the former government.

After the ousting of the authoritarian government in August 2024, the interim government nominated TIB's Executive Director to head the new *Anti-Corruption Reform Commission*, which will propose reforms to make the existing ACC a more effective, independent, and impartial institution (Dhaka Tribune 2024). Furthermore, TIB's research and reports have been used actively by the new interim government to take action against corrupt individuals of the former regime, as demonstrated when TIB's allegations against 41 ministers and MPs led to an investigation by the ACC (The Daily Star 2024).

References

Abdullah, Mamun (2023): *ACC seeks more powers to investigate money laundering cases.* Dhaka Tribune, 30 March 2023 (https://www.dhakatribune.com/bangladesh/307963/acc-seeks-more-powers-to-investigate-money, accessed 9 August 2024).

Al Jazeera (2021): All the Prime Minister's men. Reports and podcasts of Al Jazeera's investigative unit, February 2021 (www.ajiunit.com/investigation/all-the-prime-ministers-men/, accessed 10 November 2024).

Amnesty International (2023): *Bangladesh: Government must remove draconian provisions from the Draft Cyber Security Act.* Amnesty International, News, 31 August 2023 (www.amnesty.org/en/latest/news/2023/08/bangladesh-government-must-remove-draconian-provisions-from-the-draft-cyber-security-act/, accessed 7 November 2024).

Amnesty International (2024): *Bangladesh 2023.* London, Amnesty International Report 2023/24, 24 April 2024 (www.amnesty.org/en/location/asia-and-the-pacific/south-asia/bangladesh/report-bangladesh/, accessed 10 November 2024).

Amundsen, Inge (2018): *Democracy decaying in Bangladesh.* East Asia Forum, 6 March 2018 (https://eastasiaforum.org/2018/03/06/democracy-decaying-in-bangladesh/#more-113001, accessed 7 November 2024).

Amundsen, Inge (2014): *'Pay up and off you go!' Buying political positions in Bangladesh.* In Søreide, T. and A. Williams: Corruption, grabbing and development: Real world challenges, Edward Elgar Publishing.

Anam, Mahfuz (2024): TIB: The forever 'villain'? The Daily Star, 26 January 2024 (https://www.thedailystar.net/opinion/views/the-third-view/news/tib-the-forever-villain-3528166, accessed 12 August 2024).

ASK (2024): *Statistics on human rights violations.* Dhaka, Ain o Salish Kendra (ASK) (www.askbd.org/ask/statistics-on-human-rights-violations, accessed 10 November 2024).

Associated Press (2024): *Bangladesh court indicts Nobel laureate Muhammad Yunus and others on charges of embezzlement.* AP News, by Julhas Alam, 12 June 2024 (https://apnews.com/article/yunus-microcredit-bangladesh-corruption-case-grameen-174083c69d04ecd35b969cb9e10ea86b, accessed 10 November 2024).

Begum, T. and N.H. Sakib (2010): *Combating corruption in Bangladesh: Role of the anti-corruption commission.* In A.M.A Hasanuzzaman and A. Shamsul (eds): Political management in Bangladesh, pp. 249–270. Dhaka, AH: Development Publishing House.

BSS News (2024): *TIB report is one-sided, anti-government and unrealistic: Quader.* 18 January 2024 (www.bssnews.net/news-flash/168715, accessed 10 November 2024).

Byron, Rejaul Karim (2018): Govt approves country's first gold policy. *The Daily Star*, 4 October 2018 (www.thedailystar.net/frontpage/news/govt-approves-countrys-first-gold-policy-1642414, accessed 12 August 2024).

Chakravorty, N. N. Tarun (2023): Corruption in Bangladesh: Background, causes and current scenario. *Journal of Leadership, Accountability and Ethics*, 20(1), 71–83. (https://doi.org/10.33423/jlae.v20i1.6002, accessed 27 October 2024).

Civicus (2024): *Bangladesh: 'Civic space is the victim of zero-sum game politics and dysfunctional democratic institutions.* Interview, 21 June 2024 (https://civicus.org/index.php/media-resources/news/interviews/7102-bangladesh-civic-space-is-the-victim-of-zero-sum-game-politics-and-dysfunctional-democratic-institutions, accessed 8 November 2024).

CPSDG (2022): *Activities and engagements by TIB.* Citizen's Platform for SDGs (CPSDG), 22 May 2022 (https://bdplatform4sdgs.net/activities-and-engagements-by-tib/, accessed 27 October 2024).

Daily Star (2019): Mizan, Basir sued. *Star Online Report*, 16 July 2019 (www.thedailystar.net/country/ex-dig-mizan-acc-director-basir-sued-1772305, accessed 10 November 2024).

Dhaka Tribune (2024): *Profiles of chair and members of Anti-Corruption Reform Commission.* News report by Nawaz Farhin Antara, 14 October 2024 (www.dhakatribune.com/bangladesh/corruption/361768/profiles-of-chair-and-members-of-anti-corruption, accessed 7 November 2024).

Financial Express (2024): FE journalist gets TIB's IJ fellowship 2023. Financial Express, FE Online Report, 26 February 2024 (https://thefinancialexpress.com.bd/national/fe-journalist-gets-tibs-ij-fellowship, accessed 10 August 2024).

Forhad, Md. Nuruzzaman, Farhana Rahman and Md. Nure Alam (2024): *Integrity in private bus transport business.* Dhaka, TIB, 5 March 2024 (www.ti-bangladesh.org/images/2024/report/bus-transport/Executive-Summary-Private-Bus-Transport-Business-en.pdf?v=1.1, accessed 1 November 2024).

HRW (2023): *Bangladesh: Quash conviction and release rights defenders. Leaders of prominent rights group convicted on trumped-up charges.* New York, Human Rights Watch (HRW), 14 September 2023 (www.hrw.org/news/2023/09/14/bangladesh-quash-conviction-and-release-rights-defenders, accessed 11 November 2023).

ICNL (2024): *Civic freedom monitor, Bangladesh.* Washington/DC, International Center for Not-for-Profit Law (ICNL), 7 November 2024 (www.icnl.org/resources/civic-freedom-monitor/bangladesh, accessed 8 November 2024).

Iftekharuzzaman (2022): The unjust and discriminatory face of corruption. *The Daily Star*, 11 September 2022 (https://www.thedailystar.net/opinion/views/news/the-unjust-and-discriminatory-face-corruption-3116811, accessed 12 August 2024).

Islam, Mohammad Mozahidul (2013): The toxic politics of Bangladesh: A bipolar competitive neopatrimonial state? *Asian Journal of Political Science*, 2(2), 148–168, DOI: 10.1080/02185377.2013.823799 (https://www.tandfonline.com/doi/abs/10.1080/02185377.2013.823799, accessed 27 October 2024).

Islam, Mohammad Mozahidul (2023): *Why nations fail to feed the poor: The politics of food security in Bangladesh.* New York, Routledge.

Islam, Shadique Mahbub (2024): *Why is Bangladesh so weak at fighting corruption?* The Business Standard, TBS News (https://www.tbsnews.net/features/panorama/why-bangladesh-so-weak-fighting-corruption-779666, accessed 10 August 2024).

Jugantor (2024): *AL slams TIB, BNP lauds it.* Dhaka, Jugantor Report (in Bangla), 19 January 2024 (https://www.jugantor.com/politics/764925, accessed 8 November 2024).

Khair, Sumaiya (2014): UNCAC and civil society activism against corruption in Bangladesh. *Chapter in the Asian Yearbook of International Law*, 20, 115–162 (https://brill.com/display/book/edcoll/9789004379770/BP000005.xml, accessed 27 October 2024).

Knox, Colin and Tahera Yasmin (2007): *Transparency international Bangladesh impact assessment.* Governance and Social Development Resource Centre (GSDRC), 29 November 2007 (https://internationalbudget.org/wp-content/uploads/Transparency-International-Bangladesh-Impact-Assessment.pdf, accessed 27 October 2024).

Landell-Mills, Pierre (1999): *Mobilizing civil society to fight corruption in Bangladesh.* World Bank, PREM Note No 30 October 1999 (https://openknowledge.worldbank.org/entities/publication/8f74863c-2486-5ec9-a19a-d290f8294c1d, accessed 18 August 2024).

Lorch, Jasmin (2021): Elite capture, civil society and democratic backsliding in Bangladesh, Thailand and the Philippines. *Democratization*, 28(1), 81–102 (https://doi.org/10.1080/13510347.2020.1842360 , accessed 10 November 2024).

Mollah, Md. Awal Hossain (2020): *Role of civil society in Bangladesh: Challenges and prospects*, in Momen et al. (eds) (2020): *Building sustainable communities: Civil society response in South Asia*, Palgrave, Singapore, pp. 481–495 (https://ideas.repec.org/h/spr/sprchp/978-981-15-2393-9_23.html, accessed 27 October 2024).

Mustafa, Kallol (2024): How the Hasina regime became so unpopular. *The Daily Star*, 5 October 2024 (https://thegreatwave.thedailystar.net/news/how-the-hasina-regime-became-so-unpopular, accessed 10 October 2024).

Nipaa, Meherun Nisa and Mehedi Hasan (2023): The role of civil society in promoting good governance: A qualitative inquiry into bangladesh's experience. *Socio Economy and Policy Studies* (SEPS) 3(2), 91-97 (http://doi.org/10.26480/seps.02.2023.91.97, accessed 10 November 2024).

Palma, Porimol (2024): Bangladesh must listen to its youth. *UCA News,* 26 July 2024 (www.ucanews.com/news/bangladesh-must-listen-to-its-youth/105850, accessed 10 January 2025).

Parvez, Sohel (2024): Hasina's 15-year rule: A regime of crony capitalists. *The Daily Star*, 7 September 2024 (https://www.thedailystar.net/business/economy/news/regime-crony-capitalists-3696296, accessed 7 September 2024).

Rahman, Kaunain (2021): *Bangladesh: Overview of corruption and anti-corruption.* U4 Helpdesk Answer 2021:13. CMI/U4 and TI, 16 August 2021 (https://www.u4.no/publications/bangladesh-overview-of-corruption-and-anti-corruption.pdf, accessed 27 October 2024).

Reuters (2024a): *US says Bangladesh elections were not free and fair.* By Kanishka Singh, 9 January 2024 (www.reuters.com/world/asia-pacific/us-says-bangladesh-elections-were-not-free-fair-2024-01-08/, accessed 7 November 2024).

Reuters (2024b): *When Sheikh Hasina accused Nobel Winner Muhammad Yunus of "sucking blood Of poor".* Reuters, 6 August 2024 (republished in NDTV World, www.ndtv.com/world-news/when-sheikh-hasina-accused-nobel-winner-muhammad-yunus-of-sucking-blood-of-poor-6275083, accessed 7 November 2024).

Reza, Md. Hashem, Kamrun Nahar Jharna and Md. Nasir Uddin (2020): Performance and effectiveness of the anti-corruption commission in Bangladesh. *Journal of Public Administration*, 2(4), 13-24. (https://sryahwapublications.com/article/pdf/2642-8318.0204002, accessed 7 November 2024).

Rezwan (2023): The government of Bangladesh quietly passed the new Cyber Security Act 2023. *Global Voices*, 19 September 2023 (https://globalvoices.org/2023/09/19/the-government-of-bangladesh-quietly-passed-the-new-cyber-security-act-2023/, accessed 7 November 2024).

Riaz, Ali (2019): *Voting in a hybrid regime: Explaining the 2018 Bangladeshi election.* Singapore, Palgrave Macmillan.

Riaz, Ali (2020): *Bangladesh's authoritarian shift.* East Asia Forum, 18 January 2020. (https://eastasiaforum.org/2020/01/18/bangladeshs-authoritarian-shift/, accessed 27 October 2024).

Sahoo, Sarbeswar and Paul Chaney (2021): *Civil society and citizenship in India and Bangladesh.* New Dehli, Bloomsbury Publishing.

Sakib, Nurul Huda (2019a): Understanding cultural causes of corruption: The case of Bangladesh. *International Journal of Research and Innovation in Social Science* (IJRISS), 3(5), 359–368. (https://rsisinternational.org/virtual-library/papers/understanding-cultural-causes-of-corruption-the-case-of-bangladesh/, accessed 9 August 2024).

Sakib, Nurul Huda (2019b): One size does not fit all: an analysis of the corruption preventative approach of the Anti-Corruption Commission (ACC) in Bangladesh. *Asian Journal of Political Science*, 27(2), 211–234 (https://doi.org/10.1080/02185377.2019.1642773, accessed 9 August 2024).

Sakib, Nural Huda (2020): Institutional isomorphism of anti-corruption agency: The case of anti-corruption commission in Bangladesh. *Chinese Political Science Review*, 5(3), 222–252, https://doi.org/10.1007/s41111-020-00143-4.

Sakib, Nurul Huda (2022): *Community organizing in anti-corruption initiatives through spontaneous participation: Bangladesh perspective. Community Development Journal*, 57 (2), 360–379, https://doi.org/10.1093/cdj/bsaa027

SDC (2024): *PACTA - Participatory Action Against Corruption: Towards Transparency and Accountability.* Project document, 29 July 2024 (https://www.eda.admin.ch/deza/en/home/countries/bangladesh.html/content/dezaprojects/SDC/en/2020/7F10458/phase1, accessed 3 November 2024).

Tasnim, Farhat (2017): *Politicized civil society in Bangladesh: Case study Analyses.* Cosmopolitan Civil Societies: An Interdisciplinary Journal, 9(1), 98-123 (https://epress.lib.uts.edu.au/journals/index.php/mcs/article/view/5247, accessed 27 October 2024).

The Business Standard (2023): Bangladesh 12th most corrupt country in the world, 2nd in S Asia. *TBS News*, 31 January 2023. (www.tbsnews.net/bangladesh/corruption/bangladesh-remains-one-most-corrupt-countries-south-asia-corruption-perception, accessed 11 August 2024).

The Daily Star (2024): Corruption allegations: ACC to investigate 41 ex-ministers, MPs. By Dipan Nandy. *The Daily Star*, 20 August 2024 (www.thedailystar.net/news/bangladesh/crime-justice/news/corruption-allegations-acc-investigate-41-ex-ministers-mps-3681426, accessed 10 September 2024).

TIB (2014): Anti-Corruption Commission. Dhaka, *TIB Policy Brief* 37, September 2014 (www.ti-bangladesh.org/images/2014/pb-37-nicsa_acc_14_en.pdf, accessed 7 November 2024).

TIB (2019a): *Integrity in public administration: Policies and practices.* Executive Summary. By Mohua Rouf, 23 June 2019 (www.ti-bangladesh.org/images/2019/report/public-administration/Public-Admin-EX-English.pdf).

TIB (2019b): *ACC and TIB to continue joint activities against corruption.* Dhaka, 7 October 2019, (www.ti-bangladesh.org/public/index.php/articles/story/5912, accessed 15 August, 2024).

TIB (2022a): *Corruption in Service Sectors: National Household Survey 2021.* Extended Executive Summary. Dhaka, TIB, 31 August 2022 (www.ti-bangladesh.org/images/2021/report/nhs/NHS-2021-Extended-Executive-Summary-En.pdf , accessed 17 August, 2024).

TIB (2022b): *Annual report 2021-22.* Dhaka, TIB, 2022 (www.ti-bangladesh.org/images/assets/1726405474_TIB-annual-report-2022-2023.pdf, accessed 27 August 2024).

TIB (2022c): *Madaripur municipality declares final budget committing highest priority on citizen service.* Dhaka, TIB, 14 June 2022 (www.ti-bangladesh.org/articles/citizens-engagement/6617, accessed 18 August 2024).

TIB (2023a): *Digital Security Act 2018 and the draft Cyber Security Act 2023: A Comparative Analysis.* Dhaka, TIB, 30 August 2023 (www.ti-bangladesh.org/upload/files/position-paper/2023/Position-paper-on-Digital-Security-Act-2018-and-Draft-Cyber-Security-Act-2023.pdf , accessed 18 August 2024).

TIB (2023b): *CCC's public hearing in Kushtia: AC (land) advocates direct contact, discourages broker involvement.* Dhaka, TIB, 6 November 2023 (https://ti-bangladesh.org/articles/citizens-engagement/6865, accessed 19 August 2024).

TIB (2023c): *Intense battle for wit and wisdom: TIB's anti-corruption debate championship crowned JUDO as champions.* Dhaka, TIB, 23 September 2023 (www.ti-bangladesh.org/articles/story/6767, accessed 18 August 2024).

TIB (2023d): *Data journalism workshop held at JU to promote evidence-based reporting.* Dhaka, TIB, 19 March 2023 (www.ti-bangladesh.org/public/index.php/articles/story/6657, accessed 17 August 2024).

TIB (2024a): *Parliament watch. 11th national parliament.* Dhaka, TIB Report, 27 May 2024. (www.ti-bangladesh.org/images/2024/report/pw/Parliament-watch-11th-Parliament-Executive-Summary-En.pdf , accessed 11 August 2024).

TIB (2024b): *Governance challenges in the implementation of roads and highways' development projects.* Dhaka, TIB Executive Summary (in English), 9 October 2024 (https://www.ti-bangladesh.org/images/2024/report/RHD/Executive-Summary-RHD-Governance-Challenges-en.pdf, accessed 2 November 2024).

TIB (2024c): *Accessing Green Climate Fund (GCF) for vulnerable countries like Bangladesh: Governance challenges and way forward.* Dhaka, TIB Policy Brief 144/2024, May 2024 (www.ti-bangladesh.org/upload/files/policy-brief/2024/Policy-Brief-Green-Climate-Fund-144.pdf, accessed 12 August, 2024).

TIB (2024d): *Move away from blame game and confrontational power politics.* Dhaka, TIB, 23 July 2024 (www.ti-bangladesh.org/articles/commentary/7043, accessed 2 November 2024).

TIB (2024e): *Third TIB-DUMCS anti-corruption moot court competition on 6-9 March.* Dhaka, TIB, 6 March 2024 (www.ti-bangladesh.org/articles/story/6935, accessed 18 August 2024).

TIB (2024f): *Article-19 and TIB call for comprehensive personal data protection act.* Dhaka, TIB, 28 April 2024 (www.ti-bangladesh.org/articles/story/6972, accessed 7 August 2024).

TIB (2024g): *TIB provides research skills training to ACC officials.* Dhaka, TIB, 30 July 2024, (www.ti-bangladesh.org/articles/story/7049, accessed 17 August 2024).

TIB (2024h): *Information fair in Khulna to promote RTI awareness.* Dhaka, TIB, 13 February 2024 (https://ti-bangladesh.org/articles/citizens-engagement/6951, accessed 14 August 2024).

TIB (2024i): *Involve all stakeholders, including civil rights organizations, in formulating AI policy: TIB, Article 19.* Dhaka, TIB, 3 April 2024 (www.ti-bangladesh.org/articles/press-release/6956, accessed 7 November 2024).

TIB (2024j): *12th National Parliament Election Process Tracking.* Dhaka, 29 May 2024, TIB report https://ti-bangladesh.org/images/2024/report/ept/Executive-Summary-Election-Process-Tracking-English.pdf?v=1.6 (English summary), accessed 8 November 2024).

TIB website (2024): *Research themes/areas* and *our organisation.* TIB website at www.ti-bangladesh.org/ (www.ti-bangladesh.org/research and www.ti-bangladesh.org/our-organization, accessed 1 November 2024).

US Department of State (2024): *Bangladesh 2023 human rights report.* Washington, US Department of State, Bureau of Democracy, Human Rights and Labor, Country Reports on Human Rights Practices, 22 April 2024 (www.state.gov/reports/2023-country-reports-on-human-rights-practices/bangladesh/, accessed 7 November 2024).

V-Dem (2020): *Democracy report 2020. Autocratization surges – Resistance grows.* University of Gothenburg, Varieties of Democracy (V-Dem) Institute (www.v-dem.net/media/filer_public/f0/5d/f05d46d8-626f-4b20-8e4e-53d4b134bfcb/democracy_report_2020_low.pdf, accessed 7 November 2024).
V-Dem (2024): *Democracy report 2024. Democracy winning and losing at the ballot.* University of Gothenburg, Varieties of Democracy (V-Dem) Institute (https://v-dem.net/documents/44/v-dem_dr2024_highres.pdf, accessed 7 November 2024).

10

ANTI-CORRUPTION WITH A HUMAN RIGHTS LENS

Latin American Experiences of Innovation Amid Contestation

Daniela Cepeda Cuadrado

Systemic corruption and human rights violations are chronic issues in Latin America. Since the 20th century, the region has faced waves of autocratic regimes, with corruption serving to consolidate their power and facilitate human rights violations (Nash and Fuchs, 2019). Endemic corruption, as a precursor to impunity, has also allowed violence to take root in this region (Mejías, 2022). At the same time, Latin America boasts a strong regional human rights system designed to protect rights and advocate for anti-impunity measures (CIDH, n.d.), and it has made significant strides in enacting laws and establishing internal and external mechanisms to tackle corruption (Tablante and Antoniazzi, 2018). This is indeed a region of contrasts: while it possesses the institutional frameworks to address corruption and promote human rights, corruption remains widespread and human rights violations endure.

Latin America's paradoxical context is no exception to this rule: As is the case globally, anti-corruption instruments have generally concentrated on the misappropriation of resources and its impact on the economic and political stability of states. They have failed to reveal how corruption creates structural problems, such as inequality and discrimination, which harm the very people that states are meant to protect (Geneva Academy and UNHCHR, 2016).

Several institutions now acknowledge this. In 2019, the Inter-American Commission of Human Rights (IACHR or the Commission) recognised the importance of having a victim-centred approach in corruption cases. The UN Human Rights Council has endorsed several resolutions on the negative impact of corruption on human rights, and UNODC has committed to mainstreaming human rights in anti-corruption programming (IACHR, 2019; Falconi *et al.*, 2023; Human Rights Council, 2023; UNODC, 2023).

DOI: 10.4324/9781003531920-14

While there is growing realisation that corruption enables human rights violations, there is still a gap between anti-corruption discourse and practice. This is due to multiple challenges, including how to measure and quantify corruption's impact on human rights, how to establish causation and identify victims of corruption, and how to conduct strategic litigation in states that are unwilling or unable to identify and redress victims of corruption in penal, administrative, civil or preventative processes.

Despite these challenges, there is a growing number of voices questioning the effectiveness of anti-corruption efforts separate from those focused on human rights. In this context of contestation, innovative approaches have emerged in Latin America to connect both agendas. Based on a thorough literature review and key informant interviews,[1] this chapter presents examples from Colombia, Honduras, Mexico, and Venezuela, where both state and non-state actors have addressed the aforementioned challenges. In Colombia, the government has developed an indicator to measure the impact of corruption on human rights. In Honduras, Mexico, and Venezuela, civil society organisations (CSOs) have sought to assert their victim status in corruption cases that have affected them – either directly or indirectly. Their various strategies have been shaped by their countries' regulatory environments and windows of opportunity. All of these initiatives illustrate how locally grounded efforts have emerged to align the human rights and anti-corruption agendas in response to the increasing dissent against anti-corruption approaches that overlook the impact of corruption on people.

The Evolving Nexus: Anti-Corruption and Human Rights

Corruption hinders States' ability to protect, fulfil, and promote human rights. Resources lost to corruption are lost opportunities to invest in public services, undermining people's economic, social, and cultural (ECOSOC) rights. Corruption can also infiltrate the executive, legal, and judicial branches of power, threatening the accessibility and quality of electoral processes, judicial independence, and the rule of law. Corruption undermines public trust and represents a menace to the rights to due process, political participation, information, and property (Geneva Academy and UNHCHR, 2016; Falconi *et al.*, 2023).

Despite the clear linkages, international commitments on anti-corruption and human rights emerged separately. The earliest initiatives to address corruption happened in the 1990s when trade liberalisation took off and corruption was seen as an impediment to efficient business competition (IACHR, 2019). Since then, international anti-corruption instruments have aimed to equip the states with tools to tackle corruption through 'prevention, criminalisation, international cooperation, and the recovery of stolen assets' (Geneva Academy and UNHCHR, 2016).

Human rights commitments surfaced much earlier, in the 1940s. Committed to not repeating the experiences of World War II, countries established the United Nations and an associated Commission of Human Rights. In the 1990s, several Latin American countries were under peace and transitional justice processes, which required a stronger understanding of the role of human rights in advancing social justice (IACHR, 2019). Human rights instruments have focused on how to identify, protect, and repair victims, as well as developing concrete obligations for States to protect, fulfil, and promote human rights (Geneva Academy and UNHCHR, 2016; Barkhouse, Hoyland and Limon, 2018).

Since the start of the 21st century, there has been a growing understanding that it will not be possible to advance human rights in states where corruption is rampant and unaddressed (IACHR, 2019). Both corruption and human rights violations weaken the rule of law. Consequently, addressing these issues should be part of the same agenda (IACHR, 2019).

Internationally, the UN system has gradually acknowledged this. The United Nations Convention Against Corruption (UNCAC) advances key areas of human rights, such as access to information; participation in decision-making, non-discrimination, and special consideration to specific populations; the right to a fair trial and due process; whistleblowing protection; and international cooperation and asset recovery – including compensation and reparation of victims (UNODC, 2004). However, as the UNCAC does not commit States to implement its provisions following human rights standards, States' implementation is not necessarily linked to their human rights obligations (UNODC, n.d.).

The Human Rights Council (HRC) has also endorsed several resolutions on the negative impact of corruption on the enjoyment of human rights from 2012 to 2025 and had a Special Rapporteur on this issue in 2004 and 2009 (OHCHR, n.d.b; UN HRC, 2025). Nonetheless, the Centre for Civil and Political Rights reviewed all Concluding Observations adopted by the UN Treaty Bodies between 2007 and 2017 and found that corruption was addressed in limited provisions (Mutzenberg, 2018).

At the Inter-American level, the Organisation of American States (OAS) houses the Inter-American Convention against Corruption (IACC) and its associated follow-up mechanism for its implementation. The IACC advances the right of freedom of expression through its commitment to the protection of whistleblowers, and the right of freedom of association through its commitment to mechanisms that encourage civil society participation. Yet, it has not made an explicit link between corruption and human rights (OAS, 1996).

OAS' approach to human rights has been more vociferous about the link. OAS' Inter-American Court on Human Rights has ruled on several cases highlighting corruption's impact on human rights since 2009, having the greatest impact in the field of access to information. Nonetheless, there is more work to do to move beyond penal measures when addressing corruption, highlight its links to discrimination, protect whistleblowers, adapt evidentiary standards, and ensure that reparations include institutional reforms to prevent recurrence (Nash-Rojas, Bascuñan and Meza-Lopehandía, 2014). Additionally, the OAS' IACHR recognises in two of its latest resolutions (2017 and 2018) that corruption restricts the full enjoyment of human rights and is strongly linked to impunity (IACHR, 2019). In 2019, IACHR published its most comprehensive reports on the subject, illustrating the ways corruption and human rights violations intersect in the region and providing recommendations for States to address corruption from a human rights perspective (IACHR, 2019). The problem lies in its execution, as there is no current focal point to implement it (UNCAC Coalition, 2024).

Challenges in Grounding Commitments

There is still a significant gap in grounding global and regional commitments at the national level. There are three key, interrelated challenges: measuring and quantifying corruption's impact on human rights, establishing causality and identifying corruption victims, and once identified, conducting strategic litigation in states that are unwilling/unable to redress them.

First, there is the issue of causality. Ramiro Orias, human rights lawyer from the Due Process of Law Foundation (DPLF), explained that the real challenge is *'to differentiate between corruption as a context for these violations and corruption as a constitutive act of the violation'* (Interview, 2024). Corruption is understood as a cause, in a legal sense, when the proximity between the corrupt act and the human rights violation is close and strong. However, it is more likely to find corruption as one of several factors contributing to human rights violations. In these scenarios, lawyers need to prove that corruption is still a sine-qua-non condition despite all other contributing factors (Peters, 2018). However, even when the sine-qua-non condition is clear, this may not be sufficient to establish corruption as a *legal cause*. The linkage may be too remote, too old, or there are too many independent intervening acts (Interview with Roht-Arriaza, 2024).

Moreover, corruption's covert nature makes it hard to measure and quantify its human rights costs (Wickberg, 2013; Falconi *et al.*, 2023). Corruption thrives in secrecy, limiting opportunities to collect 'hard' data on its incidence and impact. Therefore, 'the challenge is to identify what to measure and the nature of the corruption damage that one wants to measure, which is also typically extremely challenging to quantify, particularly when the focus is on specific populations and contexts' (Wickberg, 2013, p.2).

Since causality is difficult to determine, this also complicates the identification of corruption victims. In some cases, especially those on petty corruption, there are individuals or communities whose rights are directly affected and can be identified. However, systemic corruption can also affect diffuse interests – that is, the rights of all members of society. Asserting victimhood then becomes incredibly difficult (Falconi *et al.*, 2023).

Even when there are clear victims, bringing them to participate in corruption cases is challenging. They might not know that they are victims (Falconi *et al.*, 2023). If they do, they might not have sufficient legal expertise and financial resources to engage in cases. Human Rights lawyer Dr Naomi Roht-Arriaza recognises that *'litigation is hard, time-consuming, and resource-consuming, and most victims of corruption are not people with time, energy, and money'* (Interview, 2024).

When victims are ready to participate, they face different obstacles. While it is gradually changing, many legal systems still consider the State as the only party affected in grand corruption cases. This has enabled judges and prosecutors to keep the legal processes airtight (Hawley, 2016). Prosecutors are also unlikely to provide space for victims, fearing they can second-guess their decisions and slow them down (Interview with Roht-Arriaza, 2024). Moreover, in many Latin American countries, the agencies responsible for investigating and prosecuting corruption cases are also co-opted by corruption. It is unlikely to have a transparent and independent judicial system ready to incorporate victims into cases (Interview with Adriana Greaves, Lawyer and Co-Director of TOJIL, México, 2024).

Nonetheless, enabling victims' participation in corruption cases has positive effects: it is a way to recognise their grievances and secure some form of redress. It also helps enhance transparency and accountability in corruption cases. Victims can be helpful to a prosecutorial mission, bringing evidence prosecutors may not have access to, monitoring the case, and keeping prosecutors' actions in check (Interview with Roht-Arriaza, 2024).

Supported by a strong regional stance on the link between anti-corruption and human rights, both government and civil society actors in Latin America are devising innovative strategies to converge on both agendas. Context-specific initiatives in Colombia, Honduras, Mexico, and Venezuela are showing a way forward.

Quantifying Corruption's Human Rights Costs: Colombia's RADAR

In December 2023, Colombia's Transparency Secretariat launched RADAR: an indicator that measures corruption's impact on ECOSOC rights (Secretaría de Transparencia, 2023). In its first cycle, RADAR measured its impact on the right to education. RADAR follows a multivariate statistical approach to summarise the associations between 43 variables related to corruption (observable and hidden), institutional capacity, and the right to education (Secretaría de Transparencia, n.d.). Its higher values reflect a stronger negative association between corruption and the violation of this right. Colombia's outer regions, where most marginalised communities reside, scored the highest RADAR values (Secretaría de Transparencia, n.d.).

RADAR conducts a principal components analysis and an exploratory factor analysis to select the most robust variables and corroborate that their correlations are statistically significant (Secretaría de Transparencia, n.d.). It follows a pioneering methodological approach to measure corruption's impact on human rights. In addition to data from sanctions, complaints, and news related to corruption, RADAR also includes proxy variables to measure non-observable corruption. These include data related to security risks, the digital divide, and illiteracy. Data on security risks were essential,

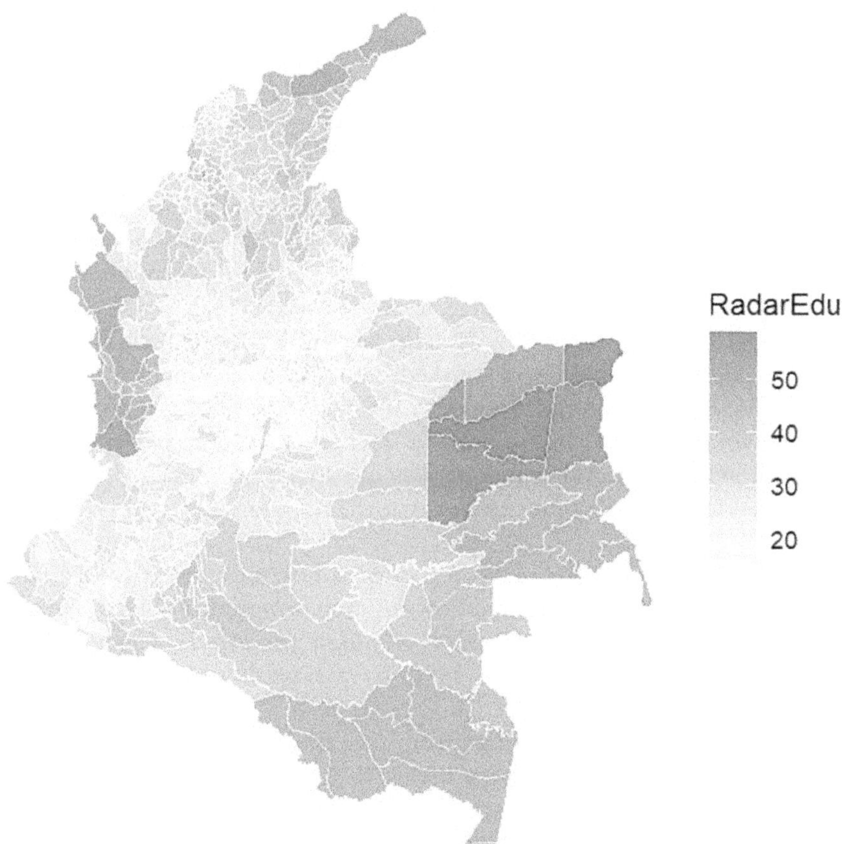

FIGURE 10.1 RADAR's findings per municipality.

Taken from the Secretariat's report on RADAR(Secretaría de Transparencia, n.d.).

as reporting corruption is unlikely to happen in territories where there is forced displacement and the presence of illegal armed groups (Secretaría de Transparencia, n.d.).

This is the first time the Transparency Secretariat has developed a composite indicator on corruption and human rights, demonstrating the national government's commitment to linking both agendas. There were two key windows of opportunity for RADAR's emergence:

First, the 2021 national protests – also known as *Estallido Social* – and the associated human rights violations experienced during this time led to the election of the first left-wing national government in 2022, which committed to the fulfilment of human rights (Colombia Informa, 2023). The guarantee of rights is a cross-cutting policy, which the Secretariat has sought to mainstream in its institutional strategy (Interview with the Secretariat's Innovation Team, 2024). Second, the Secretariat is under the leadership of former Human Rights Director of Bogotá's mayorship, Andrés Idárraga Franco, who has spearheaded the development of RADAR:

> One of the discussions that the Secretary has been emphatic about is that corruption is not only an issue that is reduced to the person captured, but it is an issue that affects the dignity and the rights of communities and territories.
> *(Interview with Christian Lesmes, Researcher at the Secretariat, 2024)*

RADAR has been a useful tool for the Secretariat, both technically and politically. As the national agency tasked with the development of anti-corruption policies, the Secretariat seeks to advance the rights of reportage and whistleblower protection. It also aims to strengthen local capacity to engage in resource monitoring and reporting acts of corruption. RADAR's data has enabled the identification of territories that the Secretariat should prioritise:

> RADAR allows us to have a heat map. It is how we present information about the violation of rights and how we can then guide public policy.
> *(Interview with Mauricio Pinzón, Coordinator of the Secretariat's Innovation team, 2024)*

RADAR also enables the Secretariat to advance the National Anti-Corruption Strategy (NACS) (Alianza Gobierno Abierto Colombia, 2023). It can provide useful information for Ministries' implementation of their commitments under NACS. The Secretariat has already shared its findings with the Ministry of Education (Interview with the Secretariat's Innovation Team, 2024).

The Secretariat recognises that RADAR's impact largely depends on the extent to which other actors also engage with its findings. Nonetheless, its development has been in-house and with limited consultation with other state and non-state actors. This may represent a challenge for buy-in from both national and local stakeholders in the future.

Moreover, there are still some methodological challenges the team is currently tackling. First, there is no centralised system to record reports/complaints on corruption, which limits data collection. Second, the indicator does not yet have a variable that measures institutional trust, but this is in progress (Secretaría de Transparencia, n.d.). Third, while RADAR has indicators to measure quality, permanence, and coverage, its methodological approach does not yet measure all the different dimensions of accessibility (physical and economic accessibility as well as non-discrimination); acceptability (relevance and cultural appropriateness); and adaptability (OHCHR, n.d.a).

RADAR's existence is nonetheless a testament to the power of political will in aligning anti-corruption efforts with human rights. RADAR represents a shift in how the Colombian government understands corruption, recognising it no longer as a victimless crime but as a serious violation that demands accountability. In a region where there is limited political will to jointly address corruption and human rights, Colombia exemplifies how government leadership can bridge the gaps between both agendas – in this case, through leveraging data. Enhancing coordination among local and national, state and non-state actors could further support efforts to align them.

Forging new paths for corruption victims: How a Honduran Indigenous group asserted victim status through advocacy and strategic litigation

In 2021, the Constitutional Chamber of the Supreme Court of Justice of Honduras granted a constitutional review (*amparo*) in favour of the Civic Council of Popular and Indigenous Organisations (COPINH), recognising their victim status in the corruption case 'Fraud on the River Gualcarque' (COPINH, 2021). This was the first time that victims could actively participate in a corruption case in Honduras (Robert F. Kennedy Human Rights, 2022). The success of COPINH, who represented the interests of the Lenca peoples directly affected, lay as much in their advocacy as in crafting a legal argument that demonstrated the causal link between corrupt acts and their human rights violations (Interviews conducted with COPINH, Abogados Sin Fronteras (ASF), and Roht-Arriaza, 2024).

The Fraud on the River Gualcarque involved the collusion between employees from the National Energy Enterprise (ENEE), the now-defunct Secretariat of Natural Resources and Environment, and the company DESA to execute the Agua Zarca hydroelectric project (PHAZ in Spanish) in the River Gualcarque (Ministerio Público, 2024a). David Castillo, while serving as ENEE's management coordinator in 2009, illicitly established DESA using two frontmen (Perdomo, 2023). A key factor enabling DESA's contract was the falsification of documents claiming prior consultation with the Lenca community of Rio Blanco, where the River Gualcarque flows and the dam was planned to be built (Irías, 2024).

In addition to violating their right to decide on issues that affected their community, PHAZ infringed upon their rights to access water, fishing, and their ancestral territory, as well as their rights to association, freedom of expression, and their right to life (ASF, 2021a; Irías, 2024). Social protests against the project were met with violent repression, culminating in the assassination of Berta Cáceres in 2016, who was spearheading COPINH's opposition to this project (ASF, 2021). Since then, COPINH has sought justice for Berta and the Lenca peoples of Río Blanco. They aim to dismantle the corruption networks that enabled PHAZ and led to her assassination (Interview with Camilo Bermúdez, COPINH's spokesperson, 2024).

As part of their strategic litigation, COPINH successfully established a direct causal link between the corrupt acts and the violation of Lenca's Indigenous rights. In 2019, the Court of Appeals removed them from the case, arguing that the legal interest at stake was that of good public administration and the State was the only party affected (Indacochea, 2020; Roht-Arriaza, 2025). In response, COPINH's lawyers demonstrated that as an Indigenous community, the development of PHAZ through corruption affected their collective property rights and limited their right to exercise control over their territories, their ways of life, and their economic development:

> COPINH developed evidence of the sine-qua-non condition. They proved that the dam would not have happened without undue influence. They could also trace changes in the quality of water and the number of species of flora and fauna to the construction of the dam.
>
> *(Interview with Roht-Arriaza, 2024)*

Lawyers cited the Honduras Criminal Procedure Code's Articles 16 and 17, which provide victim status to any person or collective whose property has been affected by a crime and enables them to participate as private prosecutors; the UN's Declaration of Basic Principles of Justice for Victims of Crime and Abuse of Power, which defines victims as those who have suffered harm through acts or omissions that violate States' criminal laws; and Convention 169 of the International Labour Organisation (ILO), which stipulates the right of Indigenous communities to exercise control over decisions affecting their interests (Indacochea, 2020).

Other contextual factors enabled COPINH's success in their strategic litigation: First, Berta's assassination elevated the profile of this case. COPINH connected the Fraud case to her murder to expose the structural discrimination faced by the Lenca peoples (Interviews with COPINH and ASF, 2024). Moreover, COPINH and other organisations commissioned an International Group of Experts (GAIPE) to conduct a separate investigation of her assassination (COPINH, 2017). GAIPE found that the actors responsible for Cáceres' murder also used undue influence to get PHAZ approved (Interview with Roht-Arriaza, 2024).

Second, COPINH started developing internal capacities to conduct strategic litigation, and they could build upon the corruption-related evidence presented by the OAS-backed Anti-Corruption Mission in Honduras (MACCIH). Although MACCIH did not establish the link to human rights violations, their work thoroughly documented the corrupt networks that facilitated the development of PHAZ (Interviews with COPINH and Roht-Arriaza, 2024).

Third, their positionality as Indigenous peoples persuaded the Constitutional Chamber to reverse the legal process so they could participate in all criminal proceedings as victims. By focusing on the collective and territorial rights of the Lenca peoples, the Chamber purposefully avoided a wider interpretation, applicable to all people's human rights (Interviews with ASF, and Roht-Arriaza, 2024). Nonetheless, this ruling is unprecedented, as the Honduran government had not considered the right to be consulted in previous interpretations of the ILO Convention (Interview with Bermúdez, 2024).

COPINH's experience in conducting human rights advocacy and establishing key alliances also helped advance their cause. COPINH engaged with other CSOs in peaceful protests and disseminated information about the case in national and international media. They partnered with law firms with expertise in human rights law, including the Law Firm for Dignity, to develop the legal argumentation; received guidance from human rights clinics at the Universities of Los Angeles and Berkeley on issues related to Indigenous rights and criminal law; and gathered support from international organisations like ASF through their submission of amicus curiae to the Constitutional Court (Interviews with COPINH and ASF, 2024).

> Our insistence on making the cases public, broadcasting them, and providing ongoing communication throughout the process is a relatively new concept in Honduras. This helps prevent corrupt structures from influencing corruption cases. The more visible a justice operator is, the better they tend to perform.
>
> *(Interview with Bermúdez, 2024)*

On 3 May 2024, the National Court of Sentencing with Jurisdiction over Organised Crime and Corruption found three defendants guilty in the Fraud case, among them David Castillo, who had already been convicted in the murder of Cáceres (Perdomo, 2024). Six months later, the Supreme Court issued its final ruling, finding Castillo and two other public officials guilty of fraud and falsification of documents (Ministerio Público, 2024b). The next step is to secure reparations for victims, but this is unprecedented and a higher mountain to climb (Interview with COPINH, 2024). Nonetheless,

COPINH has already laid the groundwork for future reparations. Thanks to their strategic litigation and advocacy, victims were heard and PHAZ was stalled (Interviews with COPINH and Roht-Arriaza, 2024).

The Pursuit of Freedom from Corruption as a Human Right in Mexico

What can be done when a case of grand corruption has wider implications for society as a whole? The Mexican CSO TOJIL asked themselves this question after Javier Duarte, ex-governor of the state of Veracruz who embezzled millions of funds, colluded with the Attorney General Office (AGO) to get a lower sentence (Indacochea, 2020; TOJIL, n.d.). In 2018, TOJIL filed a complaint for bribery crimes before the specialised unit tasked to investigate AGO public servants (Indacochea, 2020). Since then, TOJIL has sought victim status, arguing that this case of bribery affected their collective interest in good public administration and the right to live free of corruption (TOJIL, n.d.). In a landmark resolution, a judge recognised TOJIL as victims, but the AGO won an appeal that removed their victim status, and TOJIL has now taken this case to the IACHR (Medina and Greaves, 2021). TOJIL's efforts have benefited from Mexico's strong institutional framework, which recognises corruption victims with diffuse interests, and the IADH's 2019 report, which asserts that corruption cases require active counterbalance from civil society. Yet, it is TOJIL's deep understanding of how judicial institutions function, expertise in strategic litigation, ability to identify key windows of opportunity, and robust networks that have enabled them to advance this case.

As governor, Javier Duarte embezzled more than 30 million USD allocated for education and health programmes (Medina and Greaves, 2021). Under his administration, state health authorities adulterated children's chemotherapy treatments, injecting them with distilled water (CNN, 2017). In 2018, he was arrested in Guatemala and extradited to Mexico to answer for alleged abuse of power. While his initial charges were organised crime and money laundering, he negotiated a plea bargain with the AGO to avoid trial and be prosecuted for criminal association instead of organised crime. The result was a more lenient sentence: nine years in prison – instead of 55 years – and a fine of less than 3000 USD (Indacochea, 2020; Medina and Greaves, 2021).

Knowing there were no legally recognised victims who could challenge this plea bargain, TOJIL filed a criminal complaint against the federal prosecutors who negotiated it in 2018. They attributed the terms of the plea bargain to suspected bribery and sought recognition as victims (Medina and Greaves, 2021). TOJIL saw two windows of opportunity to do so: first, the government of López Obrador had been elected on a strong anti-corruption agenda, and it was unlikely that they would oppose the investigation. Second, the news on the children's tempered chemotherapy treatments had wide media coverage, making Duarte's case even more emblematic (Interview with Greaves, 2024).

There was also a legal precedent to base TOJIL's claim. TOJIL argued that the collusion between Duarte and the AGO affected their right to an environment free from corruption. Two years before, a judge ruled that the government agencies responsible for misusing 160 million USD through irregular contracts, also known as the Master Swindle case, had violated the fundamental right to live free of corruption (Medina and Greaves, 2020).

TOJIL's claim was also viable under Mexico's legal framework on victims. The 2008 penal reform attributed victims the right to justice, reparation, and clarification of facts. The State recognises that there is no crime without victims, and victims are entitled to participate in the judicial process (Angulo Nobara, *et al.*, 2019). Mexico also has two types of victims: the victim, which is directly affected, and the offended party, which is indirectly affected but has the same prosecutorial rights as victims (Interview with Greaves, 2024). Nonetheless, prosecutors were not actively including victims/offended parties in corruption cases. TOJIL took on Duarte's case to rectify these institutional patterns:

> We said, this would change everything. If you give a victim in a case of corruption the possibility to get involved, they're going to be able to push the case forward judicially, even skipping over the weakest link which is the prosecutor's office, which is where they always bribe, or which depends on the executive branch.
>
> *(Interview with Greaves, 2024)*

In addition to citing the UNCAC's article 13 – which identifies civil society as key actors in the fight against corruption – TOJIL cited Mexico's General Law on Victims' article 4, which acknowledges that civil society can be victims in cases of collective damages (Medina and Greaves, 2021). The AGO initially denied TOJIL's claim, arguing that Duarte's collusion had not directly affected TOJIL (Procuraduría General de la República, 2018). TOJIL appealed this decision and in 2019 an *amparo* judge ruled to restitute TOJIL's victim prosecutorial rights. This was the first time in Mexico when a judge recognised a CSO as a corruption victim (Medina and Greaves, 2021). This ruling, however, was revoked by a Collegiate Court, where only one judge, who was influenced by two amicus curiae and the 2019 IACHR's report, considered that TOJIL's collective rights had been violated (Lopez Benitez, 2019; TOJIL, 2023a).

Together with DPLF, TOJIL's Directors, Estefania Medina and Adriana Greaves, submitted a petition to the IACHR in 2020 on this case. They argued that the Mexican authorities' refusal to recognise TOJIL's victim status violated their right to defend human rights. In October 2023, the IACHR admitted this case for revision (TOJIL, 2023a, 2023b). This is exceptional, as *'it's the first case where a State is being sued for institutional corruption"* (Interview with Greaves, 2024). Should the IACHR rule in favour of Medina and Graves, there will be a regional legal precedent for civil society to actively participate in corruption cases (TOJIL, 2023a).

Additionally, two other factors have shaped TOJIL's strategic litigation: their support networks and their inside knowledge of the AGO. TOJIL has closely collaborated with other national and international experts. For example, two legal clinics from universities in Mexico submitted amicus curiae to the Collegiate Court, and more recently, DPLF has served as their communication link with IACHR in Washington (Angulo Nobara, *et al.*, 2019; Interview with Greaves, 2024).

Moreover, TOJIL has drafted the appeals on their own. TOJIL is composed of criminal lawyers with plenty of technical experience, and most employees – including the directors – had previously worked at the AGO. Unlike many other CSOs engaging in strategic litigation, TOJIL *'knows how the AGO works, what the areas of opportunities, as well as the Achilles heels, are'* (Interview with Greaves, 2024).

Ms Greaves recognises that in retrospect, they could have invested more in advocacy, especially when they presented the case to the Commission. Nonetheless, TOJIL's strategic litigation has been exemplary – not only did they manage that the national authorities attribute victim status to a CSO, even if this was short-lived, but they also successfully submitted the first case against a State for institutional corruption at the IACHR.

Corruption and Cancer: The Quest for Justice beyond Venezuela's Borders

If establishing a link between institutional corruption and human rights violations in democracies is challenging, doing so in repressive states may seem impossible. Civil society in Venezuela has taken up this challenge, using regional mechanisms to advocate for people's rights violated by corruption. In 2023, a group of health, human rights, and anti-corruption CSOs petitioned IACHR to address the Venezuelan State's failure to comply with its precautionary measures from 2020, which aimed to guarantee quality healthcare for 12 breast cancer patients. They requested IACHR to submit this case to the Inter-American Court so the latter could order provisional measures, arguing that grand corruption had weakened the health system's capacity to fulfil these patients' right to health (Transparencia Venezuela, 2023). Despite Venezuela's contested exit from the OAS and the heightened levels of repression, the CSOs have managed to keep this case alive. Their strategic litigation – which has mainly focused on regional advocacy – is sustained through strong alliances with international legal experts and CSOs.

In 2019, several health and human rights organisations filed a petition for precautionary measures to the IACHR in favour of 12 breast cancer patients in Venezuela. They claimed that the Venezuelan health system had failed to provide adequate medical treatment, putting their lives at risk (Pulido, 2020). In 2020, the IACHR granted precautionary measures and requested the Venezuelan State to protect these women's lives, personal integrity, and health (Pulido, 2020). Nonetheless, the State never took measures to comply with the IACHR's ruling (Transparencia Venezuela, 2023).

Up until then, neither the CSOs who submitted the petition nor IACHR had considered corruption as a key driver. The Covid-19 outbreak changed this. In 2020, 15 health, human rights, and anti-corruption CSOs submitted a report to IACHR on corruption in Venezuela's health sector. They argued that the military and high-ranking officials of the Ministry of Health had captured the health system. This impacted the functioning of medical facilities and the availability of medicines and equipment. By March 2020, 35.2% of the intensive care units were not operational and some states reached medicines shortages of up to 80%. Consequently, the State had failed to fulfil patients' right to health (DPLF *et al.*, 2020). Collaborating for this report marked the start of a joint strategy to link the 12 women's cases to corruption:

> From that point on, we began to develop a closer relationship with NGOs in the health sector. In 2021, we started discussing whether another action could be taken because the precautionary measure had been notified in Venezuela, but the government did not respond, and by that time, two of the 12 patients had already passed away.
>
> *(Interview with national CSO,[2] 2024)*

Keeping momentum for this case was challenging. The government had denounced the Inter-American Convention on Human Rights in 2013, and while the Commission continued having competencies in Venezuela, this limited the Court's jurisdiction to cases submitted before this date (OAS, 2013). In 2017, they also formally requested its exit from the OAS. This was meant to be executed two years later, but in 2019, OAS member states accepted Juan Guaidó's envoy as representative of Venezuela (Melimopoulos, 2019). This institutional limbo put into question the applicability of IACHR's measures in Venezuela. Yet, those cases submitted to IACHR up until 2019 remain valid, and this includes the case of the 12 women.

The coalition of national CSOs, together with DPLF, decided on the safest bet. Instead of submitting a new case to the Court, which could bring up questions of admissibility, they opted to continue with the case already opened at the IACHR:

> We had to show that this wasn't a new case, but rather one that stemmed from a precautionary measure already recognised by the Commission, which should then ask the Court to issue provisional measures.
>
> *(Interview with Orias, 2024)*

Petitioners' complaint focused on establishing a link between grand corruption and the violation of these women's human rights. They pointed out that the UN system and OAS had recognised corruption's impact on ECOSOC rights in previous statements, including the 2019 IACHR's report. They argued that corruption had negatively impacted cancer research and the availability of medicines and equipment for cancer patients, contributing to a high mortality rate. They concluded that the State's failure to comply with the precautionary measures had worsened the situation for the ten patients who were still alive and three more who joined this case (Interviews with DPLF and national CSO, 2024).

Asking the Commission to submit a case to the Court, *motu proprio*, was quite extraordinary. While Article 24 of the IACHR's Rules of Procedures stipulates that the Commission can refer cases to the Court, it is unusual for externals to request this practice. In the past, the IACHR used this article extensively, especially in cases from countries under military dictatorships, but at present, the Commission has too many cases and its capacity is much more limited (Interview with Orias, 2024).

CSOs have not only strategised ways to navigate the legal implications of Venezuela's contested exit from the OAS, but also carefully considered how to mitigate the risk of state reprisals against their organisations and victims. In the build-up to the 2024 Venezuelan elections, Venezuelan authorities perpetrated numerous attacks on civic space (Amnesty International, 2024). After the elections in July 2024, the State violently repressed 115 out of 300 protests and arbitrarily detained 1350 people (CIDH, 2024; WOLA, 2024). In August, the National Assembly approved an 'anti-society' law, obligating CSOs to seek government authorisation for their operations and disclose any foreign financing (CEPAZ, 2024).

In the face of repression, CSOs have relied on their alliances with international organisations to safeguard their identity. While national CSOs keep documenting violations, international CSOs focus on enhancing their advocacy at the Commission. Meanwhile, it is the victims' international lawyer the one who publicly takes the case forward (Interviews with DPLF and national CSO, 2024).

Despite – or perhaps as a result of – these challenges, there is a silver lining: today, there are more meaningful collaborations amongst human rights, health and anti-corruption CSOs. These proactive engagements have enabled health CSOs to recognise the impact corruption has had in this sector (Interview with Orias, 2024).

IACHR's decision on the petition submitted in 2023 is still pending (as of September 2024). Yet, what is clear is that Venezuelan CSOs, in collaboration with regional partners, have developed innovative strategies to engage the Inter-American system in addressing the impact of corruption on Venezuelan patients. When the State fails to respond, regional mechanisms may offer a path forward.

Reimagining Anti-Corruption through a Human Rights Lens

Tackling corruption and advancing human rights in silos has not only been ineffective in Latin America – it has delegitimised both struggles. The result has been a paradoxical state of affairs, where the institutional infrastructure to address corruption and human rights violations exists, but the challenges remain chronic.

In recent years, both the UN and the Inter-American Human Rights system have recognised that corruption can enable human rights violations. Yet, the dissonance lies in operationalising this at the national level, given multiple challenges: Methodologically, it is difficult to quantify and measure corruption's impact on human rights. Legally, it is challenging to establish causality between an act of corruption and the human rights violations it may engender, and therefore, identify victims. Institutionally, there might not be frameworks in place to identify and redress victims of corruption, and when there are, the authorities may not apply them.

Contesting this reality has given way to new ways of thinking and approaching both struggles. In some countries, like Colombia, governments are officially recognising this. In others, civil society is demanding and shaping joint efforts on anti-corruption and human rights. Today, we are living through a transition phase, with innovative approaches materialising the link between both agendas.

Innovation has been locally grounded, context-driven, and responsive to key windows of opportunity. In Latin America, the robustness of the Inter-American human rights system, the existence of strong civil society groups tied into regional and global networks, the legal frameworks in place, and in some cases, changes in government, have fed into pioneering strategies to converge anti-corruption and human rights efforts. While the actions taken in Colombia, Honduras, Mexico, and Venezuela are completely different, their goal has been the same: to move beyond the silos created to tackle corruption and human rights violations.[3]

In Colombia, the Transparency Secretariat developed an innovative methodological approach to measure corruption's impact on human rights. The political commitment to converge these agendas came as a result of the 2021 *Estallido Social*, which led to the election of a government on a strong human rights platform. In Honduras, Mexico, and Venezuela, the political will to connect both agendas in legal cases was non-existent. Yet, civil society conceived innovative legal strategies to advance the identification and recognition of corruption victims. Whenever this was not possible at the national level, they engaged the Inter-American system.

Civil society faced different challenges in developing their legal arguments. Whereas COPINH in Honduras could demonstrate that corruption under PHAZ had violated the Lenca peoples' rights, neither TOJIL in Mexico nor the Venezuelan CSOs could make such a direct assertion. TOJIL's goal was to defend the right to live in an environment free of corruption. In Venezuela, civil society sought to link breast cancer patients' poor healthcare access to the endemic corruption that had weakened Venezuela's health system.

Human rights violations and corruption are problems of social order, and the kind of social order we pursue should dictate the anti-corruption measures we must take (Jackson et al., 2026). These countries' regulations and specific windows of opportunity shaped civil society's strategies. They offer a perspective on how to engage in strategic litigation to assert victim status in corruption cases across different contexts:

In some countries like Honduras, the regulatory environment does not fully recognise corruption victims. If it is possible to demonstrate how corrupt acts impact individual or collective victims, civil society could engage in strategic litigation and work with legal experts to strengthen their legal arguments. They could also engage in protests and dissemination through media outlets to increase visibility. The more public the legal process is, the more likely it is that prosecutors include victims in the process.

In other countries like Mexico, there are regulations in place that recognise victims with direct and diffuse interests in penal cases, but prosecution officers do not apply them in corruption cases. Here, civil society could legally demonstrate how their collective interests – for example, in good administration – have been threatened. Since it is difficult to establish a clear sine-qua-non condition in cases with diffuse interests, civil society must ensure their legal arguments are sound. For this purpose, it is essential to understand how the country's AGO operates. When national mechanisms are exhausted, the next step is to submit their cases to the Inter-American system. Civil society could develop alliances with international CSOs to guide their international strategic litigation.

In non-democratic countries like Venezuela, repression obstructs any opportunity for national strategic litigation. CSOs' demands for recognition of corruption victims must happen through regional mechanisms. Yet, as the threat of reprisals is imminent, civil society must avoid putting their and the victims' lives and integrity at risk. Therefore, they must consider alliances with international lawyers and CSOs, so that they can publicly take them forward.

Anti-corruption measures are the most effective when they are not taken in isolation from other social struggles. In the case of Latin America, it is not possible to address human rights violations without dealing with the associated corruption, especially when corruption is systemic. There is an undeniable overlap between corruption and human rights violations, and this means that one cannot be addressed without addressing the other. The examples from Colombia, Honduras, Mexico, and Venezuela are part of a growing regional trend to ground the global recognition of the nexus between anti-corruption and human rights.

Notes

1. From 15 July to 8 September 2024, I conducted seven key informant interviews with 11 stakeholders, including civil society in Venezuela, Honduras, Mexico, and the US, as well as government officials in Colombia.
2. For security reasons, this interviewee cannot be identified.
3. For a summary of these case studies, see Table 1 in the Annex.

References

Abogados sin Fronteras Canada (2021a) *Caso fraude sobre el Gualcarque*. Tegucigalpa, Honduras: Abogados sin Frontera Canadá, Estudios para la Dignidad – Bufete de Derechos Humanos, and COPINH. Available at: https://asfcanada.ca/wp-content/uploads/2022/10/ficha_gualcarque_2021_10.pdf.

Abogados sin Fronteras Canada (2021b) 'Caso Gualcarque: una oportunidad para avanzar en la protección de los derechos de las víctimas en Honduras'. Available at: https://asfcanada.ca/es/medias/caso-gualcarque-una-oportunidad-para-avanzar-en-la-proteccion-de-los-derechos-de-las-victimas-en-honduras/ (Accessed: 1 August 2024).

Alianza Gobierno Abierto Colombia (2023) *V Plan de Acción Nacional de Datos Abiertos en Colombia (2023–2025)*. Bogotá: Alianza Gobierno Abierto Colombia.

Amnesty International (2024) *Venezuela: Alarmante Escalada de Persecución Contra Voces Críticas y Disidentes, Amnistía Internacional*. Available at: https://www.amnesty.org/es/documents/amr53/7949/2024/es/ (Accessed: 24 September 2024).

Angulo Nobara, J. *et al.* (2019) 'Amicus Curiae'. Available at: https://victimasdecorrupcion.tojil.org/wp-content/uploads/2024/07/6-amicus-curiae.pdf.

Barkhouse, A., Hoyland, H. and Limon, M. (2018) *Corruption: A human rights impact assessment | Universal Rights Group*. Universal Rights Group and Kroll. Available at: https://www.universal-rights.org/urg-policy-reports/corruption-human-rights-impact-assessment-2/ (Accessed: 18 March 2024).

CEPAZ (2021) 'A un año de las medidas cautelares de la CIDH las mujeres con cáncer de mama siguen sin obtener respuesta del Estado venezolano', *CEPAZ*, 18 October. Available at: https://cepaz.org/a-un-ano-de-las-medidas-cautelares-de-la-cidh-las-mujeres-con-cancer-de-mama-siguen-sin-obtener-respuesta-del-estado-venezolano/ (Accessed: 5 August 2024).

CEPAZ, C. (2024) 'En el contexto más fuerte de represión es aprobada la Ley Antisociedad en Venezuela', *CEPAZ*, 19 August. Available at: https://cepaz.org

/en-el-contexto-mas-fuerte-de-represion-es-aprobada-la-ley-antisociedad-en-venezuela/ (Accessed: 24 September 2024).

CIDH (2024) *Venezuela: CIDH y RELE condenan graves violaciones a derechos humanos denunciadas durante la represión en las protestas poselectorales*, *Comisión Interamericana de Derechos Humanos (CIDH).* Available at: https://www.oas.org/es/CIDH/jsForm/?File=/es/cidh/prensa/comunicados/2024/174.asp (Accessed: 24 September 2024).

CIDH (n.d.) *CIDH :: Observatorio de impacto :: Impacto: historias de la CIDH*, *Comisión Interamericana de Derechos Humanos (CIDH).* Available at: https://www.oas.org/es/CIDH/jsForm/?File=/es/cidh/observatorio/historias.asp (Accessed: 30 March 2025).

CNN (2017) *El estado de Veracruz investiga falsas quimioterapias a niños con cáncer*, *CNN.* Available at: https://cnnespanol.cnn.com/2017/01/18/el-estado-de-veracruz-investiga-falsas-quimioterapias-a-ninos-con-cancer (Accessed: 21 September 2024).

Colombia Informa (2023) 'El estallido social de 2021: Cuando la gente se levantó – Colombia Informa Un día como hoy', 28 April. Available at: https://www.colombiainforma.info/el-estallido-social-de-2021-cuando-la-gente-se-levanto/ (Accessed: 8 September 2024).

COPINH (2017) 'Declaración pública del Grupo Asesor Internacional de Personas Expertas (GAIPE), a un año del asesinato de Berta Cáceres', *GAIPE Grupo Asesor Internacional de Personas Expertas*, 1 March. Available at: https://gaipe.net/declaracion-publica-del-grupo-asesor-internacional-de-personas-expertas-gaipe-a-un-ano-del-asesinato-de-berta-caceres (Accessed: 15 September 2024).

COPINH (2021) *Fraude Gualcarque*, *Berta Cáceres.* Available at: https://berta.copinh.org/tag/fraude-gualcarque/ (Accessed: 2 August 2024).

DPLF *et al.* (2020) *Corrupción en el sistema de salud público de Venezuela en el contexto de la pandemia del COVID-19: Informe de audiencia presentado a la Comisión Interamericana de Derechos Humanos en el marco del 177º periodo de sesiones.*

Falconi, F.F. *et al.* (2023) *Victims of corruption: Back for payback.* Washington, DC: World Bank. Available at: https://doi.org/10.1596/40818.

Geneva Academy and UNHCHR (2016) *Human rights and countering corruption.*

Hawley, S. (2016) 'Compensation for victims of corruption: Why does it matter?' Available at: https://uncaccoalition.org/compensation-for-victims-of-corruption-why-does-it-matter/ (Accessed: 7 September 2024).

Human Rights Council (2023) *Resolution on the negative impact of corruption on the enjoyment of human rights, 53/17.*

IACHR (2019) *Corruption and human rights in the Americas: Inter-American standards.* OEA/Ser.L/V/II. OAS. Official records.

Indacochea, U. (2020) *La participación de la sociedad civil en la lucha contra la corrupción.* DPLF.

Irías, G. (2024) 'Análisis Semanal | "Fraude sobre el Gualcarque": principales aprendizajes en la lucha contra la corrupción extractiva – Cespad', 6 May. Available at: https://cespad.org.hn/analisis-semanal-fraude-sobre-el-gualcarque-principales-aprendizajes-en-la-lucha-contra-la-corrupcion-extractiva/ (Accessed: 2 August 2024).

Jackson, D., Williams, A. and Amundsen, I. (2026) 'Introduction', in *Anti-Corruption in a discordant world: Contestation, abuse and innovation.* Routledge.

Lopez Benitez, L.M. (2019) 'Voto particular'. Available at: https://victimasdecorrupcion.tojil.org/wp-content/uploads/2024/07/12-voto-particular.pdf.

Medina, E. and Greaves, A. (2020) *¿Existe un derecho a vivir en un ambiente libre de corrupción? - El Juego de la Suprema Corte - Blog de la revista Nexos*. Available at: https://eljuegodelacorte.nexos.com.mx/existe-un-derecho-a-vivir-en-un-ambiente-libre-de-corrupcion/ (Accessed: 22 September 2024).

Medina, E. and Greaves, A. (2021) 'Litigating on Behalf of Victims of Corruption: The Duarte Case from Mexico | UNCAC Coalition'. Available at: https://uncaccoalition.org/litigating-on-behalf-of-victims-of-corruption-the-duarte-case-from-mexico/ (Accessed: 21 September 2024).

Mejías, S.A. (2022) *¿Por qué América Latina es la región más violenta del mundo?* Prosegur Research.

Melimopoulos, E. (2019) *OAS recognises Guaido's envoy until new Venezuela elections held*, *Al Jazeera*. Available at: https://www.aljazeera.com/news/2019/4/10/oas-recognises-guaidos-envoy-until-new-venezuela-elections-held (Accessed: 23 September 2024).

Ministerio Público (2024a) *MP logra condena contra tres involucrados en el caso "Fraude sobre el Gualcarque"*. Available at: https://www.mp.hn/publicaciones/mp-logra-condena-contra-tres-involucrados-en-el-caso-fraude-sobre-el-gualcarque/ (Accessed: 10 September 2024).

Ministerio Público (2024b) *MP obtiene condena de 5 años de cárcel para involucrados en caso "Fraude sobre el Gualcarque", causa relacionada con lucha que libró la ambientalista Berta Cáceres*. Available at: https://www.mp.hn/publicaciones/mp-obtiene-condena-de-5-anos-de-carcel-para-involucrados-en-caso-fraude-sobre-el-gualcarque-causa-relacionada-con-lucha-que-libro-la-ambientalista-berta-caceres/ (Accessed: 23 March 2025).

Mutzenberg, P. (2018) 'How UN Treaty Bodies can better address corruption and its negative impact on human rights | Universal Rights Group'. Available at: https://www.universal-rights.org/how-un-treaty-bodies-can-better-address-corruption-and-its-negative-impact-on-human-rights/ (Accessed: 18 March 2024).

Nash, C. and Fuchs, M.-C. (2019) *Corrupción, estado de derecho y derechos humanos*. Fundación Konrad Adenauer: Bogotá, Colombia. Available at: https://www.corteidh.or.cr/tablas/r39615.pdf (Accessed: 30 March 2025).

Nash-Rojas, C., Bascuñan, P. and Meza-Lopehandía, M. (2014) *Corrupción y derechos humanos: Una mirada desde la jurisprudencia de la Corte Interamericana de Derechos Humanos*. Universidad de Chile. Available at: https://repositorio.uchile.cl/bitstream/handle/2250/142495/Corrupcion-y-derechos-humanos.pdf?sequence=1&isAllowed=y (Accessed: 14 January 2025).

OAS (2013) *OAS secretary general regrets Venezuela's withdrawal from the American convention on human rights*, *OAS - Organization of American States*. Available at: https://www.oas.org/en/media_center/press_release.asp?sCodigo=E-338/13 (Accessed: 23 September 2024).

OAS (1996) *Inter-American convetion against corruption*. Available at: https://www.oas.org/en/sla/dil/inter_american_treaties_B-58_against_Corruption.asp (Accessed: 1 September 2024).

OHCHR (n.d.a) *d) General comment No. 13: The right to education (article 13) (1999)*, *OHCHR*. Available at: https://www.ohchr.org/en/resources/educators/human

-rights-education-training/d-general-comment-no-13-right-education-article-13-1999 (Accessed: 23 March 2025).
OHCHR (n.d.b) *Resolutions*, *OHCHR*. Available at: https://www.ohchr.org/en/good-governance/resolutions (Accessed: 25 August 2024).
Perdomo, M. (2023) 'Declaran sin lugar recurso que buscaba favorecer con "amnistía" a David Castillo', *Criterio.hn*, 17 November. Available at: https://criterio.hn/declaran-sin-lugar-recurso-que-buscaba-favorecer-con-amnistia-a-david-castillo/ (Accessed: 1 August 2024).
Perdomo, M. (2024) 'Culpables tres imputados en caso Fraude sobre el Gualcarque, incluido coautor del asesinato de Berta Cáceres', *Criterio.hn*, 4 May. Available at: https://criterio.hn/culpables-tres-imputados-en-caso-fraude-sobre-el-gualcarque-incluido-coautor-del-asesinato-de-berta-caceres/ (Accessed: 2 August 2024).
Peters, A. (2018) 'Corruption as a violation of international human rights', *European Journal of International Law*, 29(4), pp. 1251–1287. Available at: https://doi.org/10.1093/ejil/chy070.
Procuraduría General de la República (2018) 'Se notifica acuerdo'.
Pulido, M.C. (2020) *RESOLUCIÓN 68/2020. Medida cautelar No. 545-19. 12 mujeres con cáncer de mama respecto de Venezuela, 14 de octubre de 2020.* Comisión Interamericana de Derechos Humanos.
Robert F. Kennedy Human Rights (2022) *Honduras: Retraso judicial vulnera acceso a la justicia en caso "Fraude sobre el Gualcarque", Robert F. Kennedy Human Rights.* Available at: https://rfkhumanrights.org/our-voices/honduras-retraso-judicial-vulnera-acceso-a-la-justicia-en-caso-fraude-sobre-el-gualcarque/ (Accessed: 2 August 2024).
Roht-Arriaza, N. (2025). *Fighting grand corruption: Transnational and human rights approaches in Latin America and beyond.* Cambridge: Cambridge University Press.
Secretaría de Transparencia (2023) *Secretario Idárraga evidenció riesgos en la garantía de la educación por la corrupción y en el índice de transparencia en entidades públicas.* Available at: https://www.secretariatransparencia.gov.co:443/secretario-id%C3%A1rraga-evidenci%C3%B3-riesgos-en-la-garant%C3%ADa-de-la-educaci%C3%B3n-por-la-corrupci%C3%B3n-y-en-el-%C3%ADndice-de-transparencia-en (Accessed: 8 August 2024).
Secretaría de Transparencia (n.d.) *Radar de Corrupción & DESC: Derecho a la Educación.* Bogotá: Secretaría de Transparencia.
Tablante, C. and Antoniazzi, M. (2018) *Impacto de la corrupción en los derechos humanos.* Querétaro, Mexico: Instituto de Estudios Constitucionales del Estado de Querétaro.
TOJIL (2023a) 'Caso Duarte', *TOJIL*, 30 July. Available at: https://tojil.org/2023/07/30/caso-duarte/ (Accessed: 31 August 2024).
TOJIL (2023b) 'Comunicado TOJIL 25/OCT/2023', *TOJIL*, 26 October. Available at: https://tojil.org/2023/10/26/comunicado-tojil-25-oct-2023/ (Accessed: 12 July 2024).
TOJIL (n.d.) 'Comisión Interamericana de Derechos Humanos | víctimas de corrupción'. Available at: https://victimasdecorrupcion.tojil.org/comision-interamericana-de-derechos-humanos/ (Accessed: 31 August 2024).
Transparencia Venezuela (2023) *En Venezuela la corrupción discrimina a las mujeres: El caso de las mujeres con cáncer de mama.*

UN Human Rights Council (2025) 'The negative impact of corruption on the enjoyment of human rights' (7 July 2025), UN Res.A/HRC/RES/59/6.

UNODC (2004) 'United Nations Convention Against Corruption'.

UNODC (2023) *UNODC pledge for the human rights 75 initiative*, *United Nations : Office on drugs and crime*. Available at: https://www.unodc.org/unodc/en/humanrights/pledge.html (Accessed: 6 September 2024).

UNODC (n.d.) *Challenges faced and best practices applied by States in integrating human rights into their national strategies and policies to fight against corruption, including those addressing non-State actors, such as the private sector*. Vienna: UNODC.

Wickberg, S. (2013) *Literature review on costs of corruption for the poor*. Bergen: U4 Anti-Corruption Resource Centre.

WOLA (2024) *Venezuela: Condenamos la sistemática represión por parte del gobierno contra personas defensoras de Derechos Humanos y manifestantes*, *WOLA*. Available at: https://www.wola.org/es/2024/08/venezuela-condenamos-sistematica-represion-gobierno-contra-personas-defensoras-derechos-humanos-manifestantes/ (Accessed: 24 September 2024).

Annex

TABLE 10.1 Summary of case studies

	Honduras	Mexico	Venezuela	Colombia
Challenge addressed	- Establishing causality and identifying corruption victims, and once identified, conducting strategic litigation in states that do not have the legal infrastructure to recognise them and redress them. - Strategy - Legal argument: direct causality	- Establishing causality and identifying corruption victims, and once identified, conducting strategic litigation in states that have the legal infrastructure but are unwilling to redress them. - Strategy - Legal argument: diffuse causality	- Establishing causality and identifying corruption victims, and once identified, conducting strategic litigation in repressive states. - Strategy - Legal argument: diffuse causality	- Measuring corruption's impact on human rights - Strategy – development of a composite indicator on corruption and human rights (RADAR)
Actor(s) spearheading innovative approaches	- Civil society	- Civil society	- Civil Society	- Government (Transparency Secretariat)
Regulatory/policy environment (on corruption and human rights)	- Unfavourable regulatory environment - No previous recognition of indigenous communities as victims in corruption cases	- Favourable regulatory environment - Mexico's penal reform and General Law on Victims - Legal precedent recognising the right to live in an environment free of corruption (the Master Swindle case)	- Unfavourable regulatory environment - Lack of judicial independence / dictatorship / repressive state - Venezuela's government denounced the Convention on Human Rights in 2013 and requested to exit the OAS in 2017. However, formalising Venezuela's exit in 2019 was unclear, as the OAS admitted an envoy from political opponent Juan Guaidó.	- The guarantee of rights is a cross-cutting policy, which the Transparency Secretariat has sought to mainstream in its institutional strategy

(*Continued*)

TABLE 10.1 (Continued)

	Honduras	Mexico	Venezuela	Colombia
Windows of opportunity from context	- The assassination of Berta Cáceres gave high visibility to the case. - Honduras is a party to the ILO Convention 169 (rights of indigenous peoples) - COPINH's internal capacities and expertise in human rights advocacy	- Newly elected government on an anti-corruption platform. - Duarte's corruption and its impact on children with cancer – high visibility to this case. - TOJIL's inside knowledge of the AGO. - 2019 IACHR Report. - Member of the OAS.	- No windows of opportunity to engage in strategic litigation at the national level. - However, cases admitted by IACH before the State's exit from the OAS are still in force. The Commission admitted the case of the 12 women with breast cancer in 2019. - 2019 IACHR Report.	- 2021 *Estallido Social*, which led to the election of a government on a strong human rights platform. - The Secretariat is under the leadership of a human rights expert.
Alliances	- International support in developing and presenting the legal argument (both through technical support and the submission of amicus curiae)	- National legal clinics: amicus curiae - DPLF: communication with Washington/IACHR	- National health and anti-corruption CSOs' close collaboration - Alliances with international human rights organisations and lawyers.	- N/A

(*Continued*)

TABLE 10.1 (Continued)

	Honduras	Mexico	Venezuela	Colombia
Strategy	- Continuous advocacy, both nationally and internationally, to bring visibility to the case. - Development of a causal argument where the sine-qua-non condition is fulfilled, with the support of national and international legal experts.	- No systematic focus on advocacy/public dissemination of this case. - Internal development of the legal argument, presenting TOJIL's as an affected party with the same prosecutorial rights as victims. - Use of regional mechanisms when national ones were exhausted.	- No public dissemination of the case, due to fears of reappraisals. - Use of regional mechanisms, as national ones are non-existent in practice: • Request to the IACHR to submit the case to the Court as motu proprio. • Advocacy through IACHR's ex-officio hearings. - More support from international actors to take the case forward, as government repression limits national CSOs and victims to engage in this case publicly.	- RADAR follows a pioneering methodological approach to measure corruption's impact on human rights. In addition to data from sanctions, complaints, and news related to corruption, RADAR also includes proxy variables to measure non-observable corruption. - RADAR has been a useful tool for: • easier identification and prioritisation of territories • progress on the National Anti-Corruption Strategy (NACS).

Source: Author's own compilation

11

STRENGTHENING ANTI-CORRUPTION THROUGH TRANSLOCAL APPROACHES

Nurturing More Resilient Forms of Collective Action

Cheri-Leigh Erasmus, Blair Glencorse, and Jean Scrimgeour

Introduction

Corruption is arguably a central challenge that states face, both externally and internally, as a weaponised threat. State-sponsored, anti-democratic forces are focused on undermining efforts to build accountability at home and abroad. In this, they are aided by new ways to spread mis- and dis-information and technologies that better allow efforts to survey citizens, restrict freedoms and clamp down on speech. Politically, we have seen recently in countries as diverse as Kenya, Bangladesh, and Slovakia, that corruption breeds deep resentment of the political class and generates movements to transform governance systems (Amundsen, 2024). In addition, there is clear overlap between corruption and related polycrises including democratic decline and the rise of autocracy, massive global wealth disparities and the climate emergency (Jamil, B. et al 2023). These problems are global in nature but finding and agreeing on shared solutions is increasingly difficult in a multipolar world.

Collective action will increasingly be an important pathway for changes in governance because it can induce political office holders to act on corruption even if it may not be in their direct interests to do so. In this chapter, "collective action" refers to joint anti-corruption initiatives that are *inclusive* of local communities and civil society, not just public-private partnerships. Consider the Movement Against Electoral Corruption (MCCE) in Brazil in 2008, through which forty-four civic groups pushed for Ficha Limpa ("clean slate") legislation which prevented those convicted of corruption and other crimes from running for office. The bill was introduced through a massive petition and significant pressure led to its passage despite opposition from many sitting representatives (Kasm, 2015).

DOI: 10.4324/9781003531920-15

Collective action practice requires some further thinking, however. Initiatives may be too isolated, underfunded, lack broader support, face political pushback, or be caught up in donor-funding traps. Pippidi (2013) indicates that too often, the ingredients that make collective action for meaningful change a success – a dense network of voluntary associations for example – do not exist. In recent times within the anti-corruption space, collective action has come to refer to efforts to bring the private sector into these issues in particular – and while some helpful progress has been made (examples include the Maritime Anti-Corruption Network, for example), the absence of a focus on meaningfully local, citizen-driven efforts in these approaches is noticeable (Basel Institute 2018). Anti-corruption collective action efforts can be exclusive, hierarchical and can in fact benefit one sub-group at the cost of others (Marquette and Peiffer, 2015).

Ideas about how to make collective action more robust are essential. The argument in this chapter is that the principle of translocalism can be a frame through which collective action initiatives against specific corruption problems can develop greater resilience. The essence of translocalism is in how locally rooted networks and organisations "transcend" the immediate site of the problem they address to connect outwards and upwards. Shannon *et al.* (2023) for example define translocal networks as networks rooted in specific geographies but connected to a global agenda, knowledge, and practice. Unlike traditional international NGOs which often operate top-down, translocal networks are decentralised and driven by local nodes, with global links serving to exchange support rather than control.

In this chapter, we draw on literature on translocality, examples from other fields, as well as practical experience to show how translocalism can help refine how collective action in anti-corruption is structured. We identify how a translocal perspective can be integrated into six dimensions of the organisational mechanics of collective action: their proximate and cross-cutting nature; the focus on learning; the values-based and organic nature of their growth; the centrality of narratives; the fact that they are predicated on equal partnership; and the ways in which they can protect civic space. The chapter is an argument for why and how translocal principles can make collective action more resilient in a discordant world. The main contribution of the chapter in terms of innovation is that it offers an alternative or complementary frame to structure collective action that goes beyond overly localised community initiatives or excessively top-down donor approaches. To make this happen, we suggest ways translocalism can be brought into collective action approaches, including through greater risk-taking by donors and supporters, support for organisations that are central to these ecosystems, and centring equity and indigenous expertise.

Building on Ideas of Collective Action

A starting point for this is a re-examination of how we understand innovation in this field. Taylor's useful definition of innovation includes "the coming together of ideas and the process for developing solutions" (Taylor, 2017, p. 128) which is notable in that it does not explicitly suggest entirely new approaches as much as iterative efforts to build on what exists. However, in contrast, within governance and international development spaces, innovation has come to mean entirely novel tools to solve specific problems that will somehow reach a scale that can change systems. There is a fascination within development studies and practice, and an overreliance, on new technologies and often a duplication of efforts that already exist within communities. The literature around systems innovation is also helpful as it allows us to better understand how innovation leads to changes in the production and distribution of knowledge (Midgley and Lindhult, 2021). As much as we might like them to, new technology tools do not translate into anti-corruption outcomes automatically (Adam and Fazekas, 2021). Innovation is as much about building on and pulling together extant ideas, networks, and information in new ways as it is about developing entirely new approaches. Translocality is one of these existing approaches.

Collective action theory highlights the inability of individuals to put group interests above their own, even when it would benefit the group collectively to do so (Olsen, 1965). Some forms of collective action struggle to ensure resilience due to challenging external conditions. Pippidi (2013) suggested previously that too often, the ingredients that make collective action for meaningful change a success, such as a dense network of voluntary associations, do not exist in many countries facing corruption challenges. They may also lack sufficient alliances and embeddedness in broader communities.

Across the public and private sector, organisations use collective action approaches to curb corruption. An important aspect of achieving effective collective action is for groups to achieve resilience: for them to be able to strengthen their base, grow and develop, find allies, sharpen techniques and methods, and connect to forms of knowledge and innovation elsewhere. A good example of this is the Maritime Anti-Corruption Network (MACN) through which 190 companies across shipping, ports, and logistics have come together to ensure transparency and integrity.

Translocalism as a way to structure collective action is not new. The idea of translocal networks seems to have first emerged in the writing of anthropologist Arjun Appadurai in relation to local ethnographic inquiry (Appadurai, 1996). Conceptually, the idea of translocal networks has been used widely, in relation to issues including migration (Sakdapolrak, 2016; Brickell *et al.*, 2011), financial cooperatives (Avelino, 2018), food systems, eco-villages, renewable energy, and just economies (Loorbach *et al.* 2020). Translocal approaches have also existed within the service delivery and arts space for a long time. However, despite the growth of global coalitions, networks, peer groups, and regional organisations in anti-corruption, there are few that apply meaningful translocal approaches. We think there are ways to operationalise translocalism for collective action within the corruption space.

The translocal perspective aligns conceptually and politically with the "localization" agenda in that it supports local agency and leadership, and is predicated on the understanding that local people and communities have the ideas, trust, and motivation to take advantage of opportunities to create positive change (Slim, 2021). With localisation now being a core goal of large donors within the anti-corruption space, translocal anti-corruption efforts provide a set of principles and vehicles by which funders and others can shift power and meaningfully ensure their work is led by those closest to developmental challenges. At the same time, translocal networks can build on more traditional conceptions of collective action and networks, because in addition they can create "spaces of agency and overcome the constraints posed by a nation-state bounded view…[T]hey both transgress and transcend locality and have the ability to change the local spaces from which they emerge" (Banerjee, 2011, p. 334).

As further examples below will illustrate, a translocal perspective may help to address some central challenges outlined earlier in this book in relation to anti-corruption – including isomorphic mimicry (Andrews *et al.*, 2017); the lack of meaningful collective action around governance issues (Mungiu-Pippidi, 2013; Johnston and Kpundeh 2002); and the failure of one-size-fits-all approaches that insufficiently account for local dynamics (Mutebi, 2008).

Operationalising Translocal Principles in Collective Action

A translocal approach involves local forms of collective action *transcending* the immediate site of their problem or challenge. It describes the process of connecting people, communities, and organisations across different localities to share knowledge, coordinate, and collaborate to achieve shared goals. This section describes specifically the way collective action against corruption can be structured in a discordant world with a translocal perspective. Building on the work of Loorbach *et al.* (2020), which outlines how transformative innovations are diffused through translocal networks, we would argue that this kind of approach has 6 main elements.

Closing the Gap between the Site of a Problem and Levers of Change

Translocal does not necessarily mean global, but rather that the network connects outwards and upwards beyond where a particular problem is felt to levers of change that exist beyond that community. In this way, proximity is reimagined as moving from closeness to a problem to closeness to levers of change, whether those be local, national, or international. This is innovative because it nuances the idea of local solutions for local problems which may not be fully effective when acting against a multi-source problem like corruption.

When communities recognise that local corruption is fuelled by outside forces (such as global markets or foreign actors), it validates globally accepted anti-corruption norms as relevant, making it harder for local leaders to dismiss reform efforts as "imposed" or irrelevant. The rationale for local, community-level efforts to fight corruption such as greater ownership, legitimacy, and accountability is well known (Robbins, 2000; Mansuri and Rao, 2012). But in and of itself, proximity is not enough; these efforts can reach limits when national-level actors specifically covet local resources and engage in institutional capture to obtain them (Klein *et al.*, 2021). At the same time, anti-corruption efforts often target either the local or the national/international, without sufficient attention to the connections between these levels (Burai, 2020). Translocal networks allow us to cross-cut dichotomies such as local and global, and connect local efforts to larger dynamics (Marcus, 1995).

La Via Campesina, an international farmers' organisation, exemplifies how a translocal network of this kind can generate meaningful governance change across levels (Juarez, 2015). As one of La Via Campesina's founding coalitions in 1993, the Landless Workers' Movement of Brazil (MST) achieved a level of land reform unparalleled almost anywhere else in the world. The basis of its success is translocal. The movement's objectives are set by chapters of landless farmers in local communities, but information and lobbying efforts are shared on the national and global stage (Tricontinental: Institute for Social Research, 2024). For example, members of the MST in Goiânia are very focused on claiming illegally closed-off land in Goiânia, but they also benefit from the support that comes with being part of a larger network. This model strengthens the MST because individuals can unite and use their collective strength for success, with large enough numbers of people pushing the Brazilian Congress to recognise peasant rights, for example. Or they are widely spread enough that it is more challenging for corporations to intimidate and isolate advocates (Plummer and Ranum, 2002). This local-national dynamic has allowed the MST to protect 18.75 million acres of land from extractive industries corporations through land occupations and "successfully pressuring local authorities to build more than 2,000 public schools in agrarian reform settlements" (Tricontinental, 2024, p. 28).

Adapting and Learning from Alternative Sources That Transcend Immediate/Local Knowledge Flows

Translocalism is also about how networks evolve in ways that allow for learning to be disseminated across the network to inform and improve practice.

Translocal networks feature an exchange of information, ideas, and identities, (Peth, 2019) or open systems. While there is a strong focus on exchanges, a substantial share of information on context originates from the local communities. These networks are locally active but globally connected around learning. The goal of this iterative learning is to allow stakeholders, ranging from citizens to officials to academics, to find new interpretations of their communities. Nodes in a network can draw on local lessons from elsewhere and integrate these ideas into their own specific contexts as needed and as they grow.

The challenge here arises in maintaining a decentralised network where nodes remain facilitators of knowledge and action rather than centralised units of power and decision-making within the network. Some larger international NGOs, such as Christian Aid, center adaptive learning in what they do and the evidence indicates that this leads to better developmental outcomes (Gray 2022). However, part of the power of translocal approaches is that they do not necessarily involve the imperative to achieve predetermined outcomes as tends to be central to most donor funded anti-corruption programming. Decentralised knowledge production is a core part of the translocal approach by default. There is not a "center" that directs what does and does not count as knowledge but organisations within the network can build on learning from each other to inform collective approaches. This activates a decentralised knowledge base that may be otherwise unavailable.

From the community financial management sector there is much we can learn about translocal knowledge and adapting from Stokvels, a South African mutual savings fund program commonly known as a "rotating savings and credit association" (ROSCA). Traditionally, Stokvels' programmes were an important poverty alleviation method amongst disadvantaged, predominantly black South African women (Matuku et al, 2014). A recently published Ipsos study revealed that South Africa's R50 billion ($2.5 billion) Stokvel sector is made up of more than 800,000 Stokvel groups and 11 million members, a vast network of dynamic "human banks." So, while a sense of community and tradition remain at the heart of the Stokvel model, by working together these groups draw on alternative forms of knowledge and take on more modern investment strategies and technology tools that increase their ability to quickly adapt and to leverage financial opportunities (Ipsos, 2024). In 1988, the National Stokvel Association of South Africa (NASASA) was established to support, share learning, and build academic knowledge about this unique informal financial structure. The association's research desk employs field coordinators and Stokvel community leaders to organise engagements and retrieve information to inform the formulation and implementation of development plans that improve effectiveness (NASASA, 2024).

Development and Diffusion via Values

Translocal networks can grow and replicate organically as they evolve, improve, and connect. This contrasts with larger, often international organisations, which can have a very specific objective of scaling up and run into problems as a result. The international development field tends to encourage scale in terms of reach instead of impact, and this can push organisations beyond their capabilities. Elements of frameworks for scaling up outlined by the likes of Hartmann and Linn (2008) have become central to donor decision-making. But examples of ethical failures among larger NGOs such as Oxfam and Save the Children, organisations that have grown dramatically and as a result failed their communities, are instructive (Dolšak et al., 2018).

Within the anti-corruption space, in which political dynamics are partly local and solutions must be driven by incentives within specific places, a pre-determined emphasis on scale is problematic. Instead, translocal networks can encourage the diffusion of local values and approaches. A good example is People Powered, which is a global hub for participatory democracy. Participatory democracy is essential to anti-corruption efforts because it can generate transparency, build accountability, improve public oversight and engagement, and overcome political divisions. Since 2019, People Powered has grown quickly but organically, drawing in local members from over the world, 58 of whom (from 28 countries) set the initial mission, vision, commitments, priorities, and importantly, values, from the outset. This co-creation provided buy-in to the network and the space for additional members at the local, national, and regional level from across civil society to join. Each pays dues (as they can afford) to keep the network going, and contributes to and benefits from collective tools, training, and opportunities. In relation to anti-corruption, member organisations within People Powered such as Alma Civica in Paraguay and K-Monitor in Hungary have collaborated to scale a free participatory mapping platform, which has supported citizens to hold their governments accountable for public spending. Nodes within these kinds of networks can provide support, and some degree of permanence, but do not become ossified, larger structures that prevent adaptive approaches over time. This approach echoes Elinor Ostrom's finding that peer-monitoring and mutual accountability can sustain collective initiatives without top-down enforcement (Ostrom, 1990).

Identity Building through Positive Narratives

Collective action infused with translocalism can help to create a shared discourse and identity implicitly in what the network does and explicitly through the messaging around the cause. All networks do something of this kind but the most effective translocal networks, we would argue, do this in ways that are grounded in positivity. This allows networks to build narratives for change that provide an alternative to the status quo and the entrenched systems that perpetuate it. It is very hard for us to think what a different reality might be like until there are collective voices and local allies helping us imagine it in practice. Research indicates that narratives and policy stories can help citizens (including those unaffected) imagine how and why issues may occur and consider possible solutions and their impacts (Oliver *et al.* 2012). The construction of effective, positive narratives has been a huge missing piece of the anti-corruption puzzle. Translocal networks are particularly well-positioned to construct and spread these positive narratives across locales.

This also relates to the significant academic research which indicates that punishment and enforcement (the approach around which most anti-corruption practice is centred) should be balanced with encouragement and recognition to ensure better outcomes (Scott, 2023). It builds on the idea of "positive deviance" which derives from "observable exceptions" – outliers who succeed against all odds as they deviate in a positive way from the norm (Pascale, 2010). Positive deviance was piloted as an approach in the 1990s in Vietnam and as a development practice has altered the lives of millions of people. It provides an entry point for us to better understand the dynamics of social change, and then to design approaches that are based on that enhanced understanding. Efforts based on the idea of positive deviance have contributed to everything from the reduction in corruption in Kenya to increased success of black entrepreneurs in South Africa (Pascale, 2010). Positive deviancy can also address the challenge identified (Peiffer et al 2023) that greater emphasis on graft through anti-corruption campaigns can reinforce the sense that corruption is ubiquitous and in turn reinforce participation in corrupt systems.

At Accountability Lab, one example of how we do this translocally is through the Integrity Icon campaign, an effort to "name and fame" honest government officials rather than "name and shame" those that may be engaging in corrupt behaviours. The campaign works through developing local, positive stories about integrity and connecting them across contexts to build a sustained, meta-narrative. It flips this narrative by publicly highlighting civil servants with integrity and providing them with a national platform to showcase their values. This begins to build a different story that people can get behind: ensure solidarity among reformers across contexts, encourage young people to join government and make values-based decisions, and even shift the norms that drive corrupt behaviour in the first place. Through the campaign we have seen clearly that positive deviance, especially in anti-corruption, is a more resilient form of framing and way of sustaining action. Other related translocal networks such as the International Observatory on Participatory Democracy (IOPD) and larger international efforts such as the Open Government Partnership (OGP) also host awards to encourage citizen-focused governance and help to share learning across member organisations in divergent contexts which are critical to the change needed within the anti-corruption space (IOPD and OGP, 2025).

Facilitating Solidarity through Collective Action

Effective translocal approaches allow organisations to find ways to partner to support each other and amplify their efforts. This means partnership not in the transactional sense but in the sense of solidarity and acting as allies during difficult times. Here again, we can draw from the literature around social movements, which outline how collective efforts can be prioritised over individual actions and external solidarity is generated through empathy and care (Santos, 2019). In this, translocal networks are not unlike other networks in the anti-corruption practice. For example, the efforts of Indonesian civil society to protect the Anti-Corruption Commission (Komisi Pemberantasan Korupsi or KPK) in the early 2000s, through a massive coalition-building effort including more than 100 civil society groups, legal non-profits, women's groups, student groups, youth collectives, and labour groups operating from the national to the hyper-local levels, drawing on learning and connections with partners based elsewhere in the world (Beyerle, 2014). Allying in intelligent ways to build out social media campaigns and collaborate with mural painters, celebrities, and former government officials, the "gecko" campaign was ultimately successful in ensuring the release of KPK leaders and protecting the Commission (Kasm, 2015). A central reason for the success of the *Gecko* movement was the solidarity it created across class, religious and economic lines (Beyerle, 2014). Such solidarity means that when one group comes under attack, others rally in support, making it harder for authorities to isolate and eliminate any single effort – thereby ensuring the *continuity* of the anti-corruption movement.

The Otpor (resistance) movement in Serbia clearly demonstrates elements of translocality (or what Waisanen (2013) has called "glocal recursion") in the partnerships and learning it has generated since the ousting of the Milosevic regime in 2000. Otpor grew from a small civic protest into a large-scale movement that centred creative approaches using humour, the arts, and pop culture in unorthodox ways to achieve its goals. Local anti-corruption and pro-democratic actors from Egypt to Belarus to Zimbabwe have adapted and integrated Otpor techniques and tactics ever since. Indeed, founding Otpor members set up the Center for Applied Nonviolent Action and Strategies (CANVAS) to support them to do so. In Georgia in 2003, CANVAS support for Kmara (Enough!) helped to precipitate a peaceful transition of power. In Ukraine in 2004–2005, CANVAS efforts supported the coordination of the youth movement against the authoritarian government. In translocal partnerships, the emphasis tends to be in a larger sense on sharing resources and capacities and putting the field ahead of individual or organisational recognition or goals. Many networks support collective goals within a specific domain. Translocal networks support the larger ecosystem.

Pushing Back against Closing Civic Space

Finally, innovation through collective action with a translocal approach can help support the anti-corruption field to nullify dynamics of contestation and abuse. Political efforts of citizens at the grassroots that are supported to transcend their local sites of problems can provide an effective alternative to overly localised or top-down forms of collective action. This is particularly the case during time-specific windows of opportunity – to address an emergency, or after a change in government, for example, when collaboration with reformers within systems may also be possible. One illustration of this within the anti-corruption space is the way that graft-fighting organisations came together during the COVID-19 pandemic to ensure transparency of the billions of dollars that flowed into pandemic response efforts around the world. In Africa, the COVID-19 Transparency and Accountability Project (CTAP) brought together local civil society organisations – and international groups, along with philanthropies – to track pandemic interventions in Cameroon, Ghana, Kenya, Liberia, Malawi, Nigeria, Zimbabwe, Senegal, and Sierra Leone. This was a period of democratic backsliding and abuse in that many of these governments were using emergency measures to restrict civic space and participation; and avoid checks and balances as they related to public spending (Akinyetun, 2023).

The CTAP network worked together to track more than $62 billion in pandemic funds that flowed to these 9 countries, improve procurement data transparency and track resources to the sub-national level. Importantly, these efforts also led to additional local coalition-building efforts – among CSOs, the media, young people, and health care workers – that generated additional demands for government accountability – as with the #FixTheCountry movement in Ghana for example (Flores *et al.*, 2022). The CTAP initiative has since evolved into a larger joint effort to advocate around healthcare policy and provide information to citizens around vaccinations more broadly.

It is also the case in places where civic space is restricted or authoritarian or autocratic actors are actively working to shut down demand for better governance. Our own experiences working in places where this is the case are instructive – the value of Accountability Lab's translocal network has repeatedly been clear as we have mobilised hubs across the network to share ideas (for example around how to respond to mid/dis-information during disasters or pandemics), provide solidarity (either privately or publicly when needed – for example during recent aid cuts), and ensure visibility when space for accountability work has shrunk (for example by highlighting each other's work within international networks).

We have found that governments that use scare and intimidation tactics against local populations are less likely to employ these tactics against those that have access to networks outside of the country. In Nigeria, for example, after a period of sustained advocacy by Accountability Lab and partners against social media bans and the imprisonment of journalists in Nigeria, an insider-outsider approach involving government ministers, journalists, and citizens has drawn attention to the reforms needed around digital rights, promoting an open internet and preventing the erosion of civic space.

It is important that these are not necessarily seen to be "international" networks per se in ways that can then be manipulated to further paint local allies as agents of foreign actors. The translocal essence of the network can provide external validity and internal credibility in ways that can mitigate against reprisals. The #KeepItOn campaign and coalition, led by Access Now, is an excellent example of similar work on a larger scale among organisations that collaborate to identify, verify, and document incidents of internet shutdowns to raise awareness and prevent recurrence. When space for dissent closes, there is power in numbers, making it more difficult for vested interests to harm individuals (Beyerle, 2014).

Table 11.1 summarises these six dimensions of translocal approaches in terms of what they might bring to anti-corruption efforts, why these ideas are important, and some conditions for success to bear in mind across these domains.

What Kind of Anti-Corruption Approaches Do We Need in a Discordant World?

The six elements outlined above are central to the kind of translocal approach for collective action that could provide a bulwark against corruption in the future. Integrating approaches of this kind into anti-corruption efforts and collective action mechanisms makes sense. A practical question emerges with this in mind: how can decision-makers and leaders at every level and across organisations best support or adapt them meaningfully within the anti-corruption space, given the political, economic, and social constraints that exist?

First, it means bringing collective action efforts that take a translocal approach together to ensure "mutual recognition and strategic collaboration" (Avelino, 2018). As Avelino points out, the European Network for Community Led Initiatives on Climate Change and Sustainability (ECOLISE) is one such example within the environmental space. There are others within the development field more broadly including the Movement for Community Led Development (MCLD) and the #ShiftthePower effort led by the Global Fund for Community Foundations (GFCF). A similar meta-effort to mainstream, support, and inspire community led action on anti-corruption would

TABLE 11.1 The six dimensions of translocal approaches

Translocal dimension	What a translocal approaches might bring	Why this is important for anti-corruption efforts	Conditions for success
Proximity	Communities close to the effects (victims) of corruption	Greater ownership, legitimacy, and accountability for anti-corruption efforts	The bigger picture is not lost while focusing on the proximate
Adapting and Learning	Ideas and lessons from elsewhere can be adapted to local contexts	Avoids isolation and encourages new perspectives on anti-corruption	Learning is not centralised and adaptation is not simply replication
Development and Diffusion	Organic, bottom-up growth of connections and agendas	Builds larger coalitions for anti-corruption and integrates anti-corruption into other policy areas	Resistance from vested interests can be overcome
Identity Building	Robust communities built on shared narratives, values, and identities	Challenges the status quo and the official understanding of the corruption problem (and possible abuse of anti-corruption)	Effective leaders who can create narratives, share values, and create identities
Solidarity	Collective action, partnerships, alliances, and solidarity across sectors	Builds broader alliances and support for anti-corruption	Alignment of incentives and energy across actors
Civic Space	External validity, internal credibility, and collective legitimacy	Can open space for civil society and collective action, and mitigate/ defuse reprisals	Ability to overcome divide and rule tactics and repression

Source: Author's own compilation

be transformative. New technologies could also support this kind of effort and open new pathways to forge translocal connections.

Second, it means those in positions of power within the social sector (donors in particular) taking more risks to allow organisations and movements as they grow to consolidate, amplify, and adapt what they do. This begins with an understanding that anti-corruption is a systemic problem but solutions emerge when they are tailored to specific, local problems around which communities can mobilise (Khan *et al.*, 2019), and can grow endogenously from that point. This also means moving beyond prescribed project log frames and predetermined understandings of what anti-corruption interventions may or may not achieve. In rapidly changing political contexts and when working with adaptive networks it does not make sense to lock anti-corruption efforts into deliverables that may rapidly become obsolete. Partnerships require flexibility that allows network members to build relationships over time but also adapt quickly as moments emerge during which anti-corruption actions can be most effective.

One might ask how donors and partners might ensure accountability of these kinds of approaches, but accountability is embedded into peer-based, relational systems. In "Governing the Commons," Ostrom proposes "mutual monitoring" through which conformity reduces infractions over time (1990). Creating transparency mechanisms through both self-monitoring and peer-monitoring reduces the risk of inconsistency and can increase coordination. On the resourcing side, this might mean looking at other models that could be adapted to the anti-corruption field. For example, the International Urban Poor Fund International collects funds nationally (bearing the currency and capital risk) and disburses these to savings federations working locally, who then engage in "venture financing" to seed new approaches to urban and climate issues locally. The Fund also facilitates cross-community sharing of information through learning centers (IIED, 2006). The Roddenbury Foundation +1 Global Fund is also instructive. It uses a creative network of network model to ensure pooled resources are directed to effective local efforts, around which active communities and practice are then built. Large-scale facilities of this sort do not exist in the anti-corruption space and would be worth exploring as part of a reimagined funding approach to these problems.

Third, it means supporting the ecosystem building organisations that do not just implement projects but that facilitate learning, convening, sharing, and connecting the dots between change-makers. For many reasons, either political, bureaucratic, or financial, funding for large-scale anti-corruption efforts flows to large contractors and international implementing organisations, who in turn sub-contract to smaller, local entities. Part of the push towards localisation means inverting this process to ensure it is local organisations that take the lead on anti-corruption, with the support, as needed, of external partners. Equally, we must find ways to bolster organisations that provide the connective tissue among and across these kinds of projects, both locally and internationally. As Barabasi has pointed out, highly linked nodes within a network grow fastest (Barabasi 2014), and it is support for these nodes, or ecosystem building organisations, within translocal networks that can provide the basis for larger-scale change in approaches.

Other node organisations adjacent to the anti-corruption space can play an essential role in allowing these networks to grow around them. Organisations like CIVICUS and Grassroots International do this around broader issues of civil liberties and human rights, while organisations such as Accountable Now provide support for internal civil society accountability. Groups including the Public Service Accountability Monitor (PSAM) generate and share knowledge around social accountability and citizen monitoring and advocacy tools. In the arts space, the Center for Artistic Activism brings together organisations from across West Africa and the Western Balkans to test out new tactics and ideas. Key connector organisations within the anti-corruption space across specific themes deserve similar backing. Open Ownership, for example, has been central to recent global efforts to drive beneficial ownership reforms.

Finally, it means intentionally centring equity and bridging the divides between elite, capital city centric anti-corruption organisations and grassroots efforts – "the wonks and the street" (Bellows, 2020). This is important to ensure inclusion but also to confirm we are addressing the correct problems. Previous research by U4 in Madagascar shows, for example, that corruption concerns viewed from the perspectives of local communities can look very different to those prioritised by external actors (Klein et al 2023). Building translocal networks requires bringing together both professionalised civil society organisations and more organic, local groups who may not directly operate within the anti-corruption space but can mobilise citizens around causes that affect them, including religious and community groups (Mungiu-Pippidi and Johnston, 2017). This allows these coalitions to collectively push in translocal ways, aligning goals, strategies, communications techniques, and learning. Through partnership, these networks avoid the pitfalls Bellows (2020) points out among "hybridising" organisations that attempt to build broader constituencies around their work, including a lack of understanding, grassroots connections, and sustainability.

This is not easy, and from the perspective of external actors attempting to support these efforts, it requires acknowledgment of the inequalities within development systems, around everything from decision-making to hiring practices, and active efforts to address these. In all of this, there is the danger that translocality becomes another buzzword, co-opted by organisations to build influence, and used by intermediaries or donors to feign meaningful localisation while maintaining existing project implementation and funding incentives and mechanisms. We must avoid this at all costs and ensure we bear the six key translocal qualities in mind when understanding what sort of networks to build within the anti-corruption space.

Conclusion

Corruption is a problem that is not bounded by borders – and is inherently connected through dynamic relationships to other places. The failure of anti-corruption efforts is often seen as an implementation problem, as those effective policies and institutions derived from Western models cannot be adequately consolidated elsewhere. In practice, these initiatives fail because of the "design-reality" gap. The policies and institutions themselves have not been designed with the context, values, organisational culture, and work processes at the core (Heeks, 2011). They are driven by contractors and other entities that in many cases have a financial incentive not to share expertise in sustainable ways or to build meaningful partnerships that endure over time. Many existing anti-corruption approaches have become locked into path-dependencies, and with the sunk costs and bureaucratic structures within development organisations, these dependencies are only reinforced at a time when we should be thinking in entirely new ways. Collective action efforts using translocal approaches begin to address these challenges; generate different kinds of incentives; and provide a different understanding of place, space, and connectivity in our globalised, discordant world.

Translocal thinking is by no means a panacea. If not thought through, nodes within a network can become centralised units of power and decision-making; consensus on ways forward can be difficult when contexts are diverse; and aligning incentives and energy can be difficult. But these are challenges that exist with other kinds of approaches that exist too. Collective action with a translocal approach allows people to reimagine their identity and agency within systems that often act to prevent this kind of thinking. It allows them to connect the local to the national and the global – but not become co-opted by or subsumed within global processes that may not best defend their own local interests. These networks are linked to specific places but can fuel larger intersectional political movements that can counter complex problems like corruption. They are globally connected but locally rooted (Loorbach et al., 2020) and allow citizens to build resilience and support the flow of ideas, resources, and information across contexts. To conclude, translocal collective action – by linking local initiatives to wider change-levers, fostering cross-context learning, growing organically through shared values, building positive identities, forging solidarity, and keeping civic space open – provides a more sustainable path to fight corruption in a discordant world.

References

Adam, I. and Fazekas, M. 2021. Are emerging technologies helping win the fight against corruption? A review of the state of evidence. *Information Economics and Policy*, Volume 57. Available at: https://www.sciencedirect.com/science/article/pii/S016762452100038X (Accessed 11 September 2024)

Akinyetun, T. 2023. *Democratic backsliding in Africa: Understanding the current challenges.* Kujenga Amani. https://kujenga-amani.ssrc.org/2022/09/20/democratic-backsliding-in-africa-understanding-the-current-challenges/

Amundsen, I. "Protests in Kenya and Uganda highlight corruption at the top- but political elites don't give in without a fight" *The Conversation*, July 31st 2024: https://theconversation.com/protests-in-kenya-and-uganda-highlight-corruption

-at-the-top-but-political-elites-dont-give-in-without-a-fight-235709 (Accessed 3 April 2025)

Andrews, M., Pritchett, L. and Woolcock, M. 2017. Looking like a state: The seduction of isomorphic mimicry. *Building State Capability: Evidence, Analysis, Action.* Oxford University Press eBooks. Available at: https://doi.org/10.1093/acprof:oso/9780198747482.001.0001

Appadurai, A. 1996. Modernity at Large: Cultural Dimensions of Globalization. (University of Minnesota Press).

Avelino, F et al. 2018. Translocal Empowerment in Transformative Social Innovation Networks. *European Planning Studies* 2020, 28(5), 955–977. Available at: https://doi.org/10.1080/09654313.2019.1578339 (Accessed 15 January 2025)

Banerjee, S.B. 2011. Voices of the Governed: Towards a Theory of the Translocal. *Organization*, 18(3), 323–344. Available at: https://doi.org/10.1177/1350508411398729 (Accessed 15 January 2025).

Barabasi, A-L. 2014. Linked: How Everything Is Connected to Everything Else and What It Means for Business, Science, and Everyday Life. (Basic Books).

Bellows, A. 2020. Bridging the Elite- Grassroots Divide Among Anticorruption Activists, Carnegie Endowment for International Peace, Working Paper: https://carnegie-production-assets.s3.amazonaws.com/static/files/WP_Bellows_EliteGrassroots.pdf

Beyerle, S. 2014. Curtailing Corruption: People Power for Accountability and Justice. (Lynne Rienner Publishers).

Brickell, K. and Datta, A. 2011. *Translocal Geographies: Spaces, Places, Connections.* Ashgate, Farnham. Available at: https://kclpure.kcl.ac.uk/portal/en/publications/translocal-geographies-spaces-places-connections (Accessed 15 January 2025).

Burai, P. 2020. Overcoming the pitfalls of engaging communities in anti-corruption programme. *U4 Issue,* 4. Chr. Michelsen Institute. Available at: https://pure.mpg.de/pubman/item/item_3241301_1/component/file_3242003/overcoming-the-pitfalls-of-engaging-communities-in-anti-corruption-programmes.pdf (Accessed 15 January 2025).

Dolšak, N., Parr, S. and Prakash, A. 2018. The Oxfam scandal shows that yes, nonprofits can behave badly. So why aren't they overseen like for-profits? *The Washington Post*, 19 February. Available at: https://www.washingtonpost.com/news/monkey-cage/wp/2018/02/19/the-oxfam-scandal-shows-that-yes-nonprofits-can-behave-badly-so-why-arent-they-overseen-like-for-profits/ (Accessed 13 May 2025).

Gray, S. and Carl, A. 2022. The Difference Learning Makes: factors that enable or inhibit adaptive programming for Christian Aid Ireland and partner organizations. Available at: https://www.christianaid.ie/sites/default/files/2022-12/the-difference-learning-makes-factors-that-enable-and-inhibit-adaptive-programming.pdf (Accessed 12 December 2024).

Hartmann, A. and Linn, J. 2008. Scaling Up: A Framework and Lessons for Development Effectiveness from Literature and Practice. Wolfensohn Center Working Paper No. 5. Brookings. (Accessed 15 January 2025)

Heeks, R. 2011. Understanding success and failure of anti-corruption initiatives. *U4 Brief*, 2. Chr. Michelsen Institute, pp. 1–4. https://www.u4.no/publications/understanding-success-and-failure-of-anti-corruption-initiatives (Accessed 17 January 2025).

International Institute for Environment and Development. 2006. The International Urban Poor Fund. Available at: https://www.iied.org/g00509 (Accessed 8 April 2025).

International Observatory for Participatory Democracy (IOPD) Awards, available at: https://oidp.net/distinction/en/ (Accessed 6 April 2025)

Ipsos. 2024. Stokvels remain the untapped 'human banks' of South Africa. 13 March 2024, Available at: https://www.ipsos.com/en-za/stokvels-remain-untapped-human-banks-south-africa (Accessed).

Jamil, B., Shahbaz, M. and Yaping, S. (2023). Impact of income inequality on carbon emissions: a matter of corruption governance. *Environmental Science and Pollution Research*, 30 (37).

Johnston, M. and Kpundeh, S. 2002. Building A Clean Machine; Anti-Corruption Coalitions and Sustainable Reform. 3466, World Bank Institute. Available at: https://documents.worldbank.org/en/publication/documents-reports/documentdetail/216621468742826981/building-a-clean-machine-anti-corruption-coalitions-and-sustainable-reform. (Accessed 15 January 2025).

Juarez, P. *et al.* 2015. 'WP4 Case Study Report: La Via Campesina. *Transformative Social Innovation Theory (TRANSIT)*. Available at: http://www.transitsocialinnovation.eu/resource-hub/wp-4-case-study-report-la-via-campesina (Accessed)

Kasm, S. 2015. S. Beyerle, Curtailing Corruption: People Power for Accountability and Justice. *State Crime Journal*, 4(2). Pluto Journals. Available at: https://doi.org/10.13169/statecrime.4.2.0201 (Accessed 15 January 2025).

Khan, M. Andreoni, A. and Roy, P. 2019. Anti-corruption in adverse contexts: Strategies for improving implementation. *Anti-Corruption Evidence Research Consortium*. SOAS University of London, 13. Available at: https://ace.soas.ac.uk/publication/anti-corruption-in-adverse-contexts-strategies-for-improving-implementation/ (Accessed 15 December 2024).

Klein, B. *et al.* 2021 Enrolling the Local: Community-Based Anti-Corruption Efforts and Institutional Capture. *Targeting Natural Resource Corruption: Topic Brief*, Chr. Michelsen Institute. Available at: https://c402277.ssl.cf1.rackcdn.com/publications/1435/files/original/Topic-Brief-Enrolling-the-Local-Community-Based-Anti-Corruption-Efforts-and-Institutional-Capture.pdf?1612890192 (Accessed 15 December 2024).

Klein, B, *et al.* 2023. (Re)Interpreting corruption in local environments: Disputed definitions, contested conservation, and power plays in Northern Madagascar. *Political Geography*, Volume 107. Available at: https://www.sciencedirect.com/science/article/pii/S0962629823001518 (Accessed 21 December 2024).

Loorbach, D. *et al.* 2020. Transformative innovation and translocal diffusion. *Environmental Innovation and Societal Transitions*. Available at: https://doi.org/10.1016/j.eist.2020.01.009 (Accessed 21 September 2024).

Marquette, H. and Peiffer, C. 2015. Corruption and Collective Action, Developmental Leadership Program and U4. Available at: https://www.u4.no/publications/corruption-and-collective-action.

Matuku, S. and Kaseke, E. 2014. The role of stokvels in improving people's lives: The case in orange farm, Johannesburg, South Africa. *Social Work* (Stellenbosch). Available at: http://dx.doi.org/10.15270/50-4-388 (Accessed 17 October 2024).

Mansuri, G. and Rao, V. 2012. Localizing Development: Does Participation Work? *Policy Research Report.* The World Bank. Available at: https://doi.org/10.1596/978-0-8213-8256-1 (Accessed).

Marcus, G. 1995. Ethnography in/of the World System: The Emergence of Multi-Sited Ethnography. *Annual Review of Anthropology*, 24(1). Available at: https://doi.org/10.1146/annurev.an.24.100195.000523 (Accessed).

Midgley, G and Lindhult, E. 2021. A Systems Perspective on Systemic Innovation. *Systems Research and Behavioral Science*, 38(5). Available at: https://onlinelibrary.wiley.com/doi/full/10.1002/sres.2819 (Accessed)

Mungiu-Pippidi, A. 2013. Controlling Corruption through Collective Action. *Journal of Democracy*, 24(1). Available at: https://www.journalofdemocracy.org/articles/controlling-corruption-through-collective-action/ (Accessed).

Mungiu-Pippidi, A. and Johnston, M. 2017. Transitions to Good Governance: Creating Virtuous Circles of Anti-Corruption. (Edward Elgar Publishing)

Mutebi, A. 2008. Explaining the Failure of Thailand's Anti-Corruption Regime. *Development and Change*, 39(1). Available at: https://doi.org/10.1111/j.1467-7660.2008.00472.x (Accessed 15 January 2025).

National Stokvel Association of South Africa. 2024. Moving towards a better future for all. Available at: https://nasasa.co.za/ (Accessed 30 September 2024).

Oliver, M. *et al.* 2012. The Effect of Narrative News Format on Empathy for Stigmatized Groups. *Journalism & Mass Communication Quarterly*, 89(2). Available at: https://doi.org/10.1177/1077699012439020. (Accessed 15 January 2025)

Olsen, M. 1965. The Logic of Collective Action: Public Goods and the Theory of Groups (Harvard University Press)

Open Government Partnership (OGP) Awards: https://www.opengovpartnership.org/open-government-awards/ Accessed 6 April 2025

Ostrom, E. (1990). Governing the Commons: The Evolution of Institutions for Collective Action. (Cambridge University Press).

Pascale, R. et al. (2010) The Power of Positive Deviance: How Unlikely Innovators Solve the World's Toughest Problems, Harvard Business Press. Available at: https://books.google.co.zw/books?hl=en&lr=&id=nBgDmcy9SnkC&oi=fnd&pg=PR1&dq=positive+deviance+approach&ots=xHRbuSOzJ8&sig=9B8MuDUtIlUsR_OCz_HyvboulL4&redir_esc=y#v=onepage&q=positive%20deviance%20approach&f=false (Accessed 29 September 2024).

Peiffer, C. and Cheeseman, N. 2023. Message misunderstood: Why raising awareness of corruption can backfire. U4 Anti-Corruption Resource Center Brief: Available at: https://www.u4.no/publications/message-misunderstood-why-raising-awareness-of-corruption-can-backfire.pdf (Accessed 10 November 2024).

Peth, S.A. 2019. What is translocality: A refined understanding of place and space in a globalized world,' *TransRe Blog*, Department of Geography, University of Bonn. Available at: www.transre.org/en/blog/what-translocality/ (Accessed 26 September 2024).

Plummer, D. and Ranum, B. 2002. 'Brazil's landless workers movement--movimiento de trabajadores rurales sem terra--MST,' *Social Policy*, 33(1), 18+, available: https://link.gale.com/apps/doc/A94590272/AONE?u=anon~3a33ae52&sid=googleScholar&xid=a85707fb (Accessed 17 November 2025).

Robbins, P. (2000) The Rotten Institution: Corruption in Natural Resource Management. *Political Geography*, 19(4). Available at: https://doi.org/10.1016/s0962-6298(99)00087-6 (Accessed).

Sakdapolrak, P. *et al.* 2016. Migration in a Changing Climate: Towards a Translocal Social Resilience Approach. *DIE ERDE – Journal of the Geographical Society of Berlin*, 147(2). Available at: https://doi.org/10.12854/erde-147-6 (Accessed).

Santos, F.G. 2019. Social Movements and the Politics of Care: Empathy, Solidarity, and Eviction Blockades. *Social Movement Studies*, 19(2). Available at: https://doi.org/10.1080/14742837.2019.1665504 (Accessed).

Scott, H. K., Jain, A. and Cogburn, M. (2023). Behavior Modification. In *StatPearls*. (StatPearls Publishing).

Shannon, G. *et al.* 2023. Think Global, Act Local: Using a Translocal Approach to Understand Community-Based Organizations' Responses to Planetary Health Crises During COVID-19. *The Lancet Planetary Health*, 7(10). Available at: https://www.thelancet.com/journals/lanplh/article/PIIS2542-5196(23)00193-6/fulltext (Accessed 04 October 2024).

Slim, H. 2021. Localization is Self-Determination. *Frontiers in Political Science* 3, 708584. https://doi.org/10.3389/fpos.2021.708584 (Accessed 24 October 2024)

Taylor, S. 2017. What is Innovation? A Study of the Definitions, Academic Models and Applicability of Innovation to an Example of Social Housing in England. *Open Journal of Social Sciences*, 05(11). Available at: https://doi.org/10.4236/jss.2017.511010 (Accessed 01 October 2024).

The Political Organisation of Brazil's Landless Workers' Movement (MST)-Tricontinental Dossier No.75: https://thetricontinental.org/dossier-75-landless-workers-movement-brazil/

Waisanen, D. 2013. (Trans)national Advocacy in the Ousting of Milosevic: The Otpor Movement's Glocal Recursions. *Communication Studies*, 64(2). Available at: https://doi.org/10.1080/10510974.2012.752756. (Accessed 30 September 2024).

12

AI TO INNOVATE ANTI-CORRUPTION

Exploring Development Models for Governmental and Non-Governmental Applications

Carolina Gerli and Fernanda Odilla

Introduction

Artificial Intelligence (AI) is gaining momentum as a powerful ally for public, private, and civil society organisations combating corruption. Thanks to its ability to rapidly automate the collection and processing of large amounts of digital data and to generate automated content in various formats, AI holds the promise of speeding up processes, reducing the discretion of public officials, helping to hold governments and businesses accountable, and improving transparency (Köbis et al., 2022; Odilla, 2023). This is crucial in a scenario where corruption takes different forms and moves quickly within and across country borders. However, AI-based anti-corruption tools are not immune to misuse, and there are risks associated with inaccurate outputs, which can reinforce or lead to bias and unfairness (Odilla, 2024). AI systems can be exploited, and individuals can be influenced to serve private interests while designing and implementing such technologies (Köbis and Starke, 2022). Amidst the high expectations and potential risks associated with AI-based anti-corruption technologies, we still know little about how these applications are designed, developed and implemented by governmental, and non-governmental organisations.

Defining AI is challenging. Broadly, AI is often equated with computer systems that can perceive and extract information, process this data, learn from it and make decisions with some degree of autonomy to achieve pre-set goals (Russell and Norvig, 2021). Not only has AI been used to refer to a wide variety of data processing techniques, such as Machine Learning (ML) and Generative Pre-Trainer Transformers (GPTs), but it has also changed rapidly over the years. This intrinsic evolution of AI makes it difficult to properly

DOI: 10.4324/9781003531920-16

define it at one point in time – what was dubbed as the "AI effect" by the computer scientist John McCarthy, according to (Geist (2016, p.2). We can, therefore, speak of "artificial intelligences" because of the rapid development of many applications that use different techniques to produce a wide range of outputs. Similar to AI, corruption is still a concept without an agreed common definition and can be seen as an umbrella term. While AI encompasses algorithms and data processing techniques, corruption encompasses practices such as bribery, embezzlement and nepotism, as well as related concepts such as clientelism, patronage and state capture, which are associated with the abuse of power for private gain (Odilla, 2023; Rothstein and Varraich, 2017).

AI models designed to curb corruption can be seen as part of what Mattoni (2024, p.7) named anti-corruption technologies (ACTs), i.e. socio-technical assemblages with the broad, abstract goal of addressing corruption, and the more immediate, concrete aim of tackling various forms of corruption and related behaviours, ranging from petty to grand corruption. Therefore, ACTs are not treated here as mere software and hardware artefacts, as they encompass not only material but social, symbolic and political dimensions that underpin the creation and use of such technologies (see Mattoni, 2024; Odilla, 2025). Yet, for analytical purposes, in this chapter, AI-based anti-corruption technologies (AI-based ACTs henceforth) are defined as data processing systems driven by tasks or problems designed to, with a degree of autonomy, identify, predict, summarise, and/or communicate actions related to the misuse of position, information and/or resources aimed at private gain at the expense of the collective good, whose application implies the analysis of a given environment based on a set of predefined rules before acting (Odilla, 2023, p. 354).

In recent years, different applications have been deployed to combat corruption, targeting a wide range of corruption-related issues, often associated with the misuse of public funds. While in Italy the police recruited data scientists to develop an AI system aimed at detecting corruption in public procurement, a police unit in southern Brazil opted to purchase IBM Watson to analyse large volumes of big data and assist in criminal investigations. In Ukraine, both ProZorro, the open-source AI-powered system launched in 2016 by civic tech activists and data experts and later adopted by the Ukrainian government, and DoZorro, a watchdog system for citizens and businesses, have enabled the detection of procurement violations and misuse of public funds (Yukins and Kelman, 2022). Similarly, in Brazil, three tech-savvy friends created Rosie in 2016, a bot that scraped public data to identify suspicious spending by elected congressional members, tweeting its findings. Over the years, Rosie flagged thousands of suspicious expenses, although it stopped posting in 2022 (Odilla and Mattoni, 2023).

As Rosie, Watson and ProZorro, there are many other AI-based anti-corruption applications currently in place, being used and developed by governmental (public organisations) and non-governmental actors (civil society, activists, journalists) as well as by the private sector (like audit and law firms). However, we still know little about the design, development, and implementation processes of these applications, which are often shrouded in opacity. There is also limited empirical evidence on the AI-based ACTs currently in use, and on the details of their development and implementation. The same applies to the evaluation of the impact of these tools.

Retrieving information about these applications from official and unofficial sources can be complex, and details about their creation and use are rarely available. This chapter aims to advance in this regard both empirically and analytically by examining key elements of the innovation models by which civil society and governmental organisations create and deploy AI-based ACTs, shedding light on the actors involved, their decision-making processes, and other critical details that could make these tools more transparent and accountable.

First, the chapter provides an overview of emerging theories on AI in anti-corruption, highlighting associated opportunities, challenges, and risks. Second, it outlines the methodology used to gather in-depth evidence on the design and development processes of AI-based ACTs. Third, it introduces an evidence-based typology of the main development models for these solutions. Fourth, it discusses the main drivers, potential opportunities, and pitfalls of each model. Lastly, it concludes by reflecting on how AI is reshaping anti-corruption in a fragmented and complex world.

AI in Anti-Corruption: State of the Art

Existing research shows how AI can help *exante* and *expost* to predict suspicious patterns and detect corrupt practices, respectively. As a predictive application in anti-corruption measures, AI – especially ML techniques – can prevent corruption by, for example, flagging risks based on political and economic data (Lima and Delen, 2020; Colonnelli et al., 2019), identifying politically exposed individuals and politically connected firms with accuracy (Mazrekaj et al., 2021), predicting corruption patterns from tendering documents (Rabuzin and Modrušan, 2019), and tracking diverse cartel behaviours (Fazekas et al., 2023). Ash et al. (2020) proved that targeted policy guided by machine predictions in Brazil could detect almost twice as many corrupt municipalities for the same audit rate.

When used to identify corruption, AI has been proven to detect cases related to the misuse of public funds by elected officials (Odilla and Mattoni, 2023), illegal mining through satellite imagery (Leon, 2018), fraudulent activities (Olszewski, 2014), use of "ghost" companies, also using satellite imagery (Wacker et al., 2018) and even self-reported corruption experiences on social media (Li et al., 2020). The detective function of AI is particularly used in public procurement, where AI has helped to define new red flags of corruption in the purchase of services, goods and works (Fazekas and Kocsis, 2017), potential cases of conflict of interest and favouritism in public calls for tenders (Odilla, 2023) and collusion (Popa, 2019). AI-based ACTs, whether preventive or detective, are most commonly applied to public procurement and tax fraud by academics and governments (Torres Berru et al., 2020). Civil society, however, has used these tools more broadly to address malpractice and promote transparency in areas like legislative misuse of funds, judicial delays, and public goods construction (Odilla, 2023).

AI is already improving public sector monitoring capacity by processing vast amounts of data, identifying risks and inconsistencies, and promoting greater accountability (Colonnelli et al., 2019). However, these tools require large volumes of reliable and good-quality digital data to work, which are not often easy to get, especially in anti-corruption (Aarvik, 2019). By relying heavily on incomplete data and past cases, AI might replicate potential past biases (Adam and Fazekas, 2021). Odilla (2024) provides empirical evidence from Brazil discussing the different sources of unfairness of AI-based ACTs that go from problematic data used as input (and sometimes as outputs to support decision-making) to individual and institutional (often unconscious) bias in the design and implementation of these applications. Furthermore, the functioning of these technologies is quite opaque (Aarvik, 2019), even for developers themselves who sometimes cannot explain certain outputs, and this can exacerbate any existing biases.

AI-based ACTs are also not immune to abuse. Although the debate is still in its infancy in the anti-corruption field, some academics are already discussing how these systems can be hacked and how individuals can be corrupted to serve private interests in designing, developing and implementing such technologies (Köbis and Starke, 2022). Private companies could exploit these types of AI tools to collect personal data from citizens (Aarvik, 2019), and criminal groups could even manipulate these systems to avoid detection or increase profits (Adam and Fazekas, 2021). Lessons from fields that are more advanced in terms of collecting empirical evidence on the misuse of AI, like policing and counterterrorism, highlight significant concerns about the risks posed by these tools. They have been shown to perpetuate and even worsen existing disparities, such as poverty and structural racism in policing (Edler Duarte, 2021, p.374; Dressel and Farid, 2018), while also causing civilian harm and violating laws of war and privacy in war zones (Human Rights Watch, 2024).

In light of these challenges and risks, scholars agree that AI should be considered as an auxiliary tool in anti-corruption efforts. For Aarvik (2019), AI will not solve corruption on its own, no matter how effective it may be in predicting or detecting misconduct or abuse. Sanchez-Graells (2021) argues that due to the lack of practical experience with AI, these tools can only provide incremental improvements to anti-corruption oversight. Finally, Köbis et al. (2022) emphasise that humans need to be involved in the oversight of these applications. However, it is precisely the human aspect of AI-based ACTs that remains largely underexplored, particularly regarding who is involved in creating and implementing these technologies and how they conduct this process.

Development Models in the Context of Technology Adoption

In the context of technology adoption and innovation, development models describe how an organisation creates, delivers and captures value from the introduction of new technology (Chesbrough and Rosenbloom, 2002). Extensive research on the public sector and on firms of various sizes and sectors has explored different existing development models and their main features. These studies have focused on, for example, partnerships between firms (Sen and Haq, 2011), between the public and private sectors (Kuchina-Musina and Morris, 2022), and between universities and firms (Robertson and Mayr, 2011), and universities and the public sector (Demircioglu and Audretsch, 2019). Although the literature on civil society organisations (CSOs) in the area of technological innovation is comparatively limited, it has shown an overall low level of ownership, i.e. many grassroots anti-corruption initiatives use existing digital media or technologies originally designed for other purposes, which are often beyond the direct control of anti-corruption activists (Mattoni, 2024).

Some of these studies on technological adoption highlight budget constraints (Kuchina-Musina and Morris, 2022) and the need for the right experience among key drivers to innovate through different types of arrangements. They also stress co-creation and outsourcing as primary models for driving innovation when in-house solutions are not feasible. While acknowledging the differences in definition and the potential overlap, for example, between some types of outsourcing and co-creation, we consider the following three ideal types of development models which emerged from the analysis: 1) *In-house development* refers to technologies created within a governmental or non-governmental organisation, including businesses, CSOs, and the media, by its own staff; 2) *Outsourcing* refers to the procurement of a value-added activity from an external provider (Micheli et al., 2012). Here we treat outsourcing more strictly as the purchase of "off-the-shelf technologies" or ready-to-use products; 3) *Co-creation* involves customisation based on the contractor's requirements, may involve payment, and is used to achieve complex objectives requiring diverse expertise (Robertson and Mayr, 2011).

The literature on technological innovation often examines these models in isolation, without considering the enabling conditions, opportunities and challenges associated with each model. To fill these knowledge gaps and improve understanding of the creation of AI-based ACTs, it is necessary to examine how and by whom these technologies are developed, considering the interrelated features and nuanced forms of these three models.

Methodology

This chapter takes an inductive approach, exploring various types of AI applications aimed at combating different forms of corruption to identify how governmental and non-governmental actors can design, develop, and implement these applications effectively. To do so, the chapter applies a qualitative research approach, presenting and discussing cases of AI-based ACTs from Brazil, Estonia, Germany, Italy, Ukraine, and Venezuela. The cases were selected according to the "diverse selection method" (Seawright and Gerring, 2008), i.e. they were chosen to illustrate, in the minimal sense of representing, the variety of AI-based ACTs' creation strategies.

Data collection consisted of a combination of in-depth interviews and desk research. Interviews served to gather data about, among other topics, how governmental and non-governmental actors design, develop, and implement technologies to combat different types of corruption, among them AI-based solutions. A total of 118 interviews were conducted online and offline, between March 2020 and August 2024, with public administration workers involved with the development of AI solutions or facilitating innovation (49), activists and grassroots initiators, including tech-savvy individuals (32), developers and IT designers (25), academic scholars (8), and journalists (4) using or participating in the development of such applications.

In addition to the primary data collected through interviews, extensive desk research was conducted to gather the existing data and literature from relevant reports, media sources, technical articles, databases, as well as presentations available on platforms like YouTube. This provided additional context on the technologies in use. The data collection was part of the BIT-ACT[1] project, which investigates how the grassroots are using digital media and technologies more broadly in combating corruption, as well as a doctoral research project on the use of AI-based ACTs by public authorities in public procurement.

Three Development Models for AI-Based ACTs

The analysis revealed a diverse landscape, not only in terms of the types of corruption AI-based ACTs are designed to detect or prevent, but in their wide range of applications, from chatbots to satellite image recognition. This section focuses on three creation models (and in some cases sub-models) for these technologies that, as mentioned before, emerged from the data, allowing us to identify what they do and who created them. The findings suggest that both the functionalities and the development models of AI-based ACTs are strongly influenced by the interaction between state and non-state actors, as well as their goals and responsibilities. The main characteristics of each type – in-house development, outsourcing, and co-creation – are detailed below, together with relevant cases.

In-House Development

Several AI-based ACTs have been developed in-house, whenever governmental or non-governmental organisations count on tech-savvy individuals. In the case of public administration, we observed three situations regarding the development and implementation of such applications. First, in many cases, specific units, such as the IT or data analytics department, together or separately with other internal "core business" units, design the AI solution to achieve specific goals. One example is from Estonia, where the data analytics unit of the National Insurance Fund developed two tools in-house to detect healthcare fraud in medical claims, using supervised ML and unsupervised neural networks, respectively. The unit, established shortly before these tools were created and consisting of around ten data scientists, developed these applications to achieve greater efficiency in monitoring medical claims. The Fraud Department has also started using them with promising results.

Second, civil servants individually take the initiative to leverage their expertise to develop tools within their respective units, aiming to automate and accelerate processes. This is particularly common in public units facing staff shortages and limited budgets. A notable example can be found in Brazil, where law enforcement officials have individually developed numerous AI tools to facilitate their work and improve administrative processes (Odilla, 2025). Qualified technical staff with technological expertise from the Revenue Service, the Office of the Comptroller General (CGU) and the Court of Accounts (TCU) have developed tools to combat corruption and fraud in the areas under their responsibility. For example, a Revenue Service auditor with a background in computer science had to overcome internal resistance from senior managers to develop the first version of SISAM, a system created in 2014 to analyse both audited and unaudited import declarations (Odilla, 2025). It calculates the likelihood of some 30 different types of error for each declaration, produces a dashboard, and generates a natural language report summarising the findings to assist customs inspectors in their work. In 2015, a CGU team specialised in data mining and AI created the Alice bot to conduct large-scale public purchase audits, facilitating the monitoring of tenders published daily. The code was shared with the TCU, which subsequently improved it (Interviewee_BRA_GOV_1). Based on around 40 risk typologies, Alice reads calls, analyses contracts and notices, crosschecks data, and generates personalised alerts via email to law enforcement officials and provides data visualisations on a dashboard. In 2023, Alice analysed more than 190,000 purchase transactions.

Third, tech experts are recruited to develop AI solutions in-house. This could be observed in the case of governmental organisations that are in the early stages of their digital transition and can invest time and money in hiring data scientists as part of a broader digital transformation strategy. A notable example of this model comes from Italy, where a national police force hired ten data scientists to develop a supervised ML solution to detect corruption in public procurement (in early 2024, the tool was under development; yet, by the time of writing this chapter, in December 2024, there are no updates about it). This new internal team of data scientists was working regularly with the IT staff and core business managers within the organisation to design and develop the solution, which would then be used by the organisation's local units. However, this police force emphasised that it was able to recruit data scientists to the project thanks to EU funding and as part of a wider organisational strategy to "internalise data science expertise for future purposes" (Interviewee_ITA_GOV_1).

Brazil has also seen a proliferation of in-house AI-based tools from the grassroots, in particular "civic bots". These were created by non-governmental organisations to combat various types of corruption. The first was the aforementioned Rosie bot, developed by Operation Love Serenade (*Operação Serenata de Amor*) and later transferred to the NGO Open Knowledge Brasil, which used AI to automate the process of data collection and cross-checking to detect suspected misuse of public money by elected members of Brazil's lower house, and then posted the suspicious cases and asked its followers on Twitter to help verify them. "We have been able to prove that there is room for people with advanced technical knowledge, such as data science, to contribute to society" (Interviewee_BRA_CS_12). In its early years, the initiative attracted 600 people who shared ideas in a Telegram group and over 40,000 followers on Twitter.

Rosie[2] is not the only bot designed to use X-Twitter to give visibility to its findings: the NGO OPS (Operation Supervised Politics) also had RobOPS[3] to monitor politicians' expenditures. The media company JOTA launched Rui Barbot[4] to monitor the Supreme Court proceedings. The bot tracked how long these cases remained inactive, often counting the days, or even years during which no decisions were made. All these Twitter bots, however, ceased posting. The reasons vary and often overlap. Limited usage (in terms of follower growth and interactions), lack of personnel to maintain and update the bots, and platform-imposed constraints were the main factors.

The in-house development model requires highly specialised skills. In the case of public administration, government organisations either recruit the required profile, as in Italy, or rely on existing staff, as in the case of Brazil, where many civil servants attracted by high salaries and job stability have a background in computer science, engineering, or data analysis. Recently, the Brazilian government has encouraged technological innovation by promoting competitions among civil servants and hackathons with universities and CSOs. In addition, in the case of the public sector in both Brazil and Italy, many law enforcement agencies offer employees the opportunity to pursue master's and doctoral degrees. For non-state actors, having tech-savvy people in the team or willing to volunteer is as important as having access to large amounts of good-quality open digitised data.

Outsourcing (Off-the-shelf Solutions)

AI-based ACTs are outsourced whenever an organisation – governmental or non-governmental – delegates their design, development, and implementation to external providers. This happens, as noted before, when the organisation decides to purchase an off-the-shelf (ready-to-go) AI solution from the outside, already pre-designed and developed. Whenever this is the case, internal managers/directors and IT staff of the organisation usually take part only in the implementation phase, during which the AI tool should be customised to the specific context of adoption, including its integration within the overall IT ecosystem of the organisation.

Our study observed that police forces in many countries have been opting to buy AI-based ACTs in this way. In 2016, a unit of the Brazilian Federal Police started using the IBM solution Watson to help police officers analyse large amounts of data seized during investigations and combine them with existing datasets. Watson is not an exclusive AI-based tool for countering corruption or supporting criminal investigations. In Brazil, it has also been used by hospitals to, for example, indicate the best treatments to be pursued in specific cases (Sperb, 2017). In Italy, AI is helping police forces improve their open-source intelligence (OSINT[5]) practices, speeding up the collection and analysis of data from open sources (e.g. social media, instant messaging groups, and other platforms of interest) for investigations into organised crime and terrorism, and the cross-check with different pieces of evidence collected (Gerli, 2024). A local German police body is also experimenting with outsourced solutions using ML and biometric recognition to tackle money laundering and identity fraud (Gerli, 2024).

These solutions are ready-to-use technologies that leverage multiple AI techniques, including computer vision and Natural Language Processing (NLP[6]), to enhance investigative capabilities and conduct "context-sensitive research" (Interviewee_ITA_GOV_2). As one interviewee noted, "[OSINT technologies] require huge investments, countless hours of work and multidisciplinary teams with engineers, researchers, developers. Hence, it would be unimaginable [to develop them in-house]" (Interviewee_ITA_GOV_2).

As these solutions are constantly evolving, outsourcing may be the only way to get the most up-to-date and effective version of them, according to some interviewees.

Public organisations can deploy these solutions independently from their overall IT ecosystem. For instance, the German start-up GovRadar offers public entities a tool to make public procurement procedures more efficient and transparent. Among other functions, the system has an AI chatbot, based on generative AI and ML, to help organisations select more neutral tender specifications. By the time of the interview (November 2023), public authorities had purchased the tool without integrating it into their pre-existing IT ecosystem.

Not only the availability of funds but also the need to protect their reputation can lead organisations to outsource AI-based ACTs from the private sector. A good example of this is the AI system used by the Italian development bank, Cassa Depositi e Prestiti (CDP), to analyse the risk of its private sector counterparts during the Know Your Customer (KYC)[7] process. As a financial institution that invests funds derived from citizens' postal savings, the authority must conduct rigorous checks on the companies it works with. To safeguard its reputation, CDP purchased an off-the-shelf AI solution developed by an academic spin-off specialising in economic crime investigations. This tool integrates supervised ML and NLP to assess the risk of private clients' involvement in criminal activities, including organised crime infiltration. It does so by comparing the financial statements of these clients with those of known corrupt entities.

Co-creation

AI-based ACTs are co-created when an organisation or initiative – whether governmental or non-governmental – works, in a collaborative vein, with different stakeholders to design, develop, and implement them in a tailored fashion. Depending on the configuration, this collaborative approach brings together the expertise, ideas, and resources of different actors, such as technology developers, law enforcement officials, decision-makers, anti-corruption activists, researchers, and donors, to ensure that AI solutions are tailored to the specific needs and contexts of the intended users. It is important to emphasise that, while co-created solutions may involve financial contributions or payments from/to one or more of the partners, the outcome will be highly customised AI-based ACTs.

In our analysis, this development model emerged in almost all the countries studied, with different arrangements and partnerships in each case. These configurations of collaboration and resource sharing highlight the flexibility and adaptability of the co-creation approach. As illustrated next, co-creation revolves around different types of actors.

1. Co-creation with academia

Academic research projects are seen as an opportunity for public organisations to co-create tools to directly or indirectly curb corruption, as well as a way to mitigate the risks of failure while innovating. These research projects can be national or transnational, depending on who is involved and who is funding them. One national case is the supervised ML tool developed by the Italian Court of Accounts, in collaboration with La Sapienza University, to predict the financial distress of local municipalities – a potential indicator of organised crime infiltration and corruption. The pilot originated from the master's thesis of one data scientist employed at the Court, which led to the involvement of academia in the initiative.

Examples of transnational applications of this kind, instead, include EU-funded research projects (e.g. Horizon Europe[8]), such as the Datacros project. Carried out by a research centre based in Italy, Datacros involves different authorities committed to anti-corruption from different countries, such as Lithuania, Romania, and France, to design and develop a tool that, using unsupervised ML, detects anomalies in companies' characteristics that can flag collusion, corruption, and money laundering risks. Nonetheless, not all public authorities involved in the project ultimately adopted the tool, as its usage requires access to costly private datasets, such as ORBIS[9] from Moody's.

In Brazil, a CSO (Transparência Brasil) joined forces with the Federal University of Campina Grande. Together they developed an AI-based ACT to monitor tenders and public contracts.[10] Tá de Pé Compras Emergenciais was able to extract, process and store data on emergency public contracts from two State Courts of Accounts (Rio Grande do Sul and Pernambuco). The output was offered in the form of a dashboard with a search engine.

Lastly, a hybrid case of co-creation with academia and business comes from Italy, where the financial institution CDP (mentioned earlier in the outsourcing paragraph) is co-creating a new AI solution for the KYC[11] of public sector counterparts, to predict the risks of public administrations engaging in corrupt practices, with an academic spin-off. According to interviewees, the co-creation would lead to the first-ever of this kind within the EU.

2. Co-creation with business

This type of development model differs from the outsourcing one, described above, as it implies the development of highly customised AI solutions that are designed and developed from scratch. Again, sometimes these solutions are made to help combat corruption indirectly. This is the case of ChatTCU, a generative AI tool inspired by ChatGPT that summarises case documents, including past investigations and verdicts, directly from the Brazilian Court of Accounts (TCU) online platform, allowing auditors to ask questions and receive answers. The tool was developed by the TCU team together with a private consortium of start-ups, one of the few times that the TCU has opened a public tender for technological innovation. ChatTCU is hosted on a dedicated instance of the Microsoft Azure OpenAI Service cloud platform and is designed for document analysis, legal research, translation, and administrative consultation.

Many of the cases where public-private co-creation has led to the deployment of AI-based ACTs come from public procurement. In Italy, for example, the central purchasing authority, up to September 2023, was developing an AI application that uses graph neural networks to predict the procurement behaviour of contracting authorities. The tool was being developed in collaboration with an external private provider, which brings specific AI expertise to the project and is ultimately responsible for its development. In addition, a local Italian contracting authority has developed two applications, both based on supervised NLP, as part of a wider organisational strategy to ensure impartiality in the drafting of tenders. The first tool standardises products' features, while the second one retrieves and compares information about tenders, identifying any mismatch between tenders and their corresponding contracts.

In contrast, a private and public sector co-creation effort that did not result in the implementation of any AI-based ACTs took place in Estonia, despite the attempts. The National Audit Office worked with a local AI agency to develop an application using supervised and unsupervised ML to detect potential misuse of public funds. By analysing social media and public bodies' websites, the tool aimed to identify collusion by comparing companies and individuals sponsoring government campaigns. However, the application was abandoned due to regulatory issues, as Meta and local municipalities like the city of Tallinn did not authorise the scraping of their data, arguing that the National Audit Office's institutional responsibilities did not permit such activity.

The tech industry has also been partnering with CSOs. Google, for example, often launches calls to sponsor bottom-up initiatives. Thanks to initiatives like this, Transparência Brasil developed a mobile app to monitor the construction of schools and nurseries that were already delayed. Due to the low number of downloads, the app was converted into a WhatsApp chatbot, the former developed in-house by the non-governmental organisation – the initiative, named *Tá de Pé*, was eventually discontinued because of limited use and insufficient funding. Also in Brazil, Google partially sponsored the creation of CruzaGraphos, an initiative developed by the association of investigative journalists (Abraji) and the civic tech group Brasil.io. The tool is designed to automate the collection and cross-referencing of data from multiple databases, including beneficial ownership registers, court cases, government suppliers, and campaign donations, to visually explore the connections between people and companies, including politicians, campaign donors, business partners, and contractors paid with public funds.

3. Co-creation among non-governmental organisations

Civil society organisations have also joined forces to develop AI-based ACTs. In Brazil, the chatbot repLAI, a play on the English word "reply" and the acronym for the Access to Information Law (LAI in Portuguese), was designed to generate automated responses to help anyone whose requests to access information were denied to appeal. The tool was part of a larger project to create a database of public information requests and responses, created by Transparência Brasil and Abraji, initially sponsored by the Ford Foundation. The chatbot was developed with funding from the global network Innovation for Change.

Journalists have also teamed up with each other and with CSOs to expose corruption-related crimes. A collaboration between the Venezuelan investigative outlet Armando.info and the Spanish newspaper El País used satellite data, ML and on-the-ground reporting to uncover a vast network of illegal mining in Venezuela, facilitated by corruption. The investigation took nearly a year and is called *Corredor Furtivo* (or Secret Corridors[12]). They identified over 3,000 mining sites – most of them illegal – and documented deforestation across an area equivalent to 40,000 football fields, many located near clandestine airstrips in southern Venezuela. This investigative effort was supported by an AI-powered satellite imagery analysis tool developed by Earth Genome, a civic tech organisation focused on creating technology to tackle critical climate and conservation challenges. Earth Genome is also a part of Amazon Mining Watch.

4. Co-creation among governmental and non-governmental organisations

Although more difficult to identify, this model illustrates the collaborative nature of top-down and bottom-up anti-corruption efforts. Some ACTs have emerged from hackathons sponsored by government organisations, although the research conducted for this chapter has not documented any AI-based tools from such events that have been successfully implemented. The most notable case is the aforementioned ProZorro in Ukraine, which was initially developed by civil society but later adapted for use by the public administration. It is an award-winning initiative that has not only gained recognition but also drawn international attention to the solution, which has created a unique and flexible electronic tendering system that allows governments to auction or select a winner based on price, price with consideration of non-price criteria, and best value for money. The application enhanced its functionalities thanks to partnerships with international organisations, such as the European Bank for Reconstruction and Development, businesses, and Transparency International.

Enabling Conditions, Opportunities, and Potential Pitfalls

Access to high-quality, abundant data and technical expertise in AI techniques is an essential prerequisite for the development of any AI solution, including AI-based ACTs. However, in the case of ACTs, domain-specific knowledge of corruption and anti-corruption strategies is also critical. In-house solutions often have the advantage of both IT expertise and anti-corruption knowledge, allowing for tailored development. Outsourcing models, on the other hand, tend to rely on off-the-shelf solutions created by external experts, which may not fully address the specific needs of the organisation. Co-creation models, in turn, bridge this gap by combining external AI expertise with internal anti-corruption knowledge, ensuring that the tool is both technically sound and contextually relevant for governmental and non-governmental anti-corruption actors.

Our findings also suggest that, beyond knowledge, expertise, and access to the right type of data, each of the identified development models for AI-based ACTs has different drivers, unique opportunities, and potential pitfalls, most of which are not directly related to combating corruption. In fact, many of them have more to do with the broader governance structures of the organisations involved. Additionally, our findings indicate that the selection of various types of AI-based ACTs is more closely linked to organisations' roles and duties rather than the development models of these applications. Exploring the development models and their respective enabling conditions can deepen our understanding of the key factors that enable the adoption of AI in anti-corruption efforts, as well as the advantages and disadvantages of different innovation strategies available to both governmental and non-governmental actors. From our analysis, we were able to identify the key advantages and disadvantages of each type of development model, as well as their major enabling conditions.

As illustrated in the Table 12.1, the in-house development model is highly dependent on an innovative internal organisational culture. Individual proactivity, whether from leaders, employees and volunteers (in the case of non-governmental organisations), is another key factor for innovation in-house. This model offers advantages such as ownership of the application, greater flexibility in implementation, and the ability to tailor tools to specific contexts. However, the risks identified include limited (or even the absence of) transparency in the design and development processes. Many of the home-grown tools analysed in this study are opaque, even regarding their basic functionalities. Developers, particularly those in public organisations handling sensitive data, often face constraints, or lack incentives to open their code or documentation.

TABLE 12.1 Enabling conditions, potential opportunities, and pitfalls of development models for AI-based ACTs

Development model	Enabling conditions	Potential opportunities	Potential pitfalls
In-house development	*Within the organisation:* • IT infrastructure and resources • Innovative culture *Among individuals:* • Proactivity	• Ownership over the applications • Context-specific tools • Lower costs	• Lower transparency on how the tool is designed, developed, and deployed • "Silo tools" if developed by non-communicating individuals • Slower adoption, limited scale
Outsourcing (off-the-shelf tools)	*Within the organisation:* • Financial availability • Adequate IT ecosystem • "Urge" for effective anti-corruption tools • Offer available on the market *Among individuals:* • Commitment to adopting new systems	• Access to best practices offered by the provider • Rapid adoption • Regular maintenance • Training	• Opaque selection of providers • Vendor lock-in • Low context-specific tools • Low flexibility • Copyright/Intellectual Property constraints • Concentration of (sensitive) data in the hands of private sector providers
Co-creation	*Within the organisation:* • Openness to collaborative environments • Clear governance framework • Finding partners able to help overcome limitations *Among individuals:* • Willing to share expertise and knowledge	• Multidisciplinary creation process • Inclusive AI solutions • Context-specific tools • Shared resources	• Lengthy processes due to complex decision-making • Copyright/Intellectual Property disputes • Concentration of (sensitive) data in the hands of externals

Source: Author's own compilation

In addition, slower adoption and sometimes problems in scaling up the tools to other units were observed as potential risks, due to the complexity of in-house innovation.

Outsourcing is driven mainly by the availability of financial resources and the urgent need for immediate anti-corruption solutions, as well as the existence of off-the-shelf tools. Organisations benefit from rapid deployment and sometimes access to best practices, regular maintenance, and training. However, there are risks associated with this model, such as vendor lock-in,[13] low flexibility and limited customisation of tools for specific contexts. There may also be concerns about transparency in supplier selection and constraints in adapting or upgrading due to intellectual property rights.

Once again, co-creation models are more likely to be enabled by budgetary constraints and the need for expertise in the highly specialised field of AI. More peculiar enabling conditions include the openness to a collaborative environment, a clear governance framework of the organisations involved, and, above all, finding a partner who can help overcome one's limitations – from the anti-corruption organisations' perspective, this may mean acquiring AI expertise at a lower cost except for co-creation with businesses. At the individual level, leadership, commitment and willingness to share expertise drive multidisciplinary creative processes, leading to more inclusive and context-specific solutions. Shared resources may enhance innovation, but the collaborative approach has its pitfalls, including lengthy processes due to complex decision-making and potential disputes over copyright and intellectual property, which can reduce the level of transparency and the chances of external audits.

Conclusion

The discordant world we live in, where global challenges such as political instability, social fragmentation, environmental degradation, and technological disruption are on the agenda, can create new opportunities for complex forms of corruption and exacerbate its harmful effects. Therefore, innovating anti-corruption efforts becomes imperative. AI presents a valuable opportunity for evolving anti-corruption in such complex scenarios. With its advanced capabilities to gather and process large amounts of data from different sources, AI can generate insights that would not be visible to the human eye and detect nuances and gaps faster. By doing this, AI is expected to make anti-corruption more responsive, effective, accountable, and collaborative. Our findings suggest that governmental and non-governmental actors have begun innovating anti-corruption efforts using AI as an auxiliary tool to support their daily tasks.

Innovation is not only about the type of technology being used, but also about who is designing, developing, and deploying it. This chapter explored the development models that can serve as inspiration for those who want to invest in emerging technologies. By collecting and examining empirical evidence from Brazil, Estonia, Germany, Italy, Ukraine, and Venezuela, we identified three types of development models governmental and non-governmental actors use to innovate anti-corruption efforts through AI: in-house development, outsourcing off-the-shelf products, and co-creation with multiple actors. Depending on their resources, such as technical expertise and financial availability, organisations can decide whether to develop AI internally, purchase ready-to-go solutions from the market, or co-create them with stakeholders, such as academia, CSOs, and businesses.

The typology of development models for AI in anti-corruption advanced in this chapter illustrates the broad spectrum of innovation in anti-corruption efforts. Moving beyond the conventional public-private sector dichotomy in technology adoption, they enable a more inclusive approach to designing, developing, and implementing AI solutions, according to the needs of a given organisation and the context in which these applications are created. Understanding the enabling conditions for each development model helps organisations select the one that best meets their needs and strategic objectives.

As shown, none of these models is inherently bad or good; each offers specific opportunities and faces distinct challenges. Yet, most of them are shrouded in opacity due to the highly sensitive data used in-house, copywriting and intellectual property issues, or low disclosure about the tools in place from actors involved, particularly public sector ones. This limits access to information about their main features, reducing the chances of having explainable and accountable solutions, as well as mitigating risks associated with ACTs development and use. Only in a few cases of initiatives co-created by different CSOs together or between CSOs and academia, we find open documentation, if not the codes available on GitHub. Still, these initiatives can be seen as outliers.

In conclusion, this chapter provided insights into how governmental and non-governmental organisations can integrate emerging technologies into their daily operations. Our findings shed light on how AI-based ACTs are designed and adopted and indicate that these processes remain largely opaque for most models of development – with a few exceptions from civil society. Empirical evidence suggests that organisational factors play a key role not only in shaping the development of these applications but also in determining the different types of AI-based anti-corruption solutions. By identifying the key actors and models involved in the creation of these applications, this chapter can serve as a starting point for further research aimed at increasing transparency, accountability, and explainability of these applications and their development processes. While AI holds the potential to enhance anti-corruption efforts and make them more adaptable to the complexities of our fragmented world, both governmental and non-governmental actors must prioritise transparency, accountability, and inclusivity in the design and use of these solutions. Failure to do so risks creating new opportunities for corruption and deepening discordance.

Notes

1. Bottom-Up Initiatives and Anti-Corruption Technologies, conducted at the University of Bologna and funded by the European Research Council under the European Union's Horizon 2020 research and innovation programme (grant agreement no. 802362, https://site.unibo.it/bit-act/en).
2. See https://x.com/RosieDaSerenata and https://github.com/okfn-brasil/serenata-de-amor. Accessed on September 11, 2024.
3. https://x.com/NFiscais. Accessed on September 11, 2024.
4. https://x.com/ruibarbot. Accessed on September 11, 2024.
5. Open-Source Intelligence (OSINT): collection and analysis of publicly available information from various open sources, such as public websites, social media, and satellite imagery, to gather actionable intelligence.
6. Natural Language Processing: data processing technique including speech recognition, text classification, and natural-language generation.
7. Know Your Customer (KYC): the process used by private and public sector organisations, particularly financial institutions, to verify the identity of their clients and prevent fraud and money laundering.
8. Horizon Europe: the EU's key funding programme for research and innovation of EUR 93.5 billion for the period 2021-2027 that aims to facilitate collaboration and strengthen the impact of research and innovation in developing, supporting, and implementing EU policies while tackling global challenges.
9. ORBIS: formerly a Bureau van Dijk flagship solution, now under Moody's, it is a database on private companies, including listed ones, containing detailed information about their corporate ownership structure and financial metrics.
10. See https://github.com/analytics-ufcg/ta-de-pe-dados. Accessed on September 13, 2024.
11. See reference 7.
12. See https://armando.info/la-mineria-ilegal-monto-sus-bases-aereas-en-la-selva/
13. Vendor lock-in: when a public or private organisation becomes dependent on a single supplier or service provider and finds it difficult or costly to switch to another vendor.

References

Aarvik, P. (2019) 'Artificial Intelligence – A promising anti-corruption tool in development settings?', *U4 Report* 2019:1, Bergen: U4 Anti-Corruption Resource Centre, Chr. Michelsen Institute.Adam, I. and Fazekas, M. (2021) 'Are emerging technologies helping win the fight against corruption? A review of the state of evidence', *Information Economics and Policy*, 57, p. 100950.

Ash, E., Galletta, S. and Giommoni, T. (2020) 'A Machine Learning Approach to Analyzing Corruption in Local Public Finances', *SSRN*.

Chesbrough, H. and Rosenbloom, R.S. (2002), 'The role of the business model in capturing value from innovation: Evidence from Xerox Corporation's technology spin-off companies', *Industrial and Corporate Change* 11(3), pp. 529–555.

Colonnelli, E., Gallego, J.A. and Prem, M. (2019) 'What Predicts Corruption?' *SSRN.*

Demircioglu, M.A. and Audretsch, D.B. (2019) 'Public sector innovation: The effect of universities', *J Technol Transf* 44, pp. 596–614 (2019).

Dressel, J. and Farid, H. (2018) 'The accuracy, fairness, and limits of predicting recidivism', *Science Advances,* 4, p. eaao5580.

Edler Duarte, D. (2021) 'The making of crime predictions: Sociotechnical assemblages and the controversies of governing future crime', *Surveillance & Society*, 19(2), pp. 199–215.

Fazekas, M. and Kocsis, G. (2017) 'Uncovering high-level corruption: Cross-national objective corruption risk indicators using public procurement data', *British Journal of Political Science*, 50(1), pp. 1–10.

Fazekas, M., Tóth, B. and Wachs, J. (2023) 'Public Procurement Cartels: A Large-Sample Testing of Screens Using Machine Learning', *Working Paper GTI-WP/2023:02*, Budapest: GTI.

Geist, E. M. (2016). 'It's already too late to stop the AI arms race—We must manage it instead', *Bulletin of the Atomic Scientists*, 72(5), pp. 318–321.

Gerli, C. (2024) 'AI in Public Organisations to Tackle Public Procurement Corruption: Empirical Evidence from Italy'. Working Paper presented at the International Research Society for Public Management (IRSPM) Conference 2024. April 16–18, 2024.

Human Rights Watch. (2024, September 10) 'Gaza: Israeli Military's Digital Tools Risk Civilian Harm'.

Köbis, N. and Starke, C. (2022) 'The Corruption Risks of Artificial Intelligence', *Working Paper*, Transparency International.

Köbis, N., Starke, C. and Rahwan, I. (2022) 'The promise and perils of using artificial intelligence to fight corruption', *Nature Machine Intelligence*, 4, pp. 418–424.

Kuchina-Musina, D. and Morris, J. C. (2022) 'Buying innovation: An examination of public–private partnerships and the decision process for contracting out innovation', *Politics & Policy* 50 (3), pp. 503–515.

Leon, S. (2018) 'How can we use artificial intelligence to help us fight corruption in the mining sector?', *Global Witness Blog*, November 8, 2018.

Li, J., Chen, W.-H., Xu, Q., Shah, N., Kohler, J.C. and Mackey, T.K. (2020) 'Detection of self-reported experiences with corruption on twitter using unsupervised machine learning', *Social Sciences and Humanities Open*, 2(1), p. 100060.

Lima, M. S. M. and Delen, D. (2020) 'Predicting and explaining corruption across countries: A machine learning approach', *Government Information Quarterly*, 37 (2020).

Mattoni, A. (Ed.). (2024). *Digital Media and Grassroots Anti-Corruption: Contexts, Platforms and Data of Anti-Corruption Technologies Worldwide.* Edward Elgar Publishing. ISBN: 9781802202090.

Mazrekaj, D., Titl, V. and Schiltz, F. (2021) 'Identifying Politically Connected Firms: A Machine Learning Approach', *SSRN.*

Micheli, Pietro, Magnus Schoeman, David Baxter and Keith Goffin. 2012. 'New business models for public-sector innovation', *Successful Technological Innovation for Government, Research-Technology Management* 55(5), pp. 51–57.

Odilla, F. (2023) 'Bots against corruption: Exploring the benefits and limitations of AI-based anti-corruption technology', *Crime Law Soc Change* 80, pp. 353–396 (2023).

Odilla, F. (2024) 'Unfairness in AI anti-corruption tools: Main drivers and consequences', *Minds & Machines,* 34, 28 (2024).

Odilla, F. (2025) *The Digitalisation of Anti-Corruption in Brazil.* London: Routledge. ISBN 9781032353807.

Odilla, F. and Mattoni, A. (2023) 'Unveiling the layers of data activism: the organising of civic innovation to fight corruption in Brazil', *Big Data & Society* 10(2), pp. 1–17.

Olszewski, D. (2014) 'Fraud detection using self-organizing map visualizing the user profiles. Knowledge-Based Systems', 70, pp. 324–334.

Popa, M. (2019) 'Uncovering the structure of public procurement transactions', *Business and Politics,* 21(3), pp. 351–384.

Rabuzin, K. and Modrušan, N. (2019) 'Prediction of Public Procurement Corruption Indices using Machine Learning Methods', *Proceedings of the 11th International Joint Conference on Knowledge Discovery, Knowledge Engineering and Knowledge Management.*

Robertson, G. M. and Mayr, L. M. (2011) 'Collaboration versus outsourcing: The need to think outside the box', *Future Medicinal Chemistry,* 3(16), pp. 1995–2020.

Rothstein, B. and Varraich, A. (2017) *Making Sense of Corruption.* Cambridge: Cambridge University Press.

Russell, S.J. and Norvig, P. (2021). *Artificial Intelligence: A Modern Approach.* Fourth Edition. Pearson Series in Artificial Intelligence.

Sanchez-Graells (2021) Procurement Corruption and Artificial Intelligence: Between the Potential of Enabling Data Architectures and the Constraints of Due Process Requirements. S. Williams-Elegbe and J. Tillipman (eds), Routledge Handbook of Public Procurement Corruption.

Seawright, J. and Gerring, J. (2008) 'Case selection techniques in case study research: A menu of qualitative and quantitative', *Political Research Quarterly,* 61(294), pp. 294–308.

Sen, Arup K. and Haq, Kushnood, Product Innovation by Small and Medium-Sized Firms Through Outsourcing and Collaboration (2011). *International Journal of Management and Marketing Research,* 4(1), pp. 61–73, 2011.

Sperb, P. (2017) 'Watson, a inteligência artificial a serviço da PF gaúcha'. *Revista Veja.*

Torres Berru, Y., López Batista, V. F., Torres-Carrión, P. and Jimenez, M. G. (2020) 'AI techniques to detect and prevent corruption in procurement: A systematic literature review', in *Applied Technologies: First International Conference,* Quito, December 3–5, 2019, Proceedings, Part II 1 (pp. 254–268).

Wacker, J., Ferreira, R. P. and Ladeira, M. (2018, October) 'Detecting fake suppliers using deep image features', In 2018 7th Brazilian Conference on Intelligent Systems (BRACIS) (pp. 224–229). IEEE.

Yukins, C.R and Kelman, S. (2022) 'Overcoming Corruption and War -- Lessons from Ukraine's ProZorro Procurement System', *NCMA Contract Management Magazine,* July 2022, p. 22.

PART V

Conclusion

13

ANTI-CORRUPTION IN A DISCORDANT WORLD

Reflections and Conclusions

David Jackson, David Aled Williams, and Inge Amundsen

The dimensions of discord noted in the introduction are still present as we write this conclusion. There is some continuity in these dimensions: the Russian aggression in Ukraine and the destruction of Gaza, for instance. But there is also discontinuity or change. The second Trump administration laid bare the inner workings of an emergent form of American state capture with far-reaching consequences for world order (David-Barrett 2025), saw the rapid disassembly of federal support for international development and humanitarian assistance, and the de-prioritisation of enforcement actions under the Foreign Corrupt Practices Act (FCPA) (Mullard 2025). However imperfectly, the latter had served, since 1977, as a main channel for anti-corruption law enforcement actions worldwide. Yet with change also came new developments. The UK, France, and Switzerland jointly announced in March 2025 new cooperation on international corruption prosecutions – possibly helping fill the immediate void left by the US anti-bribery enforcement vacuum (Rusch 2025).

On balance, however, anti-corruption norms and practices are even more contested and abused now than they were when we began this volume – further underlining why anti-corruption cannot stay still in these fast-moving times. Democratic backsliding, economic nationalism, populism and the rolling back of (any) rule-based international order are seriously affecting the way anti-corruption is done. It must innovate and refresh if it is to survive. We hope this book offers some initial insights into how this might be approached.

This final chapter offers some reflections rather than firm conclusions. Reflections because the empirics collected in this book represent only a small sample of all the ways anti-corruption may unfold. Even so, the diverse set of

DOI: 10.4324/9781003531920-18

chapters provides what we hope is a first layer of analysis that aims to understand anti-corruption in novel ways. We begin with reflections on the nuances the chapters bring to the themes of contestation, abuse, and innovation. The chapters show that different forms of contestation can occur; that abuse is often about selective enforcement; and that the term innovation as synonymous with "newness" may no longer be so helpful in understanding how anti-corruption can progress.

We then provide reflections on what kind of anti-corruption is needed in a discordant world. The chapters do not point to a particular set of policies but rather provide insights on underlying conditions of anti-corruption. They show where anti-corruption practice demonstrates resilience; it does so because it can *adapt* to contestation and abuse. By contrast, in chapters where outcomes were consistently poor, anti-corruption efforts were stifled – denied the freedom to evolve and effectively respond to challenges. Our tentative argument is that adaptability comes from two conditions: a sufficiently strong domestic ecology of anti-corruption and when that ecology is exposed to alternative ideas, partnerships, and political causes, both horizontally within that context, and vertically beyond that context.

Finally, we note what this means for future anti-corruption research, pointing out the need to further unpack the social orders conditioning anti-corruption practice and the kinds of anti-corruption that emerge as a result.

Insights from the Analytical Lenses

The premise of this book is that anti-corruption is unlikely to proceed according to bureaucratic and procedural logics. Plans and strategies written on paper are distorted, deformed, and reformed by the context in which they are implemented. Using the concepts of contestation, abuse, and innovation to break down how context shapes anti-corruption, our perspectives on anti-corruption have been enriched by the chapters in the book.

Contestation

We started the book by emphasising that anti-corruption is politics and is wrapped up in systems of power, of personal and group interests, of bargaining, and of matters of social justice and basic social values. It is therefore subject to contestation. We used this lens of contestation to try to peek beyond the projection of consensus by international discourse and agreements. We use contestation in neutral terms as referring to the act of challenging, disputing, or opposing a particular idea, norm, authority, or practice.

The chapters in the book point to how we can refine that basic idea into an emerging picture of different types of contestations: reinterpretation and resistance. In the chapter on Mexico by Rojas-Salazar and Vargas-Pineda, it is argued that a populist regime, in the former AMLO government in Mexico, *reinterpreted* corruption as a "moral perversion" of the political system, as deeply embedded in the state apparatus. In doing so, it contested and moved away from the liberal-democratic anti-corruption perspective with its traditional oversight and control mechanisms. The AMLO regime reinterpreted anti-corruption to be a movement that fosters "national identity" and highlights values such as honesty and loyalty. The logical endpoint was a populist leader who presented himself as the representative of the vulnerable, under-represented majority, as their saviour and moral keeper, and the only one honest and true to the people in contrast to the corrupt elite.

This form of reinterpretation was a prelude to abuse. The authors warn that with such a narrative in place and accepted by the majority, a populist leader can – legitimately – dismantle institutionalised anti-corruption measures, weaken autonomous bodies, choose whom to blame and punish, and concentrate ever more power in the presidency and the executive branch. This is, essentially, a version of state capture, whereby populists use anti-corruption rhetorics and legitimate means to concentrate executive power and weaken external oversight – creating the conditions for further power abuse.

However, other kinds of reinterpretation can more positively lead to innovation and change.

Dobson Phillips, in her chapter on the UK, focuses on the contestation of a nascent set of anti-corruption norms in the political discord experienced in the wake of Brexit. This discord provided an opportunity to challenge the effectiveness of Britain's anti-corruption architecture, contest the legitimacy of its institutions, and reshape ideas about the meaning of anti-corruption itself. This included contestation over the justification for the norms that long governed standards in British public life. It was not only the anti-corruption norms and institutions that were contested, but well-established and deeper norms of political conduct were also debated.

When reinterpretation and debate are absent, stagnation can occur. Shipley concludes in his chapter on MEL systems that donor evaluation mechanisms have largely been controlled in a way which does not seriously scrutinise assumptions, allow for contention from diverse perspectives, nor expose potential failings. As currently organised, they are not well placed to facilitate the adaptation needed to respond to the challenges of discordance. He argues that discordance demands that aid organisations and partners be more open to different perspectives on their agenda.

Resistance meanwhile is when actors fundamentally dispute, explicitly or implicitly, the legitimacy of a particular anti-corruption agenda, action or norm in their country, government, company, or community. In the chapter on the Brazilian *Operation Car Wash*, France and Siqueira demonstrate how an incredibly popular and internationally praised corruption case against members of the political class and business elite was contested and slowly turned around into criticism of the key case investigators and prosecutors. In the end, numerous convictions were overturned, several political actors were rehabilitated, penalties on companies were revised, and legal and institutional provisions that had enabled the operation came under attack. Again, contestation of the legal and institutional anti-corruption framework was led by a populist leader, Bolsonaro, "a far-right candidate known for his outspoken authoritarian leanings" according to France and Siqueira.

France and Siqueira argue that this "all-out" contestation led to legal reforms that weakened the powers of the public prosecutor, limited the ability to hold corrupt officials accountable, and weakened law enforcement agencies by nominating people sympathetic to the president. The contestation included questioning the legitimacy of law enforcement agents, the instruments they used to carry out investigations, the merits of "anti-corruption" as such, and its consequences – pointing to alleged economic and political harms caused by the anti-corruption probe.

The chapters also seem to suggest a link between increased discordance and increased contestation. The contestation described in Mexico followed years of corruption scandals, political debates on corruption, and significant reforms. The 2016 *Casa Blanca* scandal generated pressure on former president Enrique Peña Nieto, but initial anti-corruption proposals were met with scepticism. A history of impunity for the crimes of high-profile individuals led the opposition to question the impartiality of any new agency.

In the chapter on Brazil's Operation Car Wash, France and Siqueria point to Brazil's emerging power status in explaining the origins of some of its forms of contestation. The identification of mainstream anti-corruption approaches with a liberal-democratic agenda promoted by developed economies reinforced in some quarters the view that the approach taken by Operation Car Wash confused legitimate processes in a complex polity with systemic corruption. The backlash towards Operation Car Wash is also viewed against the backdrop of years of perceived entrenched corruption among political and business elites, as well as an increasingly polarised political discourse and landscape.

Likewise, Dobson Phillips argues that the discord inherent in the post-Brexit context made corruption more visible and heightened awareness of it in British institutions. It is this politically polarised and emotionally charged backdrop which made contestation over anti-corruption norms and political conduct possible. This context essentially stalled the establishment of the anti-corruption governance regime, which was vulnerable when political crisis hit.

Abuse

Our introduction to this book identifies several ways by which we know, and suspect, anti-corruption is being abused. We defined abuse of anti-corruption as misdirection, when the rhetoric and measures usually understood as anti-corruption are used for *other* purposes than to minimise the impact of corruption in society, politics, and the economy – i.e., for narrow group interests and self-interest: power, status, and wealth.

In his chapter on Russia, Konov uses original data from the last two decades to show how anti-corruption efforts in Russia had *selective enforcement* built into the mechanics of the legal system. Konov nuances the perspective of how this "subtle" abuse plays out, highlighting how the reforms reflected the intricate political economy of Russia's ruling system. Konov mentions that the Russian authorities "have demonstrated reluctance" to respond to corruption-related information provided by non-profit organisations and the media and instead subjected those who have published such materials to reprisals. Furthermore, in his careful wording, he states that "at least some facts suggest that criminal sanctioning of top officials has fulfilled some other functions and was not part of a genuine anti-corruption drive".

Bayar Dashpurev, in his chapter on Mongolia's coal theft case, also argues that the state's strategic absence from managing the resource-rich South Gobi region should be viewed as a case of anti-corruption abuse because of selective enforcement. The control mechanisms ultimately failed to address the root causes of both corruption and theft, ultimately leading to corruption protests which, as we write this conclusion, recently toppled the Mongolian prime minister.

In addition, Shipley mentions in his chapter on monitoring, evaluation and learning that "uncritical or flawed evaluation practices risk reinforcing approaches to anti-corruption programming which may be harmful" – in the sense that international aid organisations and their partners have failed to learn from their mistakes and "continued investment in the absence of demonstrable success", thus fuelling critiques that anti-corruption has become a self-serving industry (Sampson, 2010).

But the chapters also show how *abuse* is about reframing, redefining, and retargeting anti-corruption so that it is not primarily about addressing corrupt practices, but instead weaponises anti-corruption to delegitimise, weaken, and silence rivals, critics, and competitors.

In their chapter on "Transparency International Bangladesh", Sakib, Ahmed and Amundsen argue that anti-corruption was abused by the previous authoritarian government to crack down on free speech, to harass the opposition, and to censure the media, while ruling party and government bigwigs remained untouched. The link between increasing authoritarianism and the politicisation of anti-corruption was evident – abuse of anti-corruption was an integrated part of the wider power abuse which included electoral fraud, political violence, arbitrary arrests, extrajudicial killings, enforced disappearance of opposition figures, and even torture.

As argued by Ramasamy and Baniamin, Sri Lanka's "Executive Presidential System" was another case of blatant abuse of anti-corruption by a semi-authoritarian regime, that became a kleptocracy by using, among other abuses, anti-corruption rhetoric prior to elections and the nomination of loyalists to positions in the anti-corruption commissions.

The abuse of anti-corruption for pecuniary interests is hinted at in some of the chapters. This abuse entails the selective use of anti-corruption measures to block some businesses, entrepreneurs and businesspeople (deemed competitors and/or supporters of rivals or the opposition) and to create opportunities for others – giving government contracts, preferences, and privileges to the power holders and their supporters and cronies. The chapters on Sri Lanka and Bangladesh allude to the pecuniary interests behind the biased application of anti-corruption when talking about the "vested interests of political and business elites" and "entrenched patron-client relationships", but without analysing *how* this bias was instrumentalised. The chapter on Brazil is somewhat more specific, mentioning that some companies implicated in "Operation Car Wash" (that had funnelled money to politicians in the ruling party to finance election campaigns, cement alliances, and enrich those involved) were rehabilitated and their penalties revoked when the operation was shut down.

Innovation

Innovation is used as a lens in this book because we are interested not just in abuse or contestation, but in how individuals, organisations and communities respond to them. In the introduction, we began loosely defining innovation as a creative process that brings about new forms of anti-corruption practice, whether that be novel collaborations, discourses, analytical tools, or strategic action. This starting point reflected the broader literature, where definitions of innovation deployed in public policy tend to emphasise novelty. The OECD, for example, defines social innovation as "the design and implementation of new solutions to social problems" (OECD, 2019).

An important reflection is that this interpretation of what counts as innovation does not align with the innovations collected in the book. "Newness" is obviously important in anti-corruption. Anti-corruption may draw on new technologies which can be used to analyse the corruption problem and to disclose corrupt practices. Big data can be analysed to identify patterns in everything from tax evasion to social networks and can be extended into new areas and implemented in new strategies by a wider set of users. Investigative journalists have, for instance, used big data analytics on the Pandora Papers to uncover some of the biggest corruption scandals. Crowdsourcing platforms can be deployed for collecting information (Jaiyeola 2023). Artificial Intelligence (AI) can potentially uncover hidden and corrupt relationships, do real-time analyses of transactions, and can be used for more precise risk-scoring and prediction models (Jaiyeola 2023).

But newness is not the same as progress. Indeed, in this book innovation generally manifests not as something materially new; instead the chapters show that in anti-corruption innovation is expressed as a search for resilience – that is finding strategies and adjustments to make a particular form of practice – from technical know-how to collective action – sufficiently insulated from contestation and abuse.

Indeed, the chapters of the book align more with alternative concepts of innovation that emphasise innovation as enhancing impact through forging disruptions and discontinuities. For example, that social innovation is "an initiative, product or process or program that profoundly changes the basic routines, resource and authority flows or beliefs of any social system" (Cahill, 2010).

Sakib, Ahmed, and Amundsen in "Civil Society in an adverse environment" retrace how Transparency International Bangladesh's innovation came through new forms of interacting in the public space and with government, including a much stronger emphasis on collaborative rather than antagonistic approaches that helped enlarge the space for anti-corruption rather than abet its curbing by authoritarian governments. This argument is also made in an article on Cambodia (Norén-Nilsson 2024), where political space for NGOs, trade unions, and other civil society organisations working against corruption has been decreasing. Here, actors have "explored alternative approaches to engaging with the government – in particular, avoiding sensitive or controversial subjects, and leaning towards service-provision or technical-support activities instead of advocacy".

The chapters also describe sources of innovation, focusing on exposure to alternative ideas and partnerships as enabling anti-corruption to adapt to shifting contexts. Engagement with alternative ideas and partnerships is described in chapters in this book as operating both vertically and horizontally. Vertical exposure means anti-corruption practice drawing from capacity, knowledge, and relationships beyond the domestic context. Erasmus, Glencorse and Scrimgeour emphasise this "outside in" channel in their chapter on "translocal approaches". The essence of translocalism is about how locally rooted networks and organisations "transcend" the immediate site of the problem they address to connect outwards and upwards, connected to a collective global agenda, knowledge, and practice.

In the chapter on Latin America by Cepeda Cuadrado, we see in Venezuela how effective anti-corruption practice emerged via alliances with international lawyers and CSOs. Likewise, Gerli and Odilla's chapter on AI-based Anti-Corruption Technologies (ACTs) shows how in the same country, journalists teamed up with each other and with civil society organisations to expose corruption-related crimes. A collaboration between the Venezuelan investigative outlet Armando.info and the Spanish newspaper El País used satellite data and on-the-ground reporting to uncover a vast network of illegal mining in Venezuela, facilitated by corruption. That international organisations might help in-country reformers at critical junctures in time has also been argued by Guerzovich et al. (2020).

Yet, the authors of the Brazil chapter caution against over-emphasising the effect of international support. Though domestic reformers can borrow ideas, take inspiration from, and, to some extent, collaborate with foreign actors, if anti-corruption reforms appear or are presented as primarily motivated from abroad, they can easily be questioned and criticised as such and resisted and/ or shut down. This does not mean that the principles and designs associated with mainstream anti-corruption policy are entirely irrelevant in such contexts, but the Brazil chapter suggests that claims of a "foreign plot" are easily weaponized by populists who play on patriotic sentiments to weaken constitutional and institutionalised oversight and control mechanisms and to take personal charge of the anti-corruption agenda.

Various chapters emphasise the need for horizontal shifts: more multi-actor partnerships. Gerli and Odilla's chapter on AI-based Anti-Corruption Technologies (ACTs) shows how these increasingly rely on *co-creation* – a collaborative approach that brings together governments, civil society, academia, and private sector actors. The chapters show how this horizontal form of innovation spans various countries and sectors. In Italy, academia partnered with public authorities to predict municipal financial distress, while the EU-funded Datacros project used unsupervised machine learning to detect corporate anomalies. In Brazil, civil society and universities co-developed tools to monitor emergency contracts. Public-private initiatives, like Brazil's ChatTCU and Italy's AI for procurement analysis, showcase how businesses contribute technological capacity. Meanwhile, civil society-led efforts – such as chatbots for transparency or journalistic investigations into corruption – demonstrate bottom-up innovation.

What Anti-Corruption Is Needed in a Discordant World?

From one perspective, there is a clear answer to this question: that the normative vision for anti-corruption is set out in a variety of evolving international documents, agreements, as well as domestic strategies and national plans. Additional perspectives are nuancing this general vision through assessing which interventions may have the largest policy impact; indeed, the literature on anti-corruption effectiveness is growing (Johnson et al., 2012; Qudah et al., 2025; Schatz, 2013)

In this book we have tried to answer the "what kind of anti-corruption" question from a different angle. The aim of this book was to show that there is more to anti-corruption than policy plans and causal relationships between inputs and outputs. Anti-corruption is a political, social, and economic process. In understanding the kind of constraints, distortions, and evolutions that accompany anti-corruption interventions and practice, the aim was to *complement* ongoing policy thinking around effectiveness to focus on the enactment and positioning of anti-corruption in a discordant world. The question is narrowed to the kind of anti-corruption we need under conditions of volatility, unpredictability, backlash, and abuse. In a discordant world where technical and bureaucratic logics, consistent rule of law adherence, and international collaboration are increasingly unlikely, this question is fundamental.

The chapters in the book do not reveal a definitive answer to our fundamental question. Yet, across the diverse case studies, one important theme weaves throughout: where anti-corruption practice is resilient, it seems to be due to a capacity to adapt to respond to contestation and abuse, whether this adaptivity is driven by communities, activists, politicians, NGOs, or business organisations – some or all, in different configurations. In those chapters where outcomes were ultimately poor, anti-corruption was not free to adapt but was severely restricted.

Restricted anti-corruption means a policy field hemmed in, truncated or controlled by a narrow powerful elite in a way that precludes adaptation and evolution. The anti-corruption measures implemented in response to Mongolia's "coal theft case" were largely political manoeuvres, serving as tools for political factions vying for control over the nation's mineral resources, rather than genuine efforts to reform the extractive industry or enhance accountability. In Sri Lanka's authoritarian "executive presidency", anti-corruption bandwidth shrank by constitutional amendments that gave the president power to nominate loyalists to the anti-corruption commissions, which ensured large-scale corruption cases were swept under the carpet.

In the chapter on Russia, Konov describes how, in choosing the measures to use and the categories of officials to target, national decision-makers were guided not primarily by the usefulness of these measures in reducing corruption but by their effectiveness in taking, consolidating, and retaining power. In Mexico, the AMLO's government also used anti-corruption to attack and delegitimise its political adversaries and protect its political allies. Anti-corruption became a narrow policy field, used as a weapon against opponents, reducing their legitimacy, silencing critics, and forcing the exile or imprisonment of critical figures.

The kind of anti-corruption we need in a discordant world is one where anti-corruption can adapt to protect itself from threats, to expand into new frontiers, and to mobilise a broader foundation of support. But where does adaptiveness come from?

Much of the political science literature points to how regime type shapes the possibility to adapt. While more democratic regimes give space for policy debate and non-state actors, autocratising regimes tend to constrain alternative actors, hoarding power and information (Arriola et al., 2023). But the book chapters nuance this picture of regime type determining the kinds of anti-corruption we witness. The boundaries between democratic and autocratic states are not clear-cut. More than this, even within autocratising regimes, opportunities may emerge for resilient and adaptive anti-corruption. The chapter on Bangladesh points out that even under democratic constraints, Transparency International Bangladesh (TIB) was able to survive and keep up a significant information and sensitisation drive in an increasingly hostile environment. Two further chapters (on AI production and human rights) show how anti-corruption is possible in Venezuela.

The point is that there may be other variables at play than regime type. We suggest a tentative hypothesis based on the chapters in the book: adaptive anti-corruption is more likely when a sufficiently strong domestic core of anti-corruption exists, *and* that anti-corruption core is exposed and linked up to alternative ideas, partnerships, and political causes.

The chapters suggest an essential dimension of resilience in a discordant world is the continued making and remaking of a "domestic core" on anti-corruption. This core may have different elements. First, it implies a broad-based domestic constituency. In the chapter on Mexico, the authors argue that anti-corruption requires the participation of actors beyond the incumbent government, and that a pre-condition to trust an anti-corruption policy is that it is open to include different groups' interests, views, and concerns. The authors warn against mobilisation of coalitions via populism. The AMLO regime presented anti-corruption as a movement that fosters national identity and highlighted values such as honesty and loyalty. But the logical endpoint of this was a populist leader who presented himself as the *only* representative of the vulnerable, underrepresented majority.

But a domestic core is about more than just people and allied organisations. A second element is the capacity for making and remaking norms to match changing conditions. Some of the chapters affirm the importance of debates and disputes as a prelude to evolution. Dobson Phillips, in her chapter on the UK, focuses on the contestation of a nascent set of anti-corruption norms in the political discord experienced in the wake of Brexit. This discord provided an opportunity to challenge the effectiveness of Britain's anti-corruption architecture, contest the legitimacy of its institutions, and reshape ideas about the meaning of anti-corruption itself. This included contestation over the justification for the norms that long governed standards in British public life. It was not only the anti-corruption norms and institutions that were contested, but well-established and deeper norms of political conduct too.

As discussed, the potential for vertical and horizontal connectivity is an important predictor of adaptive anti-corruption. Cepeda Cuadrado emphasises that anti-corruption measures are most effective when they are not isolated from other social struggles. In the case of Latin America, it is not possible to address human rights violations without dealing with associated corruption, especially when corruption is systemic. The examples from Colombia, Honduras, Mexico, and Venezuela are part of a growing regional trend to recognise the nexus between anti-corruption and human rights. The chapter on Transparency International Bangladesh (TIB) states too that TIB was able to survive with alliance partners in the media.

Erasmus, Glencorse and Scrimgeour's arguments for how to realise translocal forms of collective action are relevant for how to sustain vertical and horizontal links in practice. They argue for stronger "umbrella" structures to enable "mutual recognition and strategic collaboration," leveraging technology to connect local actors across contexts. Also, donors and powerholders in the development sector could take greater risks and move away from rigid project log frames, pointing to innovative funding models such as the International Urban Poor Fund and the Roddenberry +1 Global Fund as examples that could be adapted to support translocal anti-corruption initiatives. Finally, they underscore the necessity of centring equity in translocal networks by bridging the gap between elite NGOs and grassroots groups – what Bellows (2020) describes as "the wonks and the street." Inclusive coalitions should incorporate diverse actors, including religious and community organisations that may not traditionally focus on anti-corruption but are deeply embedded in local life. These partnerships ensure a more accurate diagnosis of problems and broader legitimacy.

So, where anti-corruption practice is resilient, it seems to be due to a capacity to adapt to respond to contestation and abuse. But there is also a research angle to these challenges, about which we end our reflections.

Reflections on the Future of Anti-Corruption Research

Our main motivation for embarking on this volume was our observation of a discrepancy between the seemingly straightforward international consensus on the importance of anti-corruption as a policy goal, and the myriad messy ways anti-corruption appeared to be pursued around the world. We believed anti-corruption itself, rather than simply corruption, should become, much more centrally, the object of empirical examination, and suggested a conceptual framework for this empirical engagement. The resulting chapters have confirmed our belief in the value of empirically unpacking anti-corruption as it is pursued around the world today, as a means of identifying grounded ways forward in tackling corruption. To be clear, in doing so we do not question the well-known corrosive effects of corruption on polities, economies, and societies. Rather, we mean to encourage more critical thinking and deeper empirical analysis of the various ways states, their leaders, and other societal actors articulate and pursue "anti-corruption" as a policy goal.

"Anti-corruption" is not simply "anti-corruption" across time and space. History and context matter immensely in terms of what anti-corruption is and does, as do the stressors and motivators, the desires and visions, of societal groups, political parties, individual leaders, and their associates. If we are to truly understand what anti-corruption is and does, we must dig deeper into its empirical realities and engage more actively in theory development, as has to some extent already been done in the corruption-centred research literature in recent years. Below we outline a few initial reflections on what this empirical and theoretical engagement could look like.

Empirically, and as we believe is shown by the chapters contained in this book, anti-corruption research could further benefit from studies that grapple more with historical context, translocal dimensions (such as resource commodity trades) in their proper global political economy context, as well as from studies of the politics of anti-corruption of individual leaders, their political parties, and their movements, in prevailing political and economic ideologies or paradigms. The categories of anti-corruption described in this volume – authoritarian, populist, liberal-democratic, hybrid – are merely a starting point for beginning to grapple with the realities of anti-corruption around the world. They should not be viewed as constraining terms – there may well be other categories we have not considered, or some yet to emerge as anti-corruption itself continues to evolve and mutate.

Further empirical consideration of how anti-corruption operates, and what it achieves, under different contextual circumstances seems to us warranted and is, indeed, overdue. For example, the chapter on Russia shows how important it is to lift the veil of legislative activity and seemingly impressive official corruption prosecution figures. The author writes that "recent anti-corruption reforms worldwide have largely focused on non-criminal measures: asset disclosure, conflict of interest regulation, anti-corruption prohibitions and restrictions". In this light, Konov argues, "it would be intriguing to examine which layers of public officials have actually been affected by such preventive efforts in other countries and whether there has been selectivity in their implementation, similar to Russia's or perhaps different".

Theoretically, we believe there is space for further theory development specifically for anti-corruption that builds on the various disparate strands of corruption theory prevalent in recent years, but also on other social science theories. Literature on the principal-agent theory, collective action, functions of corruption, social norms approaches, and state capture, as well as theories such as the resource curse, have all tended to mainly focus on explaining "the corruption problem" as a starting point for attempting to tackle it. Such debates are highly valuable and meaningful. Yet, there is also an argument for focusing theory development from the other end of the challenge at stake: theorising explanations of "anti-corruption".

Important contributions have already been made in this space. Khan and Roy (2022) argued, for instance, that anti-corruption needs a radical rethink and that a "political settlements framework shows that the implementation of any policy depends not only on the power and capabilities of actors directly involved as enforcers (principals) and potential violators (agents), but also of other actors they have transactions with". To make anti-corruption "real", Khan and Roy argue, we must look for opportunities where actors have, or are likely to have, the "power, capabilities and interests to act against types of corruption". We do not disagree and find much value in Khan and Roy's conceptualisation of political settlements as markers of social order underpinning anti-corruption policies and actions.

What *our* argument stresses, however, is the need to further unpack the social orders conditioning anti-corruption practice and the often problematic kinds of anti-corruption that emerge as a result. Even if principals have the power, capabilities, and interests to act against corruption, to discipline violators, and enable other actors to uphold certain accountability and transparency measures, the chapters in this book show that resulting anti-corruption practices can still be at odds with broader values. We believe, therefore, that anti-corruption theory development requires further engagement with other areas of theory in the social sciences, for example regarding democratisation, autocratisation, liberalisation, oligarchy and populism, as well as their replication or perpetuation. After all, the emergence or perpetuation of social orders that enable power abuse is a concern for scholars, practitioners, and people, well beyond anti-corruption alone. Might corruption scholars be able to find more common ground with scholars and historians of authoritarianism and democracy, for example, to more meaningfully theorise anti-corruption outcomes? We believe this may indeed be possible and aligns with a more adaptive vision for anti-corruption; one that is not divorced from, but connects with, other social struggles in particular contexts.

References

Arriola, L. R., Rakner, L., and Van de Walle, N. (Eds.). (2023). *Democratic backsliding in Africa? Autocratization, resilience, and contention.* Oxford University Press.

Bellows, A. 2020. "Bridging the Elite-Grassroots DivideAmong Anticorruption Activists". Carnegie Endowment for International Peace.

Cahill, G. (2010). primer on social innovation: A compendium of definitions developed by organizations around the world. The Philanthropist, 23.

David-Barrett, E. (2025). "The economic consequences of state capture: Oligarchs are warping markets and Corrupting Economies Around the World". *Foreign Affairs.* April 4th 2025.

Guerzovich, F., Gattoni, M. S., and Algoso, D. (2020). *Seeing new opportunities:* (p. 137). Open Society.

Jaiyeola, R. A. (2023, January 13). *Deploying emergingtechnology to fight corruption.* International Federation of Accountants.

Johnson, J., Taxell, N., and Zaum, D. (2012). *Mapping evidence gaps in anti-corruption: Assessing the state of the operationally relevant evidence on donors' actions and approaches to reducing corruption.*

Khan, M., and P. Roy. 2022. *Making anti-corruption real: using a 'Power Capabilities and Interest Approach' to stop wasting money and start making progress.* SOAS Anti-Corruption Evidence Programme. Summary of Evidence. SOAS University of London. London.

Mullard, S. 2025. *With the US retreat from anti-corruption, what next for the global anti-corruption consensus?* U4 Blog. 19th March 2025. Chr. Michelsen Institute. Bergen.

Norén-Nilsson, Astrid (2024): Non-state actors and anti-corruption work in Cambodia: Gaps, opportunities, and synergies. U4 ISSUE 2024: 6 (Non-state actors and anti-corruption work in Cambodia: Gaps, opportunities, and synergies).

Qudah, A. M. A., Al-haddad, L., and Aljabali, A. A. A. (2025). Combatting medical corruption: A global review of root causes, consequences, and evidence-based interventions. *International Journal of Innovative Research and Scientific Studies*, *8*(2), 968–985. https://doi.org/10.53894/ijirss.v8i2.5397

OECD (2019). Embracing Innovation in Government – Global Trends 2019.

Rusch, J. 2025. *United Kingdom, France, and Switzerland Establish Joint Taskforce on International Bribery.* Oxford Business Law Blog. 8th April 2025. Faculty of Law. University of Oxford.

Sampson, S. (2010). The anti-corruption industry: From movement to institution. *Global Crime*, *11*(2), 261–278. https://doi.org/10.1080/17440571003669258

Schatz, F. (2013). Fight corruption with social accountability. *Public Administration and Development*, *33*(3), 161–174. https://doi.org/10.1002/pad.1648

INDEX

For Product Safety Concerns and Information please contact our EU
representative GPSR@taylorandfrancis.com
Taylor & Francis Verlag GmbH, Kaufingerstraße 24, 80331 München, Germany

'ww.ingramcontent.com/pod-product-compliance
-am Content Group UK Ltd.
'd, Milton Keynes, MK11 3LW, UK
'021724240926
'JK00030BA/2669